U•X•L Encyclopedia of
Native American Tribes

THIRD EDITION

U•X•L Encyclopedia of

Native American Tribes

THIRD EDITION

VOLUME 4

CALIFORNIA

PLATEAU

Laurie J. Edwards, Editor

U·X·L
A part of Gale, Cengage Learning

GALE
CENGAGE Learning·

Detroit • New York • San Francisco • New Haven, Conn • Waterville, Maine • London

GALE
CENGAGE Learning·

U•X•L Encyclopedia of Native American Tribes, 3rd Edition

Laurie J. Edwards

Project Editors: Shelly Dickey, Terri Schell

Rights Acquisition and Management: Leitha Etheridge-Sims

Composition: Evi Abou-El-Seoud

Manufacturing: Wendy Blurton

Imaging: John Watkins

Product Design: Kristine Julien

For product information and technology assistance, contact us at **Gale Customer Support, 1-800-877-4253.**
For permission to use material from this text or product, submit all requests online at **www.cengage.com/permissions.**
Further permissions questions can be emailed to **permission request@cengage.com**

Cover photographs reproduced by permission of Chumash Indian Pictographs, ©Marek Zuk/Alamy; Chumash Tomol Boat, Marilyn Angel/WynnNativestock Pictures/Corbis.

While every effort has been made to ensure the reliability of the information presented in this publication, Gale, a part of Cengage Learning, does not guarantee the accuracy of the data contained herein. Gale accepts no payment for listing; and inclusion in the publication of any organization, agency, institution, publication, service, or individual does not imply endorsement of the editors or publisher. Errors brought to the attention of the publisher and verified to the satisfaction of the publisher will be corrected in future editions.

LIBRARY OF CONGRESS CATALOGING-IN-PUBLICATION DATA

U•X•L Encyclopedia of Native American Tribes / Laurie J. Edwards ; Shelly Dickey, Terri Schell, project editors. -- 3rd ed.
    5 v. . cm.
    Includes bibliographical references and index.
    ISBN 978-1-4144-9092-2 (set) -- ISBN 978-1-4144-9093-9 (v. 1) -- ISBN 978-1-4144-9094-6 (v.2) -- ISBN 978-1-4144-9095-3 (v.3) -- ISBN 978-1-4144-9096-0 (v. 4) -- ISBN 978-1-4144-9097-7 (v. 5),
    1. Indians of North America--Encyclopedias, Juvenile. 2. Indians of North America--Encyclopedias. I. Edwards, Laurie J. II. Dickey, Shelly. III. Schell, Terri, 1968-

E76.2.U85 2012
970.004'97003--dc23   2011048142

Gale
27500 Drake Rd.
Farmington Hills, MI, 48331-3535

978-1-4144-9092-2 (set)	1-4144-9092-5 (set)
978-1-4144-9093-9 (v. 1)	1-4144-9093-3 (v. 1)
978-1-4144-9094-6 (v. 2)	1-4144-9094-1 (v. 2)
978-1-4144-9095-3 (v. 3)	1-4144-9095-X (v. 3)
978-1-4144-9096-0 (v. 4)	1-4144-9096-8 (v. 4)
978-1-4144-9097-7 (v. 5)	1-4144-9097-6 (v. 5)

This title is also available as an e-book.
ISBN 13: 978-1-4144-9098-4 ISBN 10: 1-4144-9098-4
Contact your Gale, a part of Cengage Learning, sales representative for ordering information.

Printed in U.S.A.
1 2 3 4 5 6 7 16 15 14 13 12

Contents

U•X•L Encyclopedia of Native American Tribes, 3rd Edition

Tribes Alphabetically

First numeral signifies volume number. The numeral after the colon signifies page number. For example, 3:871 means Volume 3, page 871.

Reader's Guide

Long before the Vikings, Spaniards, and Portuguese made land-fall on North American shores, the continent already had a rich history of human settlement. The *U•X•L Encyclopedia of Native American Tribes, 3rd Edition* opens up for students the array of tribal ways in the United States and Canada past and present. Included in these volumes, readers will find the stories of:

- the well-known nineteenth century Lakota hunting the buffalo on the Great Plains
- the contemporary Inuit of the Arctic, who in 1999 won their battle for Nunavut, a vast, self-governing territory in Canada
- the Haida of the Pacific Northwest, whose totem poles have become a familiar adornment of the landscape
- the Anasazi in the Southwest, who were building spectacular cities long before Europeans arrived
- the Mohawk men in the Northeast who made such a name for themselves as ironworkers on skyscrapers and bridges that they have long been in demand for such projects as the Golden Gate Bridge
- the Yahi of California, who became extinct when their last member, Ishi, died in 1916.

The *U•X•L Encyclopedia of Native American Tribes, 3rd Edition* presents 106 tribes, confederacies, and Native American groups. Among the tribes included are large and well-known nations, smaller communities with their own fascinating stories, and prehistoric peoples. The tribes are grouped in the ten major geographical/cultural areas of North America in which tribes shared environmental and cultural connections. The ten sections, each beginning with an introductory essay on the geographical area and the shared history and culture within it, are arranged in the volumes as follows:

- Volume 1: Northeast and Subarctic
- Volume 2: Southeast and Great Plains
- Volume 3: Southwest
- Volume 4: California and Plateau
- Volume 5: Great Basin, Pacific Northwest, and Arctic

The *U•X•L Encyclopedia of Native American Tribes, 3rd Edition* provides the history of each of the tribes featured and a fascinating look at their ways of life: how families lived in centuries past and today, what people ate and wore, what their homes were like, how they worshiped, celebrated, governed themselves, and much more. A student can learn in depth about one tribe or compare aspects of many tribes. Each detailed entry is presented in consistent rubrics that allow for easy access and comparison, as follows:

- History
- Religion
- Language
- Government
- Economy
- Daily Life
- Arts
- Customs
- Current Tribal Issues
- Notable People

Each entry begins with vital data on the tribe: name, location, population, language family, origins and group affiliations. A locator map follows, showing the traditional homelands and contemporary communities of the group; regional and migration maps throughout aid in locating the many groups at different times in history. Brief timelines in each entry chronicle important dates of the tribe's history, while an overall timeline at the beginning of all the volumes outlines key events in history pertinent to all Native Americans. Other sidebars present recipes, oral literature or stories, language keys, and background material on the tribe. Color photographs and illustrations, further reading sections, a thorough subject index, and a glossary are special features that make the volumes easy, fun, and informative to use.

A note on terminology

Throughout the *U•X•L Encyclopedia of Native American Tribes, 3rd Edition* various terms are used for Native North Americans, such as *Indian, American Indian, Native,* and *aboriginal.* The Native peoples of the Americas have the unfortunate distinction of having been given the wrong name by the Europeans who first arrived on the continent, mistakenly thinking they had arrived in India. The search for a single name, however, has never been entirely successful. The best way to characterize Native North Americans is by recognizing their specific tribal or community identities. In compiling this book, every effort has been made to keep Native tribal and community identities distinct, but by necessity, inclusive terminology is often used. We do not wish to offend anyone, but rather than favor one term for Native North American people, the editors have used a variety of terminology, trying always to use the most appropriate term in the particular context.

Europeans also had a hand in giving names to tribes, often misunderstanding their languages and the relations between different Native communities. Most tribes have their own names for themselves, and many have succeeded in gaining public acceptance of traditional names. The Inuit, for example, objected to the name Eskimo, which means "eaters of raw meat," and in time their name for themselves was accepted. In the interest of clarity the editors of this book have used the currently accepted terms, while acknowledging the traditional ones or the outmoded ones at the beginning of each entry.

The term *tribe* is not accepted by all Native groups. The people living in North America before the Europeans arrived had many different ways of organizing themselves politically and relating to other groups around them—from complex confederacies and powerful unified nations to isolated villages with little need for political structure. Groups divided, absorbed each other, intermarried, allied, and dissolved. The epidemics and wars that came with non-Native expansion into North America created a demographic catastrophe to many Native groups and greatly affected tribal affiliations. Although in modern times there are actual rules about what comprise a tribe (federal requirements for recognition of tribes are specific, complicated, and often difficult to fulfill), the hundreds of groups living in the Americas in early times did not have any one way of categorizing themselves. Thus, some Native American peoples today find the word *tribe* misleading. In a study of Native peoples, it can also be an elusive defining term. But in facing the challenges of maintaining traditions and heritage in modern times, tribal or community identity is acutely important to many Native Americans. Tremendous efforts have been undertaken to preserve native languages, oral traditions, religions, ceremonies, and traditional arts and economies—the things that, put together, make a tribe a cultural and political unit.

Comments and suggestions

In this third edition of the *U•X•L Encyclopedia of Native American Tribes* we have presented in-depth information on 106 of the hundreds of tribes of North America. While every attempt was made to include a wide representation of groups, many historically important and interesting tribes are not covered in these volumes. We welcome your suggestions for tribes to be featured in future editions, as well as any other comments you may have on this set. Please write: Editors, *U•X•L Encyclopedia of Native American Tribes, 3rd Edition,* U•X•L 27500 Drake Road, Farmington Hills, Michigan 48331-3535; call toll-free 1-800-877-4253; or fax 248-699-8097; or send e-mail via http://www.gale.com.

Words to Know

Aboriginal: Native, or relating to the first or earliest group living in a particular area.

Activism: Taking action for or against a controversial issue; political and social activists may organize or take part in protest demonstrations, rallies, petitioning the government, sit-ins, civil disobedience, and many other forms of activities that draw attention to an issue and/or challenge the authorities to make a change.

Adobe: A brick or other building material made from sun-dried mud, a mixture of clay, sand, and sometimes ashes, rocks, or straw.

Alaska Native Claims Settlement Act (ANCSA): An act of Congress passed in 1971 that gave Alaska Natives 44 million acres of land and $962.5 million. In exchange, Alaska Natives gave up all claim to other lands in Alaska. The ANCSA also resulted in the formation of 12 regional corporations in Alaska in charge of Native communities' economic development and land use.

Allotment: The practice of dividing and distributing land into individual lots. In 1887 the U.S. Congress passed the General Allotment Act (also known as the Dawes Act), which divided Indian reservations into privately owned parcels (pieces) of land. Under allotment, tribes could no longer own their own lands in common (as a group) in the traditional ways. Instead the head of a family received a lot, generally 160 acres. Land not alloted was sold to non-Natives.

American Indian Movement (AIM): An activist movement founded in 1966 to aggressively press for Indian rights. The movement was formed to improve federal, state, and local social services to Native Americans in urban neighborhoods. AIM sought the reorganization of the Bureau of Indian Affairs to make it more responsive to Native American needs and fought for the return of Indian lands illegally taken from them.

Anthropology: The study of human beings in terms of their populations, culture, social relations, ethnic characteristics, customs, and adaptation to their environment.

Archaeology: The study of the remains of past human life, such as fossil relics, artifacts, and monuments, in order to understand earlier human cultures.

Arctic: Relating to the area surrounding the North Pole.

Assimilate: To absorb, or to be absorbed, into the dominant society (those in power, or in the majority). U.S. assimilation policies were directed at causing Native Americans to become like European-Americans in terms of jobs and economics, religion, customs, language, education, family life, and dress.

Band: A small, loosely organized social group composed of several families. In Canada, the word band originally referred to a social unit of nomadic (those who moved from place to place) hunting peoples, but now refers to a community of Indians registered with the government.

Boarding school: A live-in school.

Breechcloth: A garment with front and back flaps that hangs from the waist. Breechcloths were one of the most common articles of clothing worn by many Native American men and sometimes women in pre-European/American settlement times.

Bureau of Indian Affairs (BIA): The U.S. government agency that oversees tribal lands, education, and other aspects of Indian life.

Census: A count of the population.

Ceremony: A special act or set of acts (such as a wedding or a funeral) performed by members of a group on important occasions, usually organized according to the group's traditions and beliefs.

Clan: A group of related house groups and families that trace back to a common ancestor or a common symbol or totem, usually an animal such as the bear or the turtle. The clan forms the basic social and political unit for many Indian societies.

Colonialism: A state or nation's control over a foreign territory.

Colonize: To establish a group of people from a mother country or state in a foreign territory; the colonists set up a community that remains tied to the mother county.

Confederacy: A group of people, states, or nations joined together for mutual support or for a special purpose.

Convert: To cause a person or group to change their beliefs or practices. A convert (noun) is a person who has been converted to a new belief or practice.

Coup: A feat of bravery, especially the touching of an enemy's body during battle without causing or receiving injury. To "count coup" is to count the number of such feats of bravery.

Cradleboard: A board or frame on which an infant was bound or wrapped by some Native American peoples. It was used as a portable carrier or for carrying an infant on the back.

Creation stories: Sacred myths or stories that explain how Earth and its beings were created.

Culture: The set of beliefs, social habits, and ways of surviving in the environment that are held by a particular social group.

Dentalium: Dentalia (plural) are the tooth-like shells that some tribes used as money. The shells were rubbed smooth and strung like beads on strands of animal skin.

Depletion: Decreasing the amount of something; depletion of resources such as animals or minerals through overuse reduces essential elements from the environment.

Dialect: A local variety of a particular language, with unique differences in words, grammar, and pronunciation.

Economy: The way a group obtains, produces, and distributes the goods it needs; the overall system by which it supports itself and accumulates its wealth.

Ecosystem: The overall way that a community and its surrounding environment function together in nature.

Epidemic: The rapid spread of a disease so that many people in an area have it at the same time.

Ethnic group: A group of people who are classed according to certain aspects of their common background, usually by tribal, racial, national, cultural, and language origins.

Extended family: A family group that includes close relatives such as mother, father, and children, plus grandparents, aunts, and uncles, and cousins.

Fast: To go without food.

Federally recognized tribes: Tribes with which the U.S. government maintains official relations as established by treaty, executive order, or act of Congress.

Fetish: An object believed to have magical or spiritual power.

First Nations: One of Canada's terms for its Indian nations.

Five Civilized Tribes: A name given to the Cherokee, Choctaw, Chickasaw, Creek, and Seminole during the mid-1800s. The tribes were given this name by non-Natives because they had democratic constitutional governments, a high literacy rate (many people who could read and write), and ran effective schools.

Formal education: Structured learning that takes place in a school or college under the supervision of trained teachers.

Ghost Dance: A revitalization (renewal or rebirth) movement that arose in the 1870s after many tribes moved to reservations and were being encouraged to give up their traditional beliefs. Many Native Americans hoped that, if they performed it earnestly, the Ghost Dance would bring back traditional Native lifestyles and values, and that the buffalo and Indian ancestors would return to the Earth as in the days before the white settlers.

Great Basin: An elevated region in the western United States in which all water drains toward the center. The Great Basin covers part of Nevada, California, Colorado, Utah, Oregon, and Wyoming.

Guardian spirit: A sacred power, usually embodied in an animal such as a hawk, deer, or turtle, that reveals itself to an individual, offering help throughout the person's lifetime in important matters such as hunting or healing the sick.

Haudenosaunee: The name of the people often called Iroquois or Five Nations. It means "People of the Longhouse."

Head flattening: A practice in which a baby was placed in a cradle, and a padded board was tied to its forehead to mold the head into a desired shape. Sometimes the effect of flattening the back of the head was achieved by binding the infant tightly to a cradleboard.

Immunity: Resistance to disease; the ability to be exposed to a disease with less chance of getting it, and less severe effects if infected.

Indian Territory: An area in present-day Kansas and Oklahoma where the U.S. government once planned to move all Indians, and, eventually, to allow them to run their own province or state. In 1880 nearly one-third of all U.S. Indians lived there, but with the formation of the state of Oklahoma in 1906, the promise of an Indian state dissolved.

Indigenous: Native, or first, in a specific area. Native Americans are often referred to as indigenous peoples of North America.

Intermarriage: Marriage between people of different groups, as between a Native American and a non-Native, or between people from two different tribes.

Kachina: A group of spirits celebrated by the Pueblo Indians; the word also refers to dolls made in the image of kachina spirits.

Kiva: Among the Pueblo, a circular (sometimes rectangular) underground room used for religious ceremonies.

Lacrosse: A game of Native American origin in which players use a long stick with a webbed pouch at the end for catching and throwing a ball.

Language family: A group of languages that are different from one another but are related. These languages share similar words, sounds, or word structures. The languages are alike either because they have borrowed words from each other or because they originally came from the same parent language.

Legend: A story or folktale that tells about people or events in the past.

Life expectancy: The average number of years a person may expect to live.

Linguistics: The study of human speech and language.

Literacy: The state of being able to read and write.

Loincloth: See "Breechcloth".

Longhouse: A large, long building in which several families live together; usually found among Northwest Coast and Iroquois peoples.

Long Walk of the Navajo: The enforced 300-mile walk of the Navajo people in 1864, when they were being removed from their homelands to the Bosque Redondo Reservation in New Mexico.

Manifest Destiny: A belief held by many Americans in the nineteenth century that the destiny of the United States was to expand its territory and extend its political, social, and economic influences throughout North America.

Matrilineal: Tracing family relations through the mother; in a matrilineal society, names and inheritances are passed down through the mother's side of the family.

Medicine bundle: A pouch in which were kept sacred objects believed to have powers that would protect and aid an individual, a clan or family, or a community.

Midewiwin Society: The Medicine Lodge Religion, whose main purpose was to prolong life. The society taught morality, proper conduct, and a knowledge of plants and herbs for healing.

Migration: Movement from one place to another. The migrations of Native peoples were often done by the group, with whole nations moving from one area to another.

Mission: An organized effort by a religious group to spread its beliefs to other parts of the world; mission refers either to the project of spreading a belief system or to the building(s)—such as a church—in which this takes place.

Missionary: Someone sent to a foreign land to convert its people to a particular religion.

Mission school: A school established by missionaries to teach people religious beliefs as well as other subjects.

Moiety: One of the two parts that a tribe or community divided into based on kinship.

Myth: A story passed down through generations, often involving supernatural beings. Myths often express religious beliefs or the values of people. They may attempt to explain how the Earth and its beings were created, or why things are. They are not always meant to be taken as factual.

Natural resources: The sources of supplies provided by the environment for survival and enrichment, such as animals to be hunted, land for farming, minerals, and timber.

Neophyte: Beginner; often used to mean a new convert to a religion.

Nomadic: Traveling and relocating often, usually in search of food and other resources or a better climate.

Nunavut: A new territory in Canada as of April 1, 1999, with the status of a province and a Inuit majority. It is a huge area, covering most of Canada north of the treeline. Nunavut means "Our Land" in Inukitut (the Inuit language).

Oral literature: Oral traditions that are written down after enjoying a long life in spoken form among a people.

Oral traditions: History, mythology, folklore, and other foundations of a culture that have been passed by spoken word, often in the form of stories, from generation to generation within a culture group.

Parent language: A language that is the common structure of two or more languages that came into being at a later time.

Parfleche: A case or a pouch made from tanned animal hide.

Patrilineal: Tracing family relations through the father; in a patrilineal society, names and inheritances are passed down through the father's side of the family.

Per capita income: The average personal income per person.

Petroglyph: A carving or engraving on rock; a common form of ancient art.

Peyote: A substance obtained from cactus that some Indian groups used as part of their religious practice. After eating the substance, which stimulates the nervous system, a person may go into a trance state and see visions. The Peyote Religion features the use of this substance.

Pictograph: A simple picture representing a historical event.

Policy: The overall plan or course of action issued by the government, establishing how it will handle certain situations or people and what its goals are.

Post-European contact: Relating to the time and state of Native Americans and their lands after the Europeans arrived. Depending on the part of the country in which they lived, Native groups experienced contact at differing times in the history of white expansion into the West.

Potlatch: A feast or ceremony, commonly held among Northwest Coast groups; also called a "giveaway." During a potlatch goods are given to guests to show the host's generosity and wealth. Potlatches are used to celebrate major life events such as birth, death, or marriage.

Powwow: A celebration at which the main activity is traditional singing and dancing. In modern times, the singers and dancers at powwows came from many different tribes.

Province: A district or division of a country (like a state in the United States).

Raiding: Entering into another tribe or community's territory, usually by stealth or force, and stealing their livestock and supplies.

Ranchería: Spanish term for a small farm.

Ratify: To approve or confirm. In the United States, the U.S. Senate ratified treaties with the Indians.

Red Power: A term used to describe the Native American activism movement of the 1960s, in which people from many tribes came together to protest the injustices of American policies toward Native Americans.

Removal Act: An act passed by the U.S. Congress in 1830 that directed all Indians to be moved to Indian Territory, west of the Mississippi River.

Removal Period: The time, mostly between 1830 and 1860, when most Indians of the eastern United States were forced to leave their homelands and relocate west of the Mississippi River.

Repatriation: To return something to its place of origin. A law passed in the 1990s says that all bones and grave goods (items that are buried with a body) should be returned to the descendants. Many Native American tribes have used that law to claim bones and other objects belonging to their ancestors. Museums and archaeological digs must return these items to the tribes.

Reservation: Land set aside by the U.S. government for the use of a group or groups of Indians.

Reserve: In Canada, lands set aside for specific Indian bands. Reserve means in Canada approximately what reservation means in the United States.

Revitalization: The feeling or movement in which something seems to come back to life after having been quiet or inactive for a period of time.

Ritual: A formal act that is performed in basically the same way each time; rituals are often performed as part of a ceremony.

Rural: Having to do with the country; opposite of urban.

Sachem: The chief of a confederation of tribes.

Shaman: A priest or medicine person in many Native American groups who understands and works with supernatural matters. Shamans traditionally performed in rituals and were expected to cure the sick, see the future, and obtain supernatural help with hunting and other economic activities.

Smallpox: A very contagious disease that spread across North America and killed many thousands of Indians. Survivors had skin that was badly scarred.

Sovereign: Self-governing or independent. A sovereign nation makes its own laws and rules.

Sun Dance: A renewal and purification ceremony performed by many Plains Indians such as the Sioux and Cheyenne. A striking aspect of the ceremony was the personal sacrifice made by some men. They undertook self-torture in order to gain a vision that might provide spiritual insight beneficial to the community.

Sweat lodge: An airtight hut containing hot stones that were sprinkled with water to make them steam. A person remained inside until he or she was perspiring. The person then usually rushed out and plunged into a cold stream. This treatment was used before a ceremony or for the healing of physical or spiritual ailments. Sweat lodge is also the name of a sacred Native American ceremony involving the building of the lodge and the pouring of water on stones, usually by a medicine person, accompanied by praying and singing. The ceremony has many purposes, including spiritual cleansing and healing.

Taboo: A forbidden object or action. Many Indians believe that the sacred order of the world must be maintained if one is to avoid illness or other misfortunes. This is accomplished, in part, by observing a large assortment of taboos.

Termination: The policy of the U.S. government during the 1950s and 1960s to end the relationships set up by treaties with Indian nations.

Toloache: A substance obtained from a plant called jimsonweed. When consumed, the drug causes a person to go into a trance and see visions. It is used in some religious ceremonies.

Totem: An object that serves as an emblem or represents a family or clan, usually in the form of an animal, bird, fish, plant, or other natural object. A totem pole is a pillar built in front of the homes of Natives in the Northwest. It is painted and carved with a series of totems that show the family background and either mythical or historical events.

Trail of Tears: A series of forced marches of Native Americans of the Southeast in the 1830s, causing the deaths of thousands. The marches were the result of the U.S. government's removal policy, which ordered Native Americans to be moved to Indian Territory.

Treaty: An agreement between two parties or two nations, signed by both, usually defining the benefits to both parties that will result from one side giving up title to a territory of land.

Tribe: A group of Natives who share a name, language, culture, and ancestors; in Canada, called a band.

Tribelet: A community within an organization of communities in which one main settlement was surrounded by a few minor outlying settlements.

Trickster: A common culture hero in Indian myth and legend. tricksters generally have supernatural powers that can be used to do good or harm, and stories about them take into account the different forces of the universe, such as good and evil or night and day. The Trickster takes different forms among various groups; for example, Coyote in the Southwest; Ikhtomi Spider in the High Plains, and Jay or Wolverine in Canada.

Trust: A relationship between two parties (or groups) in which one is responsible for acting in the other's best interests. The U.S. government has a trust relationship with tribal nations. Many tribes do not own their lands outright; according to treaty, the government owns the land "in trust" and tribes are given the use of it.

Unemployment rate: The percentage of the population that is looking for work but unable to find any. (People who have quit looking for work are not included in unemployment rates.)

Urban: Having to do with cities and towns; the opposite of rural.

Values: The ideals that a community of people shares.

Vision quest: A sacred ceremony in which a person (often a teenage boy) goes off alone and fasts, living without food or water for a period of days. During that time he hopes to learn about his spiritual side and to have a vision of a guardian spirit who will give him help and strength throughout his life.

Wampum: Small cylinder-shaped beads cut from shells. Long strings of wampum were used for many different purposes. Indians believed that the exchange of wampum and other goods established a friendship, not just a profit-making relationship.

Wampum belt: A broad woven belt of wampum used to record history, treaties among the tribes, or treaties with colonists or governments.

Weir: A barricade used to funnel fish toward people who wait to catch them.

Timeline

25,000–11,000 BCE Groups of hunters cross from Asia to Alaska on the Bering Sea Land Bridge, which was formed when lands now under the waters of the Bering Strait were exposed for periods of time, according to scientists.

1400 BCE Along the lower Mississippi, people of the Poverty Point culture are constructing large burial mounds and living in planned communities.

500 BCE The Adena people build villages with burial mounds in the Midwest.

100 BCE Hopewell societies construct massive earthen mounds for burying their dead and possibly other religious purposes.

100 BCE–400 CE In the Early Basketmaker period, the Anasazi use baskets as containers and cooking pots; they live in caves.

1 CE: Small, permanent villages of the Hohokam tradition emerge in the southwest.

400–700 In the Modified Basketmaker period, Anasazi communities emerge in the Four Corners region of the Southwest. They learn to make pottery in which they can boil beans. They live in underground pits and begin to use bows and arrows. The Anasazi eventually design communities in large multi-roomed apartment buildings, some with more than 1,200 rooms.

700 CE The Mississippian culture begins.

700–1050 The Developmental Pueblo period begins. The Anasazi move into pueblo-type homes above the ground and develop irrigation methods. A great cultural center is established at Chaco Canyon. Anasazi influence spreads to other areas of the Southwest.

800–950 The early Pecos build pit houses.

900 The Mississippian mound-building groups form complex political and social systems, and participate in long-distance trade and an elaborate and widespread religion.

984 The Vikings under Erik the Red first encounter the Inuit of Greenland.

1000–1350 The Iroquois Confederacy is formed among the Mohawk, Oneida, Onondaga, Cayuga, and Seneca nations. The Five Nations of the Haudenosaunee are, from this time, governed by chiefs from the 49 families who were present at the origin of the confederation.

1040 Pueblos (towns) are flourishing in New Mexico's Chaco Canyon. The pueblos are connected by an extensive road system that stretches many miles across the desert.

1050–1300 In the Classic Pueblo period, Pueblo architecture reaches its height with the building of fabulous cliff dwellings; Acoma Pueblo is a well-established city.

1200 The great city of Cahokia in the Mississippi River Valley flourishes.

1250 Zuñi Pueblo is an important trading center for Native peoples from California, Mexico, and the American Southwest.

1300–1700 During the Regressive Pueblo period, the Anasazi influence declines. The people leave their northern homelands, heading south to mix with other cultures.

1350 Moundville, in present-day Alabama, one of the largest ceremonial centers of the Mound Builders, thrives. With twenty great mounds and a village, it is probably the center of a chiefdom that includes several other related communities.

1400s Two tribes unite to start the Wendat Confederacy.

1494 Christopher Columbus begins the enslavement of American Indians, capturing over 500 Taino of San Salvador and sending them to Spain to be sold.

1503 French explorer Jacques Cartier begins trading with Native Americans along the East Coast.

1524 The Abenaki and Narragansett, among other Eastern tribes, encounter the expedition of Giovanni da Verrazano.

1533 Spaniards led by Nuño de Guzmán enter Yaqui territory.

1534 French explorer Jacques Cartier meets the Micmac on the Gaspé Peninsula, beginning a long association between the French and the Micmac.

1539–43 The Spanish treasure hunter Hernando de Soto becomes the first European to make contact with Mississippian cultures; De Soto and Spaniard Francisco Coronado traverse the Southeast and Southwest, bringing with them disease epidemics that kill thousands of Native Americans.

1540 Hernando de Alarcón first encounters the Yuman.

1570 The Spanish attempt to establish a mission in Powhatan territory, but are driven away or killed by the Natives.

1576 British explorer Martin Frobisher first comes into contact with the central Inuit of northern Canada.

1579 Sir Francis Drake encounters the Coast Miwok.

1590 The Micmac force Iroquoian-speaking Natives to leave the Gaspé Peninsula; as a result, the Micmac dominate the fur trade with the French.

1591 Spanish colonization of Pueblo land begins.

1598 Juan de Oñate sets up a Spanish colony and builds San Geronimo Mission at Taos Pueblo. He brings 7000 head of livestock, among them horses.

1602 Spanish explorer Sebastián Vizcaíno encounters the Ohlone.

1607 The British colonists of the Virginia Company arrive in Powhatan territory.

1609 The fur trade begins when British explorer Henry Hudson, sailing for the Netherlands, opens trade in New Netherland (present-day New York) with several Northeast tribes, including the Delaware.

1615 Ottawa meet Samuel de Champlain at Georgian Bay.

1621 Chief Massasoit allies with Pilgrims.

1622 Frenchman Étienne Brûlé encounters the Ojibway at present-day Sault Sainte Marie.

1634–37 An army of Puritans, Pilgrims, Mohican, and Narragansett attacks and sets fire to the Pequot fort, killing as many as 700 Pequot men, women, and children; Massacre at Mystic ends Pequot War and nearly destroys the tribe.

1648–51 The Iroquois, having exhausted the fur supply in their area, attack other tribes in order to get a new supply. The Beaver Wars begin, and many Northeast tribes are forced to move west toward the Great Lakes area.

mid-1600s The Miami encounter Europeans and provide scouts to guide Father Jacques Marquette and Louis Joliet to the Mississippi River.

1651 Colonists establish first Indian reservation near Richmond, Virginia, for what is left of the Powhatans.

1675–76 The Great Swamp Fight during King Philip's War nearly wipes out the tribe and the loss of life and land ends a way of life for New England tribes.

1680 The Hopi, Jemez, Acoma, and other Pueblo groups force the Spanish out of New Mexico in the Pueblo Revolt.

1682 Robert de la Salle's expedition descends the Mississippi River into Natchez territory.

1687 Father Eusebio Francisco Kino begins missionary work among the Tohono O'odham and establishes the first of twenty-eight missions in Yuman territory.

1692 The Spanish begin their reconquest of Pueblo land; Pecos make peace with Spaniards, in spite of protests from some tribe members.

1700 Pierre-Charles le Sueur encounters the Sioux.

1709 John Lawson discovers and writes about the "Hatteras Indians."

1729 French governor Sieur d' Etchéparre demands Natchez land for a plantation; Natchez revolt begins.

1731 The French destroy the Natchez, the last Mississippian culture. Most survivors are sold into slavery in the Caribbean.

1741 Danish-born Russian explorer Vitus Bering sees buildings on Kayak Island that likely belong to the Chugach; he is the first European to reach the Inuit of Alaska.

1760–63 The Delaware Prophet tells Native Americans in the Northeast that they must drive Europeans out of North America and return to the customs of their ancestors. His message influences Ottawa leader Pontiac, who uses it to unite many tribes against the British.

1761 The Potawatomi switch allegiance from the French to the British; they later help the British by attacking American settlers during the American Revolution.

1763 By the Treaty of Paris, France gives Great Britain the Canadian Maritime provinces, including Micmac territory.

1763 England issues the Proclamation of 1763, which assigns all lands west of the Appalachian Mountains to Native Americans, while colonists are allowed to settle all land to the east. The document respects the aboriginal land rights of Native Americans. It is not popular with colonists who want to move onto Indian lands and becomes one of the conflicts between England and the colonies leading to the American Revolution.

1769 The Spanish build their first mission in California. There will be 23 Spanish missions in California, which are used to convert Native Californians to Christianity, but also reduces them to slave labor.

1769–83 Samuel Hearne and Alexander Mackenzie are the first European explorers to penetrate Alaskan Athabascan territory, looking for furs and a route to the Pacific Ocean. Russian fur traders are not far behind.

c. 1770 Horses, brought to the continent by the Spanish in the sixteenth century, spread onto the Great Plains and lead to the development of a new High Plains Culture.

1776 Most Mohawk tribes side with the British during the Revolutionary War under the leadership of Thayendanégea, also known as Joseph Brant.

1778 The Delaware sign the first formal treaty with the United States, guaranteeing their land and allowing them to be the fourteenth state; the treaty is never ratified.

1778 The treaty-making period begins when the first of 370 treaties between Indian nations and the U.S. government is signed.

1786 The first federal Indian reservations are established.

1789 The Spanish establish a post at Nootka Sound on Vancouver Island, the first permanent European establishment in the territory of the Pacific Northwest Coast tribes; Spain and Great Britain vie for control of the area during the Nootka Sound Controversy.

1791 In the greatest Native American defeat of the U.S. Army, the Miami win against General Arthur St. Clair.

1792 Explorer George Vancouver enters Puget Sound; Robert Gray, John Boit and George Vancouver are the first to mention the Chinook.

1805 The Lewis and Clark expedition ecounter the Flathead, Nez Percé, Yakama, Shoshone, Umatilla, Siletz, and are the first to reach Chinook territory by land.

1811 Shawnee settlement of Prophet's Town is destroyed in the Battle of Tippecanoe.

1813 Chief Tecumseh is killed fighting the Americans at Battle of the Thames in the War of 1812.

1816 Violence erupts during a Métis protest over the Pemmican Proclamation of 1814, and twenty-one Hudson's Bay Company employees are killed.

1817 The First Seminole War occurs when soldiers from neighboring states invade Seminole lands in Florida looking for runaway slaves.

1821 Sequoyah's method for writing the Cherokee language is officially approved by tribal leaders.

1827 The Cherokee adopt a written constitution.

1830 The removal period begins when the U.S. Congress passes the Indian Removal Act. Over the course of the next thirty years many tribes from the Northeast and Southeast are removed to Indian Territory in present-day Oklahoma and Kansas, often forcibly and at great expense in human lives.

1831 Some Seneca and Cayuga move to Indian Territory (now Oklahoma) as part of the U.S. government's plan to move Native Americans westward. Other Iroquois groups stand firm until the government's policy is overturned in 1842.

1832 The U.S. government attempts relocation of the Seminole to Indian Territory in Oklahoma, leading to the Second Seminole War.

1838 The Cherokee leave their homeland on a forced journey known as the Trail of Tears.

1846–48 Mexican-American War is fought; San Juan lands become part of U.S. territory.

1847 Another Pueblo rebellion leads to the assassination of the American territorial governor. In retaliation U.S. troops destroy the mission at Taos Pueblo, killing 150 Taos Indians.

1848 Mexico gives northern Arizona and northern New Mexico lands to the United States. Warfare between the Apache people and the U.S. Army begins.

1850 New Mexico is declared a U.S. territory.

1851 Gold Rush begins at Gold Bluff, prompting settlers to take over Native American lands. As emigration of Europeans to the West increases, eleven Plains tribes sign the Treaty of Fort Laramie, which promises annual payments to the tribes for their land.

1851 Early reservations are created in California to protect the Native population from the violence of U.S. citizens. These reservations are inadequate and serve only a small portion of the Native Californians, while others endure continued violence and hardship.

1854 The Treaty of Medicine Creek is signed, and the Nisqually give up much of their land; the treaty also gives Puyallup lands to the U.S. government and the tribe is sent to a reservation.

1858 Prospectors flood into Washoe lands after the Comstock lode is discovered.

1859 American surveyors map out a reservation on the Gila River for the Pima and Maricopa Indians. It includes fields, but no water.

1861 Cochise is arrested on a false charge, and the Apache Wars begin.

1864 At least 130 Southern Arapaho and Cheyenne—many of them women and children—are killed by U.S. Army troops during the Sand Creek Massacre.

1864 The devastating Long Walk, a forced removal from their homelands, leads the Navajo to a harsh exile at Bosque Redondo.

1867 The United States buys Alaska from Russia for $7.2 million.

1870 The First Ghost Dance Movement begins when Wodzibwob, a Paiute, learns in a vision that a great earthquake will swallow the Earth, and that all Indians will be spared or resurrected within three days of the disaster, returning their world to its state before the Europeans arrived.

1870–90 The Peyote Religion spreads throughout the Great Plains. Peyote (obtained from a cactus plant) brings on a dreamlike feeling that followers believe brings them closer to the spirit world. Tribes develop their own ceremonies, songs, and symbolism, and vow to be trustworthy, honorable, and community-oriented and to follow the Peyote Road.

1871 British Columbia becomes part of Canada; reserve land is set aside for the Nuu-chah-nulth.

1874–75 The Comanche make their last stand; Quanah Parker and his followers are the last to surrender and be placed on a reservation.

1875 The U.S. Army forces the Yavapai and Apache to march to the San Carlos Apache Reservation; 115 die along the way.

1876 The Northern Cheyenne join with the Sioux in defeating General George Custer at the Battle of Little Bighorn.

1876 The Indian Act in Canada establishes an Indian reserve system, in which reserves were governed by voluntary elected band councils. The Act does not recognize Canadian Indians' right to self-government. With the passage of the act, Canadian peoples in Canada are divided into three groups: status Indian, treaty Indian, and non-status Indian. The categories affect the benefits and rights Indians are given by the government.

1877 During the Nez Percé War, Chief Joseph and his people try fleeing to Canada, but are captured by U.S. Army troops.

1879 The Ute kill thirteen U.S. soldiers and ten Indian agency officials, including Nathan Meeker, in a conflict that becomes known as the "Meeker Massacre."

1880s The buffalo on the Great Plains are slaughtered until there are almost none left. Without adequate supplies of buffalo for food, the Plains Indians cannot survive. Many move to reservations.

1884 The Canadian government bans potlatches. The elaborate gift-giving ceremonies have long been a vital part of Pacific Northwest Indian culture.

1886 The final surrender of Geronimo's band marks the end of Apache military resistance to American settlement.

1887 The General Allotment Act (also known as the Dawes Act), is passed by Congress. The act calls for the allotment (parceling out) of tribal lands. Tribes are no longer to own their lands in common in the traditional way. Instead the land is to be assigned to individuals. The head of a family receives 160 acres, and other family members get smaller pieces of land. All Indian lands that are not alloted are sold to settlers.

1888 Ranchers and amateur archaeologists Richard Wetherill and Charlie Mason discover ancient cliff dwellings of the Pueblo people.

1889 The Oklahoma Land Runs open Indian Territory to non-Natives. (Indian Territory had been set aside solely for Indian use.) At noon on April 22, an estimated 50,000 people line up at the boundaries of Indian Territory. They claim two million acres of land. By nightfall, tent cities, banks, and stores are doing business there.

1890 The Second Ghost Dance movement is initiated by Wovoka, a Paiute. It includes many Paiute traditions. In some versions the dance is performed in order to help bring back to Earth many dead ancestors and exterminated game. Ghost Dance practitioners hope the rituals in the movement will restore Indians to their formal state, before the arrival of the non-Native settlers.

1896 Discovery of gold brings hordes of miners and settlers to Alaska.

1897 Oil is discovered beneath Osage land.

1907 With the creation of the state of Oklahoma, the government abolishes the Cherokee tribal government and school system, and the dream of a Native American commonwealth dissolves.

1912 The Alaska Native Brotherhood is formed to promote civil rights issues, such as the right to vote, access to public education, and civil rights in public places. The organization also fights court battles to win land rights.

1916 Ishi, the last Yahi, dies of tuberculosis.

1920 The Canadian government amends the Indian Act to allow for compulsory, or forced, enfranchisement, the process by which Indians have to give up their tribal loyalties to become Canadian citizens. Only 250 Indians had voluntarily become enfranchised between 1857 and 1920.

1924 Congress passes legislation conferring U.S. citizenship on all American Indians. This act does not take away rights that Native Americans had by treaty or the Constitution.

1928 Lewis Meriam is hired to investigate the status of Indian economies, health, and education, and the federal administration of Indian affairs. His report describes the terrible conditions under which Indians are forced to live, listing problems with health care, education, poverty, malnutrition, and land ownership.

1934 U.S. Congress passes the Indian Reorganization Act (IRA), which ends allotment policies and restores some land to Native Americans. The IRA encourages tribes to govern themselves and set up tribal economic corporations, but with the government overseeing their decisions. The IRA also provides more funding to the reservations. Many tribes form tribal governments and adopt constitutions.

1940 Newly opened Grand Coulee Dam floods Spokane land and stops the salmon from running.

1941–45 Navajo Code Talkers send and receive secret messages in their Native language, making a major contribution to the U.S. war effort during World War II.

1942 As hostilities leading to World War II grow, the Iroquois exercise their powers as an independent nation to declare war on Germany, Italy, and Japan.

1946 The Indian Lands Commission (ICC) is created to decide land claims filed by Indian nations. Many tribes expect the ICC to return lost lands, but the ICC chooses to award money instead, and at the value of the land at the time it was lost.

1951 A new Indian Act in Canada reduces the power of the Indian Affairs Office, makes it easier for Indians to gain the right to vote, and helps Indian children enter public schools. It also removes the ban on potlatch and Sun Dance ceremonies.

1954–62 The U.S. Congress carries out its termination policy. At the same time laws are passed giving states and local governments control over tribal members, taking away the tribes' authority to govern themselves. Under the policy of termination, Native Americans lose their special privileges and are treated the same as other U.S. citizens. The tribes that are terminated face extreme poverty and the threat of loss of their community and traditions. By 1961 the government begins rethinking this policy because of the damage it is causing.

1955 The Indian Health Service (IHS) assumes responsibility for Native American health care. The IHS operates hospitals, health centers, health stations, clinics, and community service centers.

1958 Alaska becomes a state; 104 million acres of Native land are taken.

1960 The queen of England approves a law giving status Indians the right to vote in Canada.

1964 The Great Alaska Earthquake and tsunami destroys several Alutiiq villages.

1965 Under the new U.S. government policy, the Self-Determination policy, federal aid to reservations is given directly to Indian tribes and not funneled through the Bureau of Indian Affairs.

1968 Three Ojibway—Dennis Banks, George Mitchell, and Clyde Bellecourt—found the American Indian Movement (AIM) in Minneapolis, Minnesota, to raise public awareness about treaties the federal and state governments violated.

1969 Eighty-nine Native Americans land on Alcatraz Island, a former penitentiary in San Francisco Bay in California. The group calling itself "Indians of All Tribes," claims possession of the island under an 1868 treaty that gave Indians the right to unused federal property on Indian land. Indians of All Tribes occupies the island for 19 months while negotiating with federal officials. They do not win their claim to the island but draw public attention to their cause.

1971 Quebec government unveils plans for the James Bay I hydroelectric project. Cree and Inuit protest the action in Quebec courts.

1971 The Alaska Native Claims Settlement Act (ANCSA) is signed into law. With the act, Alaska Natives give up any claim to nine-tenths of Alaska. In return they are given $962 million and clear title to 44 million acres of land.

1972 Five hundred Native Americans arrive in Washington, D.C., on a march called the Trail of Broken Treaties to protest the government's policies toward Native Americans. The protestors occupy the Bureau of Indian Affairs building for a week, causing considerable damage. They present the government with a list of reforms, but the administration rejects their demands.

1973 After a dispute over Oglala Sioux (Lakota) tribal chair Robert Wilson and his strong-arm tactics at Pine Ridge Reservation, AIM leaders are called in. Wilson's supporters and local authorities arm themselves against protestors, who are also armed, and a ten-week siege begins in which hundreds of federal marshals and Federal Bureau of Investigation (FBI) agents surround the Indian protestors. Two Native American men are shot and killed.

1974 After strong protests and "fish-ins" bring attention to the restrictions on Native American fishing rights in the Pacific Northwest, the U.S. Supreme Court restores Native fishing rights in the case *Department of Game of Washington v. Puyallup Tribe et al.*

1978 U.S. Congress passes legislation called the Tribally Controlled Community College Assistance Act, providing support for tribal colleges, schools of higher education designed to help Native American students achieve academic success and eventually transfer to four-year colleges and universities. Tribal colleges also work with tribal elders and cultural leaders to record languages, oral traditions, and arts in an effort to preserve cultural traditions.

1978 The American Indian Religious Freedom Act is signed. Its stated purpose is to "protect and preserve for American Indians their inherent right of freedom to believe, express, and exercise their traditional religions."

1978 The Bureau of Indian Affairs publishes regulations for the new Federal Acknowledgement Program. This program is responsible for producing a set of "procedures for establishing that an American Indian group exists as an Indian tribe." Many tribes will later discover that these requirements are complicated and difficult to establish.

1982 Canada constitutionally recognizes aboriginal peoples in its new Constitution and Charter of Rights and Freedoms. The Constitution officially divides Canada's aboriginal nations into three designations: the Indian, the Inuit, and the Métis peoples. Native groups feel that the new Constitution does not adequately protect their rights, nor does it give them the right to govern themselves.

1988 The Federal Indian Gambling Regulatory Act of 1988 allows any tribe recognized by the U.S. government to engage in gambling activities. With proceeds from gaming casinos, some tribes pay for health care, support of the elderly and sick, housing, and other improvements, while other tribes buy back homelands, establish scholarship funds, and create new jobs.

1990 Two important acts are passed by U.S. Congress. The Native American Languages Act is designed to preserve, protect, and promote the practice and development of Indian languages. The Graves Protection and Repatriation Act provides for the protection of American Indian grave sites and the repatriation (return) of Indian remains and cultural artifacts to tribes.

1992 Canadians vote against a new Constitution (the Charlotte-town Accord) that contains provisions for aboriginal self-government.

1995 The Iroquois request that all sacred masks and remains of their dead be returned to the tribe; the Smithsonian Institution is the first museum to comply with this request.

1999 A new territory called Nunavut enters the federation of Canada. Nunavut is comprised of vast areas taken from the Northwest Territories and is populated by an Inuit majority. The largest Native land claim in Canadian history, Nunavut is one-fifth of the landmass of Canada, or the size of the combined states of Alaska and Texas. Meaning "Our Land" in the Inukitut (Inuit) language, Nunavut will be primarily governed by the Inuit.

2003 The first official Comanche dictionary is published, compiled entirely by the Comanche people.

2004 Southern Cheyenne Peace Chief W. Richard West Jr. becomes director of the newly opened National Museum of the American Indian in Washington, D.C.

2006 The United Nations censures the United States for reclaiming 60 million acres (90%) of Western Shoshone lands. The federal government uses parts of the land for military testing, open-pit gold mining and nuclear waste disposal. The Shoshone, who have used it for cattle grazing since the Treaty of Ruby Valley in 1863, have repeatedly had their livestock confiscated and fines imposed.

2011 The government gives the Fort Sill Apache 30 acres for a reservation in Deming, New Mexico.

2011 Tacoma Power gives the Skokomish 1,000 acres of land and $11 million.

N

Makah
Skokomish   Duwamish
    Puyallup   Lake   Spokane   Blackfoot
    Nisqually   Umatilla   Salish
Chinook   Colville   Flathead

Siletz   Yakama   Nakota
                            Nez
                            Percé   Crow   Lako

Yurok
Chilula   Modoc   Northern
    Hupa   Pit River   Northern Paiute   Northern   Cheyenne   Ari
                        Western   Shoshone
        Maidu   Shoshone   Eastern   Arapaho
Cahto   Shoshone   Pawne
Pomo
                Washoe

    Miwok
Costanoan   Kawaiisu
        Yahi and Yana   Ute   Southern
                                                Cheyenne
                Southern Paiute
                                    San Carlos
Chumash   Anasazi
                            Navajo   Pueblo   Jicarilla   Kiowa
                    Hopi   Jemez
            Mohave   Apache   San Juan   Taos   K
    Cahuilla   A
    Luiseño   Zuñi
        Yuman   White Mountain   Acoma   Pecos
                    Yaqui   Comanche
PACIFIC   Tohono O'odham   Kiowa
OCEAN   Pima
                    Chiricahua

California
Great Basin
Great Plains
Northeast
Pacific Northwest
Plateau
Southeast
Southwest

Abenaki

Menominee

Sauk

Fox

Mohawk

Iroquois

Wyandot

Narraganset

Pequot

Wampanoag

Dakota

Potawatomi

Delaware

Miami

Hopewell

Powhatan

Missouri

Shawnee

Mississippian
(Mound Builders)

Osage

Lumbee

Cherokee

Quapaw

Chickasaw

Caddo

Creek

Choctaw

Natchez

Seminole

ATLANTIC
OCEAN

Gulf of Mexico

0   100   200 mi

0   100 200 km

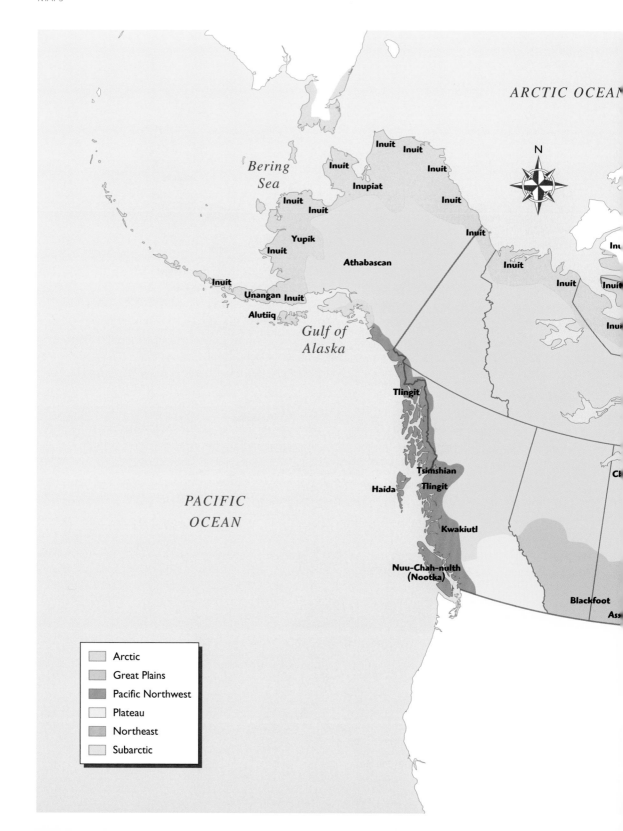

ARCTIC OCEAN

N

Bering
Sea

Inuit
Inuit
Inuit
Inuit
Inupiat
Inuit
Inuit
Inuit
Inuit
Inuit
Inuit
Inuit
Inuit

Yupik
Inuit

Athabascan

Inuit
Unangan Inuit
Alutiiq

Gulf of
Alaska

Tlingit

PACIFIC
OCEAN

Haida
Tsimshian
Tlingit

Kwakiutl

Nuu-Chah-nulth
(Nootka)

Ch

Blackfoot

Ass

Arctic

Great Plains

Pacific Northwest

Plateau

Northeast

Subarctic

Baffin
Bay

Inuit

Inuit

Inuit

nuit

Inuit   Inuit

Inuit

Inuit

Labrador
Sea

Inuit   Inuit

Inuit

Inuit

Inuit

Inuit

Inuit

Hudson
Bay

Innu

Cree

Micmac

ATLANTIC
OCEAN

Ojibwa   Algonkin

Ottawa

Huron

Wyandotte

0   250   500 mi

0   250   500 km

California

California

Although many different California Indian cultures exist, among tribes inhabiting specific territories of California—the northwest, the northeast, central, and southern California—some remarkable similarities exist between groups. In particular, methods of home construction, tool design, and the technologies used in hunting, trapping, and fishing are shared across tribal lines within territories.

Life in California before European contact

Over the centuries the density of Native populations and the patterns of Native settlement have been affected by the physical features of the land surrounding them and the availability of water, plants, and animals. Before Europeans arrived, the abundant food supply throughout California allowed Native peoples to establish villages of up to one thousand individuals, including craft specialists who produced specific goods for a living. In smaller communities, each family produced all that was necessary for survival.

History of the mission system

California lies on the West Coast of the United States and is bounded on its 700-mile-long (1,100-kilometer-long) western side by the Pacific Ocean. Native nations, the original inhabitants of the area, remained free from European influence until the mid-1500s, when Spanish explorers first laid claim to the region. Spain already had a huge colonial empire in North America before it entered California. Because the Pueblo Indians in present-day New Mexico had revolted against the Spanish in the seventeenth century, the Spaniards decided to establish their missions in Alta California (or "Upper" California; the name given to Spanish possessions in what is now the state of California) without immediately sending colonial settlers into the region. Instead of settlers, missionaries arrived first, accompanied by military authorities.

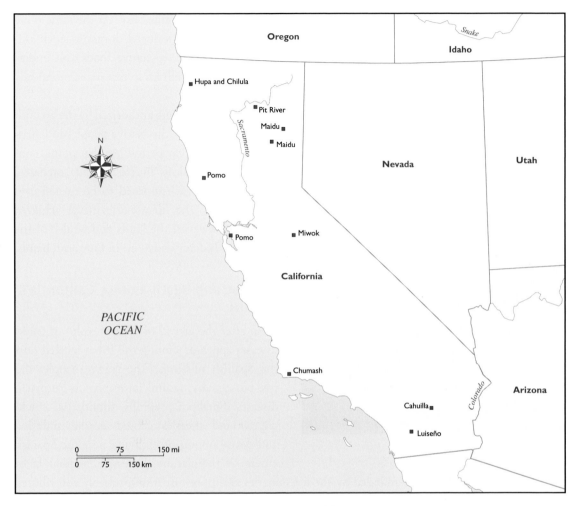

A map showing some contemporary Native American communities in California. MAP BY XNR PRODUCTIONS. CENGAGE LEARNING, GALE. REPRODUCED BY PERMISSION OF GALE, A PART OF CENGAGE LEARNING.

In 1769, Franciscan administrator Junípero Serra (1713–1784) organized in San Diego the first of twenty-one coastal missions. (The Franciscans are a religious order of the Roman Catholic Church.) Military authorities at the mission were led by Gaspar de Portolá (c. 1723–c. 1784).

California missions were essentially labor camps that benefited the Spanish colonizers and proved devastating to the Native peoples. For the most part, missionaries showed a blatant disregard for the people's traditions, customs, and rituals. Armed Spanish soldiers always escorted the Franciscans during their missionary efforts, making the presence of

Spanish Jesuit missionaries work to convert Native Americans in California in the 1600s. © PETER NEWARK AMERICAN PICTURES/THE BRIDGEMAN ART LIBRARY.

Spanish authority quite clear. At the same time, the newcomers introduced domestic stock animals that gobbled up native foods and undermined the tribes' efforts to remain economically independent.

The missions were authorized by the Spanish crown to "convert" the Native peoples to Christianity in a ten-year period. At that point, control over the missions' livestock, fields, orchards, and buildings was supposed to be turned over to the tribes. The missionaries never achieved this goal, however; the lands and wealth of the California Indians ended up in European hands.

Disease and death among California's Indians

Soon after the arrival of Spanish colonists, new diseases appeared among the tribes located near the Spanish missions. The Native peoples did not possess any natural immunity to European diseases. Smallpox, syphilis, diphtheria, chickenpox, and measles caused untold suffering and death among those living near the Spanish centers of population. Excessive manual labor demanded by the missionaries and poor nutrition probably contributed to the people's inability to survive such infections.

Even before the outbreak of these epidemics, though, a general decline in the Mission Indian population was attributed to the unhygienic environment of the neighboring Europeans. The toll was especially high for children. Sadly, the missionary practice of forcibly separating Native children from their parents and confining children from the age of six in filthy and disease-ridden quarters probably increased the suffering and death from disease. Similarly, all unmarried females from the age of six to the elderly were locked up. Many tribes lost faith in their shamans (pronounced *SHAH-munz* or *SHAY-munz*), or medicine men, when the traditional healers' efforts proved ineffective in stemming the tide of misery, suffering, and death that life in the missions caused. Frightened families eventually sought assistance from the European newcomers, who seemed to be immune to the horrible diseases that overwhelmed the Native populations.

The short life expectancy of Mission Indians led missionaries to seek out healthy laborers from tribes living farther inland from the Pacific Coast.

Native resistance

The impact of the mission system on coastal tribal life was devastating. About one hundred thousand—nearly one-third of the Native population of California—died as a direct consequence of the establishment of California missions. Missionaries destroyed the traditions of the California Indians, tore their families apart, and forced them to abandon their native territories and live in filthy, disease-ridden work camps, performing backbreaking labor.

This harsh treatment sparked several well-documented forms of resistance. More than one out of every twenty-four California Indians successfully escaped the plantation-like mission labor camps. Many Mission Indians viewed the padres (priests) as powerful witches who had to be destroyed. Consequently, several Franciscans were killed in the

Mission Indians make baskets and hair ropes in southern California, circa 1800s. © NORTH WIND PICTURE ARCHIVES.

early 1800s. Mission Indians organized widespread armed revolts against colonial authorities. After 1810, a growing number of guerrilla bands (independent fighting units) evolved in the interior. Mounted on horses and using modern weapons, these Mission Indians began raiding mission livestock and fighting colonial military forces.

Mexican takeover and the collapse of the mission system

In 1823, Mexico gained control of the area that is now the state of California. Little immediate change in policy accompanied the end of Spanish colonial rule. The vast Franciscan mission lands took up about one-sixth of the present territory of the state. Even though Mexico's 1824 constitution declared the Native tribes to be citizens of Mexico with rights to vote and hold public office, Native peoples throughout the republic continued to be treated as slaves.

In the mid-1830s, the Mexican government finally stripped the Franciscan padres of the power to force the Natives into labor. Mexico's plans to redistribute mission lands proved worthless to the Mission Indians; the policy was so restrictive that few ex-Mission Indians were eligible for the lands.

After the missions

Once freed from the missions to return to their tribal domains, the liberated California Indians were faced with the staggering task of reconstructing their devastated communities. Their population had suffered tremendous declines; their tribal lands had become transformed by the introduction of vast herds of horses, cattle, sheep, goats, and hogs; the wild game animals they had previously hunted had been driven off the land.

Outraged Native peoples banded together, and eventually a significant number of these groups formed innovative new conglomerate tribes (bands formed of groups from several different tribes). The new groups began to make systematic efforts to reassert their sovereignty (self-government) in the region. They carried out widespread, highly organized campaigns against Mexican ranchers. As resistance to the Mexican government reached its height, interior Mexican ranches were increasingly abandoned because Native stock-raiding activities had caused economic ruin.

Despite these successes in the crusade against non-Native authority, outbreaks of malaria and smallpox severely reduced the Native population of Mexican California in the 1830s. All told, the aboriginal population of approximately 310,000 had been reduced to about 150,000 since the establishment of the first Franciscan mission in San Diego back in 1769.

War and gold: The 1840s and 1850s

The poorly managed Alta California was rapidly overwhelmed by a combination of aggressive Native raids and the arrival of U.S. military forces in the summer of 1846. For two years, Mexico and the United States fought the Mexican-American War (1846–48) over territory that is now part of the southwestern United States. During this struggle, the majority of California Indians sided with the Americans. After the victory of the American forces, however, conditions for Native peoples in the area grew even worse.

With the discovery of gold in the foothills of the Sierra Nevada in the late 1840s, a horde of one hundred thousand adventurers from all over the world descended on the area, with disastrous results for the Native peoples. A deadly pattern of violence and murder developed. Groups formed whose principal occupation seems to have been to kill Native people and kidnap their children. There was also widespread random killing of Natives by individual miners. As many as one hundred thousand Native people were believed to have been murdered in the first two years of the gold rush. The survivors—by this time numbering fewer than seventy thousand—teetered near the brink of total annihilation.

Treaties made, treaties rejected

In January 1851, three federal officials were sent to San Francisco to iron out the region's land title issues. Over the next year, eighteen treaties were negotiated. According to the terms of these treaties, the federal government promised to reserve nearly 7.5 million acres of land for the California Indians. The land would be partitioned into defined areas called tracts; these tracts of land would then be divided among the signatory tribes (tribes that signed the treaties). In addition, the treaties assured the California Indians that they would receive cloth, stock animals, seeds, agricultural equipment, and assistance from American farmers, school-teachers, and blacksmiths. In return, the signatory tribes would surrender their lands to the United States. However, there were problems in the way these treaties were created. Many tribes had not been consulted in the formation of this policy, but they, too, would be bound by the terms of the treaties. During treaty negotiations most California Indians who attended meetings did not understand the English language spoken at them. Worse still, many important tribes were not contacted at all.

Upon hearing that California Indians were to receive millions of acres, most American settlers in California decided they wanted the Native tribes removed to some other territory or state. On July 8, 1852, the U.S. Senate refused to ratify, or validate, the eighteen treaties. Around the same time, a congressional commission was established to validate land titles in California. The commission was required by law to inform the California Indians that they needed to file claims for their lands and to report upon the nature of these claims. Because no one bothered to inform the Native peoples of these requirements, no claims were submitted. Through this "error," the federal government concluded that the California Indians had completely given up all claim to the land; thus, in the eyes of the U.S. government, the tribes now had no lands.

A harsh state government

Despite entering the union as a free state in 1850, the California legislature rapidly enacted a series of laws legalizing Native American slavery. In his first address to the legislature, the new governor, Peter H. Burnett (1807–1895), predicted: "That a war of extermination will continue to be waged between the races, until the Indian race becomes extinct, must be expected." Despite guarantees in the Treaty of Guadalupe Hidalgo, the 1848 agreement that settled the Mexican-American War, Native peoples were denied state citizenship, voting rights, and the right to testify in court. The California Indians were left with no legal protection.

The U.S. government decided to institute an Indian policy in California in 1854, but efforts to establish Native "reserves" and "farms" were largely marred by the corruption and incompetence of the federal government's Indian Affairs workers. The reservations and farms that were formed provided little in the way of support or even minimal refuge for the Native peoples who moved there. They lacked game, suitable agricultural lands, and sufficient water supplies. In time, they were overrun by squatters, who compounded the problems by introducing an epidemic of sexually transmitted diseases to the Native population. Most of the early reserves and farms were abandoned in the 1860s as a result of the state's slavery codes that allowed all able-bodied Native males, females, and even children to be indentured (bound to work for someone else for a given period of time) to American settlers. A great many reservation residents could not participate in the agricultural and ranching programs because their labor "belonged" to private state citizens.

Adaptation and resistance in the late 1800s

The vast majority of California Indians struggled to survive without government aid or recognition. Many on the verge of actual starvation scattered throughout their old territories and tried to support themselves as farm or ranch hands on the lands now claimed by U.S. settlers.

Organized Native resistance was reignited between 1858 and 1872. A series of Indian wars in northwestern California pitted the Yurok, Hupa, Karok, and other tribes against increasingly aggressive Americans who routinely murdered them, stole their children, and burned their villages. This burgeoning racial hatred led white militia groups (small groups of armed forces) to lash out even at nonhostile Native tribes.

The Native peoples of California were able to cope with these great hardships because of their deeply held spiritual beliefs. A religious movement called the Ghost Dance religion sprang up in the region around 1870, strengthening Native ties to the spirit world. The movement was triggered in part by a new introduction of Christian missionaries and by the massive decline in California Indian populations. Promising the return of dead relatives and the disappearance of their oppressors, the Ghost Dance religion crossed tribal lines and revitalized intratribal religious unity.

Because both state and federal authorities seriously underestimated the number of surviving California Indians, plans to remove all of them to a handful of reservations proved impractical. Several attempts to place multiple tribes on a single reservation resulted in violence, mass murder, and war. None of the California tribes wanted to be relocated outside of its aboriginal territory. Non-Native Americans could not begin to understand the intensity and depth of the Native's spiritual attachment to their lands. Not surprisingly, the Bureau of Indian Affairs showed little interest in assisting tribes affected by relocation policies.

Corruption and inefficiency plagued government programs for the California Indians. Reservation agents insisted their residents join Christian churches and give up their traditional Native ways. The General Allotment Act of 1887 (also known as the Dawes Act) forcibly divided reservation tribal lands, doling out (or "allotting") small parcels to individual Native Americans and their families. If the allottees built a house, engaged in farming or ranching, sent their children to government Indian schools, and renounced their tribal allegiance, they would—after twenty-five years—receive title to their land and U.S. citizenship. Between 1893 and 1930, approximately 2,300 allotments had been carved out of the tiny communal tribal reservation lands of California. The allotment system undermined the Native tribal system, divided populations, and rendered the Native peoples politically powerless. Widespread opposition to allotment led to the repeal of the law in 1934.

The fight for compensation

Around the turn of the century, only 6,536 Natives were "recognized" and living on reservations. Every Native person who survived to see the dawn of the twentieth century had witnessed great suffering and irreplaceable family loss. Some lineages disappeared altogether. According to S. F. Cook, a demographer (a person who studies the growth and characteristics of populations), the California Indian population declined to fewer than 16,000 individuals in 1900—an almost unbelievable descent from more than 300,000—in just 131 years of colonization.

The plight of the California Indians following colonization was terrible, but the survivors did not give up the struggle. Several reform groups blossomed before and after the turn of the twentieth century. The efforts of the Northern California Indian Association led to the creation of thirty-six new reservations and rancherías (pronounced *ranch-uh-REE-uhs*) in sixteen northern California counties. (Rancherías were very tiny parcels of land set aside for small bands of landless Native people.) No rancherías, however, were made available for landless southern California Indians.

The impact of politically active tribes and pan-Native American organizations (organizations that advocate reform for all Native American groups) was first felt in the early 1920s. Beginning with the early efforts of the Indian Board of Cooperation, several Native self-help groups began organizing legal action against the United States. The groups claimed that the U.S. government had failed to compensate California's Indians for the loss of their ancestral lands. In response, Congress passed the Jurisdictional Act of 1928, allowing the region's Native nations to sue the federal government and use the state attorney general's office to represent them.

A controversial settlement was eventually reached in 1944. The government offered more than $17 million for their failure to deliver the eighteen reservations promised in the treaty negotiations of 1851 and 1852. Less than one-third of the money was actually distributed among 36,095 California Indians. This amounted to only about $150 for each surviving person. This unfair settlement prompted California Indians to seek further legal compensation and led to the creation of the Indian Claims Commission in 1946. This federal body allowed Native groups to press for compensation over the theft of their lands in the nineteenth century. Again, the results were meager. The major problem with the process was that it was not a court proceeding and, therefore, not subject to constitutional protection. The Native nations were left with little hope that they would ever have enough money to spark desperately needed economic development in their communities.

Termination

By the 1950s, the Bureau of Indian Affairs began plans to end all federal services to California Indians and to transfer all authority over reservations to the state. This new policy, called termination, became law in California under authority of the 1958 Rancheria Act, which allowed tribes to divide communal tribal property into parcels to be distributed to its members. Distributees would receive title to their lands, be free to sell it, and be obliged to pay property tax from that time forward.

The tribes were led to believe that acceptance of termination would increase their freedom and economic independence. The U.S. government promised to upgrade squalid housing, pave roads, build bridges, improve water supplies, and even provide college scholarships in return for a vote to terminate. Between 1958 and 1970, twenty-three rancherías and reservations were terminated. Many Bureau of Indian Affairs services, such as health and education, were abruptly ended for all tribes in the state. Chronically high unemployment rates, low educational achievement, and huge medical bills soon forced many California Indians to make loans on or sell their lands. The termination policy failed miserably to improve the economic and political power of the California Indians. Instead, it stripped small tribes of their ownership of 10,037 acres of land, disrupted tribal institutions and traditions, and left the Native peoples in the region more desperate and impoverished than ever.

Hope for the future

A new civil rights–era generation of young, energetic, and highly educated California Indians emerged in the late 1960s. Understandably skeptical of the government, these new leaders were committed to protecting tribal autonomy (freedom from external control). More important, they found great value in tribal traditions and encouraged tribal religious practices, traditional ceremonies, and language retention among California's Native peoples. In recognition of the growing sophistication of California Indians, the state legislature created the Native American Heritage Commission in 1978. This all-Native commission works as a mediator between state, federal, and tribal governments. Unrecognized tribes—especially the Juaneño Band of Mission Indians, the Acagchemem Nation (formerly the Acagchemem of San Juan Capistrano), and the Muwekma Ohlone Tribe of the San Francisco Bay area—are vigorously pursuing federal recognition. (Federal recognition of Native nations allows them to negotiate as self-governing units and brings much-needed government aid to their communities.)

By the second decade of 2000, about sixty casinos had been established on tribal lands. Few private investors have come forward to work with the tribes outside the gaming industry. Without other options, reservation leaders view gaming as an important step toward greater economic independence and diversification. By 2007, California's gaming industry outranked all but Nevada's in size. That same year, Governor Arnold Schwarzenegger (1947–) signed legislation that allowed California Indian tribes to triple the size of their casino operations, provided the tribes paid hundreds of millions of dollars in annual state taxes.

The amazing adaptive capabilities of California Indians demonstrate the resiliency and genius that these misunderstood and hard-working tribes were able to achieve under the most unfavorable of circumstances. California Indians began the twenty-first century filled with optimism and have continued to make progress toward self-sufficiency and sovereignty.

BOOKS

Abbink, Emily. *Monterey Bay Area Missions in California.* Minneapolis, MN: Lerner, 2007.

Bargellini, Clara, and Michael K. Komanecky. *The Arts of the Missions of Northern New Spain, 1600–1821.* Mexico City: Antiguo Colegio de San Ildefonso, 2009.

Bibby, Brian. *Precious Cargo: California Indian Cradle Baskets and Childbirth Traditions.* Berkeley: Heyday Books, 2004.

Brower, Pauline. *Inland Valleys Missions in California.* Minneapolis, MN: Lerner, 2007.

Doherty, Craig A. *California Indians.* New York: Chelsea House Publications, 2007.

Dubin, Margaret, and Sara-Larus Tolley, eds. *Seaweed, Salmon, and Manzanita Cider: A California Indian Feast.* Berkeley, CA: Heyday Books, 2008.

DuBois, Constance Goddard. *Mythology of the Mission Indians.* Reprint. Charleston, SC: Forgotten Books, 2008.

Frank, L., and Kim Hogeland. *First Families: A Photographic History of California Indians.* Berkeley, CA: Heyday Books, 2007.

Heizer, R. F., ed. *Handbook of North American Indians.* Vol. 8: *California.* Washington, DC: Smithsonian Institution, 1978.

Hogeland, Kim, and L. Frank Hogeland. *First Families: Photographic History of California Indians.* Berkeley: Heyday Books, 2007.

Ira, Jacknis, ed. *Food in California Indian Culture.* Berkeley, CA: Phoebe A. Hearst Museum of Anthropology, University of California, 2007.

Kimbro, Edna, Julia G. Costello, and Tevvy Ball. *The California Missions: History, Art, and Preservation.* Los Angeles: Getty Conservation Institute, 2009.

LePena, Frank. *Dream Songs and Ceremony: Reflections on Traditional California Indian Dance.* Berkeley: Heyday Books, 2004.

Platt, Tony. *Grave Matters: Excavating California's Buried Past.* Berkeley, CA: Heyday, 2011.

Secrest, William B. *When the Great Spirit Died: The Destruction of the California Indians, 1850–1860.* Sanger, CA: Word Dancer Press, 2002.

Stevens, Janice. *Remembering the California Missions.* Fresno, CA: Linden Publishing, 2010.

White, Tekla N. *San Francisco Bay Area Missions.* Minneapolis, MN: Lerner, 2007.

PERIODICALS

Kelsey, Harry. "The California Indian Treaty Myth." *Southern California Quarterly* 55, no. 3 (1973): 225–38.

Kroeber, A. L. "The Religion of the Indians of California." *American Archaeology and Ethnology* 4, no. 6 (1907). Available online at *Internet Sacred Text Archive.* http://www.sacred-texts.com/nam/ca/ric/ (accessed on August 15, 2011).

WEB SITES

Beckman, Tad. "The View from Native California: Lifeways of California's Indigenous People." *Harvey Mudd College.* http://www4.hmc.edu:8001/humanities/indian/ca/intro.htm (accessed on August 11, 2011).

"California Indians." *Visalia Unified School District.* http://visalia.k12.ca.us/teachers/tlieberman/indians/ (accessed on August 15, 2011).

Castillo, Edward D. "Short Overview of California Indian History:" *California Native American Heritage Commission*. http://www.nahc.ca.gov/califindian.html (accessed on August 11, 2011).

Feller, Walter. "California Indian History." *Digital Desert*. http://mojavedesert.net/california-indian-history/ (accessed on August 11, 2011).

The George and Mary Foster Anthropology Library. "Indians of North America—California" *University of California*. http://dpg.lib.berkeley.edu/webdb/anthpubs/search?all=&subjtext=Indians+of+North+America--California&subjectid=1962&page=2 (accessed on August 11, 2011).

Giese, Paula. "Federally Recognized California Tribes." *California Tribes: Main Access Map and Tribes Listing*. http://www.kstrom.net/isk/maps/ca/california.html (accessed on August 15, 2011).

"A History of American Indians in California." *National Park Service*. http://www.nps.gov/history/history/online_books/5views/5views1.htm (accessed on August 15, 2011).

"Indian Gaming in California." *Institute of Governmental Studies, UC Berkeley*. http://igs.berkeley.edu/library/research/quickhelp/policy/government/indian_gaming.html (accessed on August 15, 2011).

"Indian Tribes of California." *Access Genealogy*. http://www.accessgenealogy.com/native/california/ (accessed on August 11, 2011).

Mullen, Nicole. "California Indian Food and Culture." *Phoebe A. Hearst Museum of Anthropology*. http://hearstmuseum.berkeley.edu/outreach/pdfs/teaching_kit.pdf (accessed on August 11, 2011).

"Native American Indian Profiles of Success." *California Indian Education (CALIE)*. http://www.californiaindianeducation.org/native_profiles/ (accessed on August 11, 2011).

"Short Overview of California Indian History." *California Native American Heritage Commission*. http://www.nahc.ca.gov/califindian.html (accessed on August 15, 2011).

Smith, C. R. "California's Native People." *Cabrillo College*. http://www.cabrillo.edu/~crsmith/anth6_syllabus_topics.html (accessed on August 11, 2011).

"State Parks and Museums. "Interpreting California Indian Culture and Heritage." *California State Parks*. http://www.parks.ca.gov/?page_id=24096 (accessed on August 15, 2011).

"A Virtual Tour of California Missions." *Mission Tour*. http://missiontour.org/index.htm (accessed on August 11, 2011).

Cahto

Name

The name Cahto (pronounced *KAH-toe*) comes from the Pomo word meaning "lake"; loosely translated, it means "people of the lake." It is often written Kato; earlier sources sometimes identified the tribe as Kaipomo or Kai Pomo, because of its close relationship with the Pomo. The Cahto lived in two valleys, so the Yuki named the Cahto Valley people *Lál-shiik-nom̀* ("lake black tribe") and those of Long Valley *Kol-úkŭm-nom̀* ("other valley tribe"). The Wailaki called both groups *To-chehl-keyan,* or "water wet tribe." The people called themselves *Djilbi,* for their lake and village. The Cahtoof Long Valley, who had six villages, referred to themselves as *Tlo-kyáhan,* meaning "grass tribe."

Location

The Cahto's original homeland was along Eel Creek in northern California in the hills of the Coast Range. The two bands had villages in Long Valley and Cahto Valley. Today those groups make their homes on the Laytonville Ranchería (Mendocino County) and the Round Valley Reservation (Mendocino and Trinity Counties) in California.

Population

Between 500 and 2,000 Cahto lived in fifty villages in the valleys along Eel Creek in the 1770s. The population declined by about 95 percent during the 1800s. By the 1910 U.S. Census, the number of Cahto had fallen to 51. In 1972, the Cahto tribal council reported 95 members. In the late 1990s, only 100 Cahto were living on the ranchería and reservation; by the mid-2000s, that count was up to 250.

Language family

Athabascan.

Origins and group affiliations

The Cahto are of Athabascan descent and therefore related to other Athabascan groups, such as the Apache, Navajo, Tlingit, and Haida (see entries). The Cahto may have been part of larger tribe that once included the Hupa

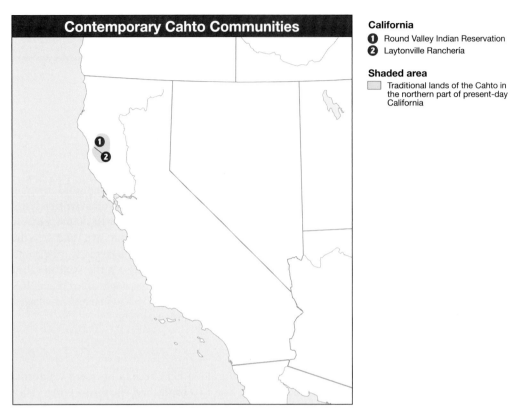

Contemporary Cahto Communities

California
1. Round Valley Indian Reservation
2. Laytonville Rancheria

Shaded area
Traditional lands of the Cahto in the northern part of present-day California

A map of contemporary Cahto communities. MAP BY XNR PRODUCTIONS. CENGAGE LEARNING, GALE. REPRODUCED BY PERMISSION OF GALE, A PART OF CENGAGE LEARNING.

(see entry), but, if so, the two bands separated long ago. The Cahto people traded extensively with their neighbors the Yuki, but the two groups often fought. They were also closely associated with other nearby tribes—the Pomo (see entry), Sinkyone, and Wailaki—but were hostile toward the latter two for trespassing on Cahto hunting grounds. The Cahto's relationship with the Pomo, though, was friendly. In fact, the two groups were so close that some early writers considered them part of the same tribe. One even listed them as bands of the Pomo: Kai Pomo, Kastel Pomo, and Kato Pomo.

The Cahto lived amid the rolling hills of the Coast Range between the headwaters of the two main branches of Eel River, where oak savannas and nearby waters provided abundant food. Rainy winters swelled the many streams that crisscrossed their land, but arid summer temperatures dried them out. The people's hunting and gathering lifestyle allowed them to adjust to their environment. Wars over territory with neighboring tribes and American prospectors, along with foreign diseases, decimated the tribe, whose population decreased drastically during the nineteenth century. By the time they moved to the reservations, much of the Cahto culture had been lost. Since that time, the tribe has been working to restore its language and traditions and to achieve economic self-sufficiency.

HISTORY

Prehistory

From available evidence, it appears that the Athabaskan arrived on the North American continent about 7,000 years ago. The various groups divided and moved north, west, and southwest into present-day Canada, United States, and Mexico. The Cahto settled in California as early as 900 CE.

Some linguists (people who study languages) believe that the Cahto and Hupa (see entry) were once part of the same tribe. They say the groups separated about 1,000 years ago. If that were so, since that time, the languages of the two groups have diverged greatly, so much so that speakers of one cannot understand the other.

Intertribal warfare

The Cahto lands were surrounded by other tribes who spoke similar languages, particularly the Wailaki to the northeast. The Yuki and Huchnom lived to the east. The Cahto maintained friendly relations with the Pomo to the south and traded with the Coast Yuki to the west. Relations with the Wailaki in the northeast and the Sinkyone to the north were generally strained. These two bands often set brush fires on Black Rock Mountain to drive out game. The Cahto, who were not normally aggressive, considered this to be deliberate trespassing on their territory and attacked the interlopers. Casualties during these battles seldom reached more than one or two people (see "Warfare rituals"), but in the 1840s, the Cahto engaged in intense fighting with the Yuki.

Important Dates

1826: Trapper Jedediah Strong Smith (1799–1831) is the first Euro-American explorer to travel through Cahto land.

1840s: Cahto engage in intense warfare with their neighbors, the Yuki.

1851: An expedition led by Redick McKee reaches Cahto territory.

1856: U.S. settlers claim Cahto land. Round Valley Indian Reservation begins as Nome Cult Farm.

1870: Ghost Dance Movement starts. Round Valley Indian Reservation is established by executive order.

1908: Missionaries purchase 200 acres of Cahto homeland for the tribe.

1967: The Cahto Tribe of the Laytonville Ranchería adopt the Articles of Association of the Cahto Tribe.

1970: Cahto tribal council is established.

2006: The Cahto approve amendments to their Articles of Association.

This battle eventually escalated until many area tribes, particularly the Wailaki, Huchnom, and Pomo, had become involved. During the fighting, the Wailaki challenged the Pomo, which led to an invitation for many coastal settlements to join the fray. The people divided themselves into sides based on kinship as well as old feuds and grudges. The main groups against the Cahto were the Sinkyone, Pomo, and Coast Yuki. Cahto allies included the Huchnom and some Wailaki; other Wailaki sided with the Yuki. (For a Cahto account of this battle, see "Warfare rituals.") The war ended when the Gold Rush started in 1949 and prospectors overran Native territory.

Relations with U.S. government

Skirmishes arose between California Indians and the miners who squatted on their homelands. To keep the peace between the two groups, Federal Commissioner Redick McKee (1800–1886) journeyed from San Francisco to Humboldt Bay in 1851. His aim was to get the various tribes to sign treaties. McKee's visit was the Cahto's first interaction with the U.S. government. McKee assured the Native nations that, unlike the Mexicans, who had enslaved many tribes to build the Catholic missions, the U.S. government was benevolent and had only the interests of the tribes at heart.

Until then, the Native nations' only contact had been with the American prospectors and settlers. Even after the United States took over the territory from Mexico, any Native man, woman, or child could be taken as a slave, and the tribes had no recourse if settlers attacked them, raped the women, or stole their land or goods. Most courts decided in favor of the settlers, even in cases where the Americans were obviously in the wrong. In addition, an 1851 law paid California citizens for ridding the state of Indians, which meant Native peoples' lives were in constant danger. McKee's promise that the tribes would see justice done and receive federal protection must have been appealing, even if it meant giving up their land.

Troubles with settlers

In 1856, two pioneers established the town of Cahto (no longer in existence). That same year, the government established the Nome Cult Farm on Yuki territory. It was one of five California reservations that the state opened in the 1850s. Although the Yuki kept a portion of their

Minutes of Meeting of Treaty Commissioner Redick McKee with Clear Lake Pomo Tribelets, August, 1851

This is part of a speech given by Redick McKee as he negotiated with the Pomo, allies of the Cahto. As many people considered the Cahto a division of the Pomo, they may well have been included in his address. A similar assurance was given to each tribe, and the Cahto, as did the Pomo, believed in the sincerity of McKee's offer.

Government agents during this time period called the president of the United States the "Great White Father." They referred to the Native peoples as his "red children," which implied that the American government intended to care for the Native people but, at the same time, dominate the relationship. The promised care was not forthcoming, however; most of the treaty terms were soon broken.

Camp Lupiyuma, August 18, 1851

The President has very many red children living beyond the big mountains, and settled happily upon lands of their own, where white men were not permitted among them; that they were cultivating the soil, raising stock, etc., and had now no cause for war, neither among themselves nor with the whites.

The President wishes to improve you in the same way, and has sent his agents among you for that purpose. He is well satisfied that is the best plan for you; if you will agree to be settled in this way you must give up all right to all other lands, and never move again without the President's permission…. Your families … must always remain at one place. The agent sent among you will settle all your difficulties and prevent the whites from injuring you, and will cause guilty Indians and guilty whites to be punished. The President will also give you teachers, farmers, and mechanics, to teach you many things and improve your condition very much.

John McKee, Secretary

SOURCE: McKee, John. "Minutes of Meeting of Treaty Commissioner Redick McKee with Clear Lake Pomo Tribelets, August, 1851." *University of California: The George and Mary Foster Anthropology Library.* http://dpg.lib.berkeley.edu/webdb/anthpubs/search?all=&subjtext=Indians+of+North+America--California&subjectid=1962&item=87 (accessed on August 11, 2011).

homeland, they were forced to share it with other tribes, many of whom were enemies. The government began rounding up members of the Pit River, Pomo (see entries), Concow, Nomlaki, Wailaki, and Cahto tribes and sending them to the reservation. Land that had once supported one band now needed to feed many more.

Even though Nome Farm had been set aside for the Native nations, many U.S. settlers moved onto the land and started farms. This influx of newcomers did more than just take Native land and hunting grounds; it introduced diseases to which Native people had no immunity, and many Native people died. The growing communities of settlers also scared away the game. When the tribes did not have enough to eat, some members began stealing cattle. Skirmishes arose between the settlers and the Natives over this issue. The settlers often retaliated by killing any Natives they saw, whether they were responsible for the thefts or not. One of the most serious incidents for the Cahto people occurred in 1859, when thirty-two Indians in Long Valley, some of them Cahto, were murdered for allegedly stealing livestock. Although U.S. soldiers were sent to the area to protect the Indians, they spent most of their time capturing tribal members who had refused to relocate and confining them to the reservation.

Changes on the reservation

In 1887, according to the terms of the Dawes Act, the government divided reservation land into five- or ten-acre plots and gave one to each head of household. They then sold the rest of the reservation land to non-Natives. Within a few decades, the government said that, to claim the land, Native owners had to pay taxes on it. Although some had managed to turn their land into profitable farms or livestock ranches, many others soon lost their property due to back taxes or poor harvests.

In 1870, a federal executive order made the Nome Cult Farm an official reservation, called Round Valley Indian Reservation. That same year, a new religion, the Ghost Dance Movement (see "Religion"), swept through many reservations in response to the suffering of the Native peoples across the country. Started by the Paiute (see entry) shaman Wodi-wob, the dance was supposed to rid the land of outsiders and restore life to the way it had been before their arrival. The Pomo taught the dance to the Cahto, who passed it on to the Wailaki and Yuki. The Ghost Dance Movement soon lost momentum when the tribes who were following this new religion saw no changes and experienced even greater cruelty and oppression from the society around them. Another Paiute, Wovoka (c. 1856–1932), revived in the dance in the 1890s. The Ghost Dance at that time was practiced with so much religious fervor that Indian agents on the reservations feared it would lead to widespread rebellion and uprisings. The government stepped in to stop it, and the Native nations had to practice their religion in secret.

Laytonville Ranchería

In 1908, missionaries purchased two hundred acres of land for the Cahto. This became the Laytonville Ranchería. When the Indian Reorganization Act passed in 1934, the Round Valley Indian Reservation set up a tribal government and wrote a constitution, which the U.S. government approved. The Cahto at Laytonville Ranchería, however, did not begin to organize under the act until 1967. That year they adopted the Articles of Association of the Cahto Tribe, and in 1970, they established a tribal council.

Mid-twentieth century and beyond

The remainder of the 1900s were marked by high unemployment and high school dropout rates, poverty, substandard housing, and struggles for survival. During that time, the Cahto culture eroded; their language and many customs were lost. Few people remained on the reservations because they could not support their families there.

By the twenty-first century, casinos and new tribal enterprises had brought in income and helped decrease unemployment and poverty. Language and culture programs were helping to restore traditions that had been lost over the previous centuries. The Cahto had started instilling in the younger generations a pride in their heritage and strengthening their people for the future.

RELIGION

The Cahto had two main deities. Chénĕsh, or T'cenes, was associated with thunder and lighting. He created animals and humans. Nághai-cho, or Nagaicho (the Great Traveler), who created mountains and streams, rode a horned beast or a huge deer through the waters. The animal then lay down to become the earth. Nághai-cho, who also plays the role of trickster, was always trying to outdo T'cenes. Their competitions with each other led to the rivalries among people on Earth

The people prayed to these two original beings. They said prayers in the morning and evening, and at meals. Praying was also done when they were sick or after they sneezed.

A Prayer for Eels

"May I eat the eels that swim up the stream with good fortune. May I eat the fish with good fortune. May the boys and girls eat them with good fortune.

"Deer, may I swallow you with good luck. You are mine. My food is sweet. Do not let it die. Let it be good," he said.

SOURCE: Goddard, Pliny Earle. "A Prayer for Eels." *Kato Texts.* Berkeley: The University Press. *University of California Publications in American Archaeology and Ethnology* 5, no. 3 (December 6, 1909): 65–238, Pl. 9.

Kato Words

Many Kato words are not just names but are also descriptions. For example, the Kato word for beaver actually means "little one who chews." Bat can be translated as "flying mammal" or "little one that flaps." Raccoon means "long hand," and horse is "big dog."

chin-ti'aalhtc	"beaver"
ch'ilhbaat'itc	"bat"
doolii	"black bear"
kooldjii	"skunk"
laa'nees	"raccoon"
lhiin'-chow	"horse"
bittc	"bobcat"
too-bittc	"housecat"
teehlaang	"whale"

The Big Head Cult Movement, or Ghost Dance Movement, began in the late 1870s. The Cahto learned this ritual from the Pomo, and they adopted the Ghost Dance that went with it. Performed at night, the Ghost Dances were supposed to restore the land to the Native peoples, bring back the animals, and get rid of the non-Natives in their homeland (see "History"). The Cahto passed the dance on to other bands on the reservation. Each group added their own variations to fit their traditions. The Cahto, dressed in regalia and headdresses, danced for four nights in row as part of their Ghost Dance ceremony. This 1870s version gradually died out, but it was later revived in 1890.

LANGUAGE

Kato, the language of the Cahto people, is part of the Athabaskan language family, which is spoken over a widespread area of North America, from western Canada and the Oregon coast to northern California and the Southwest. Kato itself was spoken only in the Cahto and Long Valley of northern California. Before European contact, between five hundred and two thousand people spoke Kato, but over the next century, the language became extinct. By the twenty-first century, no one spoke Kato as a first language, but the people were trying to revive the language.

Some experts say that Kato is a dialect, or variety, of Wailaki, a language once used by a neighboring tribe of the Cahto. Others classify Kato as a related language of its own. The two are definitely similar. For example, the number one in Wailaki is *lhai'haa'*; In Kato it is *lhaa'haa'*. Two is *naakaa'* in both languages. Three is *taak* in Wailaki and *taak'* in Kato. Yet four is *denky'en* in Wailaki and *naakaa'naakaa'* (two twos) in Kato.

GOVERNMENT

Early leadership

Before European contact, the Cahto lived in about fifty loosely connected villages. Each community had its own headman, and some had a second chief. The position usually passed from father to son, but if the headman had no sons, the people got together and selected a new chief.

The position was not one of authority. Instead, the headman served as an adviser. Decision-making power rested with the tribal council, a group of village elders. Each one expressed an opinion, after which the chief would follow the guidance of the majority. The headman's main responsibility was to be sure the people stayed moral. He often stood outside his house and gave speeches or scolded people to remind them of their duties. Whenever he spoke, people stopped to listen.

Modern government

In 1934, Congress passed the Indian Reorganization Act. As a result, reservations were to set up tribal governments and write constitutions, subject to federal government approval. The Round Valley Indian Tribes elected a seven-member tribal council and wrote a constitution that is still in use. The tribal council consists of a president, vice president, secretary, treasurer, sergeant-at-arms, and two members at large.

The Cahto Tribe of the Laytonville Rancheria came to the process much later, and in 1967, they adopted their Articles of Association, which were amended in 2006. A Cahto tribal council was established in 1970. In the twenty-first century, the tribal council elects an executive committee. The committee is composed of a chair, vice chair, secretary, and one member. Their duties include leasing and managing tribal assets, signing legal contracts, setting fees, collecting money, increasing tribal funds, enacting laws, and representing the tribe in negotiations with outside governments. As in the past, all of the committee's decisions are subject to tribal council approval.

ECONOMY

In the early days, the Cahto lived as hunter-gatherers. They also had an extensive trading network to supply their needs. The people traveled to Blue Rock to exchange arrows, clothing, and baskets with the Wailaki, and they received similar items in return. Their trips to the coast gave them a wider variety of goods. For their hazelwood bows, the Cahto received seaweed, abalone, mussels, clamshells, fish, and kelp from the Yuki. The Cahto also gathered some of their own seaweed and shellfish. The tribe even developed their own monetary system based on clamshells, flint, disk beads, and magnesite beads.

After the move to the reservation and rancheria, the people had to give up their former lifestyle and adapt to farming. Some became successful farmers or ranchers. Others lost their land because of taxes or poor harvests. Wage work became the only way for them to make a living. Most workers earned an income by hiring themselves out as ranch or farm hands or by working at a nearby lumber mill, but these jobs often paid a low wage. Layoffs occurred when the economy dipped and when aggressive, unsustainable timber harvesting caused the closing of a sawmill. At times, more than half the people were unemployed.

The Cahto people are working for a brighter future. The opening of casinos on tribal land not only added employment but also began to bring in large revenues to fund tribal programs. Many business development and economic projects have been planned to provide more job opportunities.

DAILY LIFE

Families

A Cahto woman poses for a portrait, circa 1924. © THE PROTECTED ART ARCHIVE/ ALAMY.

Labor was divided, with the men doing the hunting and fishing, and the women sewing, cooking, and gathering all foods but acorns. Everyone worked together to harvest the acorns, one of their staple foods. When a man shot game, he came home and told his wife where to find it. She followed his directions and hauled home the deer or other carcass and butchered it. Because of their duties, men owned all the hunting and war items; women's possessions included the clothing, baskets, and cooking rocks.

Buildings

Cahto homes were usually round and built over a pit about 2 feet (half a meter) deep. The roof was supported by forked posts set in a square or rectangular arrangement, with the front ones higher than those in the rear so the roof sloped from front to back. The walls and poles leaned in so that when the house was complete, it looked as if it had a conical roof, rather than square. The people stuffed slabs of wood, bark, and grasses into the openings between the posts. Dirt from the hole might be thrown around the base and on the roof. A hole in the roof vented smoke. The entrance was a narrow doorway that reached to the roof.

Sometimes only one family occupied the home, but it could provide shelter for up to three families, who cooked at the central fire. The Cahto rebuilt their homes every two years to get rid of vermin (insects and mice).

Larger villages had ceremonial lodges that could reach 20 feet (6 meters) in diameter. The Cahto built them over a deeper pit, usually about 3 or 4 feet deep (about 1 meter). These buildings were used for dances, rituals, and public meetings. They also served as sweathouses for the men.

In the summer, the Cahto camped out in their fishing and gathering areas, where they set up simple brush lean-tos.

Clothing and adornment

Both men and women wrapped a deerskin about their waists, tied their long hair up into a knot at the back of their head, and used nets knitted from iris fiber to keep their hair in place. In the summer, the deerskin was tanned, but for winter wear, the hair was left on the hide. Both sexes wore nose ornaments, deer hide bracelets, and earrings made from rings of woven grass. They made ceremonial belts by stringing large pinecones together. No shoes were worn.

Later, the Cahto made knee-length shirts sewn from two deerskins; these laced down the front. They also used moccasins.

Tattoos were done with a deer bone needle and spruce pitch that was blackened in smoke. Patterns of broken and straight lines adorned their foreheads, cheeks, chins, chests, wrists, or legs.

Food

The early Cahto lived a life of hunting and gathering. The people tamed dogs to help them with their hunting. They sometimes caught baby coyotes and bred them with the dogs. Men hunted game, such as bear, fox, wildcat, cougar, deer, rabbit, squirrel, skunk, mole, gopher, and raccoon. Quail and other birds were shot with bows and arrows or deer-hide slings. The nearby waters provided many varieties of fish, but salmon was a staple of their diet. The people sometimes ate insects, including grasshoppers, bees, caterpillars, and hornets. Trade with coastal tribes added salt, seaweed, abalone, and mussels to their food supplies.

The women broiled meat over coals or on a spit, and they cooked fish on hot rocks or in the ashes of the fires. They used baskets to boil acorn soup by dropping heated stones into the broth. The Cahto dried both meat and fish for winter use. Kelp was dried and burned to extract its salt.

Women gathered the nuts, tarweed, berries, seeds, clover, roots, bulbs, and tubers that formed the main part of Cahto meals. The most important food was the acorn, which everyone in the tribe gathered communally. Acorns had to be leached before they were used. To do this, the Cahto soaked them in water to remove the bitter tannin taste. The acorns could then be roasted for storage, added to soups and stews, or ground into flour.

Education

When the Cahto lived in the Cahto and Long Valleys, the men spent time learning various dialects. Most of them could speak every language that belonged to the people within a day's traveling distance. The sons of the chief trained especially hard because they needed to be diplomats and communicate with the neighboring tribes. Many headmen sent their sons to live with the chiefs who bordered the Cahto territory, and those chiefs sent their sons to the Cahto village.

In the mid-twentieth century, low educational levels and high dropout rates were a major concern for the Cahto. From 1952 to 1972, not even ten students graduated from high school. In addition, very few aspects of their traditional culture remained. In recent years, the Cahto have turned those dismal statistics around, and students are actively learning their language.

Healing practices

Most Cahto had a good knowledge of herbs and could cure themselves of ordinary illnesses, such as headaches, toothaches, earaches, stomach upsets, arrow wounds, and rattlesnake bites. The people had specialists—surgeons and midwives—to handle certain cases. They also called in shamans (pronounced *SHAH-munz* or *SHAY-munz*) to cure patients who needed additional help, either physically, mentally, or spiritually (see sidebar "Powers of Doctors").

ARTS

Music was an important part of the Cahto culture. In the evenings, the Cahto sat outdoors to listen to the women of the tribe sing. A pair of women tapped bones together to keep the rhythm, and the most talented

Powers of Doctors

Three types of doctors, or shamans, handled Cahto illnesses. Each had a responsibility for a different kind of sickness. Shamans were always paid even if the cure did not work. Their pay was hung from the rafters of the house or in the trees if they worked outdoors.

The ŭtiyín went through an initiation and then learned his trade from a skilled instructor. These were the only shamans who went through training. The other shamans received their calling and knowledge through dreams. The novice ŭtiyín practiced on simple cases while his instructor watched. When he had learned his skills, he handled his own cases. To heal people, the ŭtiyín sucked out disease. He also used singing, shaking rattles, and calling on Nághai-cho (see "Religion"), the father of all.

The náchŭhlna were called in when a person had a fright from an encounter with a supernatural creature. This shaman used the power of animals to heal. The náchŭhlna worked with a group of other shamans who dressed in costume and accompanied him. These healers donned wood slabs instead of clothes, put baskets on their heads, and had objects hanging from their ears. When the group entered, the sick person pointed out the one that had scared him. A shaman representing the supernatural being Nághai-cho then arrived, dressed as a giant with a buzzard-feather headdress, walking backward and twirling around. He circled the patient four times, touching the person's forehead each time. The other shamans then chased him out with sticks. That ritual removed the patient's fear, and a feast followed at the sick person's house.

The chǵhályiśh could see the future in dreams. Rather than physical ailments, they dealt with mental illness. The Cahto believed insanity was caused by seeing tái-kyhan (short, black "outside people"). During the curing ritual, singers shook their rattles and called on these tái-kyhan, who appeared. The medicine man shot one, and the others ran away. The shamans then covered the dead one and took it away. The patient recovered but sometimes had fits where he wandered around at night, singing and shouting. He also had dreams that foresaw events.

The Cahto had one other kind of shaman, the bear doctor, a shaman who murdered rather than healed. Bear doctors, who turned into grizzlies to kill others, were said to have lived among the bears to learn how to transform themselves (see Pomo entry). Unlike those of many other California tribes, Cahto bear doctors did not attack just anyone; they only went after enemies from other tribes. The fastest runners were chosen and fitted with a bear suit sewn to fit their bodies. The costume was lined with yew slats to protect it from arrows. To make the tongue look shiny, the Cahto used abalone shell. They sometimes stuck long pieces of flint in the eyes that could cut an enemy. In addition to long knives, bear shamans carried crooked staffs to trip victims who tried to escape.

Bear doctors hid with a war party near an enemy's deer traps or along a well-used path to ambush him. At other times, they tied a bear cub in the bushes to entice their victims. When the enemies heard the cub's cries, they hunted for it, and the bear shamans trapped them.

singer would begin the song. The men only listened, but they made music at other times. Initiations had both individual and group singing. Instruments were varied: the main ones were whistles, rattles (split-stick and cocoon), foot drums, bull-roarers, musical bows, and six-hole elderberry flutes.

Cahto women were known for their basketry. They made the usual twined baskets, but they also sometimes created coiled baskets.

CUSTOMS

Birth and childhood

The Cahto killed deformed babies and twins at birth. Although they did this, they were otherwise known as kind and gentle parents. Mothers sang to babies in their cradles, and parents were never harsh with their children and rarely scolded them.

Children received nicknames based on physical characteristics or some unusual action. Most had names of animals or birds.

Puberty

In the summer, teen boys, ranging from about ages twelve to sixteen, went to a solitary place outside the village with an instructor for three days. There, after being smeared with charcoal, they learned Cahto customs and rituals. Afterward, they marched to the ceremonial house, where their instructor gave them a lecture in front of the assembled villagers. The young men then plunged into the river to wash off the charcoal and returned for a feast. In the winter, they spent four months learning oral history that they then shared in front of the community.

For girls, puberty began with their first menstruation. Girls received special spiritual training, ate a diet that included no meat and very little water, did no work, and stayed in or near their homes for the next five months. A feast followed where the girl, along with all the girls and women of the tribe, danced.

Marriage

Couples arranged their own marriages. Once the girl agreed, the young man would sneak in her home to sleep with her at night. They tried to keep their relationship secret for at least a few days. People soon realized that the two were a couple, but no announcement was made, not even to the parents. Once everyone knew about their relationship, the husband usually built a house for himself and his new bride.

Divorce was as easy as marriage. Either person could leave for any reason. The mother kept the daughters; the father took the sons.

In Cahto society, couples of the same sex could marry, but usually only males did so.

Death and mourning

To prepare a body for burial, the Cahto washed it, dressed it in good clothes, and wrapped it in deer skins. Everyone in the village, crying loudly, followed the procession to the grave that had been dug in a hillside. The grave was as deep as the dead person was tall and had a floor of poles that were covered with bark and deerskins. Valuables were sometimes put into the grave with the body. Bark was put over the body before the pit was filled with earth. If a death occurred away from home, the body was cremated. Cremation had been part of the earlier burial customs.

Spouses cut their hair as a sign of mourning. Widows shaved their heads or singed off their hair. They then coated the stubble and their faces with pitch for the next year, or sometimes longer. After a year had passed, the Cahto held a ceremony, particularly if the person had been important in the village. They built a fire at the grave. The people all tossed items they valued, such as skins or baskets, into the flames. Following the ceremony, all mourners were expected to be happy.

Warfare rituals

The Cahto did not go to war unless their territory was invaded or someone from their community was attacked. Before engaging in battle, they performed rituals to ensure their success. One of the old men held up a coyote sinew tied to a human bone and chanted prayers that everyone else repeated, then everyone blew their breath toward their foe's land to weaken them. A war dance assured them of victory the next day.

Taboos

The Cahto had many different taboos. A few of them were as follows:

Children were not allowed to see live or dead raccoons.

A menstruating woman could not talk to her husband.

Names of the dead were never spoken.

The elders were forbidden to eat meat when a shaman was healing someone in the house.

Spouses could not look their in-laws in the face or speak directly to them. Sometimes they got around this taboo by addressing everyone who was present.

A war leader led the people into battle but did not participate himself. His job was to monitor the fighting and communicate to the enemy's war chief when enough people had died. Both sides stopped fighting when either side's war chief declared a halt. They then agreed when they would meet again to fight. To signal the start of a battle, one side lit the grass on fire. The rising smoke let the enemy know it was time to approach.

In the Cahto-Yuki war of the 1840s (see sidebar), the chiefs ended the daily skirmishes after a few people had been killed. They then picked a new place to fight and agreed to meet in ten days at that site. This occurred several times during the course of the battle. In all, they met in at least four different places.

The Cahto cut off the head and shoulders of their dead enemies. Back in their village, an old man prepared each one by scraping out the flesh and stuffing the skin with dried grasses. He then staked it out to dry in the sun. After it dried, he tied the head to a post that was driven into the ground. The people then invited the nearby villages to a war dance that was held inside a brush enclosure. After everyone had feasted, the Cahto threw scraps of food to the keeper of the scalps, who ate the food from the ground like an animal. Then he danced, while insulting and threatening the enemy.

Games and ceremonies

Children played acorn tops and jumped rope. The adults engaged in races, stone-throwing, shinny, and the grass game. Shinny, played by both men and women, was similar to field hockey, where players used sticks to hit a ball to a goal. The grass game was played using two identical bundles of grass, one with a stick inside. While singing, players took turns guessing which bundle in an opponent's hands contained the stick. People often bet on the winners of the game.

Ceremonies were held in winter and summer. If a person could feed many guests, neighboring communities were invited to participate. The people danced for a week, the creation story was recounted, and the headman made speeches.

The three main dances were the Acorn Dance, the Feather Dance, and the Necum Dance. The Acorn Dance celebrated the acorn harvest, in which everyone participated (see "Food"). The performers donned headdresses of buzzard or eagle feathers and cloaks. The other two dances were done for pleasure. Six men, women, and children did the Feather Dance. In the Necum Dance, six men danced on the opposite side of the fire from six women.

1840s Kato-Yuki War

This is part of a Kato (Cahto) account of the war with the Yuki, told by a Kato narrator. Most wars had few fatalities because the chiefs stopped the wars by waving their hairnets when they felt too many people had died.

> When they [the Kato and Yuki] fought, they shot with their arrows as far as from here to there (fifty to sixty yards).... The chiefs stood on each side and told each other how many had been killed. The Yuki chief said: "Six are killed." "On this side three." Then our chief said to his people, "Enough! Stop! Don't fight any more. In ten days we will begin again." So they stopped fighting....
>
> After ten days it was reported: "They want to fight again." The chief said, "Good! I have my men here." So they watched for the smoke. "There is the fire now; they are coming." Then they made a fire here too. So they came together. They dodged as if dancing, sideways. The chief would say to someone, "You have never fought before, go in." If one was killed they would carry him out and another came into his place. They were naked, sweating, and without drinking. Sometimes one side drove the other. The chief walked about, watched the battle, looked at the sun, but never shot. Then he would call, "Enough," and they stopped. "How many are killed on your side?" "Two. And on yours?" "One." "It is enough."...
>
> [Later, after several more battles, more tribes joined the war.] They lined up near Box Springs at Tocha'ns ("muddy water"). There the two chiefs said, "Go on now, fight." And they began. You cannot well hit a man at fifty or sixty yards on account of his dodging, so the Sherwood people tried to kill our men by catching them, and sometimes nearly succeeded. The women were shouting off in the woods. Then the Pomo were driven over a narrow trail. The Kato kept driving them back toward Sherwood flat.... Then the chiefs said, "It is enough," and waved their hair-nets and stopped the battle. The Kato chief said, "Now let us dance. Come here, you, and sing."... Then they all bathed in the creek ... and washed their hair with soaproot to make it shine.... They cooked and ate and gathered dry grass to sit on and keep clean; they talked, laughed, and rested before returning home.

SOURCE: Kroeber, A.L. *A Kato War.* Berkeley: University of California Archaeological Research Facility, 1973, pp. 35–40. Available online from http://digitalassets.lib.berkeley.edu/anthpubs/ucb/text/arfs006-010.pdf (accessed on August 11, 2011).

CURRENT TRIBAL ISSUES

One of the most emotionally and politically charged issues revolves around marijuana growing on the Round Valley Reservation. Although California law allows growing marijuana for medical purposes, the Round Valley tribes have set up different rules from the local government. Tribal rules allow members to grow more marijuana than the local authorities permit. The tribe views itself as an independent nation that is not governed by U.S. laws, but in 2010 nontribal officers raided tribal property and confiscated plants, property, and money. One of the concerns of both tribal police and non-Native law enforcement officers is that Mexican crime organizations are behind some of the marijuana production. Area Hispanic workers sometimes help get a garden started and then demand half of the proceeds. These gardeners are often at the mercy of the Mexican criminals, who hold the gardeners' families hostage in Mexico to force the workers to comply. In addition to the problems of illegal marijuana growing, the Round Valley tribes are concerned with the violation of their reservation's sovereignty (self-government) by outside law enforcement, a civil rights battle they have been fighting for decades.

Other concerns the Cahto face in the twenty-first century are the improvement of roads and housing, environmental cleanup, economic growth, the restoration of habitats for fish and endangered and threatened animals, the preservation of cultural artifacts and sites, language preservation and cultural programs, and the implementation of clean air, water, and wastewater systems for the communities. The Round Valley Reservation is working on developing organic gardening, aggregate mining, rangeland, and alternative energy. At the Laytonville Ranchería, a nearby landfill leaked petroleum and solvent-based contaminants, many containing heavy metals, into the ground and water systems. Since that time, the people have been working to mitigate the effects. They also have many other ongoing environmental initiatives in progress. The Cahto Environmental Protection Department initiated a five-year (2011–15) wetland restoration program, following which the Tribal Wetland Program was slated to be reevaluated and revised for the next five years.

BOOKS

Bauer, William J. *We Were All Like Migrant Workers Here: Work, Community, and Memory on California's Round Valley Reservation, 1850–1941.* Chapel Hill: University of North Carolina Press, 2009.

DuBois, Cora. *The 1870 Ghost Dance.* Reprint. Lincoln: University of Nebraska, 2007.

Kroeber, A.L. *A Kato War.* Berkeley: University of California Archaeological Research Facility, 1973: 35–40. Available online from http://digitalassets. lib.berkeley.edu/anthpubs/ucb/text/arfs006-010.pdf (accessed on August 11, 2011).

Myers, James E. "Cahto." In *Handbook of North American Indians.* Vol. 8: *California,* edited by R. F. Heizer. Washington, D.C.: Smithsonian Institution, 1978: 244–48.

WEB SITES

Anderson, Bill. "The Cahto ('Kato') Language." *California Athapascan Languages.* http://www.billabbie.com/calath/caindex.html (accessed on August 11, 2011).

"Cahto (Kato)." *Four Directions Institute.* http://www.fourdir.com/cahto.htm (accessed on August 11, 2011).

"Cahto Tribe Information Network." *Cahto Tribe.* http://www.cahto.org/ (accessed on August 11, 2011).

Powers, Stephen. "Northern California Indians: No. VI. The Pomo and Cahto." *University of California.* http://digitalassets.lib.berkeley.edu/ anthpubs/ucb/text/arf025-008.pdf (accessed on August 11, 2011).

Redish, Laura, and Orrin Lewis. "Kato Language (Cahto)." *Native Languages of the Americas.* http://www.native-languages.org/kato.htm (accessed on August 11, 2011).

Round Valley Indian Tribes. http://www.rvit.org/ (accessed on August 11, 2011).

Cahuilla

Name

The name Cahuilla (pronounced *ka-WEE-ya* or *KAW-we-ah*) is from the word *kawiya,* meaning "masters" or "powerful ones." Some sources indicate the tribe's name may have come from the Spanish interpretation of *Kawîka,* which means "mountain-ward," or from the Luiseño word *Kawîka-wichum,* which translates to "westward those-of," indicating that they lived to the west.

Location

Many Cahuilla live on or near nine small reservations in inland southern California. They are located in mostly rural areas, although part of the Agua Caliente Reservation is within the city limits of Palm Springs. The reservations are situated in the area of the tribe's traditional lands, bounded on the north by the San Bernardino Mountains, on the south by Borrego Springs and the Chocolate Mountains, on the east by the Colorado Desert, and on the west by Riverside County and the Palomar Mountains. Nearly two-thirds of traditional Cahuilla territory is desert.

Population

About 6,000 Cahuilla lived in present-day California at the time of contact with the Spanish. By the 1850s, there were 2,500 to 3,000. Following a smallpox epidemic in the early 1860s, that number dropped to 1,181 in 1865. In 1955, there were about 535; in 1970, that figure rose to 1,629. In the 1990 U.S. Census, 888 people said they were Cahuilla. The 2000 census showed 2,259 Cahuilla, and 3,435 people who had some Cahuilla ancestry.

Language family

Uto-Aztecan.

Origins and group affiliations

Centuries ago, three groups of Cahuilla occupied different regions: the Palm Springs, Pass, and Desert Cahuilla. Today, these groups are intermingled on the reservations. The Cahuilla have a long history of cultural contact, trade,

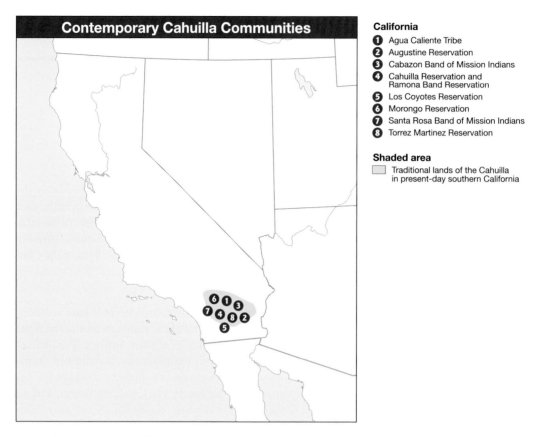

Contemporary Cahuilla Communities

California

1. Agua Caliente Tribe
2. Augustine Reservation
3. Cabazon Band of Mission Indians
4. Cahuilla Reservation and Ramona Band Reservation
5. Los Coyotes Reservation
6. Morongo Reservation
7. Santa Rosa Band of Mission Indians
8. Torrez Martinez Reservation

Shaded area

Traditional lands of the Cahuilla in present-day southern California

A map of contemporary Cahuilla communities. MAP BY XNR PRODUCTIONS. CENGAGE LEARNING, GALE. REPRODUCED BY PERMISSION OF GALE, A PART OF CENGAGE LEARNING.

and intermarriage with their neighbors—the Serrano, the Gabrieliño, and the Luiseño. The Cahuilla are sometimes called Mission Indians, along with several tribes that lived near San Diego when the Spanish began building Catholic missions there in the eighteenth century. Although the Cahuilla shared many customs with the Mission Indians, they had less contact with the missions than other tribes did.

The Cahuilla lived in a region of unpredictable weather extremes where heavy rains one year could be replaced by drought the next, and earthquakes and fires could suddenly strike. They acclimated to and took advantage of their environment. They were a friendly and generous people who would happily give away excess possessions, certain that if they were ever in need, their generosity would be repaid. Today, they live on reservations near their traditional homeland. They have adapted to their new circumstances but still retain their traditional customs.

HISTORY

Archaeologists (those who study the remains of ancient civilizations) say the Cahuilla originated in the Great Basin area of present-day Nevada and Colorado. The Cahuilla still sing what they call "birdsongs" that tell of their creation and their move to southern California some two thousand to three thousand years ago. They settled near Lake Cahuilla, which dried up hundreds of years ago and was replaced by the Salton Sea. The Cahuilla adapted to the area and found beauty in a land that many would consider harsh and barren.

Because they lived inland, the Cahuilla initially had little contact with the Spanish who took control of California in the late eighteenth century. The tribe's first meeting with Europeans took place in 1774. Spanish explorer Juan Bautista de Anza (1736–c. 1788) passed through Cahuilla territory looking for a land route from Mexico to the Monterey Peninsula. The Spanish at the Catholic mission on the peninsula hoped Anza would find a way to bring supplies overland from Mexico rather than by sea, which took a long time.

Cahuilla bands guarded their territory closely, especially the vital watering holes. They objected to Spanish trespassers and fired at them with bows and arrows. Meeting similar hostility from other tribes along their land route, the Spanish gave up their search. The Cahuilla had no more contact with them for a time, but they heard stories about Spanish ill-treatment of Mission Indians and about Spanish goods, which greatly interested them.

Important Dates

1774: Cahuilla first meet Spanish explorers.

1863: Smallpox epidemic strikes the Cahuilla.

1875–77: Various Cahuilla reservations are established.

1891: The Act for the Relief of Mission Indians establishes reservation boundaries.

1959: The Equalization Act finalizes land allotments.

1964: The Malki Museum is founded on the Morongo Reservation.

Contact with Spanish and settlers

In the early 1800s, the Cahuilla visited some of the Spanish missions near the coast. They learned Spanish, adopted European clothing, and learned new technologies, such as ironworking. In some cases, they were forced to work for the missions and were harshly treated by those in charge. Throughout the early years, however, most Cahuilla managed to retain their independence while taking advantage of European goods.

In 1822, Mexico took the mission lands away from Spain. Again, the Cahuilla remained fairly independent. They took seasonal jobs as skilled

Romantic Novel Arouses Interest in California Indians

Helen Hunt Jackson (1830–1885), a poet and writer from Massachusetts, traveled to California in 1872. While there, she became interested in the condition of the Native peoples of the West. In 1881, she published *A Century of Dishonor,* a nonfiction work that attacked the government's Indian policy and the treatment of American Indians. Because of her work, the U.S. Congress formed a special commission to investigate and suggest reforms for Native affairs.

The federal government then appointed Jackson to investigate and report on the conditions of Mission Indians. Jackson traveled throughout southern California and documented her findings in a fifty-six-page account. When Congress failed to act on her suggestions of additional schools for children and more land for reservations, she decided to bring the people's plight to the country's attention.

In 1884, she published her popular novel *Ramona,* said to be based on an actual Cahuilla woman named Ramona Lubo, whose husband had been murdered by a U.S. settler. The novel is mainly romantic fiction, not a true account of the Native peoples in the area, but it did a great deal to arouse public sympathy for the Mission Indians.

laborers on cattle ranches owned by Mexicans. In 1848, the United States officially took control of California, and shortly after that, the Gold Rush began. (The California Gold Rush was a mass migration of people to the territory after the discovery of gold there in 1848.) These two events caused tensions between the tribe and the new settlers who trespassed on Cahuilla land and water sources.

Territorial struggles

Initially, though, the Cahuilla under Juan Antonio (c. 1783–1863) existed peacefully with the settlers. Antonio even aided the U.S. Army against Ute (see entry) attacks. When a band of outlaws stole cattle and murdered people, Juan Antonio and his people tracked them down and killed all but one. After they helped control the 1851–52 Cupeño uprising, the Cahuilla expected the California and U.S. governments to ratify a treaty giving the tribe charge of their homelands. When the treaty was denied, Antonio raided settlers for several years.

During this time the tribe suffered from diseases that miners and settlers brought with them when they moved into the area. Because the Cahuilla had no immunity to these diseases, many died. In 1863, a severe smallpox epidemic reduced the Cahuilla population from 6,000 to about 2,500. Meanwhile, settlers took over the tribe's water sources, and Cahuilla crops suffered. The settlers then pressured the U.S. government to set aside reservations for the California tribes.

Starving and weakened by diseases, the Cahuilla were forced off their lands. They had no choice but to submit to the reservation system. Even then, settlers cheated them out of land.

In the decades that followed, the Cahuilla grew more resentful of federal government intervention in their lives and the continuous chiseling away of their lands. The 1891 Act for the Relief of Mission Indians, which formalized the reservation system, took still more of the Cahuilla's land when the reservation boundaries were set. Government schools and American missionaries tried to suppress the Cahuilla religion, language, and political systems. The 1887 General Allotment Act (also known as the Dawes Act) divided Cahuilla lands into individual parcels and made it impossible for them to do the kind of community farming they had done before.

Resisting assimilation

In 1919, Jonathan Tibbet organized the Mission Indian Federation. Julio Norte, from the Morongo Reservation, was grand president of the first conference. Seventy-five leaders from southern California tribes met to prevent white encroachment on their land and water supplies. They also wanted their children taught on the reservation rather than being sent away to boarding schools. The group lobbied for Native rights for many years.

During the early 1900s, the Cahuilla resisted interference in their affairs. In 1934, they regained some independence when the Indian Reorganization Act (IRA) passed; the act ended the allotment system and encouraged the formation of tribal governments. These new model governments, however, were supervised by the U.S. government. When a federal program cut off funding and supervision of the reservations in the 1950s, the Cahuilla became more involved in setting up their own health, education, and welfare programs. In the 1960s, they received funding that allowed them to manage their own affairs. They remain politically active and continue to work for their rights.

RELIGION

The unpredictable weather of their homeland convinced the Cahuilla that the world was governed by a changeable creative force. In their traditions, that force made the first two human beings, Mukat and Tamaioit. These huge and powerful beings then made everything else. With the exception of the shamans (pronounced *SHAH-munz* or *SHAY-munz*), or healers, the creatures who came after these first two did not have the same powers.

The shamans controlled rain, created food, and conducted ceremonies during which they performed amazing feats such as eating hot coals. They told stories of creation in songs and dances; special rattles made from gourds supplied the music. Shamans passed their knowledge and

Origin of the Birds

Two important figures in Cahuilla oral stories are Mukat and his brother Tamaioit, the two powerful first beings from whom all other creatures originated. The following story was told by a man named Alexandro of Morongo in 1918 to Lucile Hooper, an anthropologist (scientist who studies human cultures). Hooper claimed that Alexandro gave her a short version of the tale because it would have taken "all night to name the birds."

> When Mukat died, the people who were still living at the big house did not know where to go or what to do. They went east, west, north, south, above, and below. They could not decide which direction they were intended to take. They finally reached the edge of the water and here they saw Sovalivil (pelican). He told them how to find Tamaioit. When they found him, he asked why they came to him. "I am different from all of you," he said, "so I cannot help you, I fear. There is one thing I might suggest, however. I created the willow tree, which I forgot to bring with me; get the branches of

> that and brush yourselves with it and perhaps you will then know what to do." So they all returned and brushed themselves with the willow, then started out once more.

> A few, who became tired, stopped, and turned themselves into rocks and trees. The others reached the top of Mount San Jacinto and here they slept that night. At dawn, Isel (a bird with a yellow breast that is often seen around swamps), awoke them and made them look around. A bird which is larger than a buzzard told them not to look, that there was nothing to see. Nevertheless, they all looked around and saw many beautiful green fields. They decided to go to these. On the way, one by one, they stopped. These that stopped became birds. When the others returned that way, they named the birds.

SOURCE: Hooper, Lucile. "The Cahuilla Indians." *University of California Publications in Archaeology and Ethnology* 16 (April 10, 1920).

powers on to successors who were chosen because they exhibited certain special qualities when young.

The Cahuilla believed in a life after death. Each person had a soul spirit, *tewlavelem,* that remained in the land of the dead, located to the east. After a long, hard journey, the dead entered an afterlife much like the one they had left behind, but in the new life, only good things happened. Tewlavelem could help and advise the living.

Although their early experiences with Spanish Catholic missionaries were not pleasant, after the Cahuilla moved to reservations, missionaries renewed their efforts. In time, many Cahuilla converted to Catholicism and others to Protestantism. Today, the Cahuilla still maintain elements of their traditional beliefs and practices.

In the 1950s, the Cahuilla made a painful decision that changed the future for the people. Their children were leaving the old ways, and their language and culture dying out. No one retained enough of the old knowledge to serve as a teacher and ritual leader. They decided not to choose a *net,* or headman, and they burned their ceremonial house, ending many ties with the ancient traditions.

LANGUAGE

The Cahuilla language belongs to the Takic branch of the Uto-Aztecan stock (sometimes called Southern Californian Shoshonean) and is very close to Cupeño.

GOVERNMENT

Traditionally, the Cahuilla lived in about a dozen independent villages, each with its own name, territory, and a male ancestor common to everyone in the village. Trails connected villages with other villages and to other tribes. Each village had a headman called a *net,* who settled minor disputes, chose hunting-gathering areas, and represented the group at meetings. The position of net passed from father to son.

The net was assisted by a *paxaa?,* who made sure people behaved properly. He oversaw rituals and ceremonies, led hunting parties, and communicated the decisions made by the headman (who made them after consulting the shaman).

Traditional Cahuilla leadership was largely male-oriented, but today women are active in Cahuilla politics. Each reservation is governed by an elected business committee or tribal council. These councils are selected by the adults of the tribe, who often compose a general council. Special committees deal with economic development and other community concerns.

Cahuilla Words

Only a small number of Cahuilla speak their traditional language anymore. However, many still use some Cahuilla words, such as the many Cahuilla terms for relatives—for example, *qa?* for "father's father," and *qwa?* for "mother's father."

Some communities offer Cahuilla language classes. Thanks to Cahuilla speakers such as Katherine Siva Saubel (1920–2011), a respected elder and active political leader, books of Cahuilla grammar, stories, and vocabulary have been published. In *l'isniyatam,* her Cahuilla word book, Saubel stresses the importance of naming to the Cahuilla. She offers examples: *pal* (water), *sewet* (snake), and *huyal* (arrow), with many variations. In written Cahuilla, most letters are pronounced like English letters, with a few exceptions: a *?* sounds like a gulp; and an *x* is like a scratchy *h.*

ECONOMY

The traditional Cahuilla economy was based on a complex system of hunting and gathering, which required a complete knowledge of the hundreds of local plants and many animals. The people traded plants with other tribes for gourd rattles and baskets.

The Spanish introduced cattle to the region in the 1800s. The cattle ate many local plants, and this reduced food for game animals as well as people. Unable to hunt and gather as before, some Cahuilla went to work on farms and ranches owned by the Spanish or the Americans.

After the move to the reservations in the late 1800s, Cahuilla women earned money by making and selling woven baskets. This art is not as widely practiced today. Most reservations in the early twenty-first century run their own enterprises for the benefit of the tribe: bingo, camping facilities, and casinos, for instance. Tourism and recreation, agriculture and livestock, manufacturing, service and retail businesses, real estate development, mining, and tribal government provide additional employment opportunities for many Cahuilla. Others choose professional jobs both on and off the reservation.

DAILY LIFE

Families

Cahuilla children are born into the clan (group of related families) of their fathers. According to writers Lowell Bean and Lisa Bourgeault: "[A] typical Cahuilla community consisted of elderly men who were brothers, their wives, and their sons and nephews, together with their wives and children." All of these related people worked and played together.

Education

Children learned their adult roles by observation and through play. Boys engaged in games, such as foot races and kickball, that taught coordination and made their muscles strong so they could become quick, skilled hunters. Girls developed hand-eye coordination so they could weave baskets and pick up small seeds.

Children learned their history and religion from stories handed down from generation to generation. Elders were highly respected for their knowledge of tribal history; they advised younger people on what to do during natural disasters. Older members of the tribe also taught youngsters values and skills. Some of the values that the Cahuilla believed in were sharing, doing things slowly and in an orderly way, thinking about the consequences of one's actions, being honest and dependable, and using knowledge carefully. All children learned that if they received a gift, they must give something in return. If they did not, they were publicly ridiculed.

From the late 1800s until the 1830s, the U.S. government sent students to boarding schools to assimilate them (make them more like the rest of American society). Children were not allowed to speak their language or follow their tribe's customs, so many of them did not learn tribal traditions. In modern times, Cahuilla children attend public schools, colleges, and trade schools. Some reservations also sponsor classes in Native language and culture.

Buildings

Cahuilla homes varied widely depending on location. Some families put brush shelters over the fronts of caves; others built cone-shaped homes of cedar bark. The Cahuilla also used Y-shaped supports and thatched roofs and walls, sometimes plastering the walls. Many of these homes were dome-shaped, but some were rectangular. A *kish* was a windowless structure that had walls made from a plant called arrowwood and a slanted roof made from palm fronds. People slept inside on the earth floor and kept a fire in a circle of rocks.

At the center of the village was the largest building, the ceremonial house; the *net* lived in it or nearby. The house usually included a small area where a bundle of sacred items was kept, and a large area for religious dances. Outside was a smaller dance area. A place for preparing food for ceremonies was attached to the house. Nearby were granaries—large nest-like baskets used for storing food—and a communal sweathouse, where men went for social and ritual sweat baths, and to discuss important matters.

Cahuilla families often clustered their homes together. Unlike some tribes who had winter and summer villages, the Cahuilla had permanent villages. They built near water and food sources, often in or around canyons for protection from harsh winds. They marked the boundaries of their hunting-gathering territory with designs carved into rocks. Cahuilla homes today tend to be spread out on plots of land large enough for farming or cattle ranching.

Food

The Cahuilla diet was well-rounded and nutritious. They used a combination of hunting, harvesting, and growing. Food was gathered from four different environments: the low and high deserts, the mountains, and the area in between. Tasks were divided by gender and age—the men hunted, the women harvested plants and seeds, and children and older people cooked.

The Cahuilla knew the ripening times of hundreds of plant varieties. They even pruned and watered crops they had not planted—pine nuts, cactus, and mesquite (pronounced *meh-SKEET*) beans. Pine nuts were roasted over coals in shallow trays or baskets; cactus was boiled or eaten fresh; and mesquite beans were dried and pounded into a fine meal.

Acorns were a staple of the Cahuilla diet. They were ground into flour and then covered with boiling water to remove the poisonous tannic acid. The Cahuilla planted corn, beans, melons, and squash. They baked yucca, agave, and tule potatoes in stone-lined pits. To store food and keep it fresh, they sealed it with pine pitch. When food was scarce, they often raided birds' or rats' food stores.

Women roasted or boiled meat, or cut it into strips and sun-dried it. They cracked bones to get the marrow out or ground them into powder to mix with other foods. They drank animal blood fresh or stored it in containers made of leather or animal gut.

The Cahuilla today incorporate many traditional foods into their lives. For instance, a Cahuilla breakfast might consist of coffee, eggs, refried beans, and *sawish,* a flat bread like a tortilla. The Cahuilla still enjoy acorns and cactus buds, and they continue to eat deer and quail. Mountain sheep and antelope can no longer be hunted, but once they were highly valued for their delicious meat.

Clothing and adornment

Centuries ago the Cahuilla wore clothing made of the natural materials of their environment. They pounded mesquite bark into a soft material for women's skirts and babies' diapers. They also used mesquite bark for sandals, and they made blankets out of strips of rabbit fur. Men wore deerskin or sheepskin breechcloths (garments with front and back flaps that hung from the waist). Body paint was used for ceremonies, and facial tattooing was common.

After meeting the Spanish in the late eighteenth century, many Cahuilla began combining European-style clothing such as pants, shirts, skirts, and jackets with traditional clothing.

Healing practices

The Cahuilla believed that when the spirits were displeased, they made people sick. Shamans were then called upon. They healed by sucking directly on the affected part of the patient's body to remove the ailment, or by blowing, spitting on, stroking, or rubbing the affected area. Sometimes herbs were used, or a pit was dug and warmed with hot rocks, then the sick person would lie down in it. Those who lived near present-day Palm Springs used the hot springs there for healing. The Cahuilla have always been very concerned with cleanliness and place great importance on regular bathing and proper cleaning of cooking tools.

Shamans were men, but older women with a knowledge of herbs could help with certain conditions such as childbirth or broken bones. Ruby Modesto (1913–1980), a twentieth-century healer, or *pul,* described her life and work in her book *Not for Innocent Ears.* She noted that although many puls used power in a good way, some puls exercised their power for evil deeds like poisoning people. Modesto cured people with "soul damage"; people who had seizures, for example, were thought to have soul damage.

Whereas shamans handled spiritual health and dealt with supernatural powers, doctors handled physical illness. Most doctors were women who had learned their trade from shamans or diviners (those who could foretell the future). Doctors needed an extensive knowledge of plants and herbs. Most were older because it took a while for the community to trust them enough to consult them.

ARTS

Crafts

Once they had mastered survival in the desert, the Cahuilla had time to devote to crafts. Men made heavy baskets for practical purposes such as gathering plants and seeds. Women made beautiful coiled baskets from grasses and rushes of different colors. The baskets were decorated with designs of rattlesnakes, turtles, stars, and eagles. Gift-giving was a part of

A Cahuilla woman stands with a large basket on her head, circa 1924. © BUYENLARGE/ GETTY IMAGES.

every Cahuilla ceremony, and often the gifts were baskets or gift items presented in a basket.

Cahuilla pottery was thin, breakable redware. To form it, women patted it with wooden paddles against a rounded stone. They then carved designs into it or painted it. They made ollas (large clay pots) to store seeds and grains.

Music

The Cahuilla recorded their oral history in song. They enjoyed music of all kinds, and it accompanied games, dancing, shamans' work, hunting, and food gathering. Songs were accompanied by a variety of instruments, including pan-pipes, gourd or turtle shell rattles, sticks, dried cocoons, seashells, whistles, and flutes made of bone or wood.

CUSTOMS

Society

The tribe was divided into two groups based on male ancestors—Wildcats and Coyotes. These were divided into three to ten clans who spoke different dialects (varieties of the language). They all worked together in times of war as well as when gathering food or performing rituals. Each of these groups owned a village, but clan territory could be used by everyone.

Ceremonies and festivals

The Cahuilla placed a special emphasis on death. When a close relative died, the person's home and belongings were burned to set the spirit free so it could enjoy the possessions in the next world. The Cahuilla's most important ritual was an annual ceremony mourning the dead. The tradition continues today with a Memorial Day fiesta, celebrating Cahuilla culture and honoring Cahuilla men who died in service during World War II (1939–45; a war in which Great Britain, France, the United States, and their allies defeated Germany, Italy, and Japan).

Other rituals include the eagle ceremony. For this, the people form a large circle outside the ceremonial house. In the middle of the circle, the dancer, wearing an eagle feather headdress and skirt, imitates the movements of an eagle while hitting two sticks together to direct the people in singing. The ceremonial house remains an important center for culture and community, even to those Cahuilla who live and work away from the reservation.

Games

The Cahuilla enjoyed playing games, and moieties (units or parts of the tribe) often challenged each other. In most games, endurance was important, and betting was common. Men competed in foot races and in shooting arrows and played guessing games. Women also ran races and played guessing games. They tried to outdo each other in juggling, spinning tops, balancing objects, and playing cat's cradle. Music was part of many of these activities.

Marriage

Knowing who their ancestors were was very important because the Cahuilla would not marry anyone even remotely related to them. A boy's parents chose a bride from another clan, being careful to choose someone who would be an asset to their tight-knit, hard-working community. The boy's father then offered the girl's father a gift. If her father accepted the gift, the daughter simply moved into the home of the boy's family without further ceremony.

It was difficult for a married couple to divorce because marriage ties connected clan members. If a woman could not have children or was lazy or nonproductive, a man could divorce her. If a spouse died, the surviving wife usually married her husband's brother; a man took his wife's sister.

CURRENT TRIBAL ISSUES

In 2006, a forest fire destroyed 1,200 acres on the Morongo Reservation. Lives were lost, and homes were burned. Many people assisted the tribe, because the Morongo had often helped neighboring communities during forest fires; recovery, however, will take a long time.

In 2007, the Environmental Protection Agency (EPA) fined operators of an illegal dump on the Torres Martinez Reservation in California $46 million. According to statistics, the reservation had at least twenty-six illegal dumps, which posed major environmental, health, and safety risks. Since then the tribe has worked to clean up many of the sites with the help of the EPA, including some hazardous waste sites. They have also educated the public on waste disposal and provided opportunities for people to discard appliances and other large items.

The Cahuilla work hard to preserve their culture. A major part of this effort can be seen at the Malki Museum on the Morongo Reservation. Cahuilla scholars and storytellers have done a great deal to educate others about Cahuilla culture and history. The museum also revived the fiesta system, once thought to be a lost tradition. The Malki Museum was the first Native museum ever established on a California reservation, but in recent years several other Cahuilla reservations have opened museums of their own, where they sponsor annual fiestas.

The Cahuilla remain active in political issues such as land and water conservation. Like many American Indian tribes, they must continually fight for their share of water and against the reduction of their lands by outside developers, oil companies, and highway builders.

NOTABLE PEOPLE

Ruby Modesto (1913–1980) grew up speaking Cahuilla, and because she did not learn English or attend school until after age ten, she learned a great deal about her traditional culture. Modesto became a medicine woman in her forties. In her book *Not for Innocent Ears,* she described how she became responsible for healing people possessed by demons.

Katherine Siva Saubel (1920–2011), known for her efforts to preserve the Cahuilla language, was inducted into the National Women's Hall of Fame in 1998, a first for a Native woman. Another major focus of Saubel's work was Cahuilla ethnobotany, the study of using plants. In 1972, Saubel and anthropologist John Lowell Bean published *Temalpakh: Cahuilla Indian Knowledge and Uses of Plants.*

Cahuilla political leader Juan Antonio (c. 1783–1863) fought in the 1840s and 1850s to protect Cahuilla lands from Mexican and American settlers. Other noted Cahuilla include Rupert Costo (1906–1989), a late-twentieth-century publisher and editor who founded such magazines as *Indian Historian* and *Wassaja*; the singer Joe Lomas; and the educator, author, and activist Edward Castillo (1947–).

BOOKS

Bean, Lowell, Frank Porter, and Lisa Bourgeault.. *The Cahuilla.* New York: Chelsea House, 1989.

Bradley, Donna. *Native Americans of San Diego County, CA.* Mt. Pleasant, SC: Arcadia, 2009.

Gray-Kanatiiosh, Barbara A. *Cahuilla.* Edina, MN: ABDO, 2007.

Hooper, Lucile. *The Cahuilla Indians.* Kila, MN: Kessinger Publishing, 2011.

Jackson, Helen Hunt. *Ramona.* New York: Signet, 1988.

Johnson, Gordon. *Fast Cars and Frybread: Reports from the Rez.* Berkeley, CA: Heyday Books, 2007.

Kroeber, A.L. *Ethnography of the Cahuilla Indians.* Reprint. Charleston, SC: Nabu Press, 2010.

Milanovich, Richard, "Beauty in the Desert." In *All Roads Are Good: Native Voices on Life and Culture.* Washington, DC: Smithsonian Institution, 1994.

Modesto, Ruby. *Not for Innocent Ears: Spiritual Traditions of a Cahuilla Medicine Woman.* Cottonwood, CA: Sweetlight Books, 1989.

Saubel, Katherine. *I'isniyatami (Designs): A Cahuilla Word Book.* Banning, CA: Malki Museum Press, 1977.

Secrest, William B. *When the Great Spirit Died: The Destruction of the California Indians, 1850–1860.* Sanger, CA: Word Dancer Press, 2003.

WEB SITES

Agua Caliente Cultural Museum. http://www.accmuseum.org/ (accessed on August 11, 2011).

"Agua Caliente: Overview." *Agua Caliente Indian Reservation.* http://www.aguacaliente.org/ (accessed on August 11, 2011).

"Cahuilla." *Four Directions Institute.* http://www.fourdir.com/cahuilla.htm (accessed on August 11, 2011).

"Cahuilla." *University of California.* https://eee.uci.edu/clients/tcthorne/idp/clickablecamap/Cahuilla.htm (accessed on August 11, 2011).

Cahuilla Band of Mission Indians. http://cahuillabandofindians.com/ (accessed on August 11, 2011).

"Cahuilla Indians: California Desert People." *Manataka Home Page.* http://www.manataka.org/page550.html (accessed on August 11, 2011).

Cooper, E. "A Little Information about the Cahuilla." *The Palm Springs Indians/Agua-Caliente-Cahuilla.* http://www.xeri.com/Moapa/cahuilla.htm (accessed on August 11, 2011).

Feller, Walter. "Mojave Desert Indians: Cahuilla Indians." *Digital-Desert.* http://mojavedesert.net/cahuilla-indians/ (accessed on August 11, 2011).

Morongo Band of Mission Indians. http://www.morongonation.org/ (accessed on August 11, 2011).

"Native Americans of the Salton Basin-Colorado Delta." *San Diego State University.* http://www.sci.sdsu.edu/salton/NativeAmericansSaltonBasin.html (accessed on August 11, 2011).

Ramona Band of Cahuilla Indians. http://www.ramonatribe.com/ (accessed on August 11, 2011).

Torres Martinez Desert Cahuilla Indian Tribe. http://www.torresmartinez.org/ (accessed on August 11, 2011).

Chumash

Name

The name Chumash (pronounced *CHOO-mash*) may have come from the word the tribe used to refer to the inhabitants of one of the Santa Barbara Channel Islands. The people called themselves "the first people," although many tribal elders today say that Chumash means "bead maker" or "seashell people." The Spanish used the name "Chumash" to refer to every group of Native Americans living on the islands and along the southern coast of California. The Chumash are sometimes called the Santa Barbara Indians.

Location

The Chumash used to occupy lands stretching along 200 miles (320 kilometers) of southern California coastline, plus four of the Santa Barbara Channel Islands: Anacapa, San Miguel, Santa Rosa, and Santa Cruz. Their total territory at the time of European contact comprised about 7,000 square miles (18,130 square kilometers), ranging from San Luis Obispo to Malibu Canyon in the Santa Monica Mountains outside Los Angeles. In the late 1990s, the Chumash owned only Santa Ynez Reservation in Santa Ynez, California, located about 32 miles (52 kilometers) north of Santa Barbara and 10 miles (16 kilometers) from the Pacific Ocean. It is only about 75 acres with a small, but growing, population. Many Chumash in the early twenty-first century live in Santa Barbara, Ventura, and other southern California cities.

Population

In 1770, between 10,000 and 22,000 Chumash people were known to exist. In 1920, the number had dwindled to 74. In 1972, there were 1,925 persons of Chumash descent. In the 1990 U.S. Census, 3,114 people identified themselves as Chumash and 94 said they were Santa Ynez Chumash. The 2000 census showed 3,758 Chumash lived in the United States, whereas 7,056 people claimed some Chumash heritage. The Santa Ynez Reservation was home to 122 people in 2000; tribal sources indicated that there were 283 people living there in 2004. That number had dropped to 249 in 2011, but the Chumash population had risen to almost 5,000.

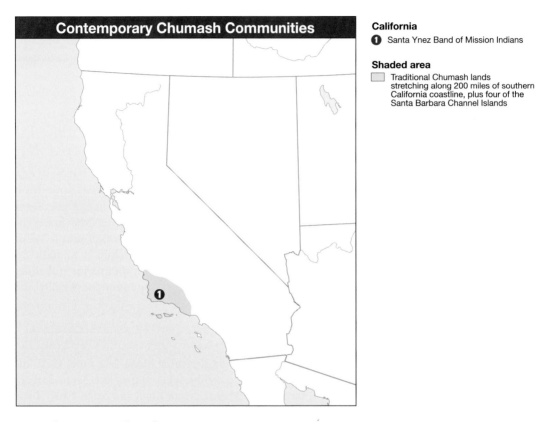

Contemporary Chumash Communities

California
❶ Santa Ynez Band of Mission Indians

Shaded area
Traditional Chumash lands stretching along 200 miles of southern California coastline, plus four of the Santa Barbara Channel Islands

A map of contemporary Chumash communities. MAP BY XNR PRODUCTIONS. CENGAGE LEARNING, GALE. REPRODUCED BY PERMISSION OF GALE, A PART OF CENGAGE LEARNING.

Language family
Hokan.

Origins and group affiliations
The ancestors of the Chumash people are believed by scientists to have migrated across the ancient Bering Land Bridge connecting Siberia (eastern Russia) to Alaska between twelve thousand and twenty-seven thousand years ago. Chumash creation stories, however, tell of a more local origin.

When the Spanish arrived, at least six groups of Chumash lived in the area; five were given the names of the Catholic missions founded in their territory beginning in the 1700s. The largest group was called the Ynezeño. Little is known about the sixth group, the Interior Chumash.

For thousands of years the Chumash sailed up and down the California coast in topols, brightly painted cedar-plank boats, that are still considered marvels of engineering. They fished in the ocean and visited and traded with tribes in faraway places. After suffering at the hands of Spanish Catholic missionaries and Mexican and American settlers, the tribe was thought to have become extinct. Chumash descendants, however, have succeeded in keeping their culture alive. They have done so quietly, hoping to retain their privacy and protect sacred artifacts from vandals and land developers. The tribe has also made great strides economically, and in doing so, they continue to practice *'amuyich,* the spirit of generosity, which is an important part of their traditional way of life. Millions in casino profits have gone to improve the surrounding community.

HISTORY

Chumash territory has been inhabited for at least nine thousand years and possibly much longer (see "Current tribal issues"). Archaeologists (scientists who study the remains of ancient cultures) speculate that the Chumash had assumed control of what is now southern California by about the year 1000. Once one of the largest Native groups in California, the tribe carried on a lively business with its neighbors, trading soapstone (a carvable soft stone made into articles such as pipes and bowls), acorns, shells, beads, fish, and other items for animal skins, herbs, seeds, and nuts. Archaeologists have unearthed remnants of these trade objects many miles from Chumash territory, so the people evidently engaged in trade far from their homes. There are theories that the early Chumash groups of hunter-gatherers all moved together for support during a drought. The confederacy then developed an organized and complex political and economic system, but the Spanish, Mexicans, and Americans who invaded Chumash lands did not record any information about the tribe's way of life. By the time people showed interest in the group's pre-contact society, there were few Chumash left who remembered the old ways.

The Chumash Indians were prosperous at the time Juan Rodríguez Cabrillo (c. 1499–1543), a Portuguese commander sailing for Spain, first made contact with them. He sailed along the Santa Barbara Coast in 1542, leading a small fleet of Spanish ships. Cabrillo was searching for riches and a northwest passage through North America when he happened upon the Chumash, a friendly, peaceful people said to be the first group of Native Californians ever encountered by Europeans.

The Chumash greeted Cabrillo in canoes carrying generous gifts. Cabrillo claimed the area for Spain but left without establishing a

Important Dates

1000–1804: The Chumash people and other California Indians use shell money.

1542: The Chumash are the first California tribe to encounter Europeans.

1772: The first of the Spanish Catholic missions in Chumash territory is built at San Luis Obispo.

1824: In the Great Chumash Revolt led by Pacomio, two thousand Native Americans rise against missionaries, holding the mission for about a month before being forced to surrender.

1855: Land is set aside near Santa Ynez Mission for a reservation.

1901: The Santa Ynez Band is officially recognized by the federal government.

1978: Chumash Indians agree to end their three-day protest at the site of an ancient burial ground.

settlement. Sixty years later, in 1602, the Spanish explorer Sebastián Vizcaíno (c. 1548–c. 1624) sailed through Chumash waters and named Santa Barbara Bay in honor of Saint Barbara's birthday as he looked for a port. For the next 160 years, the Chumash thrived and had no further visits from Europeans.

Spanish missions

Spain already had a huge empire in North America. By the sixteenth century, Spanish colonizers had laid claim to a vast expanse of land in what is now the state of California. Over the next two hundred years, Russian and British adventurers arrived in the area, threatening Spain's hold on the territory. To protect their claim, the Spanish constructed missions—combinations of a fort, a plantation, and a religious center—in California in 1769.

The Spanish government embarked on a program of "Europeanization," teaching Native peoples the Spanish language and making them into "useful" citizens. Catholic priests (*padres*) assisted in establishing the missions. The priests, who had their own goal of converting the Natives to the Catholic religion, directed the construction of the missions, using unpaid, and later forced, Native labor.

The first of the Spanish Catholic missions in Chumash territory was built in 1772 at San Luis Obispo. In all, twenty-one missions were constructed in California, five of them in Chumash territory. The missions became forced labor camps for the Native population. By the time the mission system came to an end more than sixty years later, the Chumash economy had been virtually destroyed and the culture critically disrupted.

Becoming "Mission Indians"

The Spanish introduced livestock to Chumash territory. The cattle and other animals destroyed local plant life, greatly reducing the food supply. Game animals dependent upon the plants became scarce. With their way of life disrupted, the Chumash were drawn into the colonial economy out of necessity. Some of them sought refuge at the missions after a serious earthquake in 1812. By 1824, all of the Channel Island Chumash had been coaxed into the mission system. Spanish soldiers sometimes kidnapped those who did not join the missions and forced them into it. The Chumash and other tribes who belonged to the missions are often referred to as Mission Indians.

California Indians who converted to Christianity and were baptized into the Catholic faith were called *neophytes* (pronounced *NEE-oh-fites*; beginners). Because Spanish law required that neophytes live near the missions, these converts had to leave their villages and live in camps outside the missions.

At age five or six, Chumash children were taken from their families and forced to live in barracks that were filthy and disease-ridden. At the mission, they attended religious services, performed physical labor without pay, and were trained in carpentry, agriculture, and other occupations the Spanish considered useful. Chumash parents could do little to change things because men, women, and children were beaten, imprisoned, and sentenced to harsh physical labor for disobeying the missionaries.

Mexican control

In 1824, the Chumash revolted. Neophytes from several missions rose up in protest. Abandoning their own missions, they occupied La Purísima Mission for more than one month, but they surrendered after an assault by Spanish troops and artillery. Several of the Chumash who led the rebellion were executed.

In 1823, Mexico gained control of present-day California. A decade later the Mexican government took over the California missions. The neophytes were freed, and some attempts were made to help them. Mexican officials promised the people land—the same land where the Chumash had hunted and built villages for thousands of years—but never delivered on the promise. Instead, Mexican settlers flooded into California, hoping to obtain some of the rich and developed former mission lands for themselves.

A people divided

Between 1769, when the first mission was built, and 1832, just before the Mexicans took over, nearly two-thirds of the Chumash population died from disease and mission life. The survivors had few, if any, connections to their ancient villages and way of life. Some remained in positions as unpaid laborers under Mexican rather than Spanish control. Others scattered to find employment in Los Angeles and various towns along the coast. Some headed away from the coast and into the California interior to find new homes among different tribes. Many became rebels; they stole livestock from Mexican cattle ranches—or died trying.

In 1848, the United States took California from Mexico, and a year later, gold was discovered in the area. Americans poured into California country, resulting in terrible consequences for the Natives. The Spanish and the Mexicans had used the Native people as slaves; the Americans wanted them out of their way. In only a few years, American settlers killed thousands of California Natives, including many Chumash, through new epidemics (outbreaks of disease) and outright murder.

Reservation difficulties

In 1851, the U.S. government decided to resolve California's Native American situation by establishing a reservation system. It originally created reservations on military reserves to protect Natives from the violence of the settlers. In reality, government reserves served fewer than two thousand Native Americans at any given time. The vast majority of California Indians survived as best they could on their own.

A reservation was set aside for the Chumash in 1854, but it quickly fell apart due to the corruption of its administrators. The Chumash scattered. Like other California Indians, they withdrew to remote areas away from settlers, but violence against them continued. Murder of individuals, raids by vigilantes (groups that posed as volunteer police, but went beyond the law), and even occasional army massacres took place.

It was not until 1901 that a small group of Chumash living near the former Santa Ynez Mission was finally granted 120 acres there; this amount was later reduced by almost half. The site officially became California's smallest reservation, the Santa Ynez Chumash Reservation. Seventy-five acres was not enough land to support many people. Because the reservation provided no employment, many Chumash only lived on the reservation temporarily. They came and went, living in small groups throughout their former territory.

Because American settlers continued to mistreat Natives in California, the Chumash culture went underground (became secret). Their withdrawal led some observers to believe that the entire tribe was extinct.

Although the Chumash population was reduced to a small fraction of its once great size, the group and its traditions managed to survive and were again growing in the early twenty-first century.

RELIGION

The Chumash believed the universe was divided into three worlds: the Sky World, the World of the People (Earth), and the Lower World (where evil beings lived). According to Chumash tradition, animals were Earth's first creatures. When death appeared on Earth, some animals rose into the sky to escape it and turned into heavenly bodies such as the Sun, Moon, Morning Star, Evening Star, and Sky Coyote.

The Chief of the Sky People was Eagle, who held up the sky with his wings. Eclipses occurred when Eagle covered the Moon with his wings. If the Sky People became upset, terrible storms rained down on the World of the People. If the two serpents that held up the World of the People became restless and moved, earthquakes and other disturbances shook the earth. Dead people journeyed through the heavenly bodies before reaching the afterworld.

A central feature of the Chumash religion was consumption of a drug called *toloache,* which is obtained from a plant called jimsonweed. The drug causes those who take it to go into a trancelike state and see visions. Chumash religious leaders were priest-astrologers, who could read meanings in the positions of the heavenly bodies. Under the influence of *toloache,* the priest-astrologers painted pictographs in sacred caves. (See "Arts.") The exact meaning of these pictographs is not known, but they may have been attempts to communicate with the spirit world. *Toloache* was also consumed by sons of wealthy families as part of their training for a religious society called an *antap.*

Some Chumash became Catholics reluctantly and returned to their traditional religious practices when the mission system ended. Many, however, retained the Christian belief in a supreme being. Although many modern-day Chumash identify themselves as Catholic, few attend mass on a regular basis.

LANGUAGE

At least six languages belonged to the Chumash language family, but the speakers were separated from each other for generations. Over time, the groups lost the ability to understand each other.

Chumash Words

haku	"hello"
he	"yes"
'ap	"house"
mimi	"finger or toe"
muhu	"horned owl"
muhuw	"beach"
'alqapač	"animal"
towič	"to go/be fast"
uštanin	"to understand"
'ištanitap'	"Please come in."
suk' a pitaq?	"What did you hear?"
kun e'ni?	"Who is this?"

Because of the heavy Spanish influence in Chumash areas during the late eighteenth and early nineteenth centuries, most Chumash spoke Spanish by the early 1900s. Their children, however, learned English in public schools. The last person known to have spoken a Chumash language died in 1965.

GOVERNMENT

Under the Indian Reorganization Act (IRA) of 1934, tribes were encouraged to form tribal governments modeled after the U.S. system. The Chumash created a general council, composed of all members of the tribe aged twenty-one and over. The tribe also has an elders council, open to all members over the age of fifty. They are governed by a five-member Business Committee that oversees the legal and business affairs of the tribe and handles the tribe's economic growth. Committee members are elected by the general council, which must approve all decisions made by the Business Committee. The Santa Ynez Gaming Commission is responsible for the casino.

ECONOMY

Traditional economy

Before the Spanish came, the Chumash economy revolved around gathering and trading activities. Each region provided different resources for the tribe. The Chumash processed and traded these materials with other groups. For example, those who lived on the islands collected shells, which they traded for grain and skins from the mainland dwellers. Tribe members shaped these shells into small disks to use as currency.

Many Native peoples worked cooperatively, with large numbers of community members tending fields or hunting. The Chumash people were unique in that they developed craft specialties such as fishing or basket making. Experts in these specialties belonged to organizations called guilds, much like the ones that operated in Europe during the Middle Ages (c. 500–c. 1500).

The guild system resulted in a surplus of certain objects, so villages traded their excess goods. Guild members set prices for their goods and services. The most expensive items—those priced too high for most villagers—were purchased by the wealthiest families. Villages sometimes held fairs. Guild members set up booths at a designated marketplace, and interested customers from far and wide traveled to the market to buy and trade goods.

Poverty and recovery

After the Spanish and later the Mexicans came, the Chumash people worked as slaves for nearly one hundred years. Some Chumash later worked on ranches or farms as servants or laborers. Those who fled into the interior of California faced many hardships and struggled to find enough food to live. When the U.S. government finally set aside a tiny reservation for the Chumash, some families moved there, but there was never enough land to support many people.

By the 1990s, the area surrounding the reservation had become a thriving tourist and farming region, but poverty remained a serious problem among the Chumash. Many families were headed by women (who often earned less money than men), and both women and men had to find work in nearby towns to support their families.

After the tribe opened its casino in 1994 and then turned it into the Chumash Casino Resort in 2004, the economy improved. In the early twenty-first century, the resort is the largest employer in the Santa Ynez Valley, providing jobs for more than 1,700 residents. The tribe has used gaming revenues to fund tribal housing and road improvements, educational programs, and cultural activities. They have also donated millions to help the surrounding communities through their Santa Ynez Chumash Foundation.

DAILY LIFE

Families

Chumash families were large and usually consisted of a husband and wife, their married sons and their wives, their unmarried children, and other close relatives of the husband. As many as forty to seventy people lived together in the same house.

Buildings

Most Chumash built large, dome-shaped houses—some up to 50 feet (15 meters) wide. These homes were situated in long, neat rows separated by narrow streets. (The Chumash who lived in the interior of California built smaller, single-family homes.) The coastal people covered the willow frames of their houses with mat shingles made of tule (pronounced *TOO-lee*; a cattail) or other grasses. In the center of each home, smoke from the cooking fire was vented through a hole in the ceiling. The families divided their sleeping quarters with grass mats hung from the ceiling to serve as curtains. This type of sleeping room was unusual among California tribes.

Most villages had sweathouses—secluded houses or caverns heated by steam and used for ritual cleansing, meditation, and purification. Chumash sweathouses, located partly underground, were entered through a hole in the roof. Men and women usually used separate sweathouses. Other buildings included houses for storing goods, for ceremonies, and for gambling. Villages might also contain dance grounds, game fields, and cemeteries.

Clothing and adornment

Because the climate in Chumash territory is mild, the people's clothing was very simple. Men generally wore nothing more than a string around the waist; from it they hung tools and food. Sometimes they wrapped an animal skin around their hips if the weather was cool. If it was very cold, they might wear cloaks made from animal skins. Only the rich and powerful wore bear and other fur; an ankle-length fur cloak was a sign of a man's high position in the village. The poor wore clothes made from grasses and shredded bark.

Women wore two aprons—a large one hung from the waist in back and a smaller one from the front. They made these of buckskin, shredded bark, or grass and hung a fringe of shells from them. Although people usually went barefoot, sometimes they wore deerskin socks or fiber sandals. Moccasins were used only on special occasions.

Some Chumash males had pierced noses, and many had pierced ears; the ear holes were large enough to hold containers for carrying tobacco. For special occasions they painted their entire bodies. The paint served a practical purpose by acting as a sunscreen. Ceremonial costumes representing animals and birds might be made from an entire bearskin or from all the plumage taken from the giant California condor.

Food

The Coastal and Island Chumash were blessed with abundant food and water. They had to move to follow the food supplies as the seasons changed, but the moves did not take them very far. Life was harder for the Chumash who lived in the rugged California interior. For the most part, Chumash women gathered food and men hunted, but sometimes widows became hunters in order to provide for their families.

By far, the most important item on the Chumash menu was acorns. The Chumash encouraged the growth of oak trees by setting fires to burn out the plants with low fire resistance. This practice also encouraged large deer populations. (Since the practice of selective burning has been abandoned in California, the state's forests are no longer dominated by oak trees.) During acorn-gathering season, people from several Chumash villages joined forces, dividing into small groups to make sure the entire region was harvested. Acorns were then ground into flour.

The Chumash also ate nuts, wild seeds, and roots. They ate raw pine nuts and wild strawberries, ground buckeyes and chia seeds into flour, and roasted nuts from the California laurel. The people hunted the abundant deer, mule deer, elk, rabbit, squirrel, duck, and goose on their land. The rivers teemed with fish, and the ocean supplied saltwater fish, clams, mussels, abalone (a type of shellfish), crab, and crayfish. Hunters in canoes harpooned seal, sea otter, and porpoise.

Education

Although few details are known about the education of Chumash children before the arrival of the Spanish, they probably learned mostly by observing their elders and through apprenticeships to adults. During the mission period, children were taught the fundamentals of the Catholic religion. They also learned about farming, weaving, and pottery making—trades the Spanish considered useful. The European settlers did not want to teach the Chumash to read because they feared that a young generation of educated children might become restless and dissatisfied with the mission system. In fact, teaching Native children to read was outlawed in California until the 1920s.

The U.S. government established a school on the reservation early in the twentieth century, but it did not stay open for long. Chumash children—the majority of them speaking only broken English—later attended public schools at Santa Ynez near the reservation, where they faced racial prejudice. By the mid-1990s, little more than half of the reservation population had completed high school.

With casino profits, the tribe funded educational programs intended to reverse this situation. They provide scholarships for college students. They also offer tutoring and academic mentoring to encourage students to remain in school. Vocational training programs, a computer lab, language and culture classes, and a partnership with Allan Hancock College in California offer additional opportunities for tribe members of all ages.

A new generation of Chumash people is working to save the tribe's sacred cultural sites. They have organized special education classes where historians and archaeologists teach their methods of preservation. These classes are important to the Chumash, who wish to learn more about their ancestors and traditional ways. They also want to take control of their ancient sites, because tribal cemeteries were looted in the nineteenth century, and the artifacts were sold to art collectors.

Healing practices

The Spanish who first encountered the Chumash described them as healthy; many lived to a very old age. The person responsible for curing the sick was the shaman (medicine man; pronounced *SHAH-mun* or *SHAY-mun*). The shaman's medical kit included herbs, charmstones (highly polished rocks believed to have great power), and a special tube for blowing or sucking out a disease-causing object. (The object might be a stone or even a small animal.) The shaman then performed a ritual that included singing and dancing. Today, many people on the reservation receive dental, medical, and mental health care at the Santa Ynez Tribal Health Clinic. Others travel to Santa Barbara for medical, dental, and hospital care.

ARTS

The Chumash have always had a rich artistic life. They are probably best known for their pictographs. (See "Religion.") Historians believe these brilliantly colored images of humans, animals, and abstract circles were part of a religious ritual. The Chumash Painted Cave State Historic Park near Santa Barbara preserves samples of this art.

Beautiful bowls and animal figures were carved from a soft stone called steatite (pronounced *STEE-uh-TITE*; also known as soapstone). The people made watertight fiber baskets interwoven with twine that

An intricately woven Chumash treasure basket is one of only a few of its kind to have survived into modern times.
© BILDARCHIV PREUSSISCHER KULTURBESITZ/ART RESOURCE, NY.

they dyed black. Most of the baskets that survive date from the mission period; they were admired by the Spanish and are prized by museums and art collectors.

CUSTOMS

Class system

Chumash society had an upper, middle, and lower class. Shamans, priest-astrologers, and the brotherhood of the *tomol* (the guild that made cedar-plank canoes) belonged to the upper class. Skilled, healthy workers belonged to the middle class. The lower class consisted of people lacking special skills or those in poor health.

Birth

When a pregnant Chumash woman began to feel contractions, she would dig a pit on the exact spot where she stood when the first pain came; then she would lie down in the pit. The woman went through the labor and delivery without physical help, but with a shaman present. After giving birth, the mother immediately broke her infant's nose bone because a flat nose was considered attractive. The child was named by the shaman, who consulted the stars and heavenly bodies for inspiration. Shaman and priests could be either men or women.

Puberty

As Chumash girls approached puberty, they had to observe certain rules, one of which was refraining from consuming meat and grease. Both boys and girls celebrated reaching puberty by taking *toloache,* a drug that sent them into a trance, where they encountered their guardian spirit (see "Religion").

Marriage

An ordinary Chumash man chose his bride from his own village or one nearby. A wealthy man might choose a bride from a faraway village. By forming such a relationship, he helped ensure a large and united Chumash nation.

Except for the chief and his assistants, Chumash men had only one wife. After a wedding ceremony highlighted by much singing and dancing, the couple moved into the home of the groom's family.

War and hunting rituals

The Chumash did not wage war often, but if a conflict could not be avoided, they sometimes held a mock battle. The opposing sides—dressed in full war costume—lined up facing one another. Taking turns, one member from each side shot an arrow at the other side. After one person was killed, the battle was over.

Before a hunt, men purified themselves in the sweathouse. Some Chumash hunters even slept in the sweathouse because sexual contact with women was believed to diminish a man's hunting abilities. The hunters rubbed their bodies with special substances to disguise their natural human scent. To keep from frightening deer, they wore deerskin headdresses and horns and made movements like those of a deer as they approached their prey.

Death rituals

The Chumash were extremely respectful of the dead. After several mourners sat overnight by the body of the deceased person, the corpse was carried to the cemetery, which was considered a sacred place. Mourners gathered and smoked tobacco, sang, and cried. The body was then buried face down. Sometimes, a pole was placed atop the grave. From it hung objects that had special meaning to the dead person (such as fishing gear for a fisherman). If the dead person were important enough, his pole was painted. If he were especially important, he might be burned along with his entire house. The Chumash still observe the custom of burning a dead person's possessions. Every few years a ceremony is held to honor the souls of all the dead.

Festivals

Two of the most important festivals celebrated the autumn acorn harvest and the winter solstice (the longest night of the year, marking the beginning of winter). Other ceremonies honored animals, the First Beings. Men and women applied body paint for these occasions, played flutes and whistles, and scattered seeds. Descendants of the Chumash host several annual festivals; at some, they still perform the ancient Crane Dance, the Blackbird Dance, the Dolphin Dance, and the Bear Dance.

Although powwows were not originally part of Chumash culture, in modern times, the people hold an annual one to introduce others to their culture. The powwow is a celebration that includes singing and dancing, as well as other activities. One tradition the tribe has revived is the Santa Barbara Channel Island crossing. Tribe members paddle a *tomol,* the plank canoe used by their ancestors. A trip in 2005 was only the third time in more than 150 years that the journey had been undertaken. Since then, the Chumash have made this a yearly event. The people see this as a way to reconnect with their heritage.

CURRENT TRIBAL ISSUES

Federal recognition and sovereignty

Efforts to keep the Chumash culture alive have been hampered by technicalities. The Chumash who live on the reservation are recognized by the federal government, which means the government recognizes them as a sovereign (self-governing) nation and gives them financial aid. The small size of the Chumash people's reservation allows only a few people to live there. Off-reservation Chumash have formed groups to preserve and maintain their culture, but they have not been successful in obtaining federal recognition.

Kote Lotah and his wife, Lin-A-lul'Koy, hold artifacts on an ancient Chumash site in Malibu, California, in 1992. © AP IMAGES/ DOUGLAS C. PIZAC.

One of these small bands, the Northern Chumash Tribal Council, does not want federal recognition. Instead, they are working toward supporting themselves with an organic farm and community businesses. They believe that by working together they can help their people achieve self-sufficiency. Another of their tribal projects is their Healing Vision Project in Avila Beach, California. Its goal is to share the Chumash culture with others. Unlike many bands, they did not want a hotel or any buildings on the property but opted for open space for camping, ceremonies, and park facilities.

Protecting culture and artifacts

Preserving sacred sites against vandals and land developers is a constant concern for the Chumash. In the 1800s, Chumash cemeteries were raided, and many of the artifacts in them were sold to museums and art collectors. A major effort to preserve sacred sites occurred in May 1978; about twenty-five Chumash began a three-day protest at the site of an ancient burial ground where utility companies wanted to construct a billion-dollar facility to hold liquefied natural gas. The plant was never constructed. An agreement was worked out in which the tribe was granted access to the area for religious practices. The tribe was also granted the right to have six tribal members on hand when any future digging took place in former or current Chumash territory.

Recently, a Mastodon kill site was discovered in San Luis Obispo County. This was of particular interest because, along with the bones, archaeologists found ancient Chumash weapons and tools. It is possible that these artifacts may be more than 20,000 years old. Pollen dating is being done on the bones, because that method can detect dates older than carbon dating can. The Chumash are working with various government groups to ensure that the area is protected and that their cultural resources are respected.

NOTABLE PEOPLE

Pacomio (José) Poqui (c. 1794–1844) was a Mission Indian raised and educated as a carpenter at La Purísima Mission. Unhappy with the way his people were being treated by the Spanish, he helped lead a group of two thousand California Indians against the missionaries in an 1824 uprising. The Native people held the mission for about a month before being forced to surrender. Although he was sentenced to ten years' labor at a local prison, it is believed that Pacomio was allowed to live out the remainder of his life in Monterey, California.

F. L. Kitsepawit (c. 1804–1915) was born into a leading family in a Chumash town in what is now Santa Cruz, California. As a young man he lived in the mission at Ventura, where he was not able to speak his native language. Later, like other Chumash, he lived in remote areas, working as a ranch hand and carpenter. Kitsepawit worked with John Harrington, a linguist (someone who studies languages) and ethnohistorian (someone who studies the cultures of different groups) from the Smithsonian Institution to record many details about Chumash culture remembered from his childhood. It is in part thanks to him that some of the traditions, history, and language were brought back to the Chumash people.

BOOKS

Bial, Raymond. *The Chumash*. New York: Benchmark Books, 2004.

Brower, Pauline. *Inland Valleys Missions in California*. Minneapolis: Lerner, 2007.

Broyles-González, Yolanda, and Pilulaw Khus. *Earth Wisdom: A California Chumash Woman*. Tucson: University of Arizona Press, 2011.

Gamble, Lynn H. *The Chumash World at European Contact: Power, Trade, and Feasting among Complex Hunter-Gatherers*. Berkeley: University of California Press, 2008.

Gibson, Karen Bush. *The Chumash: Seafarers of the Pacific Coast.* Mankato, MN: Bridgestone Books, 2004.

Grant, Campbell. *Rock Paintings of the Chumash: A Study of a California Indian Culture.* Reprint. Santa Barbara, CA: Santa Barbara Museum of Natural History/EZ Nature Books, 1993.

Hicks, Terry Allan. *The Chumash.* New York: Marshall Cavendish Benchmark, 2008.

Kennett, Douglas J. *The Island Chumash: Behavioral Ecology of a Maritime Society.* Berkeley: University of California Press, 2005.

Sonneborn, Liz. *The Chumash.* Minneapolis, MN: Lerner Publications, 2007.

WEB SITES

Applegate, Richard. *Samala Chumash Language Tutorial.* http://www.chumashlanguage.com/ (accessed on August 11, 2011).

Campbell, Grant. "The Rock Paintings of the Chumash." *Association for Humanistic Psychology.* http://www.ahpweb.org/articles/chumash.html (accessed on August 11, 2011).

"Chumash." *Four Directions Institute.* http://www.fourdir.com/chumash.htm (accessed on December 1, 2011).

"Chumash." *Mission Tour.* http://missiontour.org/related/chumash.htm (accessed on August 11, 2011).

The Chumash Indians. http://www.chumashindian.com/ (accessed on August 11, 2011).

"La Purisima Mission State Park." *California State Parks.* http://www.lapurisimamission.org/ (accessed on August 11, 2011).

Price, Nicholas Stanley. "The Great Murals: Conserving the Rock Art of Baja California." *The Getty Conservation Institute.* http://www.getty.edu/conservation/publications/newsletters/11_2/feature1.html (accessed on August 11, 2011).

Redish, Laura, and Orrin Lewis. "Chumash Indian Fact Sheet." *Native Languages of the Americas.* http://www.bigorrin.org/chumash_kids.htm (accessed on December 1, 2011).

Santa Ynez Band of Chumash Indians. http://www.santaynezchumash.org/ (accessed on August 11, 2011).

"Welcome to Chumash Indian Life." *Santa Barbara Museum of Natural History.* http://www.sbnature.org/research/anthro/chumash/index.htm (accessed on August 11, 2011).

White, Julia. "Lone Woman of San Nicholas Island (Juana Maria)—Chumash." *Woman Spirit.* http://www.meyna.com/chumash.html (accessed on August 11, 2011).

Costanoan

Name

For many years, the Ohlone were called Costanoan, which comes from the Spanish word *costeños,* which means "coast-dwellers." The people call themselves *Ohlone,* the name of a village. Today, some bands retain the name Costanoan, but most are referred to as Ohlone/Costanoan or Muwekma Ohlone. The people themselves usually prefer one of two names—*Muwekma* in the north (around San Francisco Bay) and *Amah* or *Amah Mutsun* in central California (around Monterey Bay). Both of these names mean "the people."

Location

The Ohlone inhabited the central coast of California (from San Francisco Bay to Monterey Bay) and east to the Mount Diablo mountain range. In the early 2000s, none of the Ohlone tribes was recognized by the federal government, and they had no reservation land. Most of the tribes' descendants remain scattered throughout their traditional territory.

Population

Before the 1600s, about 15,000 to 20,000 Ohlone people were known to exist. In 1770, the count was down to about 10,000. In 1832, fewer than 2,000 Ohlone remained. In the 1990 U.S. Census, 858 people identified themselves as Ohlone. The 2000 census showed that 1,325 Ohlone lived in United States, and 2,659 people claimed to have some Ohlone heritage.

Language family

Penutian.

Origins and group affiliations

For about one thousand years before the arrival of Europeans in North America, Ohlone settlements expanded along the coast from San Francisco Bay to Monterrey Bay and inland in what is now known as California. The people were divided into at least fifty independent nations, and these groups sometimes fought among themselves. The Ohlone traded with the Plains and Sierra Miwok (see Miwok entry) and the Yokuts.

Traditional Costanoan Communities

None of the Costanoan groups are recognized by the federal government. With no reservation land, most Costanoans are scattered throughout traditional Costanoan territory.

Shaded area

Traditional Costanoan lands on the central coast of present-day California from San Francisco Bay to Monterey Bay and east to the Mount Diablo range

A map of traditional Costanoan lands. MAP BY XNR PRODUCTIONS. CENGAGE LEARNING, GALE. REPRODUCED BY PERMISSION OF GALE, A PART OF CENGAGE LEARNING.

The Ohlone had a comfortable life compared to many other Native American peoples. They occupied the beautiful lands of the central California coast, where the ocean teemed with fish and game birds, and the surrounding hills provided excellent hunting grounds. Like their Chumash neighbors (see entry), the Ohlone people suffered at the hands of Spanish Catholic missionaries and Mexican and American settlers. Eventually, they were thought to be extinct, but the Ohlone people have managed to keep their culture alive despite tremendous obstacles.

HISTORY

Relationships with Native neighbors

The Ohlone people were divided into at least fifty separate and independent nations. They hunted, gathered, and traded with other Ohlone groups and with the Miwok (see entry) and the Yokuts. Ohlone traders exchanged shellfish, shells, salt, and hunting bows for pine nuts and beads made from pieces of clamshell. They maintained relations with villagers from nearby and far away; sometimes men would marry the daughters of these far-off villages, thereby establishing distant friendships and trade relations that lasted a lifetime.

The people sometimes waged bow-and-arrow wars with other Ohlone groups. These wars usually stemmed from land rights disputes, but sometimes villagers quarreled over the minerals that produced the prized red and white body paints.

Europeans arrive

The first contact between the Ohlone people and Europeans most likely took place in 1602 when Spanish explorer Sebastián Vizcaíno (c. 1548–c. 1624) encountered a group called the Rumsen (American Indians of Monterey Bay, California). Between 1602 and 1769, the Natives and non-Natives met from time to time. European traders stopped by on their way east from the Philippines or on their way to and from the Vancouver region in Canada. Frequent contact began with the 1769 founding of the Spanish colony of Monterey. Much of what is now known about the Ohlone people was written down after that by Spanish explorers, soldiers, and the Catholic missionary priests (called *padres* in Spanish) who traveled with them.

One Spanish missionary, quoted by Alan K. Brown in *The Ohlone Past and Present: Native Americans of the San Francisco Bay Region,* described a trip the Spaniards took through Ohlone territory in 1772. As usual, he wrote, the visitors offered glass beads to the Ohlone in exchange for food. Initially, the Natives were unwilling to accept the beads and seemed indifferent about forming any sort of relationship with the Spanish. They were slowly won over, though, and expressed their generosity by bringing gifts of food to the European settlers. The missionary was especially impressed by the pale skin of the Ohlone people. "They are like so many Spaniards," he declared.

Spanish missions built

By the sixteenth century, Spain had claimed a huge expanse of land in what is now the state of California. When Russian and British traders showed interest in the region, the Spanish founded the port of Monterey

Important Dates

1602: Spanish explorer Sebastián Vizcaíno encounters the Ohlone.

1769: The Presidio (military fort) of Monterey is founded in Ohlone territory.

1770: The first Spanish Catholic mission is built on Ohlone land.

1812: Ohlone Mission Indians assassinate Padre Quintana at Santa Cruz.

1960s: The Ohlone people call attention to Native rights.

1980s and 1990s: Four Ohlone tribes petition the U.S. government for federal recognition.

The Royal Presidio Chapel in Monterey, California, was founded as a Spanish mission in 1770. © DAVID MUENCH/ CORBIS.

to protect their hold on the California coast. They relied on the California Natives to expand their presence in the West. The California Indians were taught just enough of the Spanish language to be considered useful. Missionary priests in the region had their own goal of converting the Natives to the Catholic religion. The first Catholic mission in Ohlone territory was established in 1770; it was built with forced Native labor. Eventually the number of missions in California reached twenty-one; seven were in Ohlone territory. The California Indians who joined the mission came to be known as Mission Indians.

Mission Indians

Most Natives did not go willingly to the missions. The Ohlone were thrust into the mission system by misfortune: their food sources were eaten by Spanish cattle, and their population was weakened by strange new diseases brought by European traders and Spanish colonists.

Once at the missions, the Natives were baptized into the Catholic faith and called neophytes (pronounced *NEE-oh-fites*; beginners). Under Spanish law, neophytes had to live near the missions. These converts stayed in camps set up outside the missions. At ages five or six, Native children were taken from their parents and forced to live in barracks. They attended religious services and performed physical labor without pay. The children were trained in carpentry, agriculture, and other practical occupations as dictated by the Spanish.

Conditions at the missions were appalling. The people lived in filth. Medical care was virtually nonexistent. Many California Natives died from overwork, disease, and harsh treatment. Different tribes lived together and lost all connection to their villages, their customs, and their religions. Most historians agree that the establishment of the missions nearly caused the destruction of Ohlone culture.

Inevitably, conflicts developed between the missionaries and the Native people who refused to convert to the Catholic religion. Rebellious Natives banded together and raided the mission's horses to defy Spanish authority and cripple the economy of the colony.

Mexican rule

The mission system endured, even as the Mexican government took over California in 1834. The Mexicans freed the neophytes and made some attempts to help them, but these were mostly ineffective. Mexican officials ordered that mission property and livestock be divided among the Natives who lived at the missions. Most of the lands and livestock, however, passed into the hands of Mexican settlers.

Some Native peoples remained at the missions, which no longer served as religious centers but had thriving farms. (Many of the mission churches still exist and have become popular tourist destinations.) Most people, however, left to seek work on the Mexican ranches that were being built on former tribal lands. Certain Ohlone groups established Native communities with members of other tribes, but these communities grew smaller as young people left to find employment elsewhere. Many Ohlone had died under the mission system, and even more died at the hands of Mexican settlers. The rest became part of the larger California group of homeless and landless Natives.

California's rejected treaties

In 1848, the United States won California from Mexico following the Mexican-American War (1846–48); California became a state two years later. In the 1850s, the U.S. government decided to resolve the country's "Indian problem" by establishing the reservation system—setting aside pieces of land (most often undesirable ones) on which the Native peoples could live. Eighteen treaties were drawn up. California tribes agreed to give up most of their tribal lands to the U.S. government in exchange for about 7.5 million acres that would be used for reservations.

Most Californians, though, were alarmed that so much land—about 8 percent of the state—was being "given away" to the Native peoples. They also feared that their supply of slave labor would disappear onto reservations. They convinced the U.S. Senate to reject the treaties.

American settlers continued to push into California, and the mistreatment of Native groups, including the Ohlone, continued. Thousands were murdered, and thousands more became slaves. Others tried to make a living as best they could. Racial prejudice led many Ohlone to hide their ancestry and attempt to blend in with other groups. By the early years of the twentieth century, most historians believed the Ohlone people were extinct.

Ohlone Woman Sues Federal Government

According to the terms of eighteen treaties drawn up in the 1850s, California tribes agreed to give up most of their lands to the U.S. government in exchange for about eight million acres that would be set aside for reservations. The treaties never became legal, but the California Natives lost their land.

In 1928, Congress passed laws that allowed California Natives to sue the federal government for the land that had been taken from them. Every California Indian who could prove they were related to a member of a Native nation who had been alive in 1850 was entitled to participate in the lawsuit. One such person was Ann Marie Sayers, a Mutsun Costanoan/Ohlone. According to Sayers, the U.S. government finally determined that the land of her ancestors was worth 41 cents an acre. After many delays and much paperwork, in 1950, Sayers received her land settlement check—a paltry sum of $150. In 1972, she received an additional $668. Other were not so fortunate; they received nothing.

Twentieth century and beyond

The Ohlone were not extinct, however, as anthropologist (a person who studies human societies) John Peabody Harrington (1884–1961) discovered. In the 1920s, the Smithsonian Institution, a national research group in Washington, D.C., asked Harrington to conduct interviews with descendants of California Native groups. He found that some Ohlone were keeping their culture alive and were still speaking the language.

Around the same time, the U.S. government sent a representative to study the situation of the region's homeless Native peoples. Based on the representative's poorly researched report, the government determined that there was no reason to set aside land for the Ohlone people.

Several lawsuits were filed by California Natives in the twentieth century, claiming rights to lands they gave up while waiting for the eighteen treaties to take effect. Ohlone people took part in two of the lawsuits but received little satisfaction.

Beginning in the 1960s, various Native groups, the Ohlone with them, started calling for an end to construction projects that threatened cultural resources on traditional lands. In 2009, the Confederation of Ohlone Peoples formed as an educational organization, with a mission to preserve the culture, ceremonies, and traditions of the people. It has been lending support to movements to protect important cultural resources and sites. By the end of the twentieth century, these groups, along with many vocal individuals, were focusing the attention of scholars and the public on the long-neglected, but rich, culture of the Ohlone people.

RELIGION

Like other Native cultures of central California, most Ohlone believed in a creator, an animal character called Coyote, who was one of the First People. Coyote is said to have made the world and everything in it. Other important figures include Eagle and Hummingbird (and for the

Chochenyo band, Kaknu, a falcon-like being). Hummingbird, in spite of being tiny, often out-smarted Coyote, the trickster.

Keeping the animal spirits happy was a constant concern for the Ohlone people. This was accomplished by holding frequent ceremonies and offerings. Members of a religious group called the Kuksu Society were devoted to the worship of the creator. The Kuksu Society held dances in an earth-covered dance house. Dancers, who dressed in large feathered headdresses, impersonated animal spirits. During the ceremonies, boys between the ages of eight and sixteen were taught the rituals so they might one day become members.

The Ohlone believed that if the animal spirits were happy, good things would come to them (rain, for example), and disasters would be avoided. The animal spirits were also thought to appear to people in dreams to guide them in making major life decisions.

The tribes offered seeds, tobacco, and shell beads to appease the spirits. When they prayed to the sun, they blew smoke toward the sky. Sticks with feathers brought good luck in hunting or fishing. Some offerings were placed on poles—rabbit skin strips, tobacco leaves, feathers, and headdresses. Capes made of grass were used as death offerings.

Some of the Ohlone became Catholics under the mission system, but many were reluctant converts. The religion of their descendants blends Catholic elements with traditional spiritual beliefs and practices.

Mutsun Words

When the people lived at the Missions, they were forced to learn Spanish rather than their Native languages. The eight Ohlone languages, including Mutsun, gradually became extinct. The last fluent Mutsun speaker, Ascencion Solorsano, died in 1930, but through the efforts of the Mutsun Language Foundation in the early twenty-first century, many members of the tribe are learning their language and culture. Below are some words and phrases in the Mutsun dialect.

miSminTuuhis	"Hello."
hinkate-m?	"How are you?"
miSte-ka	"I'm fine."
akkuy	"Come in."
miSminmuruT	"please"
Suururu-me	"Thank you."
kusinwi-ka-mesmiSte	"Nice to meet you."
hinkaneppe?	"What is this?"
ana	"mom"
ansa	"dad"
mene	"grandmother"
papa	"grandfather"

LANGUAGE

The Ohlone spoke at least eight different languages; all of these dialects belong to the language family called Ohlone. The varieties that scholars know about are called Karkin, Chochenyo, Tamyen, Ramaytush, Awaswas, Mutsun, Rumsen, and Chalon. After the 1930s, there were no remaining speakers of the ancient languages.

Costanoan/Ohlone Groups Seek Federal Recognition

Federally recognized tribes are those who have a legal relationship with the U.S. government. Without federal recognition, the tribe does not exist in the eyes of the government and is therefore not entitled to financial aid and other help or reservation lands.

In order to obtain federal recognition, a tribe must meet certain conditions. A new tribal constitution must be adopted, and a new tribal government must be formed. Nine groups (sometimes called bands) of Costanoan/Ohlone have filed for federal recognition since the 1980s, including the Amah/Mutsun Band, the Carmel Mission Band, the Indian Canyon Band, the Ohlone/Costanoan Esselen Nation, the Costanoan Ohlone Rumsen-Mutsen Tribe, Costanoan-Rumsen Carmel Tribe, and the Muwekma Ohlone Tribe. As of 2011, none of the groups had achieved federal recognition.

GOVERNMENT

The Ohlone people were organized into about fifty independent groups or organizations that are sometimes called tribelets. A tribelet consisted of one main settlement surrounded by a few minor settlements. Tribelet chiefs could be either men or women, but usually the job passed from father to son. A group of elders advised the chief, who took responsibility for overseeing hunting and fishing expeditions and caring for the poor. The Ohlone people valued their personal freedom highly and obeyed an authority figure only during wartime.

By the twenty-first century, the descendants of the Ohlone were scattered throughout California. Four groups have applied for federal recognition. As part of that process, they have organized councils to oversee their tribal government.

ECONOMY

Before European arrival, the Ohlone economy depended largely on gathering and trading activities as well as hunting and fishing. Because of their clever management of the land, the Ohlone were able to supply their own food needs and have surplus to trade with neighboring groups. The region also had abundant shells and the material to make dyes used for decorative items and body paints.

The tribe's extensive trade network reached as far as Nevada, where a string of 8,600-year-old Olivella beads was found. The Ohlone quarried cinnabar (a red mineral) in what is now Santa Clara County, California. Tribes from as far away as Washington State came to trade or fight for it. The Ohlone were also known for other trade goods, such as abalone shells, obsidian, dogs, tobacco, hides, hunting bows, baskets, salt, acorns, and fish.

Under the mission system, the Ohlone were forced to become farm and ranch laborers. Later they were compelled to blend into the larger California community, which is where they find employment today.

DAILY LIFE

Families

Families usually consisted of a father, a mother, their children, and the father's relatives. Ten to fifteen people made up a household.

Buildings

Most Ohlone built domed dwellings, although some groups constructed cone-shaped homes from redwood. The domed structures were covered with thatch (plant material), which was attached to poles and tied at the top. A rectangular doorway led directly to a central fireplace. Homes contained beds made of bulrush mats and skins. The beds were covered with blankets woven from strips of sea otter or rabbit skins or duck feathers or down.

Sweathouses for men and women (no children were allowed) were dug out of stream banks. Adults retreated to sweathouses for solitude and purification rituals that helped strengthen their spiritual well-being. The people held dances in circular enclosures or in large, dome-shaped thatched structures.

Clothing and adornment

Few males wore any kind of clothing, but women wore tule (a kind of plant) and buckskin aprons suspended from the waist in front and back. Both sexes wore long robes in cold weather, and men sometimes covered their bodies with a special mud to keep warm. No shoes or hats were worn.

The Ohlone people had fairer hair than most other Native Californians, and they usually wore it long. Men tied theirs with cords decorated with feathers, whereas women let theirs hang loose. Many of the men had long, flowing beards.

Tattoos covered various parts of the body, and red and white paint was sometimes applied to decorate the face and body. Ornaments such as flowers or feathers hung from pierced ears, and some men had pierced noses. Both sexes wore necklaces made of shells.

Food

Ohlone lands were so rich in food resources that the Native people did not have to farm. Even so, they lit fires to clear and fertilize land for sowing the seeds of wild grasses. The grasses provided them with food and attracted game animals.

In the spring, the people moved from their villages on the coast to take advantage of the newly ripening plants, bulbs, greens, and grass seed found farther inland. They gathered a variety of berries to eat raw or to cook. When autumn came, some villagers departed to gather acorns. These and other nuts and seeds were then processed and eaten. Acorns were often ground into flour.

The bounty of the Pacific Coast ensured ample supplies of abalone (pronounced *AB-uh-LONE-ee*; a Rumsen word for a type of edible shell-fish), crabs, mussels, oysters, sea snails, shrimp, clams, steelhead, sturgeon, and lampreys (an eel-like fish). Salmon were netted and hauled aboard sturdy rafts or boats made of tule (*TOO-lee*; a type of cattail). The Ohlone did not hunt whales or sea lions, but if any happened to wash ashore, the people gladly roasted and ate them. They caught otter and seal in addition to other game.

All sorts of birds were hunted. Mourning dove, quail, robin, wild turkey, and hawk were part of the diet, but buzzards, eagles, owls, and ravens were not eaten. The people attracted several varieties of geese by using dried and stuffed goose decoys made by skilled craftspeople. Rabbit, deer, elk, antelope, mountain lion, and grizzly bear added variety to the diet. Smaller game included ground squirrel, rat, skunk, mice, mole, dogs, snake, and lizard. Frogs and toads were never eaten.

Education

Little is known about the education of Ohlone children prior to the arrival of European missionaries. Children most likely learned by observing adults. During the mission period, children were taught the fundamentals of the Catholic religion. They also learned about farming, weaving, and potterymaking—trades the Spanish considered useful. The European settlers did not teach the Ohlone to read because they feared that a young generation of educated youth might become restless and dissatisfied with the mission system. In fact, teaching Native children to read was against the law until the 1920s.

At the end of the twentieth century, descendants of the Ohlone had organized classes in their native language as well as in basketmaking and folklore at cultural centers in California. In 1997, a museum was built at Indian Canyon. A joint undertaking between the Ohlone Indians and the University of California–Santa Cruz, the museum is lighted using solar power because the canyon does not have electricity. It displays Ohlone items, such as an arrow, games, weaving, and a tule house.

Ohlone Medicine

The Ohlone had an extensive knowledge of herbs and roots for curing sicknesses. They treated medical problems ranging from headaches and stomach aches to internal disorders and rheumatism. Treatments were available for snakebites, burns, and wounds. Family members applied remedies to cure these common problems. Those who needed additional help might consult an herbalist. Illnesses that did not respond to the usual treatments were referred to the shamans for spiritual healing, because those hard-to-heal diseases were believed to result from supernatural causes.

To avoid snakebites, the Ohlone placed Oregon ash tree leaves in their sandals. If they were bitten, they drank a tea made from rattlesnake weed.

Not only did the Ohlone set bones using splints, but they also made casts. They boiled bark from the cottonwood tree into a sticky syrup. They wrapped the fracture in buckskin coated with this thick paste and tied on a splint. By the next day, the cottonwood gum had hardened into a cast, so they could remove the splint and buckskin.

The Ohlone squeezed juice from violets to put on open sores, then boiled the plants and used the liquid as additional treatment the next day. Heated yarrow leaves reduced swelling. Smoking or chewing yerba santa leaves or drinking teas made of herbs relieved the symptoms of coughs and colds.

The Ohlone had many cures for rheumatism to ease the pain of elders' achy joints. After the patient took a sweatbath, they rubbed the sore areas with a mix of fat from a hog's kidneys and California wild rose. Chewing herbs or drinking teas to relieve pain also helped.

Children used different medicines from adults. For high fevers with convulsions, parents rubbed their children's bodies with pineapple weed salve. Colicky babies drank warm sagebrush tea to soothe their stomach pains. When children had trouble sleeping, their parents put California poppy flowers underneath their beds, which helped them relax.

Ohlone herbal knowledge also extended to products to make them more appealing. To get rid of dandruff, they made a shampoo from crushed soaproot bulbs and stems. A paste of wild cucumber or bracken rubbed into the scalp prevented baldness.

Healing practices

According to Ohlone belief, diseases were caused by objects placed inside the sick person's body by angry spirits. Medicine men called shamans (pronounced *SHAH-munz* or *SHAY-munz*) were consulted to restore the victim's health. A shaman usually began his task by performing a ceremonial song and dance, then cured the disease by piercing the patient's skin and sucking out the disease-causing object. Shamans also used herbs

Coyote and His Wife

A group of tales about Coyote were collected in the early 1900s from two elderly women who remembered some of the Ohlone oral traditions. Many of these stories are short, and this one, as do many of them, includes the death of a main character. This time, however, death is not final.

> Makewiks is an animal that lives in the ocean and sometimes comes to the surface. Coyote went to the ocean with his wife. He told her not to be afraid. He told her about the sea lion, about the mussels, about the crabs, and the octopus. He told her that all these were relatives; so when she saw them she was not afraid. But he did not tell her about the makewiks. Then when this rose before her it frightened her so that she fell dead. Coyote took her on his back, carried her off, built a fire, and laid her by the side of it. He began to sing and dance and jump. Soon she began to come to life. He jumped three times and brought her to life.

SOURCE: Kroeber, A. L. "Indian Myths of South Central California." *University of California Publications American Archaeology and Ethnology* 4, no. 4 (1907). Available online at http://www.sacred-texts.com/nam/ca/scc/scc06.htm (accessed on August 11, 2011).

as medicine, mixing them together in a special small container called a mortar.

Some Ohlone doctors claimed to be able to kill their enemies by turning themselves into grizzly bears; these doctors were greatly feared. Rumsen grizzly bear doctors wore bearskins and had bear teeth and claws filled with poison to kill their victims. When they were suspected of witchcraft or murder, the tribe killed them.

ARTS

The California tribes, ranked among the world's best basket makers, produced two different types of baskets: coiled and twined. The Ohlone specialty was twined baskets, made from willow, rushes, and grasses. These tightly woven baskets were both beautiful and functional; they were used for carrying, storing, and processing acorns; snaring fish; carrying and storing water; and as cooking pots and utensils.

Oral literature

The Ohlone liked to tell stories about how death came into the world. There are two common elements in these stories: a supernatural power creates death and then is sorry when a relative dies, and the decision to create death is irreversible—it cannot be changed.

Music

Songs were used during ceremonies and dances and to tell stories, but they could also be sung as love or hunting charms. They were accompanied by flutes made from wood or bird bones and rhythm instruments such as split sticks that were banged against the hand, rattles made from cocoons, and a bow whose strings were plucked by hand.

CUSTOMS

Childbirth

After giving birth to her baby, a new mother would undergo a ritual cleansing in the ocean or in a stream. Then, for several days, she and her newborn child would rest on a mattress in a pit lined with hot rocks. Ohlone tradition dictated the mother's diet; there were certain foods she could not eat. Shortly after birth, the baby boy or girl's ears were pierced.

Puberty

Ohlone girls who had reached puberty did not eat certain foods or drink cold water during their menstrual period, and they went through a special ritual in a corner of the home at the onset of puberty. Menstrual blood was considered powerful and possibly even dangerous. Boys at puberty took a drug called *toloache,* obtained from a plant called jimsonweed. When consumed, the drug caused them to go into a trancelike state and see visions.

Marriage

A class system existed among the Ohlone, and members of the elite, or highest, classes married members of their same class living in tribes throughout central California, even if they did not speak the same language.

Marriages began when the groom's family bestowed a small gift upon the bride's family. The newlyweds lived in the home of the husband's father. Sometimes an Ohlone man took more than one wife, usually his wife's sister. The resulting families all lived together. If a couple decided to divorce, the mother kept the children.

War rituals

Most often war occurred over territory. Battles were conducted either by surprise attack or by prearrangement. The Ohlone killed their captives, except for young women, and placed the heads of their enemies on pikes (sticklike weapons with a sharpened end). Raiding parties also burned the villages.

Death

In keeping with Ohlone tradition, a corpse was wrapped in feathers, beads, and flowers, laid out on a stack of wood, and cremated (set on fire). A deceased person who had no family members to gather firewood for the funeral fire was buried instead. The mourners chanted and expressed their wishes for the soul's easy trip to the next world. Widows and female relatives cut off their hair and beat themselves on the head and breast with pestles (the pounding and grinding implement used with a mortar). After her husband was buried, a widow would remain in mourning for a year. The tribe held an annual memorial service for all the dead.

Festivals and ceremonies

Shamans were the main performers at many Ohlone festivals. They organized dances to bring a good acorn crop, plentiful fish, and stranded whales. Acorn season was the most festive time of the year and lasted only a few weeks. After gathering all day, at night the people danced, traded, gambled, and feasted.

The tribes held a variety of dances—devil's dance, bear dance, dove dance, coyote dance, and puberty dance. The Chochenyo had a pair of dances that were done by all men (*Hiwey*) and all women (*Loole*). The Hiwey doctor wore a skirt of raven feathers and a feathered headdress. He painted his arms and face and sprinkled down feathers over his face. He also wore a live snake wound around his forearm. He leapt through fire and caused the ground to tremble when he hugged a tree and talked to the devil. This Hiwey doctor cured all different diseases.

CURRENT TRIBAL ISSUES

Obtaining tribal recognition and preserving sacred sites are important issues to the modern Ohlone. Because they became part of the missions and later lost their land, the Ohlone tribes have had a difficult time establishing a continuously documented history—one of the main requirements for federal recognition. The Muwekma Ohlone Tribe received a positive decision in U.S. district court in 2006, which they expected would move their case along more quickly, but as of 2011, a decision had not been made.

Ann Marie Sayers, the tribal chairperson of the Indian Canyon Mutsun Band of Costanoan, holds the title to a section of Indian Canyon, a 275-mile (443-kilometer) piece of land in the San Francisco Bay area. In the nineteenth century, Indian Canyon served as a refuge for Ohlone Indians fleeing the Spanish missions. From her home there, Sayers and other like-minded individuals are carrying on the struggle for federal recognition of California's nonrecognized tribes. Sayers's property is a Living Indian Heritage Area, where today Native people live and hold traditional ceremonies. The canyon is used for ceremonies; every year about five thousand people visit the site to take part in educational programs, rituals, or vision quests. Sayers also planned a self-reliant solar village with a central, traditional-style building for ceremonial and community events, such as dances, storytelling, and healing ceremonies.

California Natives—the Ohlone among them—voice powerful opposition to major construction on their ancestral lands. A huge antidevelopment campaign in the late 1990s sought to prevent the building of a $100 million project around the San Bruno Mountain Indian Shell Mound (a site overlooking San Francisco Bay). The mound dates back five thousand years and was the site of important Ohlone ceremonies and burials. In 2000, the San Bruno Mountain lawsuit was settled in the tribe's favor, and in 2001, the Trust for Public Land agreed to purchase and protect twenty-five acres that includes the Ohlone shell mound. Another protest was launched later to prevent a large corporation from constructing a shipyard on the site of ancient Ohlone villages and burial grounds.

NOTABLE PEOPLE

Oiyugma was an Ohlone chief who led the resistance against the establishment of Mission San Jose in the late 1700s. He threatened to kill Spanish soldiers and any Native peoples who tried to help them build the mission.

Other notable Ohlone include Mutsun Ohlone Ann Marie Sayers, Rumsen Ohlone Linda Yamane, and Alex Ramirez, who are currently active in the movement to revive tribal traditions and bring them to the attention of a wider audience.

BOOKS

Abbink, Emily. *Monterey Bay Area Missions in California*. Minneapolis, MN: Lerner, 2007.

Bean, Lowell John, ed. "Introduction." In *The Ohlone Past and Present: Native Americans of the San Francisco Bay Region*. Menlo Park, CA: Ballena Press, 1994.

Brower, Pauline. *Inland Valleys Missions in California*. Minneapolis, MN: Lerner, 2007.

Davis, Thomas L., and Jack S. Williams. *Padres of the California Mission Frontier*. New York: PowerKids Press, 2004.

Giago, Tim A. *Children Left Behind: Dark Legacy of Indian Mission Boarding Schools.* Santa Fe, NM: Clear Light Publishing, 2006.

Kimbro, Edna, Julia G. Costello, and Tevvy Ball. *The California Missions: History, Art and Preservation.* Los Angeles: Getty Conservation Institute, 2009.

Margolin, Malcolm. *The Ohlone Way.* Berkeley, CA: Heyday Books, 1981.

Simons, Cynthia Vrilakas. *San Leandro.* Mount Pleasant, SC: Arcadia, 2008.

White, Tekla N. *San Francisco Bay Area Missions.* Minneapolis, MN: Lerner, 2007.

PERIODICALS

Kroeber, A. L. "Indian Myths of South Central California" *University of California Publications* 4, no. 4 (1907). Available online at http://www.sacred-texts.com/nam/ca/scc/ (accessed on August 11, 2011).

WEB SITES

Cambra, Rosemary, et al. "The Muwekma Ohlone Tribe of the San Francisco Bay Area." http://www.islaiscreek.org/ohlonehistcultfedrecog.html (accessed on August 11, 2011).

"Costanoan Indian Tribe." *Access Genealogy.* http://www.accessgenealogy.com/native/tribes/costanoan/costanoanindiantribe.htm (accessed on August 11, 2011).

Costanoan Rumsen Carmel Tribe. http://costanoanrumsen.org/ (accessed on August 11, 2011).

"Costanoan Rumsen Carmel Tribe: History." *Native Web.* http://crc.nativeweb.org/history.html (accessed on August 11, 2011).

"History: The Ohlone People." *Museum of Local History.* http://www.museumoflocalhistory.org/oldmuse/history1.htm (accessed on August 11, 2011).

Indian Canyon. http://www.indiancanyon.org/ (accessed on August 11, 2011).

Johnston, Theresa. "Those Who Came Before." *Stanford Magazine.* http://www.stanfordalumni.org/news/magazine/1998/marapr/articles/before.html (accessed on August 11, 2011).

Muwekma Ohlone Tribe. http://www.muwekma.org/ (accessed on August 11, 2011).

Ohlone/Costanoan Esselen Nation. http://www.ohlonecostanoanesselennation.org/(accessed on August 11, 2011).

"Ohlone Literature." *Indigenous Peoples' Literature.* http://www.indians.org/welker/ohlone.htm (accessed on August 11, 2011).

"Proposed Village House." *Indian Canyon Village.* http://www.indiancanyonvillage.org/ (accessed on August 11, 2011).

Redish, Laura, and Orrin Lewis. "Costanoan/Ohlone Indian Language." *Native Languages of the Americas.* http://www.native-languages.org/ohlone.htm (accessed on August 11, 2011).

Smith, Chuck. "Ohlone Medicine." *Cabrillo College.* http://www.cabrillo.edu/~crsmith/OhloneMed.html (accessed on August 11, 2011).

Hupa and Chilula

Names

Hupa (pronounced *HOO-pah*) and Chilula (*chee-LOO-lah*). The word "Hupa" comes from the name the Yurok Indians gave to the Hoopa Valley. One group of Hupa called themselves *Natinixwe* (pronounced *Nah-tin-o-whey*) or *Natinook-wa,* meaning "the people of the place by the river to which the trails return." A second group called themselves *Tsungwe,* as they still do. The valley tribe is now known as the Hoopa Valley Tribe, but the individual Native people are called Hupa.

The name "Chilula" is an Americanized version of the Yurok word *čulula,* meaning "they frequent Bald Hills" or "they pass through Bald Hills." They were known to their other neighbors as the Bald Hills Indians or Redwood Creek Indians. The Chilula called themselves *Hoil'kut.*

Location

Both the Hupa and Chilula lived in northwestern California, the Hupa along the shores of the Trinity River and the Chilula in the lower section of Redwood Creek in Humboldt County. At the start of the twenty-first century, most of the remaining Hupa and descendants of the Chilula (who no longer use the name and have become part of the other groups on the reservation) lived on the Hoopa Valley Reservation, a 144-square-mile (373-square-kilometer) area that covers one-half of traditional Hupa territory. Some Hupa also share the Blue Lake Rancheria in Humboldt County.

Population

There were an estimated 1,000 Hupa in 1850, and about 400 to 600 Chilula in the early 1800s. The Hupa population fell to 420 in 1906. In the 1990 U.S. Census, 2,386 people identified themselves as Hupa (or Hoopa); no one claimed to be Chilula. The 2000 census indicated that there were 2,589 Hupa; of that number 2,051 lived on the Hoopa Valley Reservation. The census also showed 3,207 people with some Hupa heritage living in the United States.

Language family

Athabaskan.

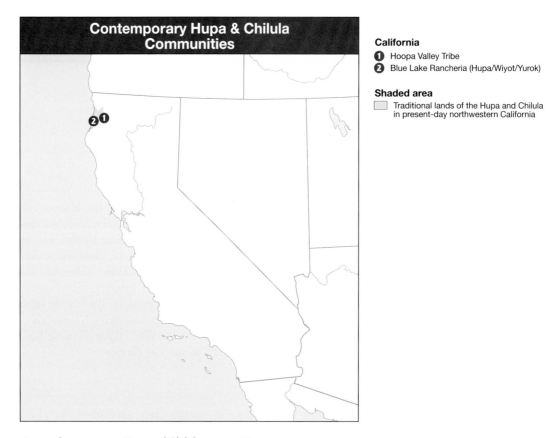

A map of contemporary Hupa and Chilula communities. MAP BY XNR PRODUCTIONS. CENGAGE LEARNING, GALE. REPRODUCED BY PERMISSION OF GALE, A PART OF CENGAGE LEARNING.

Origins and group affiliations

Archaeologists and linguists believe that the Hupa and Chilula originally lived north of California, most likely in Oregon. They probably began the move south about 1,300 years ago and completed the move around 300 years later. The Hupa had contact with the Yurok (see entry) and Karok; the Chilula also maintained a good relationship with the Yurok. The Chilula, however, did not trust the Teswan, who blocked their path to the Pacific Ocean. The two groups fought often over hunting grounds. In the early twenty-first century, the Hupa share the Blue Lake Rancheria with the Yurok and Wiyot.

The Hupa are and always have been the largest of the Athabaskan-speaking tribes living in northwestern California. They were river people whose way of life depended on the runs of salmon that still occur each fall on the Trinity River. They believe their village at the heart of the Hoopa

Valley is the center of the world and that all trails return to it. The Hupa shared a language and most customs with their less prosperous neighbors, the Chilula, who depended on the much smaller Redwood Creek for resources. The frequently damp, foggy climate, rocky cliffs, narrow stony beaches, and hardwood forests that surrounded the two tribes had more in common with the Pacific Northwest than with typical California locales.

HISTORY

Discovery of gold

Long before the coming of fur trappers in the 1800s, the Hupa and Chilula lived in secluded and prosperous villages where natural resources were fairly plentiful and life was comfortable. They were so secluded that they had almost no contact with outsiders until 1850. That year, gold was discovered on the upper Trinity River, bringing a flood of prospectors to the their homelands. The gold beds quickly ran dry, but some miners stayed in the area and built homes and planted orchards.

Throughout the United States, relations between settlers and the Native peoples were far from good. In California, where pioneers and gold seekers were pouring in, rumors spread about "wild" Indians killing "innocent" settlers. Fort Gaston was built in 1855 to protect settlers from the Hupa and Chilula. U.S. troops were stationed at the fort.

Hupa resistance to reservation

Seeking to end the growing violence Californians were showing toward the Native peoples in the 1850s, the U.S. government began talks with the tribes, urging them to give up their homelands in exchange for land on newly established reservations that turned out to be tiny and insufficient. Most California tribes were moved to areas far from their traditional homelands. Reservation land was usually unsuitable for farming and lacking in water and game.

Important Dates

1828: American trappers enter the Hoopa Valley.

1850: Gold is discovered on the Trinity River; prospectors pour onto Hupa and Chilula lands.

1859: One hundred sixty Chilula attending what they think is a peace conference are forced onto a reservation in Mendocino. Attempting to return home, most are killed by Lassik Indians.

1864: The Hoopa Valley Reservation is established.

1892: The U.S. government abandons Fort Gaston.

1950: The Hoopa Valley Tribe adopts a constitution.

1988: The Hoopa-Yurok Settlement Act is signed, giving the Hoopa Valley Tribe full rights to profits from timber harvested on the reservation.

For five years, the Hupa resisted the government's efforts to move them. Finally, in 1864, a reservation was established on their ancestral land. The Hupa people who lived on the south fork of the Trinity River, who called themselves Tsnungwe, soon joined the Valley Hupa on the reservation, as did some of their neighbors, the Yurok. The Klamath tribe moved to the same area in the early 1880s, at which point the Tsnungwe returned to their homeland on the Trinity River.

Disease and war

At the time of the move to the reservation, the presence of foreigners was taking its toll on the Native population. American settlers exposed the people of the Hoopa Valley to new diseases. Lacking immunity to those diseases, the Hupa were hit hard by epidemics (uncontrolled outbreaks of disease), and the population fell to 650 by 1864.

Between 1860 and 1872, the Hupa and other area tribes engaged in a series of Indian wars with the settlers, who had taken over Native territories, murdered Native peoples, kidnapped their children, and burned their villages. The most dramatic event occurred in 1867; it resulted in the deaths of several U.S. law enforcement agents and one Hupa man, who was suspected of robbery. More conflicts arose as U.S. troops tried to place non-valley Native peoples on the Hoopa Valley Reservation, but these disputes were relatively minor.

Chilula resistance The Chilula and the settlers were involved in far more serious clashes. The Chilula people first met gold miners and settlers in 1851, and the relationship between the two groups was instantly hostile. In response to the invasion of their territory by strangers who stole their resources, the Chilula ambushed the miners and took their supplies. The miners then shot members of the tribe on sight. Outbreaks of violence continued throughout the 1850s, as soldiers stationed at Fort Gaston and other area sites aided the settlers in their anti-Native campaign.

Chilula resistance slowed non-Native advancement onto their lands, but the tribe's skillful defense of ancestral territories fueled strong anti-Chilula feelings among the Americans. Eventually, settlers formed their own army to drive the Chilula away. On March 4, 1859, they tricked the Chilula into attending an alleged peace conference. Instead of discussing peace, the Americans rounded up about 160 Chilula (one-quarter of the tribe), forced them onto a ship, and moved them to a reservation 150 miles (240 kilometers) away in Mendocino, California.

Chilula warriors escaped from the reservation and headed home through unknown territory, guided by the sun and stars. Then, near Fort Seward on the Eel River, they were attacked without warning by a war party of the Lassik, another Athabaskan-speaking California tribe. All but one or two Chilula were killed. In retaliation, the few Chilula who remained at Redwood Creek joined the Hupa and the Whilkut and raided a Lassik summer camp.

Hearing of the violence, miners avoided the area. Finally, a U.S. government agent convinced the few remaining Chilula to join the Hoopa Valley Indian Reservation. Once there, the Chilula intermixed and intermarried with the other tribes on the reservation. In time, they lost the traits that made them Chilula until ultimately they were no longer regarded as a separate tribe.

On the reservation

On the Hoopa Valley Reservation, the Hupa began adapting to American ways of life; they settled down to farm and raise livestock and became self-supporting. They were more fortunate than many other California tribes. Because they were physically isolated from U.S. communities and because they remained on their own land and lived among the same tribes that had always been their neighbors, they were better able to preserve their traditions and their community. They did, however, encounter conflict with government agents and soldiers at Fort Gaston.

For twenty-eight years, the Hupa endured harsh treatment at the hands of occupying troops. Idle soldiers set their sights on Hupa women, fathering children. In 1892, Fort Gaston was closed, and the troops moved elsewhere. This change was a blessing for the Hupa. They gradually combined American and Native ways and prospered on their reservation. At the end of the twentieth century, the reservation had gained recognition for its many historic sites and buildings. In spite of adopting American ways, the Hupa retained a visible connection to their past and a strong cultural identity. The Athabaskan language is still spoken, and the Hupa are making efforts to preserve their customs, arts, and traditions.

RELIGION

Much more is known about Hupa religious practices than those of the Chilula. The Hupa believed that a race of Immortals (beings who would live forever) inhabited the earth prior to humans. The Immortals put

Hupa Words

To revive the Hupa language, the tribe began a Master/Apprentice Program, in which a skilled speaker is paired with a beginner. This method of learning has been increasing the number of younger speakers in the tribe. Before the program began, only a few elders spoke Hupa. By 2000, sixty-four youth between the ages of five and seventeen could speak the language. As of 2011, only six fluent first-language speakers remained, but most of the people spoke Hupa as a second language.

nosht'ah	"I don't believe it."
bo:se	"cat"
sa:ts'	"bear"
je:nis	"day"
t'e'	"blanket"
tLoh	"grass"
qo	"worm"
to	"water"
wha	"sun"
whing	"song"
xontah	"house"
wiLdung'	"yesterday"
xong'	"fire"

the earth in order for all humanity and formed rules for living on it. The ancestors of the Hupa and Chilula then sprang to life. (The Chilula believed they came from a large, hollow redwood tree.) People were only one of many important elements on the earth. Spirits were believed to be present in all things, and everything in nature was to be respected and tended.

Religion helped the Hupa and Chilula cope as they grappled with the elements, disease, fear, uncertainty, and the threat of war. The people practiced many daily rituals to promote good health, wealth, and luck. They also performed rituals established by the Immortals. These rituals were an integral part of the World Renewal Cycle (see "Festivals and ceremonies"), which guaranteed world order. Village priests were in charge of the tribe's World Renewal activities.

Christians established missions on the reservation in the late 1800s, and some Native people converted to the new religion. Their traditional rituals, however, remained a central part of their lives.

LANGUAGE

The Hupa and Chilula languages were closely related. Language was regarded as holy; nothing in the natural world was as powerful as the words used in prayers. Words could not only heal but could also do great evil. As the Chilula were absorbed into the reservation system, their language perished.

GOVERNMENT

The most important tribal unit among the northwestern California Indians was the village; no single chief headed the entire Hupa or Chilula nations. Villages were composed of groups of people who shared the same family tree. Each village maintained its own version of law and order and was guided by a chief or powerful leader, usually the wealthiest or most popular man in the village. Occasionally, a group of wealthy Hupa men gathered to resolve disputes or decide on a payment for breaking rules.

After the formation of the Hoopa Valley Reservation, the Hupa became dependent on U.S. government agents—who were not always honest or fair in their role as mediator between the Natives and non-Natives. Sometimes agents broke the laws they were supposed to be upholding, as when they allowed settlers to harvest grain planted by the Native people. The tribes then experienced a food shortage and had to ask for government support.

In the mid-twentieth century, many tribes became less dependent on the federal government as they established their own leadership. The Hoopa Valley Tribe adopted a constitution in 1950. In the early twenty-first century, they are governed by a seven-member elected tribal council and a chairperson. Members represent districts that were formerly Hupa villages. The tribal government oversees many departments including health, education, natural resources, communication, human services, finances, and tribal services. The tribe also participates in the Self-Governance Demonstration Project. This project helps tribes exercise their rights to be self-governing, structure their own programs, and use federal funds in ways that benefit the tribe. For example, after the nearby hospital closed in the late 1980s, all emergency patients had to be transported 65 miles (105 kilometers) away. Although the Hoopa came up with the funding, federal regulations prevented them from reopening the hospital. They began working to ensure that all tribes have the right to develop their own health-care systems. By 2008, they had not only opened their own hospital but had taken control of many of the programs that the Bureau of Indian Affairs had formerly operated. The Hupa now operate fifty-four programs specifically defined to meet the tribe's needs, including law enforcement, fire service, environmental management, economic development, and road-building projects.

ECONOMY

Before European contact

The Hupa were primarily fishers, and the abundant resources of the Trinity River amply supplied their needs. They traveled the river in large canoes dug out of 16- to 18-foot (5-meter) lengths of redwood and cedar, which they received in trade from the Yurok. They often journeyed by foot on well-used trails over the mountains to the Pacific Coast to trade, taking acorns and other foods they had gathered, plus shell money, to exchange for fish and dried seaweed. (They extracted salt from the seaweed.)

The Chilula had to rely on the less abundant resources of Redwood Creek. Because this waterway was too small for canoes to travel, the Chilula supplemented their needs with what they could obtain by hunting and gathering.

Repayment of debt was considered a pressing issue among the Hupa and Chilula. People who had borrowed from others and could not repay the debt had to go to work for their creditor until the debt was repaid. Records indicate that indebted men would often send their daughters to work to pay off the debt.

Unlike many tribes whose hunting and gathering lands were owned by all, the Hupa and Chilula permitted individual ownership of hunting and gathering areas. As for fishing rights, the Hupa allowed individuals to claim certain sites; the Chilula, however, did not.

Timber and tourism

By the late 1990s, the Hoopa Valley Reservation was the largest in size, population, and income in California. Rich timberlands on the reservation's 87,000 acres (primarily Douglas fir) supported four mills and created jobs in the timber industry.

With a thriving timber business, its historic sites and recreational center, gaming, and retail enterprises, the Hoopa Valley Reservation had become largely self-sufficient in the early twenty-first century. The economic downturn in the housing industry affected not only the sawmill and logging businesses but the Hupa's prefabricated-building enterprise in the second decade of the 2000s; the tribe had to lay off workers. The tribe, however, had other business to provide income. They own California Indian Manpower Corporation, which provides jobs for many different tribes. The tribal government is the second-largest employer in the county. In addition to agriculture and livestock, the reservation also owns fisheries and operates mines and a cement plant.

DAILY LIFE

Families

Northwestern California Indian families usually included a father, a mother, their children, and a few unmarried relatives. They lived in single-family homes in villages ranging in size from six to thirty homes.

Buildings

Hupa and Chilula families spent most of the year in sturdy, rectangular red-wood or cedar plank houses that lasted for generations. The wealthier the family, the bigger the house and the more desirable its location; the best sites were often on hillsides, which offered better views and protection from floods.

Houses were constructed over a pit at least 5 feet (1.5 meters) deep. A notched plank served as a staircase, leading down from the front door to the floor of the sunken dwelling. Homes often included a front porch made of rocks, where people sat and worked. In spring and fall the people moved to a gathering territory and lived in temporary shelters made of brush or bark.

Like many tribes of the West, the Hupa and Chilula built separate lodges for women who were menstruating. (The men believed that exposure to menstrual blood would ruin their good luck.) Men purified themselves before hunting and gathering by sitting in sweathouses—secluded huts or caverns heated by steam and used for ritual cleansing and meditation. Some villages also contained circular dance houses where wealthy men hosted lavish ceremonies.

Clothing and adornment

The Hupa and Chilula dressed alike. Because the climate was mild, men usually wore only an animal-skin breechcloth (a garment with front and back flaps that hung from the waist), though many of the elderly men went nude. Men wore leggings only while hunting.

A Chilula sweathouse with board walls and a flat roof is built into the side of a hill in northern California. TAKEN FROM A. L. KROEBER, *HANDBOOK OF THE INDIANS OF CALIFORNIA*, ORIGINALLY PUBLISHED IN 1925, FROM A DOVER REPRINT, 1976. PLATE 13/SMITHSONIAN INSTITUTION BUREAU OF AMERICAN ETHNOLOGY.

Women wore only a knee-length fringed apron of pine nuts braided onto grass. Over this, they tied a piece of deerskin, open down the front so the underskirt showed. Dressier skirts had clamshell and abalone decorations. Later, they adopted buckskin shirts and aprons, adding a fringed skirt threaded with shells for certain ceremonies. Chilula women sometimes wore dresses of maplewood bark.

Although the Hupa occasionally wore moccasins for long journeys, they usually went barefoot. Women wore caps to protect their heads while carrying baskets and cradles. In the winter the people donned robes of animal skin for warmth. These were made of deerskin or the fur of wildcats, raccoons, coyotes, civets, or other small mammals.

Both men and women had long hair; they parted it in the center and arranged it into two ropes that they pulled in front of the shoulders. Some men wore a single rope behind their heads. The Chilula wore headbands of yellowhammer quail feathers. Wealthy men and women wore shell ornaments in their pierced ears, and women tattooed their chins with vertical bands of color.

Food

In the Hoopa Valley The Hoopa Valley had plentiful resources and a moderate climate, so the people did not have to travel far for food. Spared the extreme summer heat that blanketed the rest of California, the region offered a rich supply of green plants for gathering all year round. Still, the Hupa focused most of their efforts on stockpiling two main food sources—salmon and acorns—that fed them well throughout the year. These foods remain an important element in Hupa celebrations.

Each spring and fall the valley tribes harvested hordes of spawning fish in the Trinity River. They broiled fresh fish on sticks over an open fire, then sliced and smoke-dried the excess. The Hupa also fished for steelhead trout, sturgeon, eels, and an assortment of smaller fish, but they hunted only rarely.

Women were responsible for gathering acorns of the tan oak. The acorns were pounded to meal (a coarsely ground flour), cooked over heated stones, and served as mush. Women sometimes cooked the ground acorns as cakes after adding nuts, berries, fruits, roots, or other plants.

Along Redwood Creek Chilula men were skilled hunters who depended on elk and deer, supplemented with acorns, as their main food source.

Deer Medicine—The Naslindiñ Young Man

In many Chilula tales, such as this one told by Tom Hill and his son, Dan Hill, animals have special powers to help people. Here, the mountain also represents supernatural powers that can aid the hunter. The young man watches the mountain grow, which will give him strength, but he does not follow the tribe's usual practice of not thinking about women before hunting. The Chilula believed that women brought bad luck to hunters.

> A young Kixunnai man came into being back of Naslindiñ. The mountain grew along with him. When he looked out at midnight the mountain had grown up higher. He used to hunt deer. He did not sleep. After a time that one who did not sleep slept. He dreamed about women. Notwithstanding he went out in the morning. The mountain which grew up with him was not there. Nevertheless he went out for deer. He climbed up into the sky. There were no deer to be seen. He heard deer snort by the eastern water. "This way it will be," he thought. "Indians will come." He came back. "I will make its medicine." Then he made it. When he looked, it (the mountain) had grown up again. In the morning he went out again and went up to the sky. A deer was standing with its face toward him "This way it is," he thought. "Indians will come. Even if he does this way, he will kill deer if he has my herb and says my formula."

This way only.

SOURCE: Goddard, Pliny Earle. "Deer Medicine—The Naslindiñ Young Man." *University of California Publications in American Archaeology and Ethnology* 10, no. 7 (1914).

The Chilula usually roasted fresh meats and cut any leftovers into strips, then dried or stored them for winter consumption. No part of an animal was wasted. Tribal law did not allow the killing or eating of any bears; the Chilula believed bears were once their relatives.

In their temporary summer and fall camps, Chilula women gathered seeds, strawberries, huckleberries, and salmonberries. During fall they dug for wild potatoes and harvested the all-important acorns. Other key foods included lettuce, clover, wild oats, wild onions, and grasses.

The Chilula fished in Redwood Creek, although it was too small to yield large catches. King salmon were taken with spears and dip nets at the base of waterfalls, and steelhead trout were caught in brushwood nets. The Chilula also developed an elaborate system of weirs (human-made

Hupa Halibut with Eggs Recipe

Serves 4.

    4 halibut fillets (about 6 ounces each)
    2 cups chicken broth
    1 small onion, chopped
    1/2 tsp salt
    1/8 teaspoon pepper
    6 juniper berries, crushed
    1 cup seaweed
    3 eggs, lightly beaten

Bring broth to a boil, add onion, salt, pepper, and juniper berries. Simmer 15 minutes.

Add halibut, but in bite-sized pieces. Simmer 10 minutes.

Add seaweed and drizzle in beaten eggs. Cook until eggs are set up.

SOURCE: Hunt, David. "Hupa Halibut with Eggs Recipe." *The Native Indian Cookbook.* East Petersburg, PA: Fox Chapel Publishing, 2007, p. 127.

dams of sticks) that slowed down eel and trout so they could be speared, harpooned, or netted. (The people who helped build the dam were said to own the spot on which it stood.) They added the bulbs of the soaproot plant to water to drug the fish, which they then scooped out of the water in nets.

Education

Children spent most of their early years playing. They were taught religion and good manners, especially proper eating habits. They learned other skills over time by observing adults. Young boys sometimes joined the men in the sweathouses; they listened to the adults' prayers for hunting success and learned hunting techniques, codes, and religious laws, which were sometimes taught through stories.

The federal government opened a day school shortly after the Hupa and Chilula were moved onto the Hoopa Valley Reservation. The school was very unpopular among Native parents; many refused to send their children there. In an effort to force school attendance, agents at one point withheld the government-issued clothing intended for reservation children. The school ended up closing after only a few years.

A boarding school was established on the reservation in 1893, but it, too, was unsuccessful. Funding was inadequate, help was scarce, and supplies were low. Many teachers quit. Those who stayed on treated the children poorly: students were beaten if they did not speak English, and some children were actually leased out to white families as servants.

The reservation is currently served by the Klamath-Trinity Unified School District, which operates schools in the area. There is a branch of the College of the Redwoods in nearby Hoopa, and Humboldt State University is located in the neighboring city of Arcata. In the early 2000s, about 72 percent of the adults on the reservation had completed high school or some college.

Healing practices

Like many tribes, the Hupa and Chilula believed that illnesses were caused by supernatural forces. A hired doctor was called in to treat and cure them.

The Chilula had two kinds of doctors: medicine healers, who treated patients with plants, and shamans (pronounced *SHAH-munz* or *SHAY-munz*), who had the ability to suck the ailment out of a sick person's body. Both men and women served as doctors, but the more powerful shamans were usually men. Their primary healing power came from language. A shaman could treat a person by speaking directly to his or her spirit with words that people did not understood. Sometimes the shaman prayed, danced, sang, and blew smoke over the patient. If the sick person did not recover or died shortly after treatment, the shaman refunded the payment for his services.

Shamans went through a long and difficult training period. The Chilula were considered the most skilled doctors in northwestern California. Chilula shaman trainees learned their trade at Dancing Doctor Rock, considered the tribe's most sacred site. At this rock, the shaman-in-training fasted, sang, danced, and looked for a vision from a spirit. Female shamans, though rare, always acquired their healing powers from Tan, the deer spirit.

In modern times, the tribe is served by its own K'ima:w Medical Center and by a hospital located in the city of Hoopa. The K'ima:w Field Health and Outreach Department offers health screenings, home visits, health education, and community support services. A dental clinic and pharmacy are also available on the reservation.

ARTS

The Hupa have always been well known for their elaborately decorated woven baskets depicting geometric figures in red, white, and black. Examples of Hupa baskets and dance costumes are on display at the Hupa Tribal Museum, a popular tourist destination. Other Hupa arts included designs carved into wooden mush paddles, horn spoons, and dentalium shells as well as articles made of bone.

The Hupa had a distinctive singing style. Most music was sung with a minimal accompaniment by wooden clappers, bone whistles, deerhoof rattles, and drums. The first rhythm instruments were planks that musicians stamped on or kicked. Later they beat on boxes covered with hide.

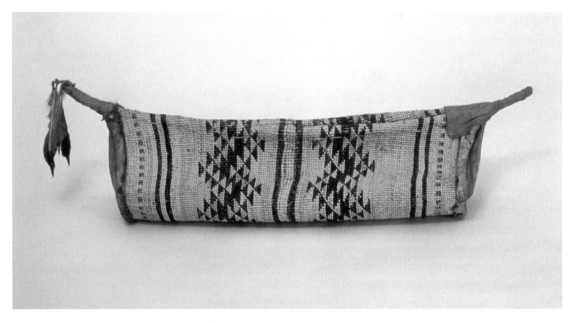

A Hupa Jump Dance basket was used as part of a traditional ceremony. © BOLTIN PICTURE LIBRARY/THE BRIDGEMAN ART LIBRARY.

These were used not only during singing, but to keep time during gambling songs. To court a woman, a Hupa man played a wooden flute.

Oral literature

The most popular subject of Hupa and Chilula stories centered on how the Immortals devised the way of life for the people to follow. Both adults and children also enjoyed humorous stories about a sly, supernatural figure called Coyote, who sometimes helped people but more often caused trouble.

CUSTOMS

Quest for riches

Being wealthy was more important to the Hupa and their neighbors than to any other Native groups in California. Wealth was measured in terms of how much money a person had (they used shells for money, strung on cords and wound with strips of fish skin). Other prized possessions of the wealthy included deerskins (especially those of unusual colors) and the scalps of the red-feathered woodpecker (attached to buckskin bands).

Rough-nose

The Hupa tell this tale of Rough-nose, whose younger brother has been kidnapped by people from the world above. Rough-nose enlists the help of several animals who assist him in reaching that world to search for his brother.

> Rough-nose caught a wood-rat and put it in his sack and then went with the rest.
>
> When they reached the world above he said to the others, "You wait here, I will go along to the place where the fire is." He changed himself into an old woman and walked with a widow's cane. He came up to the place and said, "I am only asking that I may warm myself by your fire." "You might be Rough-nose," said the old woman who was tending the fire. "Oh, yes, that fellow is likely to come here," said Rough-nose. Then the old woman ran up with a spruce tree in her hand, smashed it to pieces, and threw it on the fire. She commenced poking the bag in which the boy was hanging over the fire. "Tso, tso," he cried. "You had better roast the short ribs," she said. Rough-nose waited until he heard them eating in the house, then he caught the old woman and held her in the fire until she was dead. He stripped her clothes off and dressed himself in them. He went up to the sack and felt of his brother, who said, "Is that you Rough-nose?" "Speak softly," said Rough-nose, and then he took the boy out and put the wood-rat in his place. Then someone put his head out of the door of the house and said, "Come and eat." Roughnose putting only his head in, said, "Just throw something out here for me." When he had eaten he went to the sack and began punching it. "Tso, tso," it cried. "You better roast the short ribs," said Rough-nose.
>
> When the people had gone to bed, Rough-nose and his companions made an attack on them. All was confusion. It was dark. The fires had been put out. Some of them cried out, "My hair hurts." Others were saying, "A mouse has chewed up my bowstring." Others ran after the attacking party. When they jumped into their canoes to give chase, they filled with water and sank. The mice had gnawed holes in them. Then Rough-nose, carrying his brother, went safely home.

SOURCE: Goddard, Pliny Earl. "Hupa Texts." *University of California Publications in American Archaeology and Ethnology* 1, no. 2 (March 1904). Available online at http://www.sacred-texts.com/nam/ca/hut/index.htm (accessed on August 11, 2011).

These valuable items were only used for very important purchases, such as a bride or the services of a healer. Other evidence of a person's wealth were the site of the family home and the productivity of the fishing, hunting, and gathering places a person owned.

According to the Hupa belief system, everything that existed was a spiritual being, so a person who possessed many things would be able to harness the spirit power connected with those things. If the possessor offended the spirits, it was possible for those things—and the powers that went with them—to disappear.

Festivals and ceremonies

The two major religious ceremonies of the northwestern California Indians were the White Deerskin Dance and the Jump Dance, each of which could last up to sixteen days. Both dances were part of the World Renewal Cycle, held in late summer or early fall to ensure that natural resources would renew themselves, that life would go on as it always had, and that disasters would be averted or prevented. The Immortals laid down the exact words and order for the ceremonies, and these instructions were followed precisely. The White Deerskin and Jump dances offered major opportunities for wealthy people to display their riches. Ceremonial festivities included singing, game playing, storytelling, and, of course, dancing.

Lesser ceremonies—conducted in strategic locations—were also associated with the cycle. For example, a village near a salmon run would host a First Salmon Ceremony. Thousands of participants from villages throughout northwestern California would gather for it, and then they would move on to another village near acorn-hunting territory to take part in an Acorn Feast.

In the early 2000s, these and other ceremonies were being held each year on the Hoopa Valley Reservation. All of them were open to the public. Modern additions to the ceremonial cycle include an annual Sovereign Day Celebration to honor the day Congress recognized Hupa ownership their lands.

Puberty

No special ceremony was observed for boys who reached puberty. The onset of a Hupagirl's first menstrual period was a sacred time and was celebrated with a dance. First, the girl stayed in a secluded house for ten days, where she ate only acorn soup and salmon, and she bathed twice a day in a sacred pool. Her isolation provided her with time to think about the importance of cleanliness, independence, and patience. After the ten days were up, she was considered a woman.

The Chilula puberty rituals lasted five days. Girls stayed in their homes and avoided meat, salt, and cold water during their first menstruation. They did not touch their bodies absentmindedly, and they used a bone scratcher whenever they had an itch. After the seclusion period, the tribe held a public dance.

Courtship and marriage

Girls were considered ready for marriage at age fifteen or sixteen, and boys were ready at age sixteen or seventeen. Courtship was basically a business transaction. A boy's family sent a representative to bargain with the girl's family, and a generous price was negotiated. Following a feast and gift exchange, the newly married couple lived in the husband's village. Poor young men might arrange a "half-marriage," paying half-price for the bride and moving in with and working for her family.

The Immortals left a legacy of restrictions on the daily lives of the Hupa and Chilula; as a result, meditation and prayer accompanied most of their activities. Northwestern California Indians had a unique custom whereby men and women lived together only in the summer, even if they were married. Through the cold months and during the fall hunting season, men slept in sweathouses, and women stayed in the family home.

The birthing process

A pregnant woman avoided certain foods and offered prayers for an easy birth. When she was ready to have her baby, the mother-to-be went to the menstrual house to give birth; the father remained in the sweathouse. The newborn child was placed in a basket and held over steaming water that contained herbs; this ritual was thought to encourage the baby's soul to enter its body.

After ten days of isolation, mother and child rejoined their family at home. The baby was placed sitting up in a cradle basket and, until it could walk, was allowed outside only for exercise and bathing. It was called "baby" or a similar impersonal name until receiving a real name at about age five.

Funerals

The Hupa and Chilula differed in their treatment of the dead. The bodies of Hupa dead were disposed of quickly. They were tied to boards and buried in graves lined with planks to form boxes. Relatives were expected to wail, or cry, from the time of their loved one's death until the burial process was completed. They also cut their hair, wore necklaces to ward off dreams of the dead, and were forbidden to speak the dead person's name. The Hupa believed that the deceased's spirit haunted the village for four days before journeying on to the land of the dead.

When a Chilula person died, the family covered the body with a deerskin blanket, and it remained in the house for five days. A medicine man smoked the house with herbs to ward off evil. The gravedigger was required to observe strict codes, eating only acorn soup and dried salmon while preparing the grave. After being washed, painted, and supplied with acorns and tobacco, the body was buried with its head facing south. To avoid being haunted by the spirit of the dead, the mourners would say over the body: "You are going away from me. You must not think of me." The dead person's name could not be spoken for a full year.

CURRENT TRIBAL ISSUES

Before the arrival of American settlers, the Hupa and Chilula lived in harmony with their surroundings, taking only what they needed. They still maintain that philosophy, and they often must take a stand to protect their natural resources from exploitation. In the twenty-first century, several environmental organizations were battling with logging companies to prevent the destruction of the Chilula's ancient redwood growing areas.

The Tsnungwe, Hupa people who live on the south fork of the Trinity River, filed a petition for federal recognition in the late 1990s. Without federal recognition, the Tsnungwe have no legal relationship with the U.S. government and are not entitled to any benefits (money and other assistance). As of 2011, they were still waiting for acknowledgment.

The Hupa language is nearing the extinction. Fewer than five first-language speakers are still alive. Nonetheless, the people are determined to make their language a living one. In 2011, they applied for a grant that would provide funds to print and distribute teaching materials, implement Hupa language classes in schools, and record oral history for future generations. The Hupa also want to add more of their culture and tradition in the school curriculum, and they believe that their children's schools need to incorporate tribal values, ideas, and teaching methods.

NOTABLE PEOPLE

David Risling (1921–2005) of Hupa, Yurok, and Karok descent is a champion of improved education, legal rights, and economic advancement for Native peoples. Risling cofounded the California Indian Legal Services and the Native American Rights Fund. He grew up on the Hoopa Valley Reservation and served in the U.S. Navy during World War II (1939–45). Risling became director of the Native American Studies program at the University of California–Davis in 1970. In 1991, the university honored him with the Distinguished Public Service Award for his contributions to Native American education. He wrote and published the *Handbook of Native American Studies* and other books.

Hupa-Yurok George Blake (1944–) is a noted ceramist, painter, and carver. He was named a National Heritage fellow by the National Endowment for the Arts (NEA) in 1991.

BOOKS

Anderson, M. Kat. *Tending the Wild: Native American Knowledge and the Management of California's Natural Resources.* Berkeley: University of California Press, 2005.

Driver, Harold E., and Walter R. Goldschmidt. *The Hupa White Deerskin Dance.* Whitefish, MT: Kessinger Publishing, 2007.

DuBois, Cora. *The 1870 Ghost Dance.* Reprint. Lincoln: University of Nebraska, 2007.

Fletcher, Jill, and others, compilers. *Now You're Speaking Hupa!* Arcata, CA: Humboldt State University, 1995.

Goddard, Pliny Earle. *Hupa Texts.* Reprint. Charleston, SC: BiblioBazaar, 2009.

Goddard, Pliny Earle. *Life and Culture of the Hupa.* Reprint. Charleston, SC: Nabu Press, 2011.

Goddard, Pliny Earle. *Notes on the Chilula Indians of Northwestern California.* 1914. Reprint. Charleston, SC: BiblioBazaar, 2009. Available online from http://www.archive.org/details/noteschilula00goddrich (accessed on August 11, 2011).

Lake, Robert G. *Chilula: People from the Ancient Redwoods.* Washington, DC: University Press of America, 1982.

Tedlock, Barbara. *The Woman in the Shaman's Body: Reclaiming the Feminine in Religion and Medicine.* New York: Bantam Books, 2005.

PERIODICALS

Davis, Susan E. "Tribal Rights, Tribal Wrongs (Hoopa, Yurok, and Congress)." In *The Nation* 254, no. 11 (March 23, 1992): 376.

Lake, Robert, Jr. "The Chilula Indians of California." *Indian Historian* 12, no. 3 (1979): 14–26. Available online from http://www.eric.ed.gov/ERICWeb Portal/search/detailmini.jsp?_nfpb=true&_&ERICExtSearch_SearchValue_ 0=EJ214907&ERICExtSearch_SearchType_0=no&accno=EJ214907 (accessed on December 1, 2011).

WEB SITES

"The Chilula." *The Indians of the Redwoods.* http://www.cr.nps.gov/history/ online_books/redw/history1c.htm (accessed on August 11, 2011).

The George and Mary Foster Anthropology Library. "Chilula Indians." *University of California.* http://dpg.lib.berkeley.edu/webdb/anthpubs/search?subjec tid=844&subjtext=Chilula+Indians (accessed on August 11, 2011).

Hoopa Tribal Museum and San Francisco State University. http://bss.sfsu.edu/ calstudies/hupa/Hoopa.HTM (accessed on August 11, 2011).

Hoopa Valley Tribe. http://www.hoopa-nsn.gov/ (accessed on August 11, 2011).

"Hupa." *Four Directions Institute.* http://www.fourdir.com/hupa.htm (accessed on August 11, 2011).

"Hupa Indian Tribe." *Access Genealogy.* http://www.accessgenealogy.com/native/ tribes/athapascan/hupaindiantribe.htm (accessed on August 11, 2011).

Redish, Laura, and Orrin Lewis. "Hupa (Hoopa) Language." *Native Languages of the Americas.* http://www.native-languages.org/hupa.htm (accessed on August 11, 2011).

"The Tribes of California Present Transformations" (video). *Indian Country Today Media Network.* http://indiancountrytodaymedianetwork. com/2011/06/the-tribes-of-california-present-transformations/ (accessed on August 11, 2011).

Luiseño

Name

The Luiseño (pronounced *lew-wee-SAY-nyoh*) were named by the Spanish for the Catholic mission at San Luis Rey. Originally the Luiseño might have been called *Payomkawichum* ("the westerners") by neighboring tribes. Their own name for themselves may have been *Ataxum* ("the People"). The Luiseño at San Juan Capistrano were called *Acjachemen*. Coastal tribal members went by *Payó mkawum*.

Location

The Luiseño lived along the Pacific Coast, in inland southern California, and on the Channel Islands off southern California. They inhabited a diverse 1,500-square-mile (3,900-square-kilometer) region that extended along the coast from Aliso Creek, south to Agua Hedionda Creek, and inland to include Santiago Peak, Palomar Mountain, and part of the valley of San Jose. Their territory encompassed the northwestern section of present-day San Diego County and southwestern Riverside County. At the start of the twenty-first century, Luiseño bands were located on six reservations throughout the mid-southern California area: La Jolla, Pala, Pechanga, Pauma, Rincon, and Soboba.

Population

About 10,000 Luiseño were known to exist prior to Spanish contact. In the 1990 U.S. Census, 2,798 people identified themselves as Luiseño. The 2000 census indicated that 4,334 Luiseño lived in the United States, and 5,661 people said they were of Luiseño heritage.

Language family

Uto-Aztecan.

Origins and group affiliations

According to archaeologists and linguists, the Luiseño may have migrated into southern California from the Great Basin—an elevated region 189,000 miles (304,200 kilometers) wide in the western United States—as far back as

Contemporary Luiseño Communities

California

1. La Jolla Band and Rincon Band of Mission Indians
2. Pauma and Yuima Reservation
3. Pala Reservation and Pechanga Reservation
4. Soboba Band of Mission Indians

Shaded area

Traditional lands of the Luiseño along the Pacific Coast and inland in present-day southern California

A map of contemporary Luiseno communities. MAP BY XNR PRODUCTIONS. CENGAGE LEARNING, GALE. REPRODUCED BY PERMISSION OF GALE, A PART OF CENGAGE LEARNING.

seven thousand to eight thousand years ago. Although formerly considered a separate group, the Juaneño (as they were named by the Spanish) are now known to have been a part of the Luiseño tribe. The Luiseño had much in common with their neighbors, the Cahuilla, Yuman (see entries), Cupeño, and Gabrieliño tribes.

The Luiseño, like the Cahuilla and Chumash (see entries), are sometimes called Mission Indians because they became part of the Roman Catholic Missions built by the Spanish in California in the late 1700s. For centuries before, the bounty of the land had allowed them to live a comfortable life. They tended to keep to themselves and did not travel far to trade, although they usually married outside their own villages. The Luiseño were somewhat more warlike than other California tribes, engaging in battles when their neighbors trespassed on their lands or when they could not gain access to neighboring territory through marriage.

HISTORY

Spanish encounters

The land of the Luiseño was varied. Some groups lived along the Pacific Coast, some in the southern Channel Islands, and others in the green valleys of the California interior or on mountaintops. The climate was mild in some parts, but other areas were subject to extreme heat and periods of drought. On the whole, though, the living was fairly easy. The tribe had fished, hunted, and gathered there for centuries before white settlers came upon their territory.

The Luiseño may have had contact with Spanish expeditions as early as 1542, when Portuguese explorer Juan Rodríguez Cabrillo (c. 1499–1543) sailed along the coast, leading a small fleet of Spanish ships in search of riches and a sea lane to China. The tribe's first confirmed encounter with the Spanish occurred in 1769 when a group led by Gaspar de Portolá (c. 1723–c. 1784) ventured into California.

Missions established

The Spanish established a firm hold on California territory, but as the eighteenth century progressed, Great Britain and Russia began showing interest in the North American Pacific Coast as well. In an effort to discourage further European advancement into the area, the Spanish built a series of forts on the land. Spain claimed the land as its own and expected the California Indians to help protect this "Spanish" land as soon as they were "civilized" (schooled in European ways). The Spanish government asked Roman Catholic priests (*padres*) to assist in controlling the Native peoples. The priests had their own goal of converting the Natives to the Catholic religion, so they agreed to help and built missions with forced Native labor. Each mission had a church and a European-style farm.

The first California mission was established in 1769. Although the mission was not situated within their territory, the Luiseño were struck

Important Dates

1776: The mission of San Juan Capistrano is founded in Luiseño territory.

1798: The mission of San Luis Rey is established on Luiseño land.

1839: The first written account of the tribe's culture is written by the Luiseño author Pablo Tac.

1847: The Luiseño are massacred at Temecua by the Mexican militia and rival Cahuilla.

1875: The Luiseño sign the Treaty of Temecua with the United States; it is later rejected by the U.S. Senate.

1882: First Luiseño reservations are established.

1891: The Act for the Relief of the Mission Indians creates and allots five Luiseño reservations.

1988: San Luis Rey Indian Water Rights Settlement Act awards Luiseño $30 million for lost water rights.

1998: Access to and control of water sources continues to be a major issue for the tribe.

Spanish priests baptize Native Americans into the Catholic faith. © GIRAUDON/THE BRIDGEMAN ART LIBRARY.

hard by European diseases almost immediately. Historians estimate that the Luiseño population declined 40 percent during the mission period. San Juan Capistrano Mission was built in the Luiseño homeland in 1776 and, ravaged by the spread of disease, a weakened population found it hard to resist the priests' invitation to settle there. In 1798, Mission San Luis Rey was established on the tribe's territory, and an outpost called an *asistencia* was erected at Pala eighteen years later. The missionaries soon drew most of the Luiseño population into the mission system.

Mission Indians

Spanish settlers and missionaries used the Native people to satisfy their own goals of growth and expansion. Although the padres claimed their only interest was in converting the indigenous people to the Catholic religion, history shows that the missions survived on the sweat of the Native people. Disciplined Native labor was needed to satisfy the demands of increasing numbers of Spanish settlers in California. The missionaries taught the Luiseño the basics of the Spanish language (enough so that the Natives could understand orders). They also instructed them in farming techniques and European-style trades such as carpentry and masonry

A Spanish missionary priest speaks to Native Americans in an effort to convert them to Catholicism. © NORTH WIND PICTURE ARCHIVES.

(brickwork)—skills Spanish settlers valued. Even young children were forced to live and work at the missions.

Spanish treatment of the Luiseño differed somewhat from their treatment of other Mission Indians. Some Luiseño lived at the missions, but others were allowed to stay in their own communities and receive instruction from visiting padres. Still, many Luiseño became paid workers in trades such as carpentry, tanning (converting hide into leather), blacksmithing, and weaving—occupations far removed from their traditional lifestyle.

End of mission system

Mexico won independence from Spain in 1821 and took over the California missions in 1834. Mexican officials vowed that they would give the Mission Indians tracts of land, but Mexican settlers, who poured into California, ended up with most of the mission property. Some Luiseño became unpaid laborers on Mexican-owned ranches, but others

The Mission System

Children as young as age five or six were taken into the missions. They attended religious services and performed physical labor without pay. The children were trained in carpentry, agriculture, and other occupations that would benefit the Spanish. One former neophyte (pronounced *NEE-oh-fite*; "beginner") described life at the mission:

> When I was a boy the treatment of the Native Americans was not any good—they did not pay us for anything—they only gave us food, a loin cloth and a blanket every year, and many beatings for any mistake even if it [the mistake] was slight, it was more or less at the mercy of the administrator who ordered the beatings whenever and how many he felt like.

SOURCE: Robert F. Heizer, ed. *Handbook of North American Indians.* Vol. 8: *California.* Washington, DC: Smithsonian Institution, 1978, p. 102.

moved inland, seeking shelter among other Native groups there. Those who worked for the Mexicans were treated poorly and staged violent rebellions from time to time. However, the Luiseño who remained in their traditional villages continued to live as they had before, but now blended Spanish and lifestyles with the introduction of cattle raising and farming.

California became part of the United States after the Mexican-American War (1846–48; a war in which Mexico lost about one-half of its national territory to the United States). Droves of American settlers rushed to California. To avoid the conflicts and to get wage labor jobs, some Luiseño migrated to Los Angeles, located in the southwestern portion of the state.

Reservations established

Tensions between the Luiseño and California settlers became so high that in 1875, Luiseño chief Olegario Sal went to Washington, D.C., to request that reservations be set aside for his people. That same year, some Native people in California moved onto reservation lands. Meanwhile, the U.S. government formed a committee to investigate the condition of life among former Mission Indians and make recommendations. The committee was headed by writer Helen Hunt Jackson (1830–1885), whose books *A Century of Dishonor* and *Ramona* brought the mistreatment of Native peoples to the public's attention. Jackson's report led the government to grant more land to the Luiseño in 1882 and 1883. (For more information on Jackson and her findings, see Cahuilla entry.)

The federal government provided only minimal assistance in setting up the reservations. Then, in 1891, sixteen years after the establishment of the first Luiseño reservation, the Act for the Relief of the Mission Indians was passed. This act created five Luiseño reservations and included provisions designed to help the Native population develop an American lifestyle (a policy called "assimilation") and become self-supporting. A sixth reservation, Soboba, was officially established in 1913.

Struggle for rights

Agents from the Bureau of Indian Affairs were sent to oversee the reservations. They established schools, Native American courts of law, medical clinics, and other services, but not all agents of the Bureau represented the best interests of the Native population. Corrupt agents caused so much friction among the Luiseño that the Mission Indian Federation (MIF) was founded in 1919 to resolve the problems. The MIF worked for more independence for tribal governments, full civil rights for the tribes, more generous water rights (see "Current tribal issues"), and the elimination of the Bureau of Indian Affairs, which still exists in the early twenty-first century.

The federal government stayed involved in reservation affairs, and the Luiseño grew more and more unhappy with its methods. By the 1950s, the tribe began to assume more control, taking active leadership roles to make sure their voices were heard when decisions affecting the reservations were made by local, state, and national governments.

One of the issues of greatest concern was water rights. Dams and construction diverted much of the reservation's water supply. The tribes on the various reservations banded together to restore water to their land. In 1988, the San Luis Rey Indian Water Rights Settlement Act awarded the Luiseño $30 million for lost water rights. It also ordered the delivery of water to tribal territory. Dams were expected to release a certain amount of water annually to supply the tribe. The Soboba Band also received a $12 million settlement. Water issues, however, still presented difficulties for most Luiseño reservations into the 2000s.

Author Helen Hunt Jackson's work brought the mistreatment of Native Americans to the public's attention. © MPI/GETTY IMAGES.

RELIGION

According to ancient Luiseño traditions, a creator called Wiyót took an empty world that already existed, filled it with all things, and gave it order. Later, the Luiseño came to believe in a savior called *Chinigchinix,* who made the earth and then died and went to heaven. From there,

The Death of Wiyót, the Creator

According to the Luiseño, Wiyót was one of the first beings. He took an empty world that already existed, filled it with all things, and gave it order. Everyone was supposed to live forever, but Wiyót's own death, as described in the story below, introduced death into the world.

> Once Wiyót died, his people lost the knowledge of living forever (immortality). Rituals for the dead had to be invented so that the spirits of the dead could be freed from Earth. The Luiseño clothes-burning ceremony, for instance, releases the deceased's clothes from this world. These rituals kept the spirits happy.
>
> Wiyót was the son of Túkumit [night, or night sky] and Tamáyawùt [Earth Mother]. He was called "father" by the people who lived on the Earth. Frog was the prettiest of all the women. One day Wiyót saw her swimming, and he observed that her body was thin and not beautiful. She was repulsive to him. Knowing his thoughts, she said to herself: "My father does not like me. I will kill him by magic." She secured the aid of Badger, Gopher, and other [burrowing animals], and they [cast a spell on] him. He fell sick. Four shamans were called: Wasímal [a hawk], Sakapípi [titmouse], Púipi [roadrunner], and Chaláka [horned toad]. [But they could not cure him.] And then the people knew [a spell had been cast upon] Wiyót. The other shamans tried their power in vain. Then Wiyót called Chehémal [kingbird], and told him that after death he would appear in the sky. Soon he was dead. They placed the body on a pile of wood to burn it. Then came Coyote. He seized the heart and carried it away. Three days later the Moon appeared in the sky, and Chehémal exclaimed, "Oh, there is my father, Mâila [moon] Wiyót!"

SOURCE: Curtis, Edward. "Southern California Shoshoneans." In *The North American Indian.* Vol. 15. Edited by Frederick Webb Hodge. New York: Johnson Reprint Corporation, 1970.

he watched but seldom interfered with worldly affairs, only occasionally sending vengeful animals and other terrible punishments to those who disobeyed his teachings. Historians think the Chinigchinix religion probably developed in response to Spanish presence on tribal land.

Most Luiseño men sought membership in the Chinigchinix religion's secret society. To belong to the society, the males had to prove their physical endurance. The Chinigchinix religion had rigid rules that governed many aspects of peoples' lives, including hunting, warfare, harvesting, puberty, and mourning rituals. It also included many songs, dances, and *toloache* ceremonies. Toloache, a drug obtained from the jimsonweed plant, causes those who consume it to enter a trancelike state and see visions. Sacred knowledge was said to be revealed during these visions.

Missionaries converted many Luiseño to Catholicism, a religion that is still practiced by most of the people. Despite the strong, centuries-long Christian presence among the Luiseño, though, traditional beliefs and practices have survived.

LANGUAGE

The Luiseño were the most southwesterly speakers of the Uto-Aztecan family of languages in the United States. By the 1970s, Luiseño was spoken by only a few elder members of the tribe, but interest in the language was on the rise, language classes were being organized, and a language textbook had been written.

GOVERNMENT

The Luiseño lived in independent groups, each with its own clearly defined territory. The groups did not have political leaders, but the tribe was divided into "parties" that had religious functions (see "Society"). The head of each party was a chief called a *nó·t.* This position was usually filled by a man, but a few female nó·t are known to have existed. The nó·t oversaw warfare, economic ventures (organizing gathering projects, for example), and the activities of his or her assistant, called *paxá,* and healers that were called shamans (pronounced *SHAH-munz* or *SHAY-munz*).

During the mission period Native villages maintained the basic elements of the old style of self-government, but a new position of leadership developed—that of representative of the Luiseño to Europeans. Once the federal government began to oversee the reservations, they insisted that tribal leaders be approved by U.S. government agents.

Pechanga Words

During the early 2000s, Eric Elliott, a linguist (person who studies languages) who developed a 1,700-page English-Luiseño/Luiseño-English dictionary, began teaching language classes on the Pechanga Reservation. Adults were eager to learn and pass the lessons on to their children and grandchildren. Elliot had been taught by Villiana Hyde, a fluent speaker who has since died.

One of the difficulties of writing a language using the English alphabet is finding symbols for sounds that are not used in English. Some of the words listed here use a "$" for the Pechanga whistling "s" sound.

'ataax	"person"
kiicha	"house"
nawitmal	"girl"
tawwilash	"chair"
to'wish	"forest"
hunwut	"bear"
kupu"ilash	"bed"
$sunnganwish	"medium-sized"
temet	"day"
yot	"big"
'ao'ush	"yellow"
heelaqu$	"was singing"
hamu'tap	"the end"

The Luiseño objected to government interference in tribal affairs and managed to assume more control over them by the 1950s. In the late 1990s, each reservation elected its own tribal chairperson and tribal council. To a greater extent than most California tribes, the Luiseño are involved in state and local groups that work to promote the well-being of Native peoples.

ECONOMY

Before the Spanish settled in Luiseño territory, the Native economy was rooted in hunting and gathering, usually on sites not far from home. Some property was owned by the group, and activities such as hunting, gambling, and ceremonies took place there. Other pieces of property—stands of oaks or tobacco gardens, for example—were owned by individuals or families. Groups who lived inland had special places on the coast where they went to fish and gather at a given time each year.

The Spanish missionaries taught the Native peoples how to farm and tend cattle. Although all the Luiseño engaged in these activities by the 1850s, they did not abandon their hunting and gathering practices completely.

During World War I (1914–18; a war in which Great Britain, France, the United States, and their allies defeated Germany, Austria-Hungary, and their allies), Luiseño volunteers served in the U.S. armed forces or left the reservations to work in defense industries. After the war, some continued to work in these industries, whereas others returned to the reservations and took up cattle raising and farming. Aside from those who pursued work in agriculture, the Luiseño were employed in a variety of fields, including carpentry, education, and engineering.

By the early 2000s, many reservations had opened casinos to provide tribal income. Other important sources of employment and tribal income were tourism and recreation, services and retail, construction, mining, and manufacturing. Most bands have economic development groups to attract new businesses and increase reservation profits.

DAILY LIFE

Buildings

The Luiseño lived in cone-shaped houses. The foundation of the house was partially underground, situated on a pit that was 2 to 3 feet (up to 1 meter) deep. Construction materials included reeds, brush, and cedar bark. Dirt from the pit was piled over the brush. The only openings to the dwelling were the entrance and a smokehole. Some entrances were only gaps in the wall; others were low and covered, sloping down to the level of the pit. Near the house was a light, rectangular, porchlike structure, called a *ramada* by the Spanish, where some household chores were performed.

Settlements also contained oval-shaped earthen sweathouses, used for purification and during some curing rituals. Each permanent settlement contained a religious enclosure, called a *wamkish,* set up in the center of the village and enclosed by a brush fence. During the acorn season, the Luiseño moved to temporary camps near stands of oak trees.

Clothing and adornment

Luiseño men usually wore no clothes in warm weather. During cold weather, they wore fur capes of rabbit and deerskin; those who lived along the Pacific Coast also wore capes of sea otter skins. Women wore aprons, called *pishkwut,* made from plants such as dogbane (a tropical, often poisonous, plant with milky juice and big flowers) and milkweed, willow bark, or cottonwood bark. Both sexes let their hair grow long. Women covered their heads with coiled caps similar to baskets; men also wore caps to protect themselves when they carried loads on their heads.

The Luiseño usually wore sandals, but they put on deerskin moccasins for traveling on rough ground. They wore necklaces of bear claws, stones, and the shells of abalone (a type of shellfish), as well as bracelets and anklets made from human hair. Men pierced their ears and noses and wore decorations made from cane or bones. Men and women both had tattoos and used body paints.

Food

The Luiseño lived on acorns, wild plants, and small game. Usually men hunted and women gathered, but everyone collected the acorns produced by the six species of oak found in their territory. Acorns were stored in granaries (large above-ground baskets) until they were prepared and eaten. Various other kinds of seeds, such as sage, sunflower, manzanita (a type of evergreen shrub) and pine nuts, were also gathered. The seeds were heated and shaken in a basketry tray with embers from the fire, and then ground into flour.

Women also gathered greens, including miner's lettuce and white sage. Although not abundant in Luiseño territory, some fruits were harvested as well, including plums, manzanita berries, chokecherries, Christmas berries, currants, wild grapes, gooseberries, and elderberries. The people also gathered and roasted the fleshy parts of the prickly pear, cholla, and agave plants in earth-covered, preheated pits to make *mescal*. Yucca prepared this way was eaten as a sugary treat. The Luiseño ate grass and bulbs raw or cooked, and they used clover, watercress, peppergrass, and pigweed to spice their food. The tribe practiced a custom called controlled burning (setting fire to some land), which helped desirable crops grow better and encouraged larger rabbit populations for hunting.

Before a hunt, Luiseño men purified themselves in the sweathouse, burning white sage and other herbs on the fire. They usually hunted game like rabbits, jackrabbits, and deer. They trapped woodrats, squirrel, mice, quails, larks, and ducks, and they took black-tailed deer and antelope with bows and arrows, snares, and nets, or by clubbing. Sometimes the hunters wore deer-head disguises so they could approach their prey without being noticed.

The tribe occasionally killed bear, mountain lion, wildcat, and mountain sheep for food. Turtles and lizard were also eaten; in times of famine the people ate dogs. For most inland Luiseño, fish was a rare addition to their diet. Meat was broiled over hot coals or cooked in an earth oven.

Luiseño who lived along the coast depended on fish and mussels as their primary source of food. They also fished for trout in the upper San Luis Rey River; a common fishing technique involved drugging the fish (by throwing crushed leaves called *távaliat* in the water) and then scooping them into nets.

Education

While their parents and older siblings were off hunting and gathering, very young Luiseño children were taught traditional arts and crafts by elders who stayed behind. They also learned about goals and values, which were considered essential for their growth into responsible adults. Older men taught boys practical skills, such as how to make fishnets and arrows. In addition, these elders decided which boys would be taught to conduct ceremonies and make important decisions affecting the village. Both males and females received formal instruction during puberty rituals.

Under the mission system, children learned the Christian religion, Spanish, and skills such as farming, caring for livestock, and carpentry.

In the late 1800s, government schools were established; their main goal was to immerse the Natives in mainstream American culture. The schools were poorly run and finally closed in the 1930s. Luiseño children now attend nearby public schools. Because education is so highly prized by the Luiseño people, the reservations supplement public education with programs that teach children about their Native culture. Additionally, since the 1960s, many Luiseño have taken advantage of opportunities to attend college.

Healing practices

Traditional Luiseño healing methods used plants to treat illnesses. Wounds were treated with wild onion and cooked and crushed tule (marsh plant) leaves, for example. Still, the tribe believed that some illnesses could only be treated by a shaman. An evil shaman could make people sick by casting a spell over a lock of hair or a broken fingernail, so people were very careful when disposing of such items. Only a shaman had the power to cure a sickness caused by another shaman.

Some forms of sickness were thought to be caused by foreign objects. A common method of treatment was symbolic in nature: the shaman would dramatize the healing process by "sucking out" the object that caused the illness, usually a stone or a beetle. Other treatments included rubbing, blowing, or spurting water on the patient, or waving a bundle of hawk feathers over the person's body. Even in the twenty-first century, some of the old medicines and healing techniques were still used. In addition to traditional methods, people rely on the health clinics on the reservations and hospitals located in nearby cities.

ARTS

Crafts

The California tribes ranked among the world's best basket makers. Two types of baskets were made: coiled and twined. The Luiseño are best known for their beautiful coiled baskets with dark tan, red, and black geometric designs. To make the black fibers, they boiled sumac in water with marsh mud. Men made the larger baskets used as granaries for storing acorns. They placed them on platforms of poles or on large boulders.

Women also made pottery by the coil method, which they then shaped with a wooden paddle over a smooth stone. They fired these

A dancer wears traditional dress at a Luiseño powwow in Oceanside, California.
© NATURALIGHT/ALAMY.

unpainted pieces in a kiln (an oven for hardening clay) over bark chips. Later, they used cattle dung to bake their wide-mouthed water jars, small-mouthed jars for traveling, bowls, dishes, and pots.

Music

The Luiseño used a bullroarer to call people to feasts. This instrument was formed by stringing a wooden slat on a cord. When it was swung rapidly overhead, the cord made loud humming noise. The tribe also used wooden flutes, cane whistles, and rattles made from tortoise shells and gourds.

CUSTOMS

Society

Social divisions in the tribe related to religious ceremonies and were called "parties." A chief or *nó·t* headed each party responsible for certain rituals. A party sometimes included members from other clans. Children joined a party at puberty, usually one of their family's, but they could choose another. The position of chief was hereditary through the male line. The chief had an assistant who helped him and notified people of ceremonies.

Ceremonies and games

Most traditional ceremonies revolved around the life cycle: birth, puberty, marriage, and death. Many present-day Luiseño celebrate Catholic feast days, such as saints' days (days set aside to celebrate the lives of various saints). Catholic priests conduct rites for baptisms, confirmations, marriages, and funerals. In the 1990s, traditional singers began to perform in public and at community events.

The Luiseño still enjoy some of the same games their ancestors played. A favorite of both men and women is the peon game, a guessing game played by two teams, in which singing and magic aid the competitors.

Puberty

Complex coming-of-age ceremonies were held for boys and girls of the Luiseño tribe. Both ceremonies were conducted by a religious chief from a different village, whose role was to teach the rules of the Chinigchinix religion (see "Religion"). Boys and girls were required to watch the religious chief create a special sand painting, depicting elements of the universe such as the Milky Way and the various animals that the Creator might send to punish people. Through these sand paintings, the religious chief taught the traditions, customs, and moral codes of Luiseño society.

Boys' ritual During their puberty ritual, Luiseño boys took the drug *toloache* (see "Religion"), saw visions, and learned sacred songs and dances. They endured a number of discomforts—being lashed with nettles (prickly plants) and bitten by ants—and refrained from eating certain foods. The boys were then instructed to respect their elders and to let generosity, not greed, rule their hearts. The Luiseño believed that obeying these rules would help them live long and well; conversely, disobedience would lead to sickness and death. At the end of the lecture, the boys took a mouthful of salt mixed with white flour made from the sage plant that they then spit it onto the ground. If the lump was dry, it was a sign that the boy had been paying attention to the advice. A moist lump indicated that the boy had not been listening.

Girls' ritual Girls undergoing the puberty ritual assembled in the village's sacred enclosure and ate a lump of tobacco mixed with water. Any girl able to keep the tobacco down was considered virtuous; a girl who vomited up the mixture was not. Girls remained in a heated pit for three days and nights covered with mats or blankets. Baskets were placed over their faces, They left the pit only for short periods to eat or to reheat the pit with hot rocks. They could only drink warm water and had to use a bone scratcher whenever they felt itchy. Dancing and singing took place around them. At the end of the three days, each girl's face was painted red with a special design; a similar design was painted on a rock. This rite was conducted once a month for a year.

Like the boys, girls abstained from certain foods (meat and salt) for one year. At the end of the puberty rite, they listened to a lecture advising them on conduct and tradition.

Marriage

Marriages were arranged by parents, who usually helped choose mates from other villages so a family's access to their in-laws' resources could be expanded. (In the late twentieth century, Luiseño women often married into neighboring reservations, not to expand territory but to expand Luiseño influence.) Some marriage arrangements dated back to infancy, but a couple waited until they had reached puberty to marry. After the bride price had been paid, a religious chief performed the ceremony. Afterward, the couple moved in with the groom's family. Wealthy men might also marry their wives' sisters. A widower was entitled to marry one of his wife's sisters, if he desired.

Children

A special ceremony was performed when a child was born, confirming that the child belonged to its father's family.

Death

The Luiseño cremated their dead. As part of the ceremony, tribal members blew upward three times to release the spirit of the deceased into the sky. The mourning ceremony, which is still held in modern times, evolved after the death of the ancient Luiseño god Wiyót.

A few weeks after the cremation, the family held a *Tuvísh,* a ceremony for washing the clothes of the dead person. People assembled in a brush shelter after dark and sang. Between songs, an elder recited stories about the origin of death. Women danced in place; men pounded the ground with one foot while groaning and blowing out air to keep the dead person's ghost away. The ceremony lasted until long after midnight, and one of the final rituals was to symbolically wash the deceased's clothing with water.

About one year later a chief from another clan burned these clothes during another singing ceremony. Sometimes mourning ceremonies were held in memory of all tribe members who had died recently. Relatives made figures out of tule to represent the deceased. They burned these along with baskets, shell beads, and other property. Sometimes other villages attended these rituals.

If a dancer had died, the whirling dance was performed in his honor. The new whirling dancer painted black lines from his nose to his cheekbones and dotted them with white. He dressed in a skirt of eagle feathers and wore an owl-feather headdress. Afterward, guests from the other villages were sent home with the leftover food from the feast. Eagle-killings were done in memory of dead chiefs; these were accompanied by dancing and a feast.

CURRENT TRIBAL ISSUES

Water continues to be a constant concern for the tribe. Since the late 1800s, conflicts have arisen between people on the reservations and people in cities near them concerning water rights. The diversion of water away from reservations has ruined Luiseño farms and orchards, forcing people to move off the reservation to seek work elsewhere. Several lawsuits have been filed. Some Luiseño groups have received money to settle their claims; other cases had not been settled by the early twenty-first century.

Conflict with local law enforcement and contentious internal tribal politics plague some reservations. Over the past few years, corruption, arrests, and shootings have troubled the Luiseño people. So, too, have conflicts over land use. Many tribal members express concerns over leadership issues and decisions that they believe are detrimental to the people and/or to the environment. One major environmental concern exists on the La Jolla Reservation. In 2007, the Mount Palomar Fire burned 92 percent of the reservation, and the people lost huge forests of oak trees that had provided their ancestors with acorns. Although the homes that burned down were rebuilt with help from volunteers, donations, and federal funds, replacing the vegetation will take decades.

NOTABLE PEOPLE

Edward D. Castillo (1947–) is a university professor specializing in Native American studies. He has a doctoral degree in anthropology and has taught and lectured about Native peoples at various California universities. Castillo has published many articles and books on anthropology and Native American Studies, but he is probably best known for the chapters he wrote in volume eight of the Smithsonian Institution's massive set of reference books called *Handbook of North American Indians*.

Fritz Scholder (1937–2005) was a leading modern artist in the United States. His works often dealt with themes relating to the Native experience. Although his grandmother was a member of the Luiseño tribe, Scholder described himself as "a non-Indian Indian." His critics complain that his "pop art" is shallow and casts Native problems in a superficial light, but his work remains popular nationwide.

James Luna (1950–), of Luiseño/Diegueño heritage, is an installation and performance artist whose work explores (usually with humor) what it is like to be a Native American. His artwork, featured in museums throughout the nation, also encourages his audience to examine the ways they perceive Native peoples. One of Luna's exhibitions was dedicated to Pablo Tac (1822–1841), who at age ten was sent to Rome, Italy, to be schooled for the priesthood. He died there nine years later after completing the first outline of a Luiseño grammar book and a partial dictionary.

BOOKS

Bean, Lowell John, and Florence C. Shipek. "Luiseño." In *Handbook of North American Indians.* Vol. 8: *California,* edited by Robert F. Heizer. Washington, DC: Smithsonian Institution, 1978.

Bradley, Donna. *Native Americans of San Diego County, CA.* Mt. Pleasant, SC: Arcadia, 2009.

Du Bois, Constance Goddard. *Mythology of the Mission Indians.* Reprint. Charleston, SC: Forgotten Books, 2008.

Du Bois, Constance Goddard. *The Religion of the Luiseno Indians of Southern California.* Gloucester, UK: Dodo Press, 2010.

Lightfoot, Kent G. *Indians, Missionaries, and Merchants: The Legacy of Colonial Encounters on the California Frontiers.* Berkeley: University of California Press, 2005.

Oetteking, Bruno, Edward H. Davis, George Gustav Heye, and Frederick John Teggart. *Early Cremation Ceremonies of the Luiseño and Diegueño Indians of Southern California.* New York: Museum of the American Indian, Heye Foundation, 1921.

Shipek, Florence Connolly. "Luiseño." In *Native America in the Twentieth Century: An Encyclopedia,* edited by Mary B. Davis. New York: Garland Publishing, 1994.

Sparkman, Philip Stedman. *The Culture of the Luiseno Indians.* Reprint. Whitefish, MT: Kessinger Publishing, 2010.

Williams, Jack S. *The Luiseno of California.* New York: PowerKids Press, 2003.

Zimmerman, Larry J. *American Indians, The First Nations: Native North American Life, Myth and Art.* London: Duncan Baird Publishers, 2003.

PERIODICALS

Du Bois, Constance Goddard. "Mythology of the Mission Indians Index." *The Journal of the American Folk-Lore Society* 17, no. 72 (1906): 52–60, 73, 145–64. Available online from http://www.sacred-texts.com/nam/ca/mmi/index.htm (accessed on August 11, 2011).

Kroeber, A. L. "Two Myths of the Mission Indians." *Journal of the American Folk-Lore Society* 19, no. 75 (1906): 309–21. Available online at http://www.sacred-texts.com/nam/ca/tmmi/index.htm (accessed on August 11, 2011).

WEB SITES

La Jolla Band of Luiseño Indians. http://www.lajollaindians.com/ (accessed on August 11, 2011).

"Luiseño." *Four Directions Institute.* http://www.fourdir.com/luiseno.htm (accessed on August 11, 2011).

"Luiseno/Cahuilla Group." *San Francisco State University.* http://bss.sfsu.edu/calstudies/nativewebpages/luiseno.html (accessed on August 11, 2011).

"Luiseno Ethnozoology." *Palomar College.* http://daphne.palomar.edu/scrout/Luisenoz.htm (accessed on August 11, 2011).

"Miiyu." *Pechanga Band of Luiseno Indians.* http://www.pechanga-nsn.gov (accessed on August 11, 2011).

Pala Band of Mission Indians. http://www.palatribe.com/ (accessed on August 11, 2011).

Redish, Laura, and Orrin Lewis. "Luiseno Indian Language." *Native Languages of the Americas.* http://www.native-languages.org/luiseno.htm (accessed on August 11, 2011).

Rincon Band of Luiseño Indians. http://rinconmembers.net/ (accessed on August 11, 2011).

Soboba Band of Luiseno Indians. http://www.soboba-nsn.gov (accessed on August 11, 2011).

Sparkman, Philip Stedman. "The Culture of the Luiseño Indians Index." *Sacred Texts.* http://www.sacred-texts.com/nam/ca/coli/index.htm (accessed on August 11, 2011).

Wallace, Cathleen Chilcote. "Ìswut of San Luis Rey: A Luiseño Tale." *Native Talk.* http://www.nativetalk.org/pages/story.htm (accessed on August 11, 2011).

Maidu

Name

The name Maidu (pronounced *MY-doo*) comes from the tribe's term for "person." The Northwestern Maidu were called *Konkow* or *Concow*. Southern Maidu were known as *Nisenan*.

Location

The Maidu's traditional lands were in the northeastern and north-central parts of present-day California. They now live on and around more than a dozen rancherías (small ranches), mostly in Plumas and Butte counties, and on the Round Valley Reservation.

Population

In 1846, there were about 9,000 Maidu. By 1910, the population had decreased to 1,100. In the 1990 U.S. Census 2,334 people identified themselves as Maidu. The 2000 census showed 2,281 Maidu, and 3,857 people who had some Maidu heritage.

Language family

Penutian.

Origins and group affiliations

The Maidu, who have lived in California for thousands of years, consisted of three groups: the Mountain Maidu, Concow (or Konkow), and Nisenan. Today, the name *Maidu* refers to all three groups. The Maidu were friends with the Paiute (see entry) to the east but harbored ill will toward the Washo, Yana (see entries), and Achumawi. In the early twenty-first century, they live on rancherías with the Miwok, Pit River, Pomo (see entries), Paiute, Wintun, Washoe, and several other tribes.

In the high mountain meadows, valleys, and foothills of the Sierra Nevada range, to the floor of the Sacramento Valley and along the Sacramento River, the Maidu lived a fairly comfortable and peaceful existence of hunting, gathering, and fishing. They enjoyed a generally mild

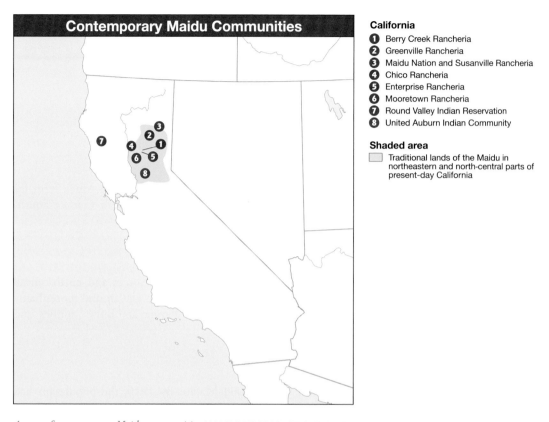

Contemporary Maidu Communities

California
1. Berry Creek Rancheria
2. Greenville Rancheria
3. Maidu Nation and Susanville Rancheria
4. Chico Rancheria
5. Enterprise Rancheria
6. Mooretown Rancheria
7. Round Valley Indian Reservation
8. United Auburn Indian Community

Shaded area
Traditional lands of the Maidu in northeastern and north-central parts of present-day California

A map of contemporary Maidu communities. MAP BY XNR PRODUCTIONS. CENGAGE LEARNING, GALE. REPRODUCED BY PERMISSION OF GALE, A PART OF CENGAGE LEARNING.

climate, plenty of food, and a rich spiritual and cultural life until the invasion of gold miners in 1848. Life changed for the tribe then, and much of their culture was lost during the early reservation years. Now the Maidu are working to restore their traditions and language. Some Maidu history and landmarks have been preserved at Plumas National Forest. They can be observed along the 67-mile (108-kilometer) Maidu Indian World Maker Route.

HISTORY

Early lifeways

The Maidu once controlled a large amount of territory in what is now California, and they were one of the most populous groups there. Their homeland in northern and central California has been inhabited for at least eight thousand years, and other peoples may have lived there before the Maidu.

Because they did not have to travel far to search for food, the Maidu built permanent villages. The majority of these hardy people usually stayed in their villages to face the winter. When the season was right, they set up temporary camps near hunting and gathering areas.

Although the California tribes tended to be the least warlike of Native American tribes, the Maidu sometimes engaged in warfare with their enemies or in feuds among themselves. They fought over such issues as trespassing on hunting grounds. They sometimes carried out sneak attacks or kidnapped or murdered hostages, but enemies often made up and resumed trading and gambling with one another.

Important Dates

1848: Gold is discovered in Maidu territory.

1851: The U.S. government negotiates a treaty that forces the Maidu to relocate to a reservation.

1958: Congress passes the Ranchería Act, terminating several Maidu rancherías.

1990s: Terminated rancherías are federally recognized again.

2002: The U.S. government places 49 acres in trust for the United Auburn Indian Community.

European contact

The Spanish were the first to build large-scale settlements in California, beginning in the 1700s, but the Maidu had little if any direct contact with them. They caught diseases such as smallpox and malaria from American trappers and traders who passed through their territory in the early 1800s, and many Maidu died. For the most part outsiders did not explore the Maidu lands until the mid-1800s because it was mountainous and difficult to travel.

The destruction of the Maidu way of life that began with the epidemics (outbreaks of diseases) increased after the discovery of gold in the foothills of the Sierra Nevada mountain range in 1848. The Maidu knew about the gold but considered it of no value. Far more interesting than gold to the tribe were the miner's ropes, which made better bridges than the grapevines they had been using.

Gold fever

Thousands of people from all over the globe poured into Maidu lands. Many merely wanted to get rich quickly and leave, giving no thought to the feelings and traditions of the Native peoples whose land they destroyed. The miners often treated the Natives with violence. The discovery of gold was a disaster from which the Maidu never recovered. From an estimated population of 9,000 in 1846, just before gold was discovered, the Maidu population fell to 1,100 by 1910.

Careless gold miners polluted the streams that supplied the Maidu with food and drove away game animals. Settlers arrived, and their cattle ate local plants and their hogs foraged for the acorns so important to the Native diet. Unable to feed themselves, some Maidu were forced to leave their villages to work in the cities or on nearby ranches and farms. They soon found themselves competing for jobs with disappointed gold miners.

Government intervention

In 1850, only two years after the discovery of gold, discussions began over what to do about the "Indian problem" in California. The U.S. government's solution was to isolate California Natives on reservations. Government officials claimed it was for the Native peoples' protection because it would prevent the extinction of tribes by hostile settlers.

Eighteen treaties were drawn up between the government and California tribes, including the Maidu, beginning in 1851. The Native peoples agreed to give up most of their lands to the U.S. government in exchange for about 7.5 million acres that would be set aside for reservations. The treaty the Maidu made with the federal government gave them a large reservation on land where there was no gold. The government expected the Maidu to farm this land.

Settlers were upset that so much land was being given away to the Native nations (about 8 percent of the state). They pressured the U.S. Senate to reject the treaties. Shortly after that, only 1.2 million acres were set aside for reservations. The Maidu received a 227-square-mile (588-square-kilometer) reservation away from their traditional homeland, where they would be confined with other tribes.

Refusal to cooperate

Over the next several years, U.S. soldiers repeatedly escorted the Maidu people to the new reservation, which was called *Nome Lackee* by the Wintun tribe of Maidu who originally owned the land. Repeatedly, the Maidu left the Nome Lackee Reservation to return to their homeland. California citizens complained about the Maidu's refusal to settle down.

In 1857, U.S. soldiers again rounded up a large group of Maidu, mostly women and children, and forced them to return to the Nome Lackee Reservation. According to Maidu who made the trip, young women had to spend the nights in trees to protect themselves from the soldiers.

Over the next four decades, the Maidu and other California Indians faced constant violence at the hands of white settlers. In 1858, 461 Natives (including some Maidu) were rounded up and forced to endure a five-day walk to Round Valley Reservation in present-day Mendocino County. Almost half of them were murdered or died on the way. Those who made it did not like conditions there. Some escaped and fled to remote areas where they tried to avoid contact with settlers. By the beginning of the twentieth century, the Maidu found themselves landless and homeless.

Rancherías established

In 1906, a system was established to address the problem of still-homeless Natives in California. The government bought small parcels of land for them, called *rancherías,* a Spanish term for a small ranch. Much of the ranchería land was located in isolated areas, was too poor to farm, and often lacked developed water sources. Several families from the same tribe settled on each of these parcels.

Between 1906 and 1934, seven rancherías were purchased for the Maidu people. Agents from the U.S. Bureau of Indian Affairs and missionaries from various churches taught the Maidu to farm and tried to make them more like Americans in other ways, a policy known as assimilation. The Maidu, however, found it nearly impossible to support themselves, and many people moved away from the rancherías or became dependent on government support.

Termination of rancherías

Government officials decided assimilation would take place more quickly if people lived and worked in cities, so they adopted a policy called termination. Termination ended the relationship between the federal government and Native nations, and the people became subject to state laws instead. Tribes received no government assistance, and tribal landowners had to pay state property taxes on their land. Since most Natives lived in poverty, taxation and no assistance meant that eventually they lost their land. Four Maidu rancherías accepted termination before the policy changed. As tribal members lost their land when they could not pay property taxes, the ranchería at Mooretown became a ghost town.

Modern times

The termination policy soon came under heavy criticism, and support for it died. The civil rights movement of the 1960s ushered in a new era of government programs and policies for Native nations. Tribes were urged to take more responsibility for their own communities and were given funds to assist them. In the early twenty-first century, the U.S. government maintained relations with tribal governments at eight Maidu rancherías; seven bands of Maidu were seeking government recognition. Despite the poverty and oppression they have endured, the Maidu people have preserved many ancient customs, which they have adapted to modern times.

RELIGION

Beliefs

Among the most important of the Maidu gods was their creator, usually called World Maker, who made a first man, called *Kúksu,* and a first woman, called Morning Star Woman. Next World Maker created a new race of people and told Kúksu and Morning Star Woman to teach them everything they needed to know about survival, law and order, dancing, and ceremonies. The new race of people—the Maidu—were sent out into the world, speaking various languages to form many tribes. The Maidu believed they were the center of all creation.

World Maker intended for people to live easy, eternal lives, so death did not exist at first. It was introduced by Coyote, a fun-loving character who sometimes helped people but also made mischief. One example of the trouble he caused the Maidu was changing the California landscape so it became more rugged, thus making life harder for the people.

Most Maidu believed in an individual soul, which they called the heart. When a person died, his or her heart was said to have left. The soul of a good person traveled along the Milky Way until it reached World Maker. The souls of bad people were reborn to live forever as rocks or bushes. The Maidu also believed that every object had a soul, which was set free when the object was destroyed.

The First Ghost Dance Movement

The Ghost Dance of 1870 was a religious move-ment founded by a member of the Paiute tribe (see entry) named Wodziwob (c. 1844–c. 1872). He was born around 1844; by most accounts he died in about 1872 or 1873, but some say he lived into the twentieth century. Wodzibwob, who lived on the Walker River Reservation in Nevada, was also known as "Gray Hair" and "Fish Lake Joe."

In the late 1860s, Wodziwob's people were mourning a number of calamities that had befallen them. They had lost much of their land and their way of life because of the westward expansion of American settlers. They were expe-riencing a drought, and many were starving. Diseases had greatly reduced the population.

Wodziwob brought a welcome message to these suffering people. He said that he had died and

visited the spirit world, but had then come back to life and had many tales to tell of his experi-ence. He brought messages for his people from their dead friends and relatives. He said the Indian dead were planning to come back to life and when they did, they would cause great fear among white people. He told his followers that if they performed the Ghost Dance, it would has-ten the day when the Indian way of life would be restored, and everyone would be happy once again.

Wodziwob's movement came to be known as the Ghost Dance. It soon spread to the Califor-nia tribes and the tribes of the Great Basin. Just as the movement was fading in the late 1800s, another Ghost Dance movement began. Known as the Ghost Dance of 1890, it was revived by another Paiute, Wovoka (c. 1856–1932), whose father, Tavibo, had assisted Wodziwob.

Religious leaders and ceremonies

Maidu priests had mystical powers and could communicate with spirits. Some had both healing power and spirit power, while others had only one of those powers.

At their frequent religious ceremonies, the Maidu made offerings to World Maker and to earth spirits; sometimes they acted out stories about their gods. In return for their offerings, the people expected a good rela-tionship with nature, which meant an abundance of game animals and wild foods along with sufficient rain.

Some Maidu embraced the Ghost Dance religion in the 1870s, add-ing variations of their own. Because of the missionaries' efforts to sup-press Maidu religious beliefs and their expression, the people today tend to keep their beliefs to themselves.

Maidu Words

maidüm	"man"
küle	"woman"
söm	"dog"
pokom	"sun"
pōmpokom	"moon"
momim	"water"
wiiti	"one"
pēne	"two"
sāpwi	"three"
tsöye	"four"
māwike	"five"

LANGUAGE

Versions of the Penutian language were spoken by a large number of California Natives. Although all the dialects were closely related, groups who spoke them often could not understand one another. Today, few speakers of Maidu are still alive; some say that William Shipley (1921–2011), a professor at the University of California, Berkeley, from 1966 to 1991, was one of the last living speakers. Shipley translated a number of Maidu myths and stories into English and published them in a book called *The Maidu Indian Myths and Stories of Hanc'ibyjim* (1991). The stories were told in 1902 to representatives of the American Museum of Natural History by Hanc'ibyjim, who was said to have been the last great Maidu storyteller.

GOVERNMENT

Before they had contact with gold miners, the Maidu were organized into tribelets—one main village surrounded by a few minor outlying villages. Communities ranged in size from one hundred to five hundred persons and were loosely headed by a headman or chief, who lived in the large central village. He had little authority except when major decisions had to be made or during ceremonies. In some tribelets, the chief (usually a man, but sometimes a woman) handed down his position to his children. In other tribelets, the chief was selected by the villagers or by a powerful person who had received a message from the spirits. The chief often acted with the advice of a council of elders.

The Indian Reorganization Act, passed by the U.S. Congress in 1934, encouraged tribes to form tribal governments that more closely resembled the American system of elective government. In modern times, Maidu rancherías elect members to a council that handles tribal government affairs.

ECONOMY

For thousands of years, the Maidu economy depended on hunting, gathering, and trade. After the influx of settlers made the traditional economy impossible, many Maidu took jobs as farmers and loggers. In the early twenty-first century, some Maidu are still employed in the forestry business and others do seasonal work in canneries. Other sources of employment include tourism and recreation, real estate development, service and retails businesses, mining, and government jobs. Casinos provide jobs and much-needed funds on some rancherías.

DAILY LIFE

Education

Traditional methods Maidu children were expected to imitate adult behavior. As soon as they learned to walk, they had the run of the village and ate and slept wherever they wished. They learned many life lessons from their grandparents, and there was a strong bond between the two generations.

When children misbehaved, their grandparents explained to them the consequences of future bad behavior. They were told, for example, that they might be kidnapped by a fearsome old lady who lurked in the woods.

Young boys in some tribelets were expected to choose a skill they wished to develop, such as fishing or hunting. Girls learned all the skills necessary to be a Maidu woman, which included a thorough understanding of plants, basket making, and gathering.

Modern methods The U.S. government got involved in the education of Maidu children around the turn of the twentieth century when they established schools, such the Greenville Indian School, where boys were given a military-style education. Girls were trained to be servants. The Greenville Indian School was later destroyed in a fire.

At government schools, children faced harsh treatment. They were forbidden to speak their own language or observe their traditional customs. Most government schools are no longer in operation, and children attend public schools in cities near the reservation. Some Maidu parents feel the public schools do not serve their children well, so the Round Valley Reservation opened the Eel River Charter School for their students. They also operate Round Valley Educational Center, a resource center that offers programs to promote Native achievement. Some rancherías supplement public school education by offering cultural programs for children during the summer months.

Buildings

Winter homes The Maidu built permanent winter homes and summer shade dwellings. Winter homes, which were partly underground, were built in the spring when the ground was soft enough to dig to a depth of 2 to 4 feet (about 1 meter). They were small, cone-shaped dwellings of cedar bark covered with earth to keep them well insulated.

Inside, shelves held large baskets full of acorns. Chairs and beds were made of a plant material called tule (cattails). Beds were covered with blankets made from duck and goose down. Near each dwelling stood thatch-covered basketware containers for more acorns.

Summer homes and other buildings When the Maidu were on the move during the hunting and gathering season, they built simple shade shelters. These were basically flat-roofed canopies of oak branches supported by wooden poles.

Other buildings might include a roundhouse, or dance house, where the people held ceremonies and the headman of the largest village often lived; sweathouses that could be used by up to four or five men at a time to purify themselves; huts where women were confined during their menstrual periods; and stations for butchering meat, cleaning fish, cutting wood, and storing acorns.

Food

The climate of central California was usually mild, and in most years the Maidu found an abundance of food within a short distance of their villages. Their major source of food was acorns. Insects and worms that got into the acorn flour during the wintertime were eaten either dried or roasted. Those who did not collect a sufficient supply of acorns were forced to seek shelter with relatives in other villages during the winter months.

In the spring, the Maidu gathered wild rye and other grass seeds in the valleys. They took to the foothills to gather pine nuts, whose shells were made into beads; the nuts were eaten whole or ground into flour. Some Maidu also gathered hazelnuts, buckeye nuts, and nutmeg. Mint tea and cider made from manzanita berries were favorite beverages. Because of their custom of digging for roots, the gold miners called the Maidu "Diggers." Other menu items included stewed eel and dried salmon.

Tobacco was the only plant grown by the Maidu. Priests offered tobacco smoke up to the spirits, and others used tobacco as a painkiller and at bedtime, because it made them sleepy.

Hunting techniques

Some Maidu left their permanent villages in the summer to hunt for deer and bear in the mountains. Groups of five or six men would gather in front of the cave of a bear about to end its winter hibernation. First the men performed a ceremony in which they requested that the bear stand up and allow itself to be shot. They then hid behind trees. One man at a time showed himself to the bear and shot it with an arrow or two. The bear chased the shooter, who led the bear to another hunter, who in turn shot it once or twice, until finally the bear was bristling with arrows and gave up. Some groups of Maidu would not eat the bear, but removed its hide to use as a costume in ceremonies.

Deer drives were sometimes organized with surrounding villages. One hunting technique was to entice a deer to approach by dressing like one. The hunter wore a deer mask and a rabbit-skin blanket; he smeared a substance on his body to disguise his own scent, and then moved in on his prey while making movements like a feeding deer. Sometimes, deer were driven into a ring of fire and then killed with bows and arrows.

Clothing and adornment

Maidu men, women, and children wore little clothing year round. Men sometimes wore buckskin breechcloths (a garment with front and back flaps that hung from the waist), and younger women sometimes wore small aprons that hung from the waist in front and back and were made of buckskin, grass, or tree bark. In very cold weather, they might wear deerskin leggings and ankle-length deerskin moccasins stuffed with grass. In extremely severe weather, they added cloaks made of feathers or the skins of rabbits, deer, or mountain lions. Snowshoes were used in winter.

Hair was worn long and loose by both sexes. A hat made of tule was favored by some Maidu women. They pierced their ears and made earrings from bone or wood decorated with woodpecker skulls or quail tips. Men preferred pierced noses. Both sexes wore necklaces made from shells and animal teeth. Tattoos and body paint added color.

Healing practices

Maidu healers, called shamans (pronounced *SHAH-munz* or *SHAY-munz*), could both cure and cause illness. In fact, shamans were so powerful they could make entire villages sick.

A shaman cured by piercing the skin and sucking out the substances that caused diseases. As late as the 1950s, some Maidu men had scars from having been cured this way. The sickness-causing agents were actually stones, crystals, bones, or even live animals that the shaman brought with him to the sickbed. Some Maidu groups also had female shamans. Although some people believed women shamans were poisoners, other Maidu groups preferred them to male shamans.

In modern times, a high percentage of Maidu people suffer from diabetes. This is not uncommon among Native peoples, whose death rate for diabetes and tuberculosis is much higher than for other Americans. The Maidu have their health-care needs attended to either at clinics on the rancherías or in health-care facilities in nearby towns.

ARTS

According to some versions of the Maidu creation story, the creator sang the world into being. Songs and music were an important part of all Maidu festivals and ceremonies. Maidu drums imitated the sound of bears. Their rattles sounded like pebbles swishing and were sometimes made from insect cocoons attached to long wooden handles and decorated with feathers and shells. Flutes, whistles, and a one-stringed bow were also played.

CUSTOMS

Marriage

Marriages between Maidu often began with the couple moving in together, at first with the bride's family for a short time and then with the groom's family. In some groups, though, contact between a mother-in-law and a son-in-law was considered bad, so the couple lived apart from the bride's family, and the husband avoided any contact with his wife's mother.

A man could choose his bride from within his own village or from another village. A husband who was a good hunter was especially prized by his wife's family because he sometimes provided them with food. No

The Horrible Bear

The Maidu, who lived in grizzly bear country, had a great respect for bears and even had a special dance they hoped would protect them from a bear attack. While many Native stories tell of a person marrying a bear, the story below is about a squirrel who married a bear.

There is a story told of a ground squirrel who had taken a mean old grizzly as his wife. One early morning when he had left for a day's hunting, the squirrel's home was visited by his half-brother, a bat. This creature was also very mean, and as he threw himself down on a bed of skins, he demanded to be fed. Growling with irritation, the grizzly supplied her brother-in-law with some acorn soup, jerky, and hazel nuts.

The bat began to throw the hazel nut shells into the face of his reluctant hostess, whose growls became increasingly threatening. Suddenly, she leapt at the bat. But he was ready for her attack. When the squirrel arrived home he found his wife dead from a poisoned arrow, and the bat gone.

Today's travelers into grizzly bear country are hopefully aware of additional ideas on coping with this beast. From the Maidu comes this traditional advice: if you drop a piece of meat on the ground, don't pick it up and eat it—or a "grizz" will one day eat you.

SOURCE: Jewell, Donald P. "The Horrible Bear." In *Indians of the Feather River: Tales and Legends of Concow Maidu of California.* Menlo Park, CA: Ballena Press, 1987.

woman had to accept a man she did not find pleasing. If either party desired a divorce, it was easily accomplished. Important men occasionally took several wives.

Pregnancy and babies

Pregnant women ate special diets that often excluded meat and fish. When her delivery time drew near, a Maidu mother-to-be was restricted to her home, and her husband stopped hunting and fishing. An experienced older woman assisted with the birth. If a baby was stillborn, both mother and father fasted for a period ranging from one to three months. Some groups considered twins unlucky, so they killed both the mother and the babies.

Names were very important and were changed several times during a Maidu's lifetime. At first, a girl received a baby name, such as "girl," "daughter," or "niece." The name then changed at important life events: at puberty, when she gave birth for the first time, and when she reached old age. A boy also received a baby name, such as "boy," another name at about age three, and yet another name if he joined a religious society (see "Puberty"). Some examples of Maidu children names were "climbing girl" and "snoring bird."

Puberty

During her first menstrual period, a girl withdrew from the community—either to her home, to a menstrual hut, or to a place in the mountains with her mother. Afterward, she took part in joyous ceremonies involving singing, dancing, bathing, face and body painting, and ear piercing.

Some very young Maidu boys were invited to join a secret religious society called the Kuksu Society. After several years spent in training, at puberty these boys took part in a secret ceremony and became members of the society.

Ceremonies and festivals

The Maidu welcomed spring with a Toto Dance. Female dancers shook beaded belts in rhythm with the music provided by men on drums, rattles, flutes, and whistles. Some groups still celebrate spring with this dance, and some still hold the bear dances that kept people safe from bear attacks.

The modern Maidu hold Indigenous Peoples Day in October. It features the Calling Back the Salmon Ceremony and traditional dances. For many years, they held Maidu Indian Days with storytelling and demonstrations of traditional crafts, such as acorn cooking and making baskets and flint tools.

Funerals

Some Maidu groups cremated the dead. Those who buried their dead dressed the bodies in fine clothing and wrapped them in animal skins. They put the bodies in unmarked graves together with some of their possessions to use in the afterworld and with offerings made by mourners. What remained of a dead man's property (hunting and fishing equipment, canoes, and clothing) was burned.

Special mourning ceremonies were held immediately following the burial and on anniversaries thereafter. At them, women wailed and emotional speeches were given. Afterward, the people ate, played games, and sang. The names of the dead were never mentioned again, but sometimes that name was passed on to a young relative.

CURRENT TRIBAL ISSUES

Some reservations and rancherías face problems with cleanup and soil contamination. Water pollution is also a major concern. During the Gold Rush days (see "History"), miners often used mercury to extract the smaller bits of gold while they were panning. The mercury got washed downstream, creating a buildup that still affects the water quality today. Many rancherías are working with various environmental groups to mitigate the dangers of mercury and other contaminants in their water. The Susanville Ranchería, which has a problem with drinking water quality, passed ordinances assessing fines of up to $1,000 a day for discharging any "chemical, physical, biological, bacteriological, radiological and other properties" into the water. Dealing with these environmental hazards is an expensive and ongoing process.

In the later part of the twentieth century, the Maidu displayed a renewed interest in their own culture. This led to a renewal of Maidu ceremonial practices, both social and religious. Since then, many Maidu have been working to restore their language and teach it to their children. In addition to reviving its traditions, the tribe is also seeking to increase its landholdings because much of its land was lost during the reservation and termination eras (see "History").

NOTABLE PEOPLE

The paintings of artist Frank Day (1902–1976) drew upon Maidu history and mythology. His father was a village headman, and Day inherited ceremonial knowledge and responsibilities from him. Day helped found a dance group called the Maidu Dancers and taught the younger dancers the songs, the meaning of the words in the songs, and the dance steps to use. Not only did he pass down Maidu traditions through dance, he also used his art to depict Maidu history and legends. He explained his interest in art: "Once in while I take up color and paint a little bit because if I do not do this, all things will be forgotten." In the early 2000s, many of his three hundred paintings were in private collections.

Artist Harry Fonseca (1946–2006) is probably best known for paintings and other graphics depicting Coyote, the cunning and irresponsible trickster of Maidu mythology.

Other notable Maidu include Tobu (born c. 1793), who led a group of Maidu warriors against European grave robbers; Frank Tuttle (1957–), a Yuki-Wailaki-Maidu dancer, painter, basket maker, and historian; and Maidu-Konkow poet Janice Gould (1949–).

BOOKS

Bauer, William J. *We Were All Like Migrant Workers Here: Work, Community, and Memory on California's Round Valley Reservation, 1850–1941.* Chapel Hill: University of North Carolina Press, 2009.

Belting, Natalia. *Whirlwind Is a Spirit Dancing: Poems Based on Traditional American Indian Songs and Stories.* New York: Milk and Cookies Press, 2006.

Burrill, Richard, *River of Sorrows: Life History of the Maidu-Nisenan Indians.* Richard Burrill; 1988.

DuBois, Cora. *The 1870 Ghost Dance.* Reprint. Lincoln: University of Nebraska, 2007.

Lepena, Frank. *Dream Songs and Ceremony: Reflections on Traditional California Indian Dance.* Berkeley: Heyday Books, 2004.

Middleton, Beth Rose. "Trust in the Land: New Directions in Tribal Conservation." Tucson: University of Arizona Press, 2011.

Riddell, Francis A. "Maidu and Concow." *Handbook of North American Indians.* Vol. 8: *California.* Edited by Robert F. Heizer. Washington DC: Smithsonian Institution, 1978.

Sarris, Greg, and Sara-Larus Tolley. *Quest for Tribal Acknowledgment: California's Honey Lake Maidus.* Norman: University of Oklahoma Press, 2006.

Shipley, William. *The Maidu Indian Myths and Stories of Hanc'Ibyjim.* Berkeley: Heyday Books, 1991.

Wilson, Norman L., and Arlean H. Towne. "Nisenan." In *Handbook of North American Indians.* Vol. 8: *California.* Edited by Robert F. Heizer. Washington DC: Smithsonian Institution, 1978.

WEB SITES

Dixon, Roland B. "Maidu Texts." *Internet Sacred Text Archive.* http://www.sacred-texts.com/nam/ca/mdut/index.htm (accessed on August 11, 2011).

Edward S. Curtis's The North American Indian. http://curtis.library.northwestern.edu/curtis/toc.cgi (accessed on August 11, 2011).

Enterprise Ranchería. http://enterpriserancheria.org/index.cfm?fuseaction=menu&menu_id=2 (accessed on August 11, 2011).

Greenville Rancheria. http://www.greenvillerancheria.com/ (accessed on August 11, 2011).

The Honey Lake Maidu. http://www.honeylakemaidu.org/ (accessed on August 11, 2011).

Konkow Valley Band of Maidu. http://www.maidu.com (accessed on August 11, 2011).

"The Maidu." *The First Americans.* http://thefirstamericans.homestead.com/Maidu.html (accessed on August 11, 2011).

"Maidu." *Four Directions Institute.* http://www.fourdir.com/maidu.htm (accessed on August 11, 2011).

"Maidu People." *City of Roseville.* http://www.roseville.ca.us/parks/parks_n_facilities/facilities/maidu_indian_museum/maidu_people.asp (accessed on August 11, 2011).

Mechoopda Maidu Indians. http://www.mechoopda-nsn.gov/ (accessed on August 11, 2011).

"Memory and Imagination: The Legacy of Maidu Indian Artist Frank Day." *Oakland Museum of California.* http://www.nmai.si.edu/exhibitions/memory_and_imagination/ (accessed on August 11, 2011).

Redish, Laura, and Orrin Lewis. "Maidu Indian Language (Maidun, Nisenan, Konkow)." *Native Languages of the Americas.* http://www.native-languages.org/maidu.htm (accessed on August 11, 2011).

Tsi Akim Maidu. http://www.tsi-akim.org/ (accessed on August 11, 2011).

"Visiting a Maidu Bark House." YouTube video, 1:41. Posted by "theunionvideo," October 5, 2007. http://www.youtube.com/watch?v=fw5i83519mQ (accessed on August 11, 2011).

Miwok

Name

The name Miwok (pronounced *MEE-wock* or *MEE-wuk*) is derived from *míwŭk,* the Central Miwok word for "people." It is sometimes spelled Me-Wuk, Mewuk, or Meewoc. The Lake Miwok called themselves *kó·ca,* which also means "people"; they referred to themselves as *Pomo,* however, when they spoke English.

Location

Formerly, three groups lived in more than one hundred villages in a large area in central California. Their territory stretched from the Sierra Nevada mountain range in the east to the Pacific Coast just north of San Francisco. In the early twenty-first century, the Miwok live on small, often isolated rancherías scattered throughout their former territory.

Population

In the late 1700s, there were about 22,000 Miwok. In 1910, the population was down to about 700. In the 1990 U.S. Census 3,438 people identified themselves as Miwok. The 2000 census showed 2,785 Miwok and 4,923 people who had some Miwok heritage.

Language family

Penutian.

Origins and group affiliations

Miwok groups have occupied Central California for at least three thousand years. The four Miwok groups are Coast Miwok, Lake Miwok, Bay Miwok, and Valley (or Sierra) Miwok. The Coast, Bay, and Lake Miwok were cut off from the Sierra Miwok and from each other by the Pomo, Patwin, and Wappo tribes. The Miwok married people of the Pomo and Maidu (see entries) tribes, among other neighbors. During the mid-1800s, the Valley Miwoks formed an alliance with the Yokuts to fight American encroachment on their territory. In modern times, some Miwok share reservations or rancherías with the Maidu, Pomo, and Wintun.

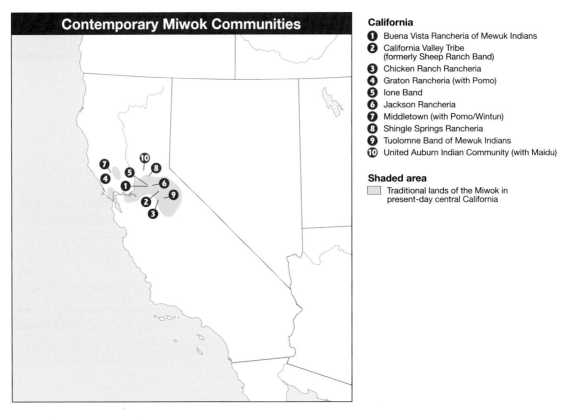

Contemporary Miwok Communities

California
1. Buena Vista Rancheria of Mewuk Indians
2. California Valley Tribe (formerly Sheep Ranch Band)
3. Chicken Ranch Rancheria
4. Graton Rancheria (with Pomo)
5. Ione Band
6. Jackson Rancheria
7. Middletown (with Pomo/Wintun)
8. Shingle Springs Rancheria
9. Tuolomne Band of Mewuk Indians
10. United Auburn Indian Community (with Maidu)

Shaded area
Traditional lands of the Miwok in present-day central California

A map of contemporary Miwok communities. MAP BY XNR PRODUCTIONS. CENGAGE LEARNING, GALE. REPRODUCED BY PERMISSION OF GALE, A PART OF CENGAGE LEARNING.

An easygoing, happy people who loved to dance, the Miwok were divided into four groups who shared a language and customs, but each was unique. Their differences stemmed from the ecology of the regions they inhabited, for a life lived in the mountains is unlike a life lived by the ocean. Like other California tribes, they lived a comfortable, peaceful life until gold was discovered on their lands. Since then, they have struggled to survive and maintain their culture, identity, and language, and to recover some of their former homelands.

HISTORY

Encounters with Europeans

The Coast Miwok were the first to meet Europeans. In 1579, the British explorer Sir Francis Drake (1540–1596) sailed into Miwok waters. He spent five days there repairing his ship, the *Golden Hind,* and he wrote an account of his meeting with the tribe. At about the same time, Spanish explorers claimed California, but they did not encounter the Miwok or build any settlements in the tribe's territory. Two centuries passed before the Miwok again encountered Europeans.

In 1769, the Spanish began building forts and missions in California to protect the land from the British and Russians. They also intended to teach Native Californians to be "useful" to future Spanish settlers. They converted the Native tribes to the Catholic religion, moved them into the missions, and taught them Spanish and skills such as farming and carpentry.

Spanish domination

Spanish missionaries baptized their first Miwok convert in 1794. Soon, most Coast Miwok had either been converted or had died from harsh treatment at the missions or from diseases brought by Europeans. Next the missionaries turned their attention to Native groups living inland. By 1811, they had reached the Sierra Miwok and forcibly took them to San Jose Mission.

Spanish soldiers rounded up those who tried to flee. Some Miwok were killed, but others joined people from the Yokuts tribe and rebelled. During the 1820s and 1830s, the Miwok learned Spanish fighting techniques and used them to carry out raids against the missions and to acquire horses from Spanish ranches. (By the late 1820s, horsemeat had become a staple in the Miwok diet, and they could only obtain it by raiding the settlements.) Horses also gave them mobility, and they soon became expert riders whose hit-and-run attacks posed a real threat to the Spanish.

The Miwok who had been taken to the missions, like the Cahuilla, Chumash, and Costanoan (see entries), endured great hardships and the near-destruction of their culture. Those who could manage it, fled; others were forced into labor at the missions or on nearby ranches. Disease spread quickly in the close quarters of the mission, and many Miwok died.

Important Dates

1579: Sir Francis Drake encounters the Coast Miwok.

1794: First known Miwok baptism takes place at San Francisco Mission.

1821: Mexican independence from Spain hastens settlement of Miwok territory.

1848: Gold Rush brings U.S. settlers in large numbers into Miwok country.

1900–20: Several rancherías are established for the surviving Miwok.

1934–72: Most Miwok rancherías are terminated.

1972–94: Tribal status is restored to several Miwok rancherías.

Mexican rule

Mexico won its independence from Spain in 1821 and ended the mission system in 1834, but for California Indians, freedom from the missions did not mean a return to their old way of life. Although Mexico had promised them land, they never received it. Instead, they were forced to work for the Mexican settlers who flooded into California. One Mexican rancher gathered a posse of other ranchers, slaughtered large numbers of Miwok, and took hundreds more as prisoners to work as slaves. Massacres and enforced labor of Native peoples became common throughout California as Mexican settlers moved northward in force.

California statehood

A third wave of settlement washed across Miwok territory after 1848. Mexico ceded (gave up) California to the United States following the Mexican-American War (1846–48; a war in which Mexico lost about one-half of its national territory to the United States). Gold was discovered in the Sierras, and shortly after the war was over, the California gold rush began. Now the Miwok of the Sierra Nevada, largely unaffected by Mexican settlement, were confronted with an invasion of prospectors and miners. The newcomers brought fatal diseases and alcohol, which caused many longstanding problems for the Miwok.

Relations between the Miwok and miners were almost instantly hostile. Whites took over Native American land, leaving the Miwok with only small plots. Some Miwok went to work for miners; others searched for gold themselves. Often, whole families worked together. Men dug and passed full baskets to their children who carried them to their mothers. The women washed the diggings in specially made grass baskets. Some Miwok made good money until prospectors ran them off and took over their claims, often stealing their gold and even killing them. Between 1847 and 1860, miners killed at least two hundred Miwok and took their land.

Treaties broken

Beginning in 1851, eighteen treaties were drawn up between the U.S. government and California tribes, including the Miwok. The tribes agreed to give up most of their lands to the U.S. government in exchange for about 7.5 million acres that would be set aside for reservations.

Settlers objected to so much land being devoted to the Natives (about 8 percent of the state). They convinced the U.S. Senate to reject the treaties. Unaware that the treaties had not been ratified, many tribes moved to the reservations they thought belonged to them. Most Miwok remained in the area of their homelands, but they had no land rights. During this time, hundreds more Miwok were enslaved or murdered by American settlers.

Rancherías for the Miwok

By 1910, the population of the Sierra Miwok had fallen to 670 from its pre-European contact high of 19,500. Only 41 Lake Miwok and 11 Coast Miwok were counted in a census about that time.

In the early 1900s, the U.S. government addressed the problem of homeless Native Americans in California by buying small parcels of land called rancherías (the Spanish word for ranch). Much of this property was located in isolated areas where settlers did not want to live. The land was poor and lacked developed water sources. The Lake Miwok moved onto the Middletown Ranchería (near Clear Lake) with the Pomo (see entry). Some Sierra Miwok went to Jackson Ranchería and Tuolumne Ranchería, both in the Sierra Nevada Mountains. Other rancherías started at that time whose residents were all or partly Miwok are Buena Vista, Chicken Ranch, Ione, Sheep Ranch, and Shingle Springs.

Natives on the rancherías were expected to farm and to assimilate, or become more like U.S. citizens. The land was so poor, however, that it was nearly impossible for the people to support themselves. Most Miwok became dependent on government aid.

Termination policy

The government, finding that its assimilation policies were not working, adopted a new policy called termination. Termination ended all U.S. government relations and cut off federal financial assistance to reservations. Those who agreed to the policy received a monetary settlement for their share of tribal assets, but they lost federal recognition.

The Ranchería Act of 1958 forced California Natives on the rancherías to decide whether to accept or reject termination. Thirty-six of the most isolated California Indian rancherías accepted termination, including most of the Miwok rancherías. Some tribe members were forced to accept termination if others on the ranchería agreed to it. The payments they received in exchange for the reservations were, in most

Ranchería Act of 1958

The Ranchería Act was passed by the U.S. Congress in 1958. It required that rancherías decide whether to accept or reject the federal government's new policy of termination. Termination would end the relationship between the U.S. government and Native tribes and instead make the tribes subject to state laws and taxes. Some tribes accepted termination, but others hesitated.

State authorities, hoping to collect taxes on this land, visited the rancherías that had not agreed. They promised that if tribal members agreed to accept termination, the state would provide new housing, road and water system improvements, and even college scholarships for the children. Before long, however, the state government realized that it would cost more to keep these promises than it would collect in taxes from the rancherías.

The termination policy soon came under heavy criticism, and support for it died. However, thirty-six of the most isolated California Indian rancherías had already accepted termination. The civil rights movement of the 1960s ushered in a new era of government programs and policies that were more friendly toward Native peoples, but it would be years before terminated tribes regained federal recognition.

cases, very small, and the people no longer had land of their own. Extreme poverty resulted.

Modern times

In 1979, a Pomo woman, Tillie Hardwick, filed a lawsuit on behalf of thirty-four terminated rancherías. The courts declared termination illegal and restored the rancherías, including several Miwok ones. By 2011, eleven Miwok reservations and rancherías were federally recognized, entitling them to federal funds and benefits and allowing them to run gaming operations. Many had opened casinos to improve their economies as well as to fund land purchases and tribal services. Five other Miwok groups were still working for federal recognition.

RELIGION

The Miwok believed in a creator, an animal god called Coyote. Other important animal gods were Coyote's son, Condor, and Condor's son, Chicken Hawk. Mount Diablo is a sacred place for the Miwok because that is where these creative forces came together. Grandfather Coyote created the Native American people at Mount Diablo, along with everything that they needed for life.

One of the most important figures in Miwok society was the spirit doctor, or sucking shaman (pronounced *SHAH-mun* or *SHAY-mun*), who could cure illnesses (see "Healing practices") and who was in charge of sacred ceremonies (see "Festivals and ceremonies").

Secret societies were common; a major one was the Kuksu Society. Young boys who were chosen to be members underwent a long training process in which they learned special dances and prayers. The society held ceremonies in a large, circular dance house. Members wore feathered headdresses and imitated the spirits while praying for favors, such as rain and an abundance of crops.

Some Miwok converted to Catholicism during the mission period (1769–1834). Many Miwok took up the Ghost Dance religion around 1872. Those who performed the Ghost Dance believed that the Native American way of life would soon be restored. Some elements of the Ghost Dance religion still survive among the Miwok.

LANGUAGE

The Miwok language has two major divisions: Eastern Miwok and Coastal Miwok. The two appear to have separated about 2,500 years ago. The Miwok spoke many different dialects of each of these language divisions.

Under the mission system, the Miwok were forced to speak Spanish. Later, facing prejudice from American settlers, many refused to speak their own languages to conceal their heritage. Government-run schools did not allow Miwok children to use their language. When Miwok elders died, the language began to die, too. Attempts are being made by the few remaining Native speakers to teach the Miwok language to the younger generation.

GOVERNMENT

The Miwok were divided into tribelets—one main settlement surrounded by a few minor outlying settlements. Each tribelet was a separate nation, headed by a chief (*hóypuh*) and one or two female leaders who oversaw either the dances or the women's ceremonial house. The woman who handled the dances was part of the Bird Cult. The other female chief directed the construction of the ceremonial house, supervised wood gathering and food preparation, sent out invitation sticks for dances, and sometimes chose the performers.

In some groups, the position of chief was handed down to a male heir. If there were no male heirs, a woman could inherit the position. If

Coastal Miwok Words and Phrases

Spelling is very important in the Coastal Miwok language. Many words are similar, except for one doubled consonant. For example, *hama* means "no" or "not," whereas *hamma* is "grandmother." *Yulu* is "to be angry," but *yullu* is a "rat." When speaking, the Miwok pronounce doubled consonants longer rather than twice.

To say "goodbye," the Miwok use the first two phrases below:

eyyamanaykanni	"Don't forget me!"
kaópyatinii	"I am going now."
kamaccaw	"I'm speaking."
'unmaccaw	"You're speaking."
oppuntowih	"Are you well?"
katowih	"I am well."
'uu	"yes"
hama	"no"
hayuusa	"dog"
'ellée	"fish"
wuki	"fire"
'umpa	"acorn"
'oolok	"ocean"

the heir was too young, a woman could rule in his place until he came of age. In other groups, an old chief and four old women chose a future chief and trained him. When he was ready to take over, the old chief stepped aside. If he refused to do so, a poisoner might be hired to remove him from office.

A chief's duties could include managing food resources, giving personal and legal advice, settling disputes, and making speeches. A Miwok chief who had morning wake-up duty was described in *The Indians of California*. At sunrise, he made the rounds of his village, calling out: "Get up! Get up! All the people get up! Wash your face. After you wash yourself, eat breakfast. Go hunt for something. You will get hungry. After you get something, you will eat it. Get up."

In modern times, there is no unified Miwok nation, but rather a dozen separate Miwok rancherías or reservations. Each is governed by an elected tribal council, with the exception of Tuolumne Ranchería, which is overseen by a community council composed of all eligible tribe members.

ECONOMY

Before contact with Europeans, the Miwok economy was based on hunting and gathering; some trading was also done. Shells, which were polished and strung into necklaces, served as money.

The Miwok had a strong sense of property. Land was not private property, but the acorn-producing oaks on it, for example, could be. Fees were charged for the use of the dance house for a girl's puberty rite. People paid to attend dances but received a refund if they were unhappy with the performance. Chiefs were paid for their services by hunters, who were required to turn over a portion of the meat they had caught.

After the arrival of the missionaries and settlers, some Miwok still supported themselves by hunting and gathering. They supplemented their income with meager wages from seasonal labor. Some worked on ranches and farms located on their former homelands. Others earned a living by logging; the forestry industry continues to be a major employer. Yosemite National Park in the Sierra Nevada range provides employment as well.

Most Miwok lived in poverty and, for some, the situation has not changed much. One economic success story is the Jackson

Miwok Ranchería Casino, which became one of the most profitable Native-owned casinos in California. It was been so successful, in fact, that in a matter of only a few years, every person living on the ranchería rose from poverty to live a middle- or upper-class life. The casino is a major employer; its profits allowed the tribe to offer free health care and substance abuse programs, hire a police force, build homes, and pave roads. Several other reservations have also improved their economies through gaming.

DAILY LIFE

Families

Miwok villages were made up of several extended families, consisting of a father, mother, children, and close relatives of the father. Usually, six to ten people lived together in one home.

Education

Miwok children learned by observing their elders. Everyone, even the smallest child, was expected to be productive. At age six or seven, boys were trained in song and dance rites, and by adolescence, they were ready to be welcomed into a variety of Miwok secret societies.

Under the mission system, children learned some Spanish and all about the Catholic religion. In modern times, Miwok children attend local public schools; some efforts are also being made to supplement their education with programs on the rancherías.

Buildings

Miwok home construction depended on where the group lived. Those in the mountains needed sturdier houses to stand up to severe weather; they built cone-shaped structures from three or four thicknesses of bark slabs with no supporting posts. At lower elevations, most buildings were conical, formed over a frame of two forked willow poles that leaned together. More poles were tied to these, and then this framework was covered with brush, grass, tule, or bark. A hole in the roof vented smoke from the central fire pit. Eastern Miwok covered their floors with digger or yellow pine needles. Tule mats (pronounced *TOO-lee*; a type of cattail) and animal hides served as beds. Chiefs sometimes had beds made of poles.

A reconstruction of Miwok bark houses stands at the Indian Grinding Rock State Historic Park in California. © NORTH WIND PICTURE ARCHIVES.

Large villages had circular sweathouses, located partly underground and used only by men; ceremonial chambers or dance houses, sometimes with separate, smaller chambers for women; cone-shaped huts for menstruating women; and acorn granaries constructed of upright poles covered with brush. Many also had a conical hut built over a large rock used during bad weather for grinding.

Transportation

The Coast Miwok made boats from tule reeds that could carry as many as eight to ten people. Although these boats sometimes became waterlogged after prolonged use, they worked well for short trips because they were light, fast, and easily steered with long poles in shallow water. Double-ended paddles were used in deep water.

Food

Gathering The Miwok were hunter-gatherers with access to a great variety of foods. The acorn was a staple food for all groups. Like acorns, buckeye nuts were gathered and prepared in a mush. Women harvested seeds and greens in season, but fruits and roots were scarce. Tobacco was both gathered and planted; men smoked it in elderberry pipes. When the Miwok raided Spanish horse herds in the 1800s, they added horsemeat to their diet.

Before they went hunting, men spent time in sweat lodges to lessen their human odor. They also rubbed their bodies with angelica and mugwort and held their bows and arrows over the fire. They then donned deer heads to lure animals to them, rather than chasing them. The Miwok caught birds using baskets, put plant bulbs in the water to stun fish, and used nets to catch salmon, geese, seagulls, and other wildlife.

Coast and lake dwellers Coast Miwok built their villages close to the shore or to lagoons where fishing was plentiful. Crabs were available all year; kelp, winter salmon runs, and late geese helped to round out their diet during cold weather. Fishing with nets and small traps began in earnest with the coming of spring. Larger fish, such as salmon, were speared, and smaller fish and eels were poisoned by throwing a root (*Marahfabaceus*) into shallow pools. Mussels and clams were important food from the sea. Small game such as rabbits, wood rats, gophers, and squirrels were eaten, but sea mammals were not.

Lake Miwok followed much the same pattern. They also hunted deer by snaring them or tracking them until the animals were worn out. Before settlers drove most of the animals away, the Miwok also shot elk and grizzly bears. Rabbits, squirrels, and ducks—hunted with clay pellets cast by a sling—also provided meat. Men caught trout with their bare hands or by using basket traps or dip nets. Both men and women fished, but only the men hunted game.

Women collected greens such as lettuce, clover, and nettles. They sometimes placed miner's lettuce near a red ant hill. As the ants walked on the leaves, they secreted a vinegar-like substance, which was used as salad dressing. In the summer women gathered wildflower seeds to make pinole. They also toasted pine seeds, pounded manzanita berries into a type of candy, and dried or baked seaweed for a salty snack.

Mountain dwellers The Sierra Miwok gathered plants and hunted deer, elk, antelope, black and grizzly bears, quail, pigeons, woodpeckers, rabbits, squirrels, and wood rats. They would not eat dogs, coyotes, or eagles. Fishing was another important source of protein, especially salmon and trout. Women dislodged seeds from the heads of plants with seed beaters and carried them in burden baskets. A few of the many plants they harvested included wild oats, balsam root, evening primrose, clarkia, gumweed, skunkweed, and California buttercup. Manzanita and madrone berries were used in a cider drink. The Miwok also picked wild plums, chokecherries, gooseberries, wild currants, and mushrooms in season.

Clothing and adornment

Clothing was fairly simple for all Miwok. Young children usually wore no clothing, whereas girls and women had two-piece skirts or double aprons made of deerskin or grass. Men wore animal-hide loincloths (apronlike flaps that hung from the waist in front and back; some were ankle-length) and sleeveless shoulder throws of deer hide or tule. In cold weather, they wore robes made from strips of jackrabbit fur held together with vine cording; these also served as blankets. Footwear was not common, but sock-like deerskin moccasins were worn in cold weather and for hunting.

Hair was worn long, either braided, loose, or gathered in a woven hair net. Some men also let their beards grow. Tattoos were common throughout Miwok territory for both men and women. They made them by rubbing poison oak ash into cuts in the skin. A popular design included several vertical lines at the chin and sides of the mouth; the lines might extend from chin to navel. Body paint and feathered belts and bracelets were worn on special occasions. The Miwok believed that body piercing contributed to a long life, so children had both their nose and earlobes pierced and wore flowers through their ears. Women wore shell earrings and nose sticks of shell or polished bone.

Healing practices

Depending on the illness, several types of doctors were available. A person sickened by evil spirits called a sucking doctor, who made a cut in the patient's body and sucked out the spirits. "Old dancers," men and women who cured the sick by dancing, singing, and playing musical instruments, were the favorite doctors. People desiring revenge would call upon a professional poisoner. This "doctor" produced illness in others by spells or by actual poison.

Special doctors took care of young girls having their first menstrual period. The most powerful doctors of all were bear doctors, whose guardian spirit was a bear. When a bear doctor put on his bearskin, the people believed he actually became a bear. Since he could either harm or cure, he was greatly feared.

Less serious diseases were treated by herb doctors who used plants to cure. Although only men smoked tobacco, some women prescribed it for themselves to cure a bad cold. Ceanothus leaves (also called California lilac) could also be used like tobacco. The Miwok chewed galls from oak trees as toothpaste and made tea from iris bulbs to treat kidney stones. They set aside some acorn mush until it aged and grew a mildew-like substance. They scraped this off and used it like penicillin.

In more recent times, the Miwok and other Native nations have faced problems with alcoholism. Medical care on the rancherías was undependable. In 1969, the Miwok and eight other California tribes formed the California Rural Indian Health Board (CRIHB). Today, the CRIHB oversees Native American health programs throughout the state. Through its efforts, health clinics have opened on or near most Miwok reservations.

ARTS

The Miwok were gifted basket weavers, and the surviving examples of their work are highly prized by modern art collectors. The tribe was also known for their decorative use of feathers, which they wove into the rims of baskets and also used for ceremonial costumes. By the early twenty-first century, some Native artists had revived the basketry tradition; examples of this as well as contemporary arts are exhibited at the Native American Invitational Art Show, held at Grinding Rock State Historical Park in conjunction with the Big Time festival (see "Ceremonies and festivals") in September.

Oral literature

Favorite Miwok stories involve the adventures and misadventures of the creator, Old Man Coyote. He displays some of the best qualities of humans, but more often the worst ones. Also popular are tales of birds, who were believed to have magical properties.

Creation of Man

After Coyote had completed making the world, he began to think about creating man. He called a council of all the animals. The animals sat in a circle, just as the Indians do, with Lion at the head, in an open space in the forest.

On Lion's right was Grizzly Bear; next Cinnamon Bear; and so on to Mouse, who sat at Lion's left.

Lion spoke first. Lion said he wished man to have a terrible voice, like himself, so that he could frighten all animals. He wanted man also to be well covered with hair, with fangs in his claws, and very strong teeth.

Grizzly Bear laughed. He said it was ridiculous for any one to have such a voice as Lion, because when he roared he frightened away the very prey for which he was searching. But he said man should have very great strength; that he should move silently, but very swiftly; and he should be able to seize his prey without noise.

Buck said man would look foolish without antlers. And a terrible voice was absurd, but man should have ears like a spider's web, and eyes like fire.

Mountain Sheep said the branching antlers would bother man if he got caught in a thicket. If man had horns rolled up, so that they were like a stone on each side of his head, it would give his head weight enough to butt very hard.

When it came Coyote's turn, he said the other animals were foolish because they each wanted man to be just like themselves. Coyote was sure he could make a man who would look better than Coyote himself, or any other animal. Of course he would have to have four legs, with five fingers. Man should have a strong voice, but he need not roar all the time with it.

And he should have feet nearly like Grizzly Bear's, because he could then stand erect when he needed to. Grizzly Bear had no tail, and

CUSTOMS

Courtship and marriage

Miwok brides were chosen not for beauty but for their love of hard work. Marriages were arranged by parents, although sometimes brides were kidnapped. Courtship began with the exchange of gifts such as beads, shells, or baskets. The bride usually moved in with her husband's family, but a poor man lived with the bride's family to prove that he would be a good provider. If a husband or wife died, the remaining spouse often married a relative of the dead mate. Marriage with members of non-Miwok tribes was common.

man should not have any. The eyes and ears of Buck were good, and perhaps man should have those.

Then there was Fish, which had no hair, and hair was a burden much of the year. So Coyote thought man should not wear fur. And his claws should be as long as the Eagle's, so that he could hold things in them. But no animal was as cunning and crafty as Coyote, so man should have the wit of Coyote.

Then Beaver talked. Beaver said man would have to have a tail, but it should be broad and flat, so he could haul mud and sand on it. Not a furry tail, because they were troublesome on account of fleas.

Owl said man would be useless without wings.

But Mole said wings would be folly. Man would be sure to bump against the sky. Besides, if he had wings and eyes both, he would get his eyes burned out by flying too near the sun. But without eyes, he could burrow in the soft, cool earth where he could be happy.

Mouse said man needed eyes so he could see what he was eating. And nobody wanted to burrow in the damp earth. So the council broke up in a quarrel.

Then every animal set to work to make a man according to his own ideas. Each one took a lump of earth and modeled it just like himself. All but Coyote, for Coyote began to make the kind of man he had talked of in the council.

It was late when the animals stopped work and fell asleep. All but Coyote, for Coyote was the most cunning of all the animals, and he stayed awake until he had finished his model. He worked hard all night. When the other animals were fast asleep he threw water on the lumps of earth, and so spoiled the models of the other animals. But in the morning he finished his own, and gave it life long before the others could finish theirs. Thus man was made by Coyote.

SOURCE: "Native American Legends: Creation of Man." *First People.* http://www.firstpeople.us/FP-Html-Legends/CreationofMan-Miwok.html (accessed on August 11, 2011).

Pregnancy

Some groups had small grass huts for birthing. Other groups had rules about what the mother should or should not eat during pregnancy. Among the Lake Miwok, for example, a woman was forbidden to eat woodpecker while pregnant; if she did, the child would cry too much after birth. Infants were named either for animals, family members, or deceased relatives.

Babies

Some tribes had rules about how many children a couple could have. For example, the Coast Miwok had a limit of three children, and any additional children were supposed to be killed. Historians do not believe this happened often, however.

Some Miwok flattened the heads of their infants because flat heads were considered attractive. Shortly after birth, they placed a baby in a cradle and tied a padded board to its forehead to mold the head.

Puberty

The various groups had different puberty rites. The Coast Miwok celebrated a girl's first period by welcoming her into a secret society and performing a circle dance for her. Girls who did not belong to dance societies stayed home, usually in a special hut. In all Miwok tribes, menstruating girls and women used a hairbrush and a scratching stick to avoid touching their hair or bodies. They also avoided fresh meat, and when they were led outside, their faces were covered. Boys usually fasted for the first time at adolescence, then went on their first hunt.

Ceremonies and festivals

Religious and social dances played an important part in Miwok ceremonies, although the Miwok were so fond of dancing they often danced to celebrate minor occasions such as killing a game bird. Ceremonial dancers pretended to be spirits to acquire luck, power, or good health. Only men participated in some dances, whereas women and children would be included in others. Male dancers often closed the smoke hole in the dance house to make the room hot, and then jumped into a nearby creek to cool off hours later.

Some popular dances included the Big Head Dance, Ghost Initiation, Old Time Dance, First Fruits ceremony, and Dance of the Dead. Often these ceremonies continued for many days: the Big Head Dance, for example, lasted four days and nights and was conducted by a caretaker and a timekeeper, both trained for the purpose.

Traditional celebrations are still held at many rancherías. The dance house at Tuolumne Ranchería is used for the September Acorn Festival. The Graton Ranchería hosts both Acorn and Strawberry Festivals. At Grinding Rock State Historical Park (called Chaw'se by the Miwok), people from several tribes gather at the dance house for the September Big Time celebration, where they dance and play Native football and the traditional handgame. Jennifer Bates described the game in *Native America in the Twentieth Century: An Encyclopedia*: "It involves the singing of songs and guessing of bones; there are two marked and two unmarked bones, and two teams play against each other for the money in the 'pot.'"

A player hides a bone in each hand inside a bundle of grass. The other team must guess which hand holds the unmarked bone.

Death

It was believed that at death, humans traveled toward the west to live with Coyote. Miwok were either cremated or buried along with their personal possessions. Mourners cut their hair short or singed it off, and older women smeared charred laurel berries on their faces. People sometimes mourned for a whole year if the dead person was important, and widows remained secluded for several months or even for years. Most groups would not speak the name of the dead person. In the summer or fall, the tribe held a mourning ceremony in memory of those who had recently died. The people gathered for three or four nights and wailed until about midnight. On the last night, they lit a large pyre and burned the dead person's property.

CURRENT TRIBAL ISSUES

By the early twenty-first century, many Miwok tribes had opened or were planning to open casinos. Reservations and rancherías that once struggled with poverty find gaming not only provides monetary benefits for individual tribe members but also funds important social, health, and educational programs. Casinos, however, have also brought difficulties to many tribes. The casino riches earned by the Jackson Miwok at the end of the twentieth century resulted in unfortunate side effects. Young people who received a monthly share of the profits saw no reason to attend school. The tribe finally issued an order that without a high school diploma, young people could not collect their share of the profits. Greater difficulties have arisen between groups who want to preserve sacred sites and those who want to build or expand the various casinos. Many projects have also become embroiled in legal controversies over who owns the land, whether casinos should be built, and who is entitled to casino profits. Legal challenges have even been made to the federal recognition status of some Miwok groups; frequently these court cases are connected to the tribe's rights to build a casino.

Another major concern of most groups is that, although they have received federal recognition, which entitles them to financial benefits and government assistance, they have little or no land. When the rancherías were terminated, that land was sold. Many tribes are working to recover their original acreage and rebuild their communities.

NOTABLE PEOPLE

Marin (d. 1834) was a Coast Miwok chief who played an important role in the early history of the San Francisco Bay area. He led his people in several successful battles against the Spanish between the years 1815 and 1824, but he was captured and imprisoned. He escaped but was recaptured. Priests from the San Rafael Mission intervened to prevent his execution. Marin later converted to Catholicism and lived close to the mission until he died there in 1834. The island where he took refuge was named after him, and some years later the entire adjacent peninsula and county were also given his name.

Other notable Miwok include the Hopi/Miwok poet, artist, and educator Wendy Rose (1948–), the Paiute/Miwok basket maker Lucy Telles (1885–1955), and the Pomo/Miwok professor and writer Gregory Sarris (1952–), who is also chairman of the Federated Coast Miwok Tribe.

BOOKS

Barrett, S. A. *Myths of the Southern Sierra Miwok.* Reprint. Charleston, SC: Nabu Press, 2010.

Bates, Jennifer. "Sierra Miwok." In *Native America in the Twentieth Century: An Encyclopedia,* edited by Mary B. Davis. New York: Garland Publishing, 1994.

Bibby, Brian. *Deeper than Gold: A Guide to Indian Life in the Sierra Foothills.* Berkeley: Heyday Books, 2004.

Dubin, Margaret, and Sara-LarusTolley, eds. *Seaweed, Salmon, and Manzanita Cider: A California Indian Feast.* Berkeley, CA: Heyday Books, 2008.

Gifford, Edward Winslow. *Miwok Moieties.* Reprint. Charleston, SC: General Books, 2010.

Gifford, Edward Winslow. *Miwok Myths.* Reprint. Charleston, SC: BiblioLife, 2010.

Goerke, Betty. *Chief Marin: Leader, Rebel, and Legend.* Berkeley, CA: Heyday Books, 2007.

Jackson, Louise A. *The Sierra Nevada before History: Ancient Landscapes, Early Peoples.* Missoula, MT: Mountain Press, 2010.

Kimbro, Edna, Julia G. Costello, and Tevvy Ball. *The California Missions: History, Art, and Preservation.* Los Angeles: Getty Conservation Institute, 2009.

La Pena, Frank, Craig D. Bates, and Steven P. Medley, compilers. *Legends of the Yosemite Miwok.* 3rd ed. Berkeley, CA: Heyday Books, 2007.

Merriam, C. Hart. *The Dawn of the World: Myths and Tales of the Miwok Indians of California.* Kila, MN: Kessinger Publishing, 2010.

Sarris, Greg. *Keeping Slug Woman Alive: A Holistic Approach to American Indian Texts.* Berkeley: University of California Press, 1993.

Thalman, Sylvia Barker. *The Coast Miwok Indians of the Point Reyes Area.* Point Reyes, CA: Point Reyes National Seashore Association, 2004.

PERIODICALS

Barrett, Samuel Alfred, and Edward Winslow Gifford. "Miwok Material Culture: Indian Life of the Yosemite Region" *Bulletin of Milwaukee Public Museum* 2, no. 4 (March 1933).

WEB SITES

Buena Vista Ranchería. http://www.buenavistatribe.com/ (accessed on August 11, 2011).

California Valley Miwok Tribe, California. http://www.californiavalleymiwoktribe-nsn.gov/ (accessed on August 11, 2011).

Clark, Galen. "Indians of the Yosemite Valley and Vicinity: Their History, Customs and Traditions." 1904. *Internet Sacred Text Archive.* http://www.sacred-texts.com/nam/ca/ioy/index.htm (accessed on August 11, 2011).

"Coast Miwok at Point Reyes." *U.S. National Park Service.* http://www.nps.gov/pore/historyculture/people_coastmiwok.htm (accessed on August 11, 2011).

"Coastal Miwok Indians." *Reed Union School District.* http://rusd.marin.k12.ca.us/belaire/ba_3rd_miwoks/coastalmiwoks/webpages/home.html (accessed on August 11, 2011).

"Culture: Coast Miwok Indians." *San Francisco State University.* http://www.sfsu.edu/~geog/bholzman/ptreyes/introclt.htm (accessed on August 11, 2011).

Edward S. Curtis's The North American Indian. Vol. 14. *Northwestern University Digial Library Collection.* http://curtis.library.northwestern.edu/curtis/toc.cgi (accessed on August 11, 2011).

Federated Indians of Graton Ranchería. http://www.gratonrancheria.com/ (accessed on August 11, 2011).

Ione Band of Miwok Indians. http://www.ionemiwok.org/ (accessed on August 11, 2011).

"Miwok." *Four Directions Institute.* http://www.fourdir.com/miwok.htm (accessed on August 11, 2011).

Miwok Archeological Preserve of Marin. "The Miwok People." *California State Parks.* http://www.parks.ca.gov/default.asp?page_id=22538 (accessed on August 11, 2011).

"Miwok Indian Tribe History." *Access Genealogy.* http://www.accessgenealogy.com/native/california/miwokindianhist.htm (accessed on August 11, 2011).

"Prospecting: Indian Gold Washing." *Oakland Museum of California.* http://www.museumca.org/goldrush/fever13-mi.html (accessed on August 11, 2011).

Redish, Laura, and Orrin Lewis. "Miwok Indian Language." *Native Languages of the Americas.* http://www.native-languages.org/miwok.htm (accessed on August 11, 2011).

Shingle Springs Ranchería. http://www.shinglespringsrancheria.com/ (accessed on August 11, 2011).

Pit River Indians

Name

The name Pit River Indians comes from the group's unique hunting technique, which involved digging pits along the river for deer to fall into. The tribe is made up of descendants of the Achumawi (pronounced *ah-CHOO-ma-wee*; also spelled "Achomawi") and Atsugewi (*at-SOO-gay-wee*). The name Achumawi comes from a word meaning "river." Atsugewi comes from *atsuke,* the Native name for a place along the Hat Creek; they were also called Hat Creek Indians.

Location

The Achumawi lived along the Pit River in northern California, in an area bounded by Mount Shasta to the northwest, Lassen Peak to the southwest, and the Warner range to the east. There were two Atsugewi groups: the Pine Tree People, who lived in the densely wooded area north of Mount Lassen; and the Juniper Tree People, who lived in the drier plains in and around Dixie Valley, northeast of Mount Lassen. Today, both groups live on several rancherías in northern California, often with members of other tribes. They also own 79 acres in the town of Burney, California, where their tribal headquarters is located.

Population

In the early 1800s, there were about 3,000 Achumawi and 900 Atsugewi. After the two groups had combined, the the 1990 census counted 1,753 people who identified themselves as Pit River Indians. The 2000 census showed 1,765 Pit River Indians; of those, 1,733 were from the Pit River Tribe of California.

Language family

Hokan.

Origins and group affiliations

The Achumawi lived in a collection of villages that were organized individually but maintained ties with one another. The Atsugewi tribe was made up of two distinct groups: the Pine Tree People and the Juniper Tree People, who

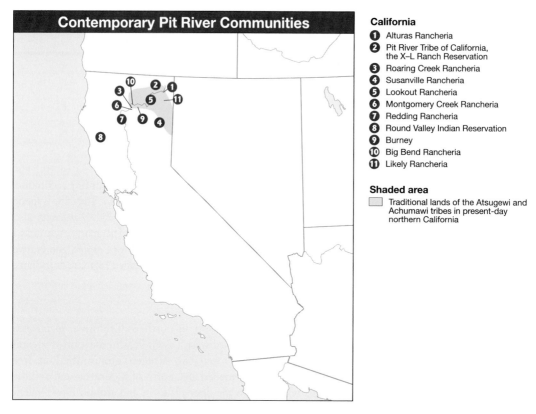

Contemporary Pit River Communities

California
1. Alturas Rancheria
2. Pit River Tribe of California, the X–L Ranch Reservation
3. Roaring Creek Rancheria
4. Susanville Rancheria
5. Lookout Rancheria
6. Montgomery Creek Rancheria
7. Redding Rancheria
8. Round Valley Indian Reservation
9. Burney
10. Big Bend Rancheria
11. Likely Rancheria

Shaded area
Traditional lands of the Atsugewi and Achumawi tribes in present-day northern California

A map of contemporary Pit River Indian communities. MAP BY XNR PRODUCTIONS. CENGAGE LEARNING, GALE. REPRODUCED BY PERMISSION OF GALE, A PART OF CENGAGE LEARNING.

shared a language. The Achumawi and the Atsugewi were on good terms and frequently renewed friendship ties through marriage. Both tribes fought with the Modoc, Paiute (see entries), and Klamath, who sent raiding parties into Pit River territory to enslave women and children. In the early twenty-first century, the eleven bands of Pit Indians share several of their rancherías with other tribes, including Yana, Maidu, Pomo (see entries), Paiute, Wintun, and others.

Although they inhabited a fairly small region, the Pit River Indians traveled every part of it, looking for food and visiting with neighbors. They rowed swiftly down California rivers in canoes they dug out of pine trees. They fished in those rivers and in countless lakes and streams. They hunted in high and low mountain regions, plains and valleys, swamps and marshes, and grasslands and meadows. Mountain groups often endured winters lasting six months. When one group fell on hard times, neighbors were always willing to help out. Today, the bands have united as one nation while living in separate communities.

HISTORY

Contact with Europeans

The Pit River Indians were a fairly peaceful people. They did not like to fight and usually did so only when provoked. When challenged, they sometimes sent a peacemaker to resolve issues with hostile tribes. The Modoc, Paiute (see entries), and Klamath made frequent invasions into their territory and captured and enslaved their women and children. Some historians think Pit River Indian slaves may have been handed over to the Spanish in the Southwest in the early or mid-1700s, marking their actual first encounters with Europeans.

American fur trappers entered the Pit River region in 1827, and soon after, the Native population was overcome by a malaria epidemic. More Native territory was taken after Mexico gave California to the United States in 1848 and after gold was discovered in 1850. Hundreds of settlers passed through on their way to the coast, followed by gold seekers. Relations were hostile, and conflicts erupted throughout the 1850s.

Edward S. Curtis, in *The North American Indian,* relates an eyewitness account of an encounter in the 1850s: "A band of white men from Red Bluff attacked the Fall River Achomawi in a camp at Beaver Creek and slaughtered the entire number except 30 or 40 men, who escaped.… About 160 were killed." In 1856, Atsugewi warriors attacked whites who had settled on their land. Three years later, an entire friendly Atsugewi group was killed by angry settlers, who mistakenly believed that their village was responsible for the murder of some whites in Hat Creek.

Outnumbered and weakened by death and diseases, the Natives were no match for the incoming hordes of U.S. settlers. By 1860, the surviving Atsugewi and Achumawi were removed to Round Valley Reservation in Mendocino County, where members of several other California tribes were already confined.

An American fur trapper explores the frontier. White trappers arrived in the Pit River region in 1827, bringing malaria with them. © MARY EVANS PICTURE LIBRARY/THE IMAGE WORKS.

Important Dates

1833: Malaria epidemic kills many Pit River Indians.

1848: Gold is discovered in California; Pit River lands are overrun by gold miners.

1859: An entire Atsugewi tribe is killed by settlers over a misunderstanding.

1860s: The Pit River Indians are forced to move to the Round Valley Reservation; most eventually leave.

1915–38: The U.S. government establishes seven rancherías for Pit River Indians.

1976: The Pit River Tribe is granted federal recognition.

1987: The tribal constitution is accepted by the federal government.

Allotments and rancherías

The government expected Native peoples on the reservation to give up their culture and become more like mainstream American society. It was not long before Pit River Indians became disenchanted with life on the reservation and made their way back to their homeland. Once there, they made do as best they could until the General Allotment Act of 1887 (also known as the Dawes Act) was passed. This act divided former tribal lands into small parcels, which were given to individual Natives to farm. Most of these parcels were not suitable for farming, and when the Pacific Gas and Electric Company offered to buy them between 1917 and 1930, many Pit River Indians sold their allotments.

Between 1915 and 1938, the U.S. government purchased seven small plots of land for the still-homeless Pit River Indians. These plots were called rancherías, a Spanish term for a small ranch. Like allotments, ranchería land was mostly unsuitable for farming. The largest of the rancherías, the X-L Ranch Reservation, consists of 9,255 acres of cattle-grazing land and is now the home base of about forty members of the Pit River Tribe.

Land claims

Beginning in 1919, the Pit River Indians took part in several lawsuits over land that was taken from them illegally. In 1963, the U.S. government and all the California Indians reached a settlement in which the Native nations agreed to share $29 million, which amounted to about $.47 an acre. The Pit River Indians rejected the settlement. The U.S. Bureau of Indian Affairs then sent a letter to all members of the tribe asking for their votes. Based on the responses they received, the Bureau said the tribe had accepted the settlement. Some tribal representatives said that those who voted in favor did not fully understand the issues. The settlement went through, but members of the tribe disagreed bitterly among themselves over the matter.

Some of the most unhappy members of the tribe joined in Native protest actions during the 1960s. Protestors complained about the unjust taking of their lands and about too much government interference in tribal affairs, among other grievances. These protests sparked a movement among Pit River Indians, who were then scattered throughout northern California. They joined together for a common goal—recognition by the U.S. government as the Pit River Tribe. Federal recognition was granted in 1976, establishing an official relationship between the tribe and the government. Recognition entitles the tribe to certain rights and privileges not received by unrecognized tribes.

In the early twenty-first century, the Pit River Tribe is made up of eleven bands who live in separate areas along the Pit River and its tributaries. The Pit River Indians are an extremely private people who are unwilling to reveal details of their history or their present way of life. They have retained many elements of their ancient culture, despite having their lives disrupted many times.

How the Pit River Indians Got Their Name

The name Pit River Indians comes from the tribe's unique hunting technique. The people dug pits 10 to 12 feet (2 to 4 meters) deep along river banks for trapping game. Brushwood and grass concealed these holes, and deer fell into them as they came to the water to drink. Later, settlers forced the Natives to abandon this hunting practice because many of their cattle and horses stumbled into the traps.

RELIGION

Achumawi beliefs

Jaime de Angulo (1887–1950), an author and linguist (person who studies languages), quoted an Achumawiman's description of the tribe's religious beliefs in an article titled "Achumawi Sketches": "All things have life in them. Trees have life, rocks have life, mountains, water, all these are full of life. You think a rock is something dead. Not at all. It is full of life."

In "The Achumawi Life Force," Angulo discussed the Achumawi belief that every person has a good soul-shadow. An Achumawi shaman (pronounced *SHAH-mun* or *SHAY-mun*; a religious leader and doctor) by the name of Son-of-Eagle said of the soul-shadow: "You can hear it sometimes in the morning, just before you wake up. It comes from over the mountains. It comes from the East. It comes singing: 'Dawn is rising. I come. I come. Dawn is rising. I come. I come.'" The people believed that if a person was unfortunate or angry, the soul-shadow could leave. People whose soul-shadows are gone may appear to be alive, but they are really half dead.

Achumawi Words

yalyú	"man"
amitéučan	"woman"
čahómaka	"dog"
čol	"sun or moon"
as	"water"
hookíči	"black"
taktakí	"red"
makmakí	"yellow"
tíwičí	"white"

The Achumawi believed in two creators who laid down codes for the people to live by. These codes covered every aspect of life, including hunting, cooking, marriage, and moral conduct.

Atsugewi beliefs

The Atsugewi religion revolves around a large group of nature spirits, who appear as people, animals, rocks, or trees. Shamans can communicate with these spirits, who live in special caves and sacred bathing areas. Old Man Spirit, for instance, lives in a cave near Lost Creek. Guardian spirits guide people during their lifetime. They can bring a person good fortune and are often called upon in times of need. Bad fortune or sickness is blamed on unhappy guardian spirits. Information on these spirits is scant, because mentioning the name of a guardian spirit is forbidden.

Some Pit River Indians were drawn to the Ghost Dance religion of 1890. The Ghost Dance was a movement started by a prophet named Wovoka (c. 1856–1932), a member of the Paiute tribe (see entry). The Ghost Dance was a circle dance during which performers often went into trances and "visited" dead friends and relatives. The Atsugewi built a dance house in 1892 to accommodate their Ghost Dancers.

By the 1920s, some had adopted the Indian Mission Church, which combined elements of Christianity and traditional Native beliefs. Other Pit River Indians have converted to Christianity. Although the Christian churches have active members, the people continue to hold traditional beliefs.

LANGUAGE

Until a report on the languages of the Achumawi and Atsugewi was published in 1905, the two groups were commonly confused as one tribe. The distinction between the two languages showed that the Achumawi and Atsugewi were two separate bands.

A few people in the Pit River region spoke Achumawi in 1966, and according to the 1990 U.S. Census, eighty-one people still spoke Achumawi at home. Thirty of those Achumawi speakers were under seventeen years of age, which meant that the Achumawi were maintaining the language by teaching it to youngsters. In 2000, only eight people were considered fluent speakers. Meanwhile, the Atsugewi language fell out of use. According to the 1990 census, no families spoke Atsugewi at home. As of 2011, no Achumawi first-language speakers remained.

GOVERNMENT

Achumawi and Atsugewi villages were independent, each led by a chief whose position was handed down to his son (either the eldest or the most popular). Atsugewi villages were often grouped into clusters presided over by a headman, who was usually a wealthy man and an excellent hunter.

The chief did not have to be wealthy, but he had to be wise and a hard worker. He did not rule by force but by persuading others of the rightness of his decisions. A chief set an example to his villagers, encouraging them to work hard and be alert to outside dangers. He acted as an adviser, gave instructions on when to hunt, and settled disputes.

When the U.S. government got involved in tribal affairs in the second half of the 1800s, many Pit River Indians complained about government interference. The Indian Reorganization Act of 1934 offered some freedom from federal intervention if tribes agreed to adopt a constitution like that of the United States. The Pit River Indians' constitution was finally accepted in 1987. It set up a tribal council with eleven members, each representing a Pit River group. Members started working together to unify a community whose people are widely scattered and have strong and differing opinions on tribal issues. Many of the rancherías also have elected tribal or business councils.

ECONOMY

The Pit River Indian economy was based on acorns, plants, fish, and other river products. The Atsugewi traded with their neighbors, but they called it a gift exchange. A person who received a gift had to return a gift. The Atsugewi traded their twined baskets for Achumawi baskets and hats and exchanged more baskets, plus hunting bows and furs, for Maidu (see entry) skins, beads, and coiled baskets. The Yana (see entry) and Achumawi shared their acorn harvest with the Atsugewi when the crop was poor. In return, the Atsugewi permitted the use of their lands for gathering root crops. The Achumawi also granted the Atsugewi use of their fishing grounds in return for access to Atsugewi root-digging areas.

Wealth was measured in terms of how many practical goods a person owned. Important property included pine canoes, furs, buckskins, cooking utensils, and fishing nets.

After settlers took over California lands, many Pit River Indians worked for them on ranches and in sawmills. Some continued to gather plants in familiar territory as they always had. In the twentieth century, the logging industry declined in their territory, and many sought logging work elsewhere in California. Others did seasonal work away from their homeland, picking fruits and vegetables, for example.

By the early twenty-first century, most tribal income was generated through gaming. Off-reservation tourism and recreation also brings in money. Most people continue to work in agriculture or forestry; a large number also work for the federal and state government.

DAILY LIFE

Families

Families consisted of a father, mother, their children, and a few relatives. Three or more families lived together in one home. The people had a great affection for children and considered them very valuable. Childless women felt shame and might consult a doctor about this problem.

Education

The Atsugewi believed strongly that hard work was the way to succeed. They arose at dawn, often to the sound of their chief urging them to get up and do something for a living. A person who rarely slept was highly regarded and received the respected nickname *Nohalal,* meaning "Going all the time."

Children were encouraged to be hard workers; they started working from the age of eight or nine under the guidance of their parents. Young girls learned that idle chatter was not permitted while doing the important work of gathering food, yet it was important to know just how much work was enough. Those who worked too hard were not considered intelligent, because lazy people often reaped the fruits of their labor.

Children also received moral training. They were taught to display modesty in the presence of the opposite sex and to refrain from lying, fighting, and disobedience, lest they be punished by a beating with a coyote's tail.

In the late 1800s, Christian missionaries and the Bureau of Indian Affairs set up religious and boarding schools for Pit River children. Since the 1930s, children have attended local public schools. At the Round Valley Reservation, children can attend the Eel River Charter School. The tribe also operates the Round Valley Educational Center, which offers support for student achievement.

Buildings

The Atsugewi lived in two types of homes: sturdy winter structures or brush huts set up near hunting and gathering areas during the summer. Their oval-shaped winter homes were dug about 3 feet (1 meter) into the ground. Split logs and bark covered the wooden frame, which the people overlaid with earth and grass. They placed a ladder next to the central post opening, which served as both an entrance and smoke hole. The interior was very simple. A thin layer of grass covered the floor, and mats made of tule (pronounced *TOO-lee*; a type of cattail) hung from the dirt walls. The Atsugewi had no furniture, and they rolled up their bedding and put aside during the daytime. These dwellings varied in size from less than 12 feet (4 meters) in length to as long as 20 feet (6 meters).

Most Achumawi villages lined the banks of the Pit River, which at 2,000 feet (610 meters) above sea level was the warmest section of their territory. During the summer, the people lived in tepees covered with tule mats. Winter homes, cone-shaped and partially underground, housed several families and measured about 15 square feet (5 square meters). The Achumawi used trees that had been felled by nature to make the support beams. A smoke-hole in the center of the roof also served as entrance and exit by way of a ladder strapped to the central post. Tule mats and skins for bedding furnished the interior. Several larger buildings—up to 20 feet by 30 feet (6 to 9 meters)—served as ceremonial houses.

Clothing and adornment

Atsugewi During the summer, Atsugewi women wore shredded cedar bark or fringed buckskin aprons that covered them in front and back. Wealthier women decorated their aprons with pine nuts or bones. Basket-like caps covered their heads. Men usually wore a white coyote-skin apron that hung down to their knees; behind this hung a second apron, with the coyote's tail still attached. During the winter, they wore fur or skin cloaks, leggings, mittens, hats, and waterproof moccasins. Wealthier people adopted the buckskin shirts more typical of the Great Basin and Plains tribes.

Men and women both grew their hair long. Men rolled their hair up into a hair net, whereas women wore pigtails wrapped in strips of mink, deerskin, or grass. Men and women groomed their hair with porcupine-tail brushes and kept their hair shiny and supple by applying deer marrow. The Atsugewi painted their bodies red, blue, and white. Girls had their chins tattooed in vertical lines. On special occasions, tribal members wore strings of beads and shells; the chief wore eagle feathers, but others wore magpie feathers.

Achumawi Achumawi clothing showed influences from east of the Rocky Mountains and the Pacific Coast. Women usually wore a fringed deerskin, shredded tule, or juniper bark apron, along with a basket-like cap. On important ceremonial occasions they wore long fringed and beaded dresses, often decorated with porcupine-quill embroidery or hummingbird feathers. To protect themselves in winter, women wore capes, moccasins, and deerskin leggings. They often dyed their clothes with minerals and plants that produced yellows, reds, blues, blacks, and whites. Achumawi women painted their faces with a mixture of grease and a red mineral. They wore braids or coiled their hair on top of their heads and tattooed their chins with three lines.

Men wore deerskin shirts and robes, leggings, and moccasins. They used badger skins for smaller garments, such as caps and capes, and they painted their faces red on special occasions. Shells hung from their pierced noses, but unlike the women, they were not tattooed.

Food

Men's work Fish and acorns were the staple foods of the tribe. Salmon was probably the most important fish, but trout was also caught. Groups who had access to salmon or acorns often invited those who did not to share in their bounty. Men were responsible for hunting and cooking meat and for fishing, although in some groups women and children drove fish into nets held by men. The bands employed a number of methods for catching fish, such as drugging them with wild parsley or hanging gill nets vertically in the water in order to trap the fish as they attempted to swim through. At night, men fished from pine or cedar canoes, attracting the fish with torches and then spearing them. This fishing method is still practiced.

The men hunted deer, antelope, elk, rabbits, badgers, and wood rats. Meat that the people did not eat fresh was dried and partially smoked for preservation and winter storage. Ducks, cranes, grebe, pelicans, coot, geese, swans, mudhens, grouse, meadowlarks, robins, and blackbirds all provided food for the bands. Men trapped waterfowl in nets placed across rivers and swamps; once caught, fowl were clubbed to death. Some groups would not eat mink, grey fox, coyote, eagle, buzzard, magpie, or crow, possibly for religious reasons.

Women's work The Atsugewi considered women more valuable than men because tribal survival during winter depended on the women's ability to gather sufficient supplies for storage. Women pounded acorns into flour and processed them with hot water to remove their bitterness. Other foods gathered by women included various roots, pine nuts, tiger lilies, wild onions, manzanita berries, gooseberries, huckleberries, and sunflower seeds.

Women usually boiled food in baskets, roasted it on hot stones, or baked it. The Achumawi did not add salt to their food because they believed it caused sore eyes. They occasionally burned large areas of grass to flush out grasshoppers, which they collected and stored until winter. Grasshoppers and the larvae of yellow jackets were considered delicacies. The only plant the people grew was tobacco.

Healing practices

The Pit River Indians believed illnesses were caused by the departure of one's soul, by bad blood, or by evil spirits sent by enemy tribes. Shamans, who had contact with healing spirits, were called upon to cure the afflicted one. The bands had three kinds of shamans: the sucking shaman, who sucked out the object that caused the disease; the singing doctor, who cured by singing to call the healing spirits; and the bear doctor. Bear doctors were men or women who could either cure or harm. Some groups believed the bear doctor could put on a grizzly bear skin and head and actually "become" a bear (see Pomo entry). This type of doctor was both respected and feared.

Village elders decided who would become a shaman-doctor. Few people wanted the job because it could be dangerous. If the shaman did not catch a disease as it left the body, it could escape and cause epidemics

An Encounter with the Tamcìye

Storytelling was usually meant for entertainment rather than to teach lessons, but children did hear stories of evil spirits who punished disobedience. Dwarfs, called *tamcìye*, were friendly spirits who often turned up in stories and lived like people did. The tamcìye brought men strength and luck. The following story describes a man's encounter with the tamcìye.

> One spring a lazy man went to the bench near Lost Creek to get pine nuts. Here he met two tamcìye women who asked him what he was doing. They said, "We don't eat that kind of food. You better go back with us." They took him to their house on the west side of Bald Mountain, where there was an earth lodge. He saw all the tamcìye people. The men were out hunting deer or fishing. In the evening they returned. The lazy man stayed with the tamcìye for a while, and they treated him with much hospitality. When he wanted to return home, the two tamcìye women made ready to go with him as his wives. He was given a buckskin shirt, pants, a bow and arrow, and other things. Before this he had been naked. The two women loaded themselves with dry meat and other things, and the three started to his home. But before they reached his home he made an excuse to go into the bushes, saying that he wanted to urinate, and as soon as he was out of sight he started running. He wanted to leave the women. They saw him running and were angry. They took back all the clothes and beads they had given him, so that he had nothing on when he arrived home. The man told his family what had happened. They were very angry with him for running away from the two women. He was a fool. If he had brought them back he would have made a good living.

SOURCE: Garth, Thomas R. "Atsugewi Ethnography." *Anthropological Records* 14, no. 2 (1953): 129–212.

(uncontrolled outbreaks of disease). To keep this from happening, a shaman who failed once too often to cure his or her patients was sometimes killed by a shaman from a neighboring tribe; the disease was then thought to die with the shaman.

Herbs and plants were also used for healing. For example, wild parsley was a remedy for colds, coughs, and stomach aches. Snakes were warded off by rubbing one's legs with chewed angelica roots.

Long after the disruption of their society by settlers, the Pit River Indians continued to rely on their traditional ways of healing. Even if they desired the services of modern medical doctors, they were often unable to secure them because they lived in remote areas. This is changing slowly. The tribe now has some medical clinics to serve its needs, but more are needed to serve people in outlying areas.

CUSTOMS

Courtship and marriage

The hardest-working woman was the most-prized bride. If she came from a wealthy family, so much the better—she was considered more valuable than a man. Once the bride's parents checked on the good reputation of the groom's family, who did some checking of their own, the families exchanged presents, and the wedding took place. Often, the wedding ceremony simply consisted of the groom spending the night with his bride.

A man could divorce a lazy wife by returning her to her family. If he could afford the wedding gifts, he might try out several brides before settling on one. If one partner died, his or her family "owned" the survivor, who had to marry another member of the same family.

Pregnancy and childbirth

Some pregnant women returned to the parents' home to give birth. Mothers assisted in the birthing and often offered a drink made from oak bark to prevent blood poisoning. The grandmother made the baby's first cradle.

Puberty

Although the people were usually too busy to engage in ceremonies, an exception was made for the beginning of puberty. The practice varied from group to group, but a girl's ritual was often similar to this: When her first period began, her father sent her into the hills, asking the spirits to aid her. At midnight on the first day, she began to dance. For the next four or five days, she continued to dance, stopping only to dig for roots if it was summertime or to collect firewood in winter. She got little or no sleep. The more energy she displayed, the better a worker she was believed to become. The ceremony ended with the piercing of the girl's ears or nose, which meant she was at last a woman.

When a boy's voice broke, he went on a power quest. His father or a respected village elder lectured him about his conduct and whipped him with a coyote's tail or a bow string before sending him into the mountains for two or three days. The boy fasted, lit fires, and sometimes cut his arms or legs with a sharp object. If the boy reported hearing a fawn call, the people believed he had a future of good hunting ahead of him. If he heard a groan, it was a sign that he should become a shaman.

Funerals

The dead were either buried or burned without much ceremony, together with clothing, personal valuables, and a basket of water. Women mourners shaved their heads and covered them with soot or a sticky liquid. The dead were feared, and it was forbidden to speak their names, because they might return looking for a traveling companion on their journey through the western mountains. When an important tribal member died, the people often burned his house along with two or three unpopular people who would become his traveling companions in the afterlife.

War and hunting rituals

In some groups, before warriors departed for battle, they carried out a mock fight against the women of the village, screaming and pretending to go after them with drawn bows. After the warriors left, the women danced war dances. Upon the warriors' return, women anointed them with roots and tea. Warriors sometimes cremated their fallen comrades in the battlefield and brought the ashes back to the village.

A skilled hunter was greatly respected, especially a man who killed grizzly bears, because he was thought to receive the bear's powers. A man who returned from a hunt empty handed, however, was ridiculed. Of all the animals hunted by the tribe, deer were the most prized. Sometimes, a chief summoned a group of men to a communal deer hunt by sending around a message consisting of knots on a piece of string, the number of knots indicating how many days until the hunt.

The night before the hunt, the men gathered in the sweathouse, where they drew up a hunting scheme. They sometimes charmed deer and antelope with singing. Other times they wore a deer-head disguise to get close to the animals.

Festivals and ceremonies

The Atsugewi people worked so hard that ceremonies were a rare luxury. At regular intervals, though, village chiefs ordered a day of rest; men gambled and women cooked. The Pit River Indians sometimes attended Maidu ceremonies if they happened to be passing Maidu villages at the right time.

CURRENT TRIBAL ISSUES

The Pit River Indians continue to gather plants for eating and healing. Other tribal issues remain private according to the wishes of the tribal council. A tribal representative once explained that many historical accounts about the tribe are inaccurate; however, she was unwilling to identify them.

As with many other Native nations, the Pit River Indians need to fight to protect sacred ground or ancient burial sites. In 2011, they passed a resolution to protect Sogorea Te, also known as the Glen Cove Shellmound Burial, as a sacred site. They camped out at the Glen Cove site to prevent construction on this ancient burial ground.

In spite of casinos bringing additional funds to many bands, unemployment and poverty remains high on many reservations or rancherías. The Pit River Indians are no exception. One concern is adequate housing and water supplies for their people. Statistics released in 2010 showed that less than half the Pit River people had access to acceptable water and sewage systems. Close to half could not afford crucial medical prescriptions. Although casinos and other business enterprises have funded some social service projects, many others still need to be attended to.

NOTABLE PEOPLE

Darryl "Babe" Wilson (1939–), the son of an Achumawi father and an Atsugewi mother, is a member of the Pit River tribe. He has worked to preserve the oral traditions of all Native people and has written essays, short stories, and poetry. His book *Wilma Mankiller: Principal Chief of the Cherokee Nation* was published in 1995.

BOOKS

Curtain, Jeremiah, and Roland B. Dixon, eds. *Achomawi and Atsugewi Myths and Tales.* Reprint. Sandhurst, UK: Abela Publishing, 2009.

Curtis, Edward S. *The North American Indian.* Vol.13. 1924. Reprint. New York: Johnson Reprint Corporation, 1970. Available online from *Northwestern University Digital Library Collections.* http://curtis.library. northwestern.edu/curtis/viewPage.cgi?showp=1&size=2&id=nai.13. book.00000192&volume=13#nav-Edward (accessed on August 11, 2011).

De Angulo, Jaime. *Indian Tales.* Santa Clara, CA: Heyday Books, 2003.

Dixon, Roland Burrage. *Achomawi and Atsugewi Tales.* Reprint. Charleston, SC: BiblioBazaar, 2009.

Du Bois, Cora. *The 1870 Ghost Dance.* Lincoln: University of Nebraska Press, 2007.

Margolin, Malcolm. *The Way We Lived: California Indian Stories, Songs, and Reminiscences.* Reprint. Heyday Books, Berkeley, California, 2001.

Wilson, Darryl J. *The Morning the Sun Went Down.* Berkeley, CA: Heyday, 1998.

Wilson, Darryl J. *Songoochaeba.* New York: BookSurge Publishing, 2006.

Woiche, Istet, and C. Hart Merriam. *Annikadel: The History of the Universe as Told by the Achumawi Indians of California.* 2nd ed. Tucson: University of Arizona Press, 1992.

PERIODICALS

De Angulo, Jaime. "The Achumawi Life Force." *The Journal of California Anthopology* 2, no. 1 (1975).

De Angulo, Jaime. "Achumawi Sketches." *Journal of California Anthropology* 1, no. 1 (1974).

Dixon, Roland B. "The Mythology of the Shasta-Achomawi." *American Anthropologist* 7. (1905): 607–12.

Dixon, Roland B. "Achomawi and Atsugewi Tales." *Journal of American Folklore* 21. (1908): 159–77.

WEB SITES

"The Achumawi." *Far Western Anthropological Research Group.* http://www.farwestern.com/crookscanyon/page05.htm (accessed on August 11, 2011).

"Achomawi." *Four Directions Institute.* http://www.fourdir.com/achomawi.htm (accessed on August 11, 2011).

"Achomawi Indian Tribe History." *Access Genealogy.* http://www.accessgenealogy.com/native/tribes/shastanfamily/achomawi.htm (accessed on August 11, 2011).

"Constitution of the Pit River Tribe." *Native American Rights Fund.* http://www.narf.org/nill/Constitutions/pitconst/pitriverconsttoc.htm (accessed on August 11, 2011).

"Native Americans: Achumawi." *College of the Siskiyous.* http://www.siskiyous.edu/shasta/nat/ach.htm (accessed on August 11, 2011).

"Pit River/Hat Creek Baskets." *California Baskets.* http://www.californiabaskets.com/pages/pitriverhatcreekhome.html (accessed on August 11, 2011).

Pit River Indian Tribe. http://www.pitrivertribe.org/home.php (accessed on August 11, 2011).

Redish, Laura, and Orrin Lewis. "Achumawi Language (Achomawi, Pit River Indians)." *Native Languages of the Americas.* http://www.native-languages.org/achumawi.htm (accessed on August 11, 2011).

"Shasta Indian Tribe History." *Access Genealogy.* http://www.accessgenealogy.com/native/tribes/shastan/shastaindiantribe.htm (accessed on August 11, 2011).

Susanville Indian Ranchería. http://sir-nsn.gov/ (accessed on August 11, 2011).

Pomo

Name

Pomo (pronounced *PO-mo*) means "at red earth hole" or "those who live at red earth hole." The name most likely refers to magnesite (pronounced *MAG-nuh-site*), called *po* by all the tribes, a mineral used to make red beads, or to the red clay mined in that area, often mixed with acorn flour to flavor and color bread.

Location

The Pomo lived in northern California along the Pacific Coast and some distance inland, near Clear Lake and the Russian River in present-day Mendocino, Sonoma, and Lake Counties. In modern times, they live on or near about two dozen mostly tiny, isolated rancherías and reservations located throughout their homeland.

Population

In the early 1800s, there were between 13,000 and 20,000 Pomo. In the 1990 U.S. Census, 4,766 people identified themselves as Pomo. The 2000 census showed 5,092 Pomo, and 8,011 people claimed to have some Pomo heritage.

Language family

Hokan.

Origins and group affiliations

The Pomo have lived in the hills and valleys north of present-day San Francisco for more than ten thousand years. Historians believe that early Pomo lived around the shores of Clear Lake, but a western branch split off from the rest, settling along the Russian River and near the Pacific Coast. There were more than seventy Pomo tribes divided into seven groups: Northern Pomo, Central Pomo, Southern Pomo, Southwestern Pomo or Kashaya, Eastern Pomo, Southeastern Pomo, and Northeastern Pomo.

For thousands of years, the Pomo lived calm, well-ordered lives filled with laughter and song. Their story after contact with Europeans

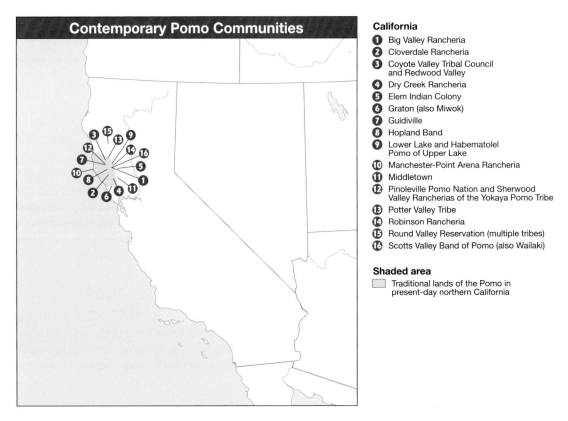

Contemporary Pomo Communities

California
1. Big Valley Rancheria
2. Cloverdale Rancheria
3. Coyote Valley Tribal Council and Redwood Valley
4. Dry Creek Rancheria
5. Elem Indian Colony
6. Graton (also Miwok)
7. Guidiville
8. Hopland Band
9. Lower Lake and Habematolel Pomo of Upper Lake
10. Manchester-Point Arena Rancheria
11. Middletown
12. Pinoleville Pomo Nation and Sherwood Valley Rancherias of the Yokaya Pomo Tribe
13. Potter Valley Tribe
14. Robinson Rancheria
15. Round Valley Reservation (multiple tribes)
16. Scotts Valley Band of Pomo (also Wailaki)

Shaded area
  Traditional lands of the Pomo in present-day northern California

A map of contemporary Pomo communities. MAP BY XNR PRODUCTIONS. CENGAGE LEARNING, GALE. REPRODUCED BY PERMISSION OF GALE, A PART OF CENGAGE LEARNING.

is a tragic one. They suffered brutality at the hands of Russians, Spanish, Mexicans, and Americans, who polluted their lands, enslaved them, and slaughtered innocent men, women, and children. By the late nineteenth century, only one thousand or so Pomo remained, homeless on their own former lands. The tribe regained some Pomo land in the twentieth century, and their population began to grow.

HISTORY

Russians in Kashaya Pomo territory

Little information is available about Pomo history and ways of life before the arrival of white settlers in the nineteenth century. The Pomo may have had a brief encounter with British explorer Francis Drake (1540–1596) after his 1579 landing in Coastal Miwok territory (see entry) to the south of the Pomo. If there was such an encounter, it was not recorded.

Groups of Pomo were spread out over a large territory, so they did not all encounter the same nationalities of outsiders. Each incoming group—first Russians, then Spanish, then Mexicans, and finally U.S. citizens—played a part in the near-destruction of this large and important California tribe.

The Kashaya Pomo lived along the Pacific Coast in present-day northwestern Sonoma County. They were the only Pomo group to encounter the Russians, who established Fort Ross in 1811 on Bodega Bay. The Russians took advantage of the big profits to be made from sea otter furs, but they also kidnapped and enslaved Pomo women and children and used them as hostages to force Pomo men to hand over furs and food.

Like the Tlingit tribe (see entry) to the north, the Pomo resisted the Russian invaders, but the resistance mostly consisted of a few escapes and small-scale attacks on individuals. By the time the Russians left in 1842, many of the Kashaya Pomo had died from murder, overwork, or diseases brought by Europeans.

Important Dates

1811: The Russians establish Fort Ross in Kashaya Pomo territory.

1817: The first Spanish mission is founded on Pomo land.

1850: The U.S. Army massacres most residents of a small Pomo village.

1856: Many Pomo move to the Mendocino and Round Valley Reservations.

1881: Pomo chiefs organize a fund-raising drive to buy rancherías.

1958: The state of California terminates the status of many Native American tribes, including the Pomo rancherías.

1983: Tillie Hardwick wins her case, and federal reservation status is restored to seventeen California rancherías.

Spanish and Mexicans exploit Southern Pomo

Meanwhile, the Spanish, who claimed California as their own, feared its takeover by the Russians or British and established forts and missions there. The forts protected the Spanish settlements in California, and the missions tried to convert California Natives to the Roman Catholic religion and teach them skills so they could become slaves or laborers for the Spanish settlers.

The Southern Pomo came under the control of Spanish missionaries when a mission was built at San Rafael by 1817. About six hundred Pomo people were baptized at San Rafael Mission and at San Francisco de Solano Mission.

In 1822, California became part of the Mexican Republic, and the missions were closed. Mexicans took over Pomo lands, resulting in skirmishes between the new ranchers and the Pomo people. This was especially true in the Clear Lake region. One Mexican landowner, Salvador Vallejo, tried to force a group of Eastern Pomo to harvest his crops. When they refused, he sent Mexican troops after them, and the soldiers massacred some of the men, who were sitting peacefully in their sweathouse. Thousands of Pomo were captured or died between 1834 and 1847 at the hands of Mexican soldiers. Trade in Native slaves along with epidemics of smallpox and cholera claimed thousands more lives.

Pomo mistreated by American settlers

The United States won California from Mexico in 1848, and California became a state in 1850. American settlers immediately poured in and seized Native lands. They soon reached Pomo groups who had previously had little contact with outsiders: the Northern Pomo, Northeastern Pomo, and Central Pomo. Hostile relations flared between these new settlers and the Pomo people, just as they had with the Mexican settlers.

Matters came to a head after two white landowners, Andrew Kelsey and Charles Stone, were killed. For three years, the pair had been forcing hundreds of Pomo to work on their ranch, even though slavery was by then illegal in California. Tired of being starved, beaten, and even shot, some Pomo slaves rebelled, killed both of their tormentors, and fled into the hills.

U.S. Army soldiers sent to capture those responsible for the killings came upon a peaceful group of Eastern Pomo gathered on a small island on Clear Lake. They slaughtered innocent men, women, and children at the site, which was later renamed Bloody Island by the Pomo. The soldiers continued eastward, killing as they went, though their victims had nothing to do with the murders of Kelsey and Stone.

Pomo forced onto reservations

In 1851, hoping to end the violence taking place throughout California, the U.S. government sent agents to discuss treaties with Native nations. In these treaties, California tribes, including the Pomo, agreed to give up most of their lands to the U.S. government in exchange for a total of about 7.5 million acres that would be set aside for reservations.

California citizens were horrified that so much land was being given away (about 8 percent of the state). They were also afraid that the Native peoples they had been using as slave labor would disappear onto reservations. They pressured the U.S. Senate to reject the treaties. In the end, only 1.2 million acres were set aside for reservations.

The Pomo people were rounded up and forced to move to the Mendocino and Round Valley Reservations, along with Native peoples from several other tribes. Settlers immediately took over Pomo lands. Ten years later, in 1867, the Mendocino Reservation was abruptly closed, and many of the remaining Pomo were left homeless. Some returned to the area of their homeland, only to find the best land had been taken over by American settlers. The Pomo ended up on poor, unwanted pieces of land in the region. Their population continued to decline as people died from diseases. At the same time, their traditions and beliefs began to disappear.

By the turn of the century, the remaining Pomo, numbering little more than one thousand, lived a poverty-stricken existence. They survived on fish, game, plants, and the few items they could afford to buy in stores. California citizens treated the Pomo as second-class citizens or worse, discriminated against them, and kept them apart from the rest of society.

Landowners again

Native groups began to rally, however, and they united to buy pieces of their former land. The Pomo pooled the meager sums they earned by working on non-Native-owned ranches and the money earned by selling their beautiful feathered baskets. They bought the rancherías of Pinoleville and Yokaya. (Ranchería is a Spanish term for a small ranch.)

Religious groups and some government officials became involved in the ranchería movement, and the Indian Reorganization Act of 1934, which was partly designed to counteract the damage done by previous Indian policies, supplied funds to buy more reservations and rancherías. The Pomo bought additional land. They also became skilled at using the American justice system to their advantage. In 1907, an Eastern Pomo named Ethan Anderson won a lawsuit that gave non-reservation Native people the right to vote. Legal actions by the Pomo and other Native groups resulted in all Native peoples being granted full U.S. citizenship in 1924.

Termination

New federal government policies in the 1950s resulted in a change of status for California rancherías, including many Pomo settlements. If the rancherías agreed to terminate their special relationship with the federal government (a relationship called federal recognition), they were promised help from the Bureau of Indian Affairs (BIA) in improving life on the rancherías. These promises of help never materialized. Instead, Pomo land was divided among members of the rancherías, and many of the owners later lost their property because they could not make mortgage or tax payments.

Pomo activists

In 1979, when it became obvious that the BIA was not going to fulfill its promises, a Pomo woman named Tillie Hardwick filed a class action lawsuit against the United States of America on behalf of thirty-four illegally terminated rancherías. She finally won in 1983, and several rancherías were successful in regaining federal recognition. (Federal recognition means the tribes and groups have a special legal relationship with the U.S. government as sovereign, or self-governing, nations. The relationship entitles them to certain benefits and financial assistance.) During the 1980s and 1990s, the members of the remaining Pomo rancherías fought to regain their status. By the turn of twenty-first century, all Pomo reservations and rancherías were once again federally recognized.

Many Pomo activists brought attention to the plight of the Native peoples during the 1970s and 1980s. By taking over unoccupied public buildings and making demands, they received publicity as they fought for many of the rights they had long been denied. Although many of these takeovers ended in arrests, others were successful. A Central Intelligence Agency base, vacant for more than a decade, was eventually transferred to the tribe. It is now the home of Ya-Ka-Ama, meaning "Our Land" in Pomo, an American Indian Learning Center. This is one of the many ways the Pomo are working to keep their culture, language, and traditional arts alive. At the same time, they continue to explore ways to work within the American system to expand their land base and to find ways to earn money from the tourists who flock to their beautiful homeland.

RELIGION

The Pomo believed in many spirits, including a creator-hero who gave his name to the secret religious society called Kuksu. The Kuksu Society was open only to a small group of men who were selected as children to go through a long training process. Once they became members, they were responsible for carrying out many of the village's ceremonies and public affairs. At ceremonies, Kuksu dancers pretended to be spirits and wore special headpieces made of sticks with feathers at the ends. They generally painted their bodies black. The dance rituals ensured good luck, such as abundant acorn and fruit harvests or protection against natural disaster and enemy attack.

A lesser religious society called the Ghost Society was open to all young men and, in some Pomo groups, to women too. The Ghost Society performed dances like those of the Kuksu to honor the dead. Both the Ghost and the Kuksu societies were led by professional spiritual guides, or shamans (pronounced *SHAH-munz* or *SHAY-munz*).

Ghost dances and dream dances

After their society was disrupted by the forced move to reservations, the Pomo adopted the Ghost Dance religion of 1870. (For more information, see Maidu entry.) When that religion failed to deliver on its promise to rid the world of white people, the Bole-Maru, or New Ghost Dance religion was adopted.

Bole-Maru translates roughly as "spirits of the dead." The Bole-Maru religion combined elements of the old Ghost Society and the Ghost Dance religion. Its leaders were people who had received visions in dreams; some of those visions included songs and dances, which they then taught to men and women of the tribe. The religion stressed moral behavior as well as belief in an afterlife and a supreme being. It opposed drinking, fighting, and stealing. The religion inspired hope in a desperate people, enough hope that the Pomo began to buy land of their own where they could preserve their culture (see "History"). They still practice the Bole-Maru religion.

LANGUAGE

There were originally seven Pomo languages; three remained in use in the early twenty-first century. The 1990 U.S. Census reported that 112 Pomo spoke their language in the home. By the early 2000s, only two or three people still spoke the Southern Pomo dialect, but not fluently. Statistics published in 2010 indicated that several dozen people spoke Kashaya,

Pomo Words

Although the seven Pomo languages were related and occasionally used identical or similar words, they were not enough alike that speakers of each language could understand each other. Interestingly enough, one word all the tribes shared in common was *po,* the name they used for the red mineral magnesite.

Pomo Words

English	Central Pomo	Eastern Pomo	Northern Pomo
"man"	baiya	gauk	ba
"woman"	mata	da	mata
"dog"	hayu	haiu	hayu
"sun"	da	lā	da
"moon"	iweda	duwɛlā	diweda
"water"	ka	xa	ka
"white"	kale	pit'au	kale
"yellow"	tsakat	xošilī	tsakat
"red"	tas	g'ida	ta'ts
"black"	kili	gili	katse

the most vigorous and well-documented dialect. Pomo language education programs and a growing number of published books on the subject are helping to keep interest in the language alive.

GOVERNMENT

At one time, there were more than seventy independent Pomo tribes. They were further divided into groups called tribelets, which ranged in size from 125 to more than 500 persons. A tribelet is a type of organization in which one main village was surrounded by a few minor outlying settlements. Villages were made up of one or more family groups, who chose one group to be leaders.

Some villages had only one chief in charge, whereas others had as many as twenty. Women have always held a high position in Pomo society; some groups had female chiefs. The right to become a chief passed from a chief to his sister's son, if the young man showed leadership qualities.

In modern times, most Pomo reservations and rancherías are governed by elected tribal councils. Some tribe members, though, had difficulty adopting a U.S. pattern of government because it did not conform to their traditional matriarchal (passed down the line through the mother) form of leadership.

ECONOMY

Traditional economy

The Pomo economy was based on hunting and gathering; they also had a brisk trading economy that used money. Pomo money came in two forms: clamshells, which were ground into regular circles, had a hole bored into them, and were strung on strings like beads; and beads made from a mineral called magnesite. When the mineral was treated with fire, it turned different shades of pink, orange, and tan. The value of clamshell disks depended on the age of the clamshells, the thickness of the disk, and the length of the strung disks. Magnesite beads were considered more valuable and were traded individually rather than strung.

Food and other products were bartered at trade-feast gatherings. Direct money transactions—beads for fish, for example—were a common occurrence, allowing Pomo people to establish a surplus of goods. Magnesite beads were often used for gambling.

Because of their use of money, the Pomo developed a reputation as great counters; they dealt in sums in the tens of thousands without using multiplication or division. Their knowledge of money proved useful when it came time for the Pomo to buy land from the U.S. government.

After confinement on reservations

Pomo rancherías have always been too small to support many people. By the late nineteenth century, the people were forced to seek seasonal work on non-Native-owned lands. They picked fruit and hops (a plant used in making beer), traveling from farm to farm to follow the crops. Women wove baskets to sell and worked doing others' laundry. Meanwhile, traditional Pomo hunting and gathering practices were all but lost.

Both World War I (1914–18) and World War II (1939–45) brought employment to Pomo men, who left to serve in the military or take jobs in cities. Women went to work in cities as maids. In modern times, only about one-third of the population remains on the rancherías and reservations. The Pomo continue to struggle to support themselves. Some members farm tribal land, but much of it is not suitable for agriculture. Tribal government provides some jobs. Most groups have opened businesses to cater to the region's many tourists, and many have casinos to provide employment and fund tribal programs. In addition, the Ya-Ka-Ama Indian Education and Development Center in Sonoma County provides training and job leads for the unemployed.

DAILY LIFE

Families

The Pomo placed a strong emphasis on the importance of families, as they still do. Their traditions include sharing land and homes with family members in close-knit communities.

Pomo women were rare among Native nations in enjoying a fairly high status. They could be chiefs. Some became members of the tribe's secret societies, but they were barred from certain other societies, which held "devil-raising" performances carried on to frighten women.

Young couples often lived with the bride's family in homes occupied by several families. The oldest wife in the house was its owner. The modern history of the Pomo often makes mention of the many skilled women whose beautiful baskets were sold to collectors to support the tribe during hard times and to build up a land base for the Pomo people after they became homeless.

Buildings

Four types of structures were common to all Pomo groups: dwelling houses, temporary or seasonal shelters, sweathouses, and ceremonial houses built partly underground. Building materials and shapes of houses varied because some tribelets lived where redwood was plentiful, whereas others resided in the valley-foothill region.

A Pomo woman sits in a shelter made of tule, circa 1924.
© BUYENLARGE/GETTY IMAGES.

For groups in the redwood forest, a typical family structure was a conical house made of slabs of redwood bark. These were small, only 8 to 15 feet (2 to 5 meters) in diameter and perhaps 6 feet (2 meters) in height. Although generally single-family dwellings, they could house as many as twelve people. The assembly or ceremonial houses were much larger, up to 70 feet (21 meters) in diameter, supported by beams and partially covered by earth so that, from a distance, they appeared to be tiny hills.

Valley and Lake Pomo groups built circular, rectangular, or L-shaped structures of brush or reeds. The Clear Lake groups used the abundant tule (pronounced *TOO-lee*; a plant material) from the marshes for the construction of multifamily dwellings up to 40 feet (12 meters) in length that housed twenty people. The tule reeds were dried and bound together with split grape vines.

Food

All Pomo groups had abundant natural resources, and they were keenly aware of the proper times for hunting and gathering the various foods. Naturally, the Pomo diet varied depending on a group's environment; more seafood was eaten along the coast, whereas more game was consumed inland.

Lake, stream, and river fish were caught with spears, basketry traps, or nets by fishermen in lightweight, raft-like canoes. Clear Lake Pomo groups dried much of their catch, usually carp and blackfish, with salt that they acquired through trade with the Northeastern Pomo. The Pomo people hunted deer, elk, and antelope. Deer might be stalked by one person wearing a deer-head mask or by groups. The Pomo hunted bear with bows and arrows, spears, and clubs. Although they ate some birds, others, such as the crow and owl, were not killed because they had an important place in Pomo religious life.

The people also gathered and ate insects, particularly grasshoppers and caterpillars. They ate various grasses, roots, berries, nuts, bulbs, and edible greens when these foods were in season, but their favorite food was the acorn. They ate ground acorn meal daily, generally served as a mush along with dried blackfish. Although their methods of obtaining food have changed over time, the Pomo continue to eat traditional foods.

Education

Young people respected elder Pomo men and women, with whom they spent a great deal of time. Elders tended the fires and the home, allowing the younger adult members of the tribe to hunt and gather.

Pomo Bear Doctors

In 1906, a Pomo man who had once been a bear doctor told this story. According to his account, which began in the days when animals were human, a small bird carried a bear carcass to the village so all could eat. The bird received a bear-skin in payment. Later, he got one for his brother. The two of them stitched up the bearskins until they looked real. Wearing the skins, they killed other animals, then returned to their village and pretended to be sad about the deaths.

> When they put on their suits it was only necessary to say in what direction they wished to go and what they wished to do, and the suits would bear them thither by magic.... Upon this occasion they went eastward, and finally, in the late afternoon, met Wildcat carrying upon his back a very heavy load. They immediately attacked and killed him, but did not cut him to pieces as they

had Wolf. It is a custom, even now, among bear doctors never to tear to pieces or cut up the body of a victim who is known to have in his possession valuable property. Hence they stabbed Wildcat only twice. When they looked into the burden basket which he had been carrying they found a good supply of food and a large number of beads of various kinds. They took only the bag of beads, which one of them secreted inside his suit. Upon reaching their place of seclusion they removed their suits and were soon back in the village....

[After Wildcat's funeral] when the people heard of the killing of two more hunters by two bears, they suspected the brothers, and formulated a plan to spy on them. All were to go hunting and certain ones were to keep a close

---

Special bonds formed between elders and youngsters. In some groups, for example, a young boy slept with his grandfather. He kept the old man warm at night, and in return, the grandfather taught the boy tribal history.

After they moved to reservations, Pomo children faced many hard-ships. Nearby towns refused to allow them to attend public schools. Pomo parents filed lawsuits challenging this practice. In one instance, the local school board established a separate school for Native children. In 1923, a Pomo man named Stephen Knight took action on behalf of his daughter; his lawsuit resulted in the end of school segregation in Men-docino County. (Segregation is a policy of separating one race or class of people from the rest of society.)

watch on these two, and see just where they went and what they did....

Finally, one of the hunters on the east side of the lake saw the bears and shouted, "Look out there; two brother deer are coming down the hill!" There were two trees standing some distance apart with a thick, brushy place on each side. One hunter hid behind each tree. A third hunter … was but a few feet from these trees when the bears came close to him, so he dodged between the trees and the bears followed.

Immediately the two hunters behind the trees attacked the bears from the rear with their clubs and jerked the masks from their heads. The other hunters came up armed with clubs, bows and arrows, and stones, and found the bear doctors standing very shame-facedly before their captors.

They finally confessed to the murders, and took the hunters to their hiding place. Here they exposed their entire secret and told all the details of their work: how they dug the cavern, how they made the ceremonial outfits, and how they killed people. The hunters then stripped the bear doctors and took them, together with all their paraphernalia, and the property they had stolen, back to the village, placed them in their own house, tied them securely, and set fire to the house. Thus ended the bear doctors. That is how the knowledge of this magic was acquired. It has been handed down to us by the teaching of these secrets to novices by the older bear doctors ever since.

SOURCE: Barrett, S. A. *Pomo Bear Doctors.* Berkeley: University of California Press, 1917. Available online at http://www.sacred-texts. com/nam/ca/pbd/index.htm (accessed on August 11, 2011).

Clothing and adornment

Pomo men usually wore no clothing but sometimes put on a breech-cloth, a garment with front and back flaps that hung from the waist. Women wore long skirts of shredded bark or tule. Both sexes sometimes wore mantles, cape-like garments consisting of long pieces of hide or woven plant fibers that tied at the neck and were belted around the waist. Wealthy people kept warm with blankets made of rabbit hides or other skins. The poor had to make do with shredded willow bark or other fiber.

Generally, the Pomo went barefoot, but for special occasions they put on deer-hide boots and tule moccasins. Women also donned finely shredded skirts and hide mantles, and men wore feather headdresses.

A Pomo woman weaves a gambling tray. © INGA SPENCE/ ALAMY.

Hair was worn long by both sexes, either loose or tied at the nape of the neck. Women wore ear ornaments decorated with beads and feathers. Clamshell beads, abalone shells, and feathers were used in belts, neckbands, and wristbands, but these were usually saved for special occasions. Some women wore dance headdresses made of fur, feathers, and beads.

Healing practices

Pomo healing was closely connected with their religion, because healers (shamans) were also heads of the Kuksu Society (see "Religion"). Shamans (pronounced *SHAH-munz* or *SHAY-munz*) set broken bones and treated ailments, such as stomach problems, with herbs. Most illnesses, however, were thought to be caused by the patient, who had broken some rule that had angered the spirits or had earned the dislike of another member of the group. Shamans cured these illnesses by singing or by sucking out the sick-making poison. There were also bear doctors, who were paid an annual fee for their position. They wore a bear's skin and head and were thought to have the power to both heal and cause illness (see sidebar).

ARTS

Crafts

The Pomo were known for their many basket-weaving techniques using a large variety of roots and other fibers, as well as shells and feathers. Men as well as women traditionally made baskets. Pomo basketry and other crafts have been kept alive by internationally known basket weavers such as Elsie Allen (1899–1990), Mabel MacKay (1907–1993), and Laura Fish Somersol.

Oral literature

Coyote the trickster played an important role in Pomo literature. Coyote brought the Pomo people the sun and did other favors, but he could also be cruel. Tribal stories tell of Coyote flooding the world to punish people for being cruel to his children. Other tales tell of Coyote bringing food and water to the Pomo during a terrible drought. Many birds are also featured in Pomo stories.

CUSTOMS

Festivals and ceremonies

Dancing and singing have always been an important part of Pomo ceremonies and trade-feasts. The tradition continues into modern times, and some rancherías have built dance houses. The Pinoleville Band of Pomo Indians began hosting an annual Big Time Cultural Awareness Gathering in 1994. The Big Time, which they opened to the public, gives the Pomo people an opportunity to reunite and participate in traditional songs and dances; it also helps create bonds among other Native tribes who attend.

Gambling was part of many Pomo gatherings, and a skilled gambler was highly honored. Families always welcomed son-in-laws who were good gamblers. Even the Pomo religion sanctioned gaming, so everyone in the tribe participated. Members tried not to win too much or take too many of another's valuable possessions, because it could cause hard feelings.

A woman performs a seldom-seen traditional Pomo dance at a powwow. © ARMAND HARRIS/ALAMY.

Courtship and marriage

Marriages were arranged by parents. Children were not forced to take suitors picked by their parents, but they could not marry someone else without their parents' approval. Many Pomo couples experimented with a trial period of living together in the woman's dwelling before the families exchanged gifts and the marriage took place. After marriage, the young couple lived for a time at the home of one of the families before settling in the home of the other. Some couples remained with the groom's or bride's parents until they had children; then they cut a new door in the home and added a new fire and sleeping area. Young couples did not generally move out on their own; only in the case of a very full house would a new one be constructed.

Childbirth

A woman normally gave birth in her family's home. Afterward, both sides of the family presented her with gifts, usually lengthy ropes of clamshell beads with up to eight hundred disks each. Among the Eastern Pomo, the father could not leave his home for eight days after the birth and was forbidden to hunt, gamble, or dance for a month. Children were given two names, one each chosen by their mother's brother and their father's brother. They were often named after deceased relatives.

Puberty

Special ceremonies were performed for boys and girls when they reached puberty. Eastern Pomo girls were purified in a steaming ceremony, in which they lay on tule mats with hot coals all around. On the fourth night, the girl bathed and was given a basket of acorns. She performed the complicated acorn preparation process and then served acorn mush to her family.

Throughout their youth, boys were given songs to learn and at age twelve were presented with a bow and a fancy beaded hair net. A few boys were chosen each year to begin the long training to become a member of the Kuksu Society (see "Religion").

Death and funerals

At death, the body lay in the house for four days so that its spirit might leave. Mourning was public and dramatic, with female relatives crying and scratching themselves deeply enough to leave scars. Mourners cut their hair short, and others in the tribe brought them gifts. The Pomo then took the body outside and burned it, face down and pointing toward the south. They also often burned the home and its contents. After 1850, the U.S. government largely stopped these burning ceremonies.

CURRENT TRIBAL ISSUES

Since the 1970s, the Pomo have been battling attempts by big businesses to build on sacred grounds. The waters of Clear Lake have been polluted by wastes from old, abandoned mines, from homes and resorts built along the shore, and from pleasure boats that race on the lake. Another primary issue for the Pomo is acquiring more land and providing housing for tribal members.

Casinos can bring in much-needed income to Native nations, whose people are suffering from unemployment, poverty, inadequate housing, high rates of disease, and other social ills. They also bring challenges—disruption to nearby communities, misuse of funds, illegal dealings, and lawsuits from disgruntled tribe members, employees, contractors, or neighboring towns. Some Pomo communities struggle with problems such as these in the twenty-first century.

NOTABLE PEOPLE

Elsie Allen (1899–1990), who at age eleven was taken away from her family and sent to boarding school, became a well-known Pomo basket weaver, scholar, educator, cultural preservationist, and writer. She not only kept the art of basketweaving alive but created a worldwide interest in it. Her illustrated book *Pomo Basketmaking: A Supreme Art for the Weaver* (1972) tells her life story.

Pomo/Wintu/Patwin basket weaver, doctor, and cultural preservationist Mabel McKay (1907–1993) is the subject of a biography by Pomo/Miwok writer and professor Gregory Sarris (1952–) called *Weaving the Dream.* As the title suggests, McKay dreamed the design of her baskets.

Pomo elder, chief, and tribal historian William Benson (1860–1930) was one of the few Pomo men who made beautiful baskets. He turned to this craft when there was no longer a need for the basketry fish traps that Pomo men usually made.

A Pomo Childhood

Basket maker Elsie Allen (1899–1990), who grew up during the early 1900s, describes this incident from her childhood in *Pomo Basketmaking: A Supreme Art for the Weaver*:

> My mother used to hide me whenever the white people came because we had heard of Native American children who had been kidnapped. My great-grandmother said that when she was young, a number of Native American children were brought down from the north by whites riding on mules. Her aunt fed about 7 or 8 of these small children, who were being carried south to be sold to ranchers. They were so starved, they swallowed their food whole. My people wept when these children were taken away.

SOURCE: Allen, Elsie. *Pomo Basketmaking: A Supreme Art for the Weaver.* Healdsburg, CA: Naturegraph Publishers, 1972.

BOOKS

Allen, Elsie. *Pomo Basketmaking: A Supreme Art for the Weaver.* Healdsburg, CA: Naturegraph Publishers, 1972.

Barrett, Samuel Alfred. *Ceremonies of the Pomo Indians and Pomo Bear Doctors.* University of California Publications in American Archeology and Ethnology. 1917. Reprint. Whitefish, MT: Kessinger Publishing, 2010.

Barrett, Samuel Alfred. *Pomo Indian Basketry.* 1980. Reprint. Whitefish, MT: Kessinger Publishing, 2010.

Barrett, Samuel Alfred. *Pomo Myths.* Whitefish, MT: Kessinger Publishing, 2007.

Castillo, Edward D. *The Pomo.* Austin: Raintree Steck-Vaughn, 1999.

Clark, Cora, and Texa Bowen Williams. *Pomo Indians: Myths and Some of Their Sacred Meanings.* Reprint. Charleston, SC: Literary Licensing, 2011.

DuBois, Cora. *The 1870 Ghost Dance.* Reprint. Lincoln: University of Nebraska, 2007.

Patrick, K.C. *The Pomo of Lake County.* Mt. Pleasant, SC: Arcadia, 2008.

Ryan, Marla Felkins, and Linda Schmittroth. *Tribes of Native America: Pomo.* San Diego, CA: Blackbirch Press, 2002.

Tiller, Veronica E. Velarde. *Tiller's Guide to Indian Country: Economic Profiles of American Indian Reservations.* Albuquerque, NM: BowArrow Publishing Company, 2005.

PERIODICALS

Martinez, Antoinette. "Excavation of a Kashaya Pomo Village in Northern California." *Berkeley Archaeology.* Fall 1995.

Poole, William. "Return of the Sinkyone." *Sierra* 81 (November/December 1996): 52–5, 72.

WEB SITES

Big Valley Band of Pomo Indians. http://www.big-valley.net/index.htm (accessed on August 11, 2011).

Coyote Valley Band of Pomo Indians. http://coyotevalleytribe.com/ (accessed on August 11, 2011).

Dry Creek ranchería Band of Pomo Indians. http://www.drycreekrancheria.com (accessed on August 11, 2011).

Giese, Paula. "California Pomo: Tribal Information." *Native American Resources.* http://www.kstrom.net/isk/maps/ca/pomopage.html (accessed on August 11, 2011).

"History." *Robinson Ranchería Pomo Indians.* http://www.robinsonrancheria. org/history.htm (accessed on August 11, 2011).

Hopland Band of Pomo Indians. http://www.hoplandtribe.com/index. php?option=com_content&view=article&id=58&Itemid=2 (accessed on August 11, 2011).

"Native American Literature: The Pomo." *Reed College.* http://academic.reed. edu/english/courses/English201NAL/Pomo.html (accessed on August 11, 2011).

"The Pomo and the Paiute." *Gold, Greed & Genocide: The Story of California's 1849 Gold Rush.* http://www.1849.org/ggg/pomo.html (accessed on August 11, 2011).

"Pomo People: Brief History." *Native American Art.* http://www.kstrom.net/isk/ art/basket/pomohist.html (accessed on August 11, 2011).

Redish, Laura, and Orrin Lewis. "Pomo Language and the Pomo Indian Tribe (Pomoan, Kulanapan, Shanel, Kábinapek, Gallinomero)." *Native Languages of the Americas.* www.native-languages.org/pomo.htm (accessed on August 11, 2011).

Yahi and Yana

Name

Both Yana (pronounced *YAH-nuh*) and Yahi (pronounced *YAH-hee*) are composed of the noun *ya,* meaning "people." The suffix *na* was used in northern dialects and *hi* (or *xi*) in southern ones. The Yahi were a southern group of the Yana. The Witun name for the Yana was *Nozi* or *Nosa.* The Northern Yana called themselves *Garii*; the Central Yana were *Gatai.* The name *Yahi* was not used until the last survivor, Ishi, emerged in 1911. Settlers called the Yahi and Yana the Deer Creek Indians, Mill Creek Indians, or Lassen Indians.

Location

The Yahi occupied the area along Deer and Mill Creeks, bordered on the west by the Sacramento River and on the east by Mount Lassen in northern California. The Yana lived in the east section of the upper Sacramento River Valley, from Pit River in the north to as far south as Rock Creek.

Population

In the early 1800s, there may have been between 1,500 and 3,000 Yana people, of whom 200 to 300 were Yahi. The last Yahi, Ishi, died on March 25, 1916. There were an estimated twenty Yana in 1973, but in the 1990 census, no Yana were counted. Some descendants of the Yana tribe live on the Redding Ranchería; total population for this ranchería in 2000 was 72 people, but this number also included Wintun and Pit River Indians.

Language family

Hokan.

Origins and group affiliations

The Yana lived in northern California for more than three thousand years before contact with non-Natives. The Yana were composed of four groups: the Northern Yana, the Central Yana, the Southern Yana, and the Yahi. The Yahi were friendly with the Yana, the Nomlaki, and the Wintun; the Yahi

Contemporary Yana & Yahi Communities

California

① Redding Rancheria (Yana/Wintun/Pit River Indians). In 1990 no one identified themselves as Yahi or Yana in the census polls.

Shaded area

☐ Traditional lands of the Yahi and Yana in present-day northern California

A map of contemporary Yahi and Yana communities. MAP BY XNR PRODUCTIONS. CENGAGE LEARNING, GALE. REPRODUCED BY PERMISSION OF GALE, A PART OF CENGAGE LEARNING.

often hunted and camped in Wintun territory. They were enemies of the Maidu (see entry). The Yana feuded and often fought with many of their neighbors, such as the Wintun and the Achumawi.

Yana territory in northern California has been described by the historian Alfred Kroeber (1876–1960) as "a region of endless long ridges and cliff walled canyons, of no great elevation but very rough, and covered with scrub rather than timber. The canyons contain patches of brush that is almost impenetrable [impossible to get through], and the faces of the hills are full of caves." In this rough land, the Yana and Yahi thrived, but they perished soon after the American settlers came. Only a few Yana descendants shared the Redding Ranchería in the early twenty-first century, but Yahi and Yana memory is preserved in the Ishi Wilderness, a rugged portion of the Lassen National Forest.

HISTORY

Arrival of settlers

Little is known about Yana life prior to contact with American settlers. The people lived in the foothills of Mount Lassen for many years. Some groups may have had contact with Europeans as early as 1821, when the Spanish explorer Captain Luis Arguello (1784–1830) journeyed east from San Francisco. Between 1828 and 1846, the Yana probably encountered British fur trappers from time to time, but they had little real interaction with outsiders until the late 1840s. That is when non-Natives began to settle in the Yana homelands, and the theft of Yana lands and destruction of their people began.

In 1848, rancher Peter Lassen (1800–1859) led new settlers over the Sierra Nevada mountains into the Sacramento Valley along the ridge between Mill Creek and Deer Creek. This route became known as the Lassen Trail and was used frequently until 1850. The California-Oregon Trail also crossed Yana territory.

Settlers' cattle ate the Natives' food, causing much hardship for Yana peoples. The Yana got even by stealing cattle—since it was grazing on their land, they believed they were entitled to it, and they needed food to feed their families. Relations between two groups grew so tense that the Yana hid their food supplies. That way, if settlers chased them out of their homes, they would still have something to eat.

Massacres begin

Settlers often took violent action in response to the Yana's stealing of food. In 1846, U.S. Army captain John Frémont (1813–1890) led the first major attack when he surprised a peaceful Yana group on Bloody Island in the Sacramento River. Many other massacres occurred during this period; often thirty or more Yana were killed at one time. In one instance, forty to sixty Yana were killed for stealing some cattle. The last 181 people of the Southern Yana were removed from their homelands

Important Dates

1840s: Settlers moved into Yana territory.

1846: The first major assault against the Yana is launched by Captain John Frémont.

1848: Settlers travel through the Yahi territory on the Lassen Trail. Conflicts begin.

1858–65: Hundreds of Yana are moved to reservations.

1864: Whites almost succeed in destroying the Yana.

1908: The last band of Yahi are disturbed by surveyors, who take all of their winter supplies.

1916: Ishi, the last Yahi, dies of tuberculosis.

1923: Redding Ranchería is established; the Yana join the Wintun and Pit River Indians there.

1959: Redding Ranchería is terminated.

1985: Federal recognition is restored to Redding Ranchería.

Ishi, the last Yahi survivor, sits for a portrait in 1911.
AMERICAN MUSEUM OF NATURAL HISTORY.

in 1858 and taken to the Nome Lackee Reservation. Many of these people were very sick, and they died when the reservation was abandoned several years later.

The fighting went on and on as settlers sought to destroy the entire Yana nation or remove the people to reservations. Sometime between 1858 and 1865, U.S. Army officers led 277 Yana to Round Valley Reservation in Mendocino County. Many died on the way or were too sick to finish the journey.

Around 1864, white citizens killed most of the surviving Yana in response to the murder of two white women. Another terrible massacre followed, in which three hundred Yana who were attending a ceremony were killed. Only a handful of Yana survived that slaughter. Seventy-four Yahi were killed in 1865; the following year, forty were murdered during the Three Knolls Massacre and thirty-three in the Dry Camp Massacre. In 1867, forty-five or more bodies lay on the ground because there were not enough Yana to left bury them.

Violence continues

Still, the violence did not end. In the 1860s, the settlers appealed to the U.S. Army for assistance with their "Indian problem," and soldiers were sent out to punish the Native peoples for raiding settlers' homes. Yahi living on Mill Creek were considered the most troublesome, and army troops had orders to round up their leaders and imprison them on Alcatraz Island. The cycle of raiding and retaliation continued.

In 1862, after the Yahi killed three children, the settlers vowed to destroy every Yahi who could be found. After the Kingley Cave Massacre in 1871, few Yahi were left alive. The remaining Yahi went into hiding. Over the years, they were seen from time to time by settlers, but no one was able to catch them. They lived in concealment, leaving no trace of their existence. They learned to hop among the rocks, never leaving a footprint on the earth. They practiced walking without breaking twigs or vegetation, which would indicate a trail. They were spotted so rarely that by the early 1900s, it was believed that the Yahi had all been wiped out.

Last of the Yahi

In 1908, a team of surveyors (people who measure the boundaries and other features of an area) accidentally stumbled upon a hidden Yahi village. They reported that an old man and a middle-aged woman escaped. (Ishi, the last Yahi survivor, later said that he thought they jumped to their deaths.) The surveyors also found a partially paralyzed elderly woman, lying on the ground, wrapped in a blanket. The surveyors helped themselves to the contents of the camp. They took bows, arrows, baskets, and blankets—everything the little band of Yahi needed to survive the winter.

The surveyors visited the camp the following day to find that its inhabitants had fled. Three years after this disturbance, Ishi emerged from his homeland. He spent the rest of his life with scientists who wanted to learn about him and his culture. What is known about the Yahi and Yana is mostly due to Ishi's willingness to share his knowledge with these scientists. With his death in 1916, the Yahi ceased to exist.

On August 29, 1911, a tired, starving, frightened man left the forests of his Yahi homeland and wandered into an Oroville, California, slaughterhouse in search of food. He had been living alone in hiding, terrified of the settlers who had murdered his people and taken over his land. When he was discovered, the sheriff put him in jail because he did not know what to do with this man.

Local Natives were brought to speak with him, but Ishi could not communicate with any of them. He was the only person left who could speak in his Native Yahi tongue. Professor Thomas Waterman of the University of California took him to San Francisco. There Alfred Kroeber (1876–1960), a curator at the anthropology museum that became the man's home, gave him the name Ishi, which means "man" in Yana.

Ishi had apparently gone into hiding at about the age of ten. From the year 1872 forward, he and his people had to stay completely out of the sight of settlers. One of his hiding places was a concealed area called the Grizzly Bear's Hiding Place. It was occupied by Ishi, his mother, his sister, and two men. In 1908, some surveyors happened upon Ishi while he was fishing. He scared them away. Shortly after that, another party of surveyors found the Grizzly Bear site. Ishi's mother, who was sick, was there, wrapped in a blanket. The men took all useful items, including food and implements, and left the dying woman behind. Ishi returned to move his mother, but she died a few days later. The others in his small group had disappeared, and Ishi was totally alone for nearly three years.

After surfacing in public, Ishi lived for five years in the University of California's museum as a live exhibit. He demonstrated to Waterman, Kroeber, and the visitors his skills in making bows, arrows, harpoons, spears, and other tools. Ishi was given a job as an assistant to the head janitor, which allowed him to earn a small salary. In May 1914, Waterman, Kroeber, and Dr. Saxton Pope took Ishi on a trip back to his homeland. For three weeks, Ishi displayed his intimate knowledge of the landscape and ways of survival.

Ishi had very little resistance to the diseases of the Californian settlers. He was often sick while living at the museum, and on March 26, 1916, he died of tuberculosis.

The strangeness of the world he had entered may have overwhelmed Ishi at first, but he showed remarkable adaptability and quickly made close friendships with the people involved in his life. Alfred Kroeber's wife, Theodora, who later published a book about Ishi, wrote of his shyness and dignity, saying, "He was interested, concerned, amused, or delighted, as the case might be, with everything and everyone he knew and understood." His doctor, Saxton Pope, wrote upon Ishi's death, "And so, stoic and unafraid, departed the last wild Indian of America. He closes a chapter of history. He looked upon us as sophisticated children—smart, but not wise.… His soul was that of a child, his mind that of a philosopher."

Thomas Waterman wrote in *Ishi, the Last Yahi* that Ishi "convinced me that there is such a thing as a gentlemanliness which lies outside of all training, and is an expression of a purely inward spirit. He never learned how to shake hands but he had an innate [natural] regard for the other fellow's existence, and an inborn considerateness, that surpassed in fineness most of the civilized breeding with which I am familiar."

RELIGION

Little is known about the religious beliefs and practices of the Yana. Their religious leaders were also healers, called shamans (pronounced *SHAH-munz* or *SHAY-munz*), who were usually male, but sometimes female. The people believed that both humans and non-humans possessed supernatural powers, which allowed them to live forever. Some historians think they had a secret religious society called the Kuksu Society, which held religious dances.

In 1871, the Northern Yana adopted the Ghost Dance religion, which they learned from the Maidu (see entry). Members believed that if they performed the Ghost Dance, the earth would swallow up all non-Natives, and life would be as it was before they came.

Between 1872 and 1873, some Yana became believers in the Earth Lodge cult, an offshoot of the Ghost Dance religion. Members of the Earth Lodge cult danced to bring on the end of the world. When it came, believers would be protected in underground earth lodges. After the destruction was over, believers could live on in peace. Dreams, songs, and dances were important parts of the Earth Lodge cult.

LANGUAGE

Yana groups living in different regions spoke different dialects (varieties) of the Hokan language. They could understand each other, but not perfectly.

An interesting feature of the Yana language is its division into genders. When men talked among themselves, they spoke one form of the language; women talking among themselves spoke another. Men, however, used the female form of speech when talking with women, although women never used the male form of speech. Both sexes understood each other's language.

The forms of the language used by men and women might differ in this way: Women would take the ending off the "male" form of a word. So *Yana,* meaning "person," becomes *Ya* when spoken by a woman (or spoken by a man when he was talking to a woman); *auna,* "fire" and *hana* "water," become *auh* and *hah.*

In *Ishi in Two Worlds,* the author Theodora Kroeber, who spent a great deal of time with Ishi, discussed how Yana people might converse with their relatives. Men did not look directly at or continue a long conversation with their mother-in-laws or daughter-in-laws. Women behaved the same way toward their father-in-laws or son-in-laws. This way of speaking was considered a sign of respect and is illustrated by Ishi's behavior when visiting the home of his doctor, Saxton Pope. Pope wrote, "His attitude toward my wife or any other woman member of the household was one of quiet disinterest. Apparently his sense of [what was proper] prompted him to ignore her. If spoken to, he would reply with courtesy and brevity [few words], but otherwise he appeared not to see her."

GOVERNMENT

The Yana lived in independent groups and each group dwelled in one large village and a number of smaller surrounding settlements. Usually, the chief lived in the large village. In Northern Yana territory, a chief and

The Story of Alcatraz Island

Alcatraz Island is a small, barren, rocky place located in San Francisco Bay. In 1859, it became a U.S. military prison, and some Yana people may have been imprisoned there in the 1860s. The military moved out in 1933, at a time when gangsters were becoming a national problem. The federal government decided it needed a prison for the worst of these criminals, a remote place that would allow no escape and no communication with the outside world. Alcatraz Island, called "The Rock" by inmates, became America's first super-prison.

The prison closed in 1963, in part because Americans were rethinking many social policies, including that of imprisoning people without giving them any chance to rehabilitate (reform) themselves. At this time, policies toward Native nations were being rethought, too. Natives had become frustrated and angry at U.S. government actions that took away their lands and aimed to break up their reservations. They showed their displeasure in a number of ways, including the takeover of Alcatraz Island.

One hundred years before the takeover, the federal government had agreed that Native nations who were not given reservation lands could claim abandoned forts, prisons, and other facilities no longer wanted by the government. In November 1969, three hundred people, mostly college students, calling themselves the Indians of All Tribes seized the abandoned prison on Alcatraz Island and claimed it as their own under this one-hundred-year-old government policy. They were led by Richard Oakes (1942–1972), a Mohawk (see entry).

The Indians of All Tribes offered to pay the government $24 in glass beads and other trinkets. This was a mocking reference to the 1626 Dutch purchase of Manhattan Island (in New York City) from the Canarsee tribe for $24 in trinkets. The Indians of All Tribes offered to care for poor white people on Alcatraz Island, a mocking reference to the federal government "taking care" of Native peoples. In a biting allusion to long-standing government and missionary efforts to make Native peoples more like mainstream American society, the Indians of All Tribes declared: "We will offer them [non-Natives on Alcatraz Island] our religion, our education, our life-ways, in order to help them achieve our level of civilization and thus raise them, and all their white brothers up from their savage and unhappy state."

The Indians of All Tribes occupied Alcatraz Island for nearly two years before being forcibly removed in June 1971. On the island they set up a sanitation council, a daycare, a school, housing, and cooking facilities. They demanded that the federal government turn over the island to them and pay for a cultural center, a university, and a museum.

Many considered the protest a failure, but the protestors drew national attention to the problems Native nations faced in dealing with poverty and the destruction of their cultures. During their occupation the U.S. Senate voted to return Blue Lake, a sacred site, to the Taos Pueblo peoples (see entry) of New Mexico. After the occupation, a Native university was established near the University of California at Davis.

one or two subchiefs governed the larger villages. The chief was wealthier than other villagers and had two wives. He was also the only one in the tribe allowed to keep a vulture as a pet. The position of chief was passed from father to son.

Village members helped the chief by giving him items of value; for example, a successful hunter might share his deer carcass. The chief served his group by making speeches and acting as a dance leader. He did not tell people what to do, but only made suggestions, then listeners chose whether or not to take his advice.

The descendants of the Yana who live on the Redding Rancheria with the Wintun and Pit River Indians (see entry) are governed by a ten-member tribal council. Officers (chairperson, vice chairperson, secretary, treasurer, plus six additional members) serve two-year staggered terms. The constitution was written in 1986 and amended in 1989.

ECONOMY

The Yahi and Yana economy was based on hunting, gathering, and trading. In spite of feeling unfriendly toward their neighbors, the Yana actively traded with them. They received arrows, woodpecker scalps, and wildcat quivers from the Atsugewi (also called Pit River Indians; see entry) in exchange for shells and salt. Clam disk beads came from the Maidu (see entry) or Wintun, dentalium shells from the Wintun, and obsidian points from the north. The Yana gave these tribes deerskins, buckeye fire drills, and baskets in return.

In 1995, the three tribes—Wintun, Pit River, and Yana—formed the Redding Rancheria Economic Development Corporation (RREDC) to develop and oversee tribal enterprises. In the early twenty-first century, the casino and hotel, along with service and retail businesses, provide income and employment. The tribal government also supplies many jobs.

DAILY LIFE

Buildings

The shapes of houses and the materials used in constructing them depended on where a group lived. Some built cone-shaped, single-family houses made of slabs of cedar or pine bark. They rose three to four feet (roughly one meter) above ground level over a pit that was about two feet (half a meter) deep. Banks of earth placed around them prevented ground water from seeping into the homes. The entrances faced south. Other groups had similar, but larger, houses that accommodated several families. There was a smoke hole in the roof that some groups used as an entrance, whereas others built separate doorways.

Other buildings included earth-covered sweathouses, meeting houses, and huts where women were confined during their menstrual periods (menstrual blood was considered powerful, even dangerous). During the hot summer months, the Yana made seasonal trips to higher and cooler elevations, where they built temporary grass and bark houses.

The housing materials and building methods of the Yahi changed after contact with the settlers. Ishi's village, for example, was built to hide its inhabitants, and it used native and non-native materials. In *Ishi in Two Worlds,* Kroeber described the village, called *Wowunupo mu tetha* ("Grizzly Bear's Hiding Place"). It consisted of a cookhouse, storehouse, smokehouse, and living house. The cookhouse contained a fireplace, stones for grinding acorns, cooking baskets, cooking stones, and utensils. It was covered with a brush roof to provide shelter from the sun and rain and to "diffuse the smoke," so that no one could detect their hiding place. The smokehouse, used to smoke salmon, was built of driftwood with a roof of old canvas taken from a pioneer's covered wagon. The storehouse was shaped like the letter *A.* It had a pole framework tied together and thatched with bay branches. Inside it was separated into two rooms for the storage of baskets, food, and tools. The living house was also an A-shaped building. It was covered with strips of bark and laurel.

Food

The Yana people got their food by hunting and gathering. Women did most of the cooking and gathering, but some Yana husbands built the roasting pits, collected the fuel, and cooked the roots and tubers (underground vegetables such as potatoes) gathered by the women.

Acorns were a staple food. If the acorn harvest was meager, people could starve. Men and women both participated in gathering acorns in September and October; men shook the acorns from the trees while women collected them. The Yana usually made the acorns into a mush. Other important foods included bulbs, buckeyes, clover, berries, sunflower seeds, hazelnuts, and sugar-pine and digger-pine nuts.

The men hunted large game such as deer, elk, and bear, and smaller game such as rabbit, duck, quail, and goose. Some Yana groups fished in the

Sacramento and Pit Rivers, but fish was considered an important food source only to the Yahi, whose Deer and Mill creeks were filled with salmon. The Yahi speared salmon and caught trout with hooks, poisoned them with cucumber pulp dumped in trout pools, or captured them behind a wicker net. Salmon were broiled on heated rocks, roasted over the fire, or dried and stored.

Clothing and adornment

Women wore buckskin dresses and aprons or skirts made from shredded plant material. Behind the apron, some wore a large piece of buckskin or plant material to cover the back of the body. Wealthier women decorated their clothing with leather fringes and braided tassels made of grass and pine-nut beads or bones, adding belts of braided human hair. Women covered their heads with basket-like caps, which were painted with black and white patterns.

Men wore aprons and robes of deer, rabbit, wildcat, coyote, and bear skins. They tied the robes around their chests with buckskin string or wide elk skin belts. In cold weather, wealthy men wore leggings that stretched from their hips to their ankles, whereas poor men wore a deer hide skirt that left their legs uncovered. Sometimes they used robes made of three or four deer hides sewn together that they threw over their shoulders; these also served as sleeping blankets. The different groups wore a variety of shoes, including deer hide moccasins, sandals, and snowshoes.

Men and women wore their hair long. Men usually tied their hair in back or on the top of their heads. They plucked out their facial hair with a split piece of wood. Women parted their hair in the middle and wore it in two braids shaped into rolls that they wrapped in mink or buckskin.

Both sexes wore necklaces made of bear claws, shells, clamshell disks, bones, juniper berries, and a mineral called magnesite (pronounced *MAG-na-site*). Other decorations included feather and skin headbands, woodpecker-scalp belts, leather earrings covered with beads, and shell and wood jewelry worn through their pierced noses. Some people tattooed their bodies, but tattoos were not common.

Healing practices

Ishi described Yahi healing practices to Dr. Saxton Pope. He said that older women cured minor ailments with herbs, but shamans tackled major medical problems.

Like many Native groups of northern California, the Yahi thought that most pain was caused by foreign objects in the body. These objects might be spines, thorns, bee stingers, or pins. The job of the shaman was to suck these pains out of the sick person's body or grab them from the air around the sick person. Once he removed the object, the shaman placed it in a container, often a bird carcass, which was sealed with pitch (a sticky substance obtained from pine trees) so that the sickness could not escape and cause further harm. A shaman who did not perform his job properly, or who practiced evil or bad medicine, was sometimes killed.

Dr. Pope wrote that when Ishi was feverish he did not want to bathe with water because he believed it was important to sweat out the illness. Pope also wrote about some of Ishi's personal healing practices. Ishi had a hole in his nose, in which he wore a small piece of wood. When he had a cold, he placed a twig of juniper or baywood into this hole. When Ishi inhaled the scent of the twig, his airways opened. Ishi treated rattlesnake bites by binding a frog or toad to the bitten area.

CUSTOMS

Festivals and games

There is very little information about Yana festivals. The people are known to have been fond of dancing. They painted their faces red and white, and the men put on net caps or headdresses made of wildcat skin when dancing or for special occasions. Dancers might be accompanied by the music of rattles, flutes, and whistles.

The Yana enjoyed playing games. Author Jerald Jay Johnson wrote that the men enjoyed a game called double-ball shinny, usually played only by California Native women. Shinny was similar to field hockey; settlers called it the "stick game." Johnson said they took pleasure in "ring and pin, cat's cradle, throwing sticks at a stake, a ball game, and several forms of the grass or hand game" (a team gambling game where players tried to guess which hand held an object).

War and hunting rituals

Although the Yana were not on friendly terms with their neighbors, they were not in the habit of waging wars. Yana warriors sometimes accepted payment from the Pit River Indians to join them in battle against the Wintun. Occasionally, the Yana began a war in retaliation for trespasses on their hunting grounds or the kidnapping of Yana women. In preparation for fighting or entering dangerous situations, they wrapped their hair around the top of the head and tied it in a topknot.

Hunting was done both by individuals and groups. When a young boy made his first kill, the tribe struck him with the animal carcass to ensure his good luck in future hunts.

On bear hunts, several men surrounded the animal, holding flaming torches. As the bear tried to escape, the men aimed their arrows at its mouth. This continued until the animal became too exhausted to fight and died.

Ishi told Dr. Saxton Pope that Yahi men knew many animal calls and would hide and wait to ambush the animal. Deer hunters wore stuffed deer head decoys to attract the deer's attention and lure it closer so it could be killed with bows and arrows.

Courtship and marriage

Yana marriages were arranged by the young couple's parents. A young man's parents offered gifts to the parents of the woman he desired to marry. If the gifts were accepted, the man had permission to marry her. Among the Yahi, if a man died, his brother had to marry his wife. A man married his wife's sister if his spouse died.

Childbirth

Shortly before a woman gave birth, she moved to a birthing hut and stopped eating meat and salmon. The father could not hunt or fish during this time. The mother was attended by several helpers, including her own mother. If it was a difficult birth, a shaman was called in.

After giving birth the mother lay in a shallow pit heated with hot rocks. When the child's umbilical cord dropped off, the parents purified themselves by performing a sweating ceremony and returned to normal living.

Naming

The Yana did not name a child until after six years of age. Ishi said he never had a real name; because he had been all alone, there had been no one to give him a name. The name "Ishi" was given to him by Alfred Kroeber.

Puberty

Women who were menstruating were considered bad luck. During a girl's first menstrual period, she stayed by herself in a menstrual hut and ate only acorn mush and berries. She was forbidden to touch herself

The Creation of Men

Yana stories explained past events and traditions; many contained moral messages. The Yana believed that animals were the creators of people. In this creation story, the place where people were created, *Wama'rawi,* is near Battle Creek in the approximate center of Yana territory.

> Lizard, Gray Squirrel, and Coyote lived in a big sweat-house at Wama'rawi. They had no wives or children. Coyote wanted to make people, but the others thought that they themselves were enough. Finally Lizard agreed, "We'll make people, different kinds of people." So Lizard went out and cut three sticks like gambling sticks. The others wanted to know how he was going to make people out of these. Lizard said, "I'll show you." One stick he took for the Hat Creeks … one for the Wintun … and one for the Pit Rivers…. When he looked at them he said, "There is something lacking." Coyote asked, "Who has been left out?" Lizard said, "The Yana." So he took any kind of stick, broke it up into little pieces, and put them in a pile for the Yana. The stick for the Hat Creeks he placed in the east, the stick for the Wintun in the west, the stick for the Pit Rivers in the north.

> All three, Lizard, Gray Squirrel, and Coyote, then made a big basket, heated rocks, put water in the basket, and heated the water by putting the hot rocks into the basket. Then Lizard put the sticks into the boiling water, put in more hot rocks to boil the sticks. All then went to sleep, after setting the basket outside on the roof and covering it up. Before they slept Lizard said, "Early in the morning you will hear some one when the basket turns over. That will be because there are people. You must keep still, must not move or snore."

> Early in the morning they heard people falling down, heard the basket turn over. By and by they heard the people walking about outside. They got up, then covered the door with a large rock to keep the people out. They did not talk or answer those outside. For a long time the people were talking. One called out, "Where is the door?" Coyote said, "Keep still, that talk does not sound right." Others then spoke, asked also. Then Coyote said, "Now it sounds right," and then they opened the door. Then all the people came crowding in, all came into the sweat-house. Then the three said, "It is well. There are people."

SOURCE: Sapir, Edward. "Yana Texts." *University of California Publications in American Archaeology and Ethnology* 9, no. 1 (1910). Available online at http://www. sacred-texts.com/nam/ca/yat/yat24.htm (accessed on August 11, 2011).

with her fingers, so she used a wooden or bone scratcher when she had an itch. After completing this initial menstrual ritual, every woman was required to rest in the menstrual lodge for six days each time she had her period.

Death rituals

The Yana buried their dead, but the Yahi burned them. Before burial a body was washed, dressed in fine clothing, placed in a flexed position, wrapped in a deerskin blanket, and tied with rope. The dead person's belongings were broken before being placed in the grave with the body. This prevented grave robbery. At the gravesite mourners danced, cried, cut their hair short, and painted their heads with pitch. After burial, the Yana avoided saying the name of the dead person.

The Yahi cremated a body immediately after death to release the person's soul to begin its westward journey to the Land of the Dead. Once the soul reached its destination, deceased family and friends met the soul and directed him or her to a place at a campfire. If the person was not cremated, his soul remained in the Land of the Living, wandering about unhappy, lonely, and causing trouble to the living. After cremation, the ashes and bones were gathered in a basket, which was buried under a rock to mark the grave and keep animals away.

CURRENT TRIBAL ISSUES

Steven Shackley and Jerald Johnson are archaeologists (people who study the remains of past human cultures) who have a theory that Ishi may not have been a full-blooded Yahi. During Ishi's childhood, California was in a state of turmoil. Native nations were being forced onto reservations with members of other tribes. The theory is that Ishi may have been of mixed ancestry or descended from a different tribe altogether. Shackley examined arrowheads made by Ishi and said they are more similar to those of neighboring tribes than of the Yahi type. Johnson stated that Ishi looked more like the Maidu, Wintun, or Nomlaki than the Yana.

Edward Castillo, a historian who has studied California Natives, responded to these theories with the counter that Ishi may have learned different tool-making techniques because of his unusual lifestyle away from his own people. Conversely, because Ishi spent five years in the University of California's museum, surrounded by different types of arrowheads, he may have observed them closely enough to reproduce them.

Ishi had shown he was able to adapt to different ways of doing things. For example, he switched to glass for making arrowheads when traditional materials became hard to get. Ishi's goods are on display at the University of California–Berkeley's Phoebe Hearst Museum.

BOOKS

Bibby, Brian. *Precious Cargo: California Indian Cradle Baskets and Childbirth Traditions.* Berkeley: Heyday Books, 2004.

Curtin, Jeremiah. "The Yanas." In *Creation Myths of Primitive America.* Boston, MA: Little, Brown, and Company, 1903.

DuBois, Cora. *The 1870 Ghost Dance.* Reprint. Lincoln: University of Nebraska, 2007.

Isenberg, Andrew C. *Mining California: An Ecological History.* New York: Hill and Wang, 2005.

Johnson, Jerald Jay. "Yana." In *Handbook of North American Indians.* Vol. 10: *Southwest,* edited by Alfonso Ortiz. Washington, DC: Smithsonian Institution, 1983.

Justice, Noel D. *Stone Age Spear and Arrow Points of California and the Great Basin.* Bloomington: Indiana University Press, 2002.

Kroeber, Alfred Louis. *Handbook of the Indians of California.* New York: Dover Publications, 1976.

Kroeber, Karl, and Clifton B. Kroeber. *Ishi in Three Centuries.* Lincoln: University of Nebraska Press, 2003.

Kroeber, Theodora. *Ishi in Two Worlds: A Biography of the Last Wild Indian in North America.* Berkeley: University of California Press, 2004.

Lightfoot, Kent G. *Indians, Missionaries, and Merchants: The Legacy of Colonial Encounters on the California Frontiers.* Berkeley: University of California Press, 2005.

Nabokov, Peter. *Where the Lightning Strikes: The Lives of American Indian Sacred Places.* New York: Viking, 2006.

O'Connor, Mike, Yusef Komunyakaa, and Scott Ezell. *Songs from a Yahi Bow: A Series of Poems on Ishi.* New York, NY: Pleasure Boat Studio, 2011.

Sackman, Douglas C. *Wild Men: Ishi and Kroeber in the Wilderness of Modern America.* New York: Oxford University Press, 2010.

Secrest, William B. *When the Great Spirit Died: The Destruction of the California Indians, 1850–1860.* Sanger, CA: Word Dancer Press, 2002.

Starn, Orin. *Ishi's Brain: In Search of America's Last "Wild" Indian.* New York: W.W. Norton, 2004.

WEB SITES

Compton, W. J. "The Story of Ishi, the Yana Indian." *Ye Slyvan Archer.* July 1936. http://tmuss.tripod.com/shotfrompast/chief.htm (accessed on August 11, 2011).

"A History of American Indians in California: Ishi's Hiding Place." *National Park Service.* http://www.nps.gov/history/history/online_books/5views/5views1h39.htm (accessed on August 11, 2011).

"Hunting with the Bow and Arrow, I: The Story of the Last Yana Indian." *The Archery Library.* http://www.archerylibrary.com/books/pope/chapter01.html (accessed on August 11, 2011).

Redding ranchería. http://www.redding-rancheria.com/ (accessed on August 11, 2011).

Rockafellar, Nancy. "The Story of Ishi: A Chronology." *University of California, San Francisco.* http://history.library.ucsf.edu/ishi.html (accessed on August 11, 2011).

"Yanan Tribes." *Four Directions Institute.* http://www.fourdir.com/yanan_tribes.htm (accessed on August 11, 2011).

Yurok

Name

Yurok (pronounced *YOOR-ock*) comes from the word *yuruk,* meaning "downriver" in the Karok language. The Yurok sometimes called themselves *Olekwo'l* ("the people") or *Pulikla* ("downriver"), but they usually used village or clan names rather than a general tribal name. Yurok tribes were known as the Pohlik-la, Ner-er-er, Petch-ik-lah, and Klamath River Indians.

Location

The Yurok lived in the northwestern corner of California along the lower Klamath River and along the Pacific Coast. In the 1800s, the U.S. government moved the people to a reservation and several small rancherías. The Yurok Reservation is now located near the Pacific Coast in northwestern California about 30 miles (50 kilometers) south of the Oregon border. Yurok territory extends 1 mile (1.6 kilometers) on either side of the Klamath River from the mouth upriver for 44 miles (71 kilometers). The rancherías are also located in northwestern California near the Oregon border.

Population

Before the Europeans arrived, approximately 2,500 Yurok lived in fifty villages. In 1910, the U.S. Bureau of the Census counted the population at 688 Yurok; in 1930, there were 471. The Bureau of Indian Affairs showed 1,917 Yurok in 1981. The 2000 census indicated 4,029 Yurok lived in the United States, and 5,873 people had some Yurok blood. The Yurok tribe was California's largest Native nation, with more than 5,500 enrolled members as of 2011. In the early years of the twenty-first century, most of the people lived on the Yurok Reservation (formerly the Hoopa Extension Reservation).

Language family

California Algic (Ritwan), related to Algonquian.

Origins and group affiliations

The Yurok traded with and maintained friendly relations with many neighboring tribes such as the Hupa, Chilula (see entry), Shasta, Wiyot, Tututni, and Karok. These tribes sometimes intermarried. Today, the Yurok share

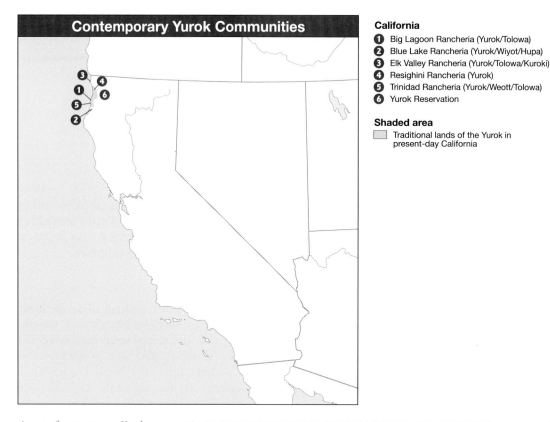

Contemporary Yurok Communities

California

1. Big Lagoon Rancheria (Yurok/Tolowa)
2. Blue Lake Rancheria (Yurok/Wiyot/Hupa)
3. Elk Valley Rancheria (Yurok/Tolowa/Kuroki)
4. Resighini Rancheria (Yurok)
5. Trinidad Rancheria (Yurok/Weott/Tolowa)
6. Yurok Reservation

Shaded area

Traditional lands of the Yurok in present-day California

A map of contemporary Yurok communities. MAP BY XNR PRODUCTIONS. CENGAGE LEARNING, GALE. REPRODUCED BY PERMISSION OF GALE, A PART OF CENGAGE LEARNING.

rancherías with the Hupa, Tolowa, Weott (Wiyot), and Kuroki. (*Ranchería* is Spanish for a small farm.)

About ten thousand years ago, ancestors of the Yurok lived near the Pacific Coast of California. The ocean and redwood forests protected them from invasion. Natural resources provided abundant food and allowed them to live in permanent, year-round villages. A peaceful people, they generally maintained good relations with neighboring tribes and learned to speak other languages so they could communicate. Although they built plank houses like many Northwest tribes, they also shared similar religious and cultural practices with other California Indians. In modern times, the Yurok have recommitted to their traditions and attempt to keep the world in balance through "good stewardship, hard work, wise laws, and constant prayers to the Creator."

HISTORY

Early history

Archaeologists (scientists who study objects of the past) found evidence of Yurok civilization dating back to 1310 at present-day Patrick's Point State Park. This village operated until American settlement occurred in the nearby area of Trinidad in 1850. Scientists also discovered a site off the coast of Patrick's Point believed to be an ancient Yurok ceremonial spot that was filled with sea lion skulls.

Prior to the arrival of Europeans, the Yurok lived along the coast or in the interior either on lagoons, at the mouths of streams, or along the lower course of the Klamath River. Similar to many California tribes, they rarely engaged in war, except for revenge. The worst battle occurred in the early 1800s between the village of Rekwoi and a Hupa (see entry) village. Both settlements were destroyed. Generally, though, the Yurok had good relations with all of their neighbors.

The tribes of the area established laws and boundaries. If a member of another tribe committed a crime in Yurok territory, Yurok law applied, and the Yurok imposed the penalties. Conversely, if a Yurok wronged someone on Hupa or Karok lands, he or she was subject to the laws of those tribes. To facilitate intertribal relations, most Yurok spoke their own language as well as that of their immediate neighbors. Some tribe members spoke additional languages.

The thirty to fifty Yurok villages traded among themselves and with other area tribes. They were different from many Native peoples in that wealth determined status in the tribe. The Yurok believed in individual ownership not only of portable objects, but also of land.

First European contact

Because the groups were sheltered from land contact, the first explorers reached them by sea. In 1775, Juan Francisco de la Bodega (c. 1743–1794) reached Trinidad Bay and spent several days there. He noted that the

Important Dates

1310: Yurok village at Patrick's Point is established.

1775: The Yurok first encounter Europeans.

1850: California becomes a state.

1851: Gold Rush begins at Gold Bluff.

1983: The Yurok, Karok, and Tolowa win a ten-year battle over a sacred site in Six Rivers National Forest.

1988: Hoopa-Yurok Settlement Act divides the reservations.

1993: The Yurok write a constitution.

1994: The people form the Yurok Tribal Council to govern the reservation.

2007: Department of the Interior awards Yurok tribe $90 million—their share of the Hoopa-Yurok Settlement Act.

Yurok were already using iron. Other writers mentioned that the Yurok had a system of math and a calendar.

Other than providing the people with trade goods, the few vessels that arrived in Yurok territory during the eighteenth century did not have much impact on Yurok culture. It was not until 1827 that Europeans arrived among the inland peoples. Fur traders from the Hudson's Bay Company were the first. The following year, Jedediah Smith (1799–1831), a fur trader, sailed down the Trinity River and traded beads and tools for beaver pelts. Later, the Spanish established missions.

California statehood

In 1850, California became a state. That year, the state passed the Act for the Government and Protection of Indians, a law that turned many Native rights over to the state. Native peoples could not testify against California citizens in court; unemployed Natives could be arrested and hired out; and non-Natives could take custody of Native children. Laws also protected the settlers' rights to land and water supplies.

Gold Rush

In 1851, a small Gold Rush began at Gold Bluffs in present-day Redwood National Park. Within a year, many Yurok worked for prospectors in several different settlements. Violence, though, between the prospectors and Native nations was common, and during the first year twenty-seven Native Americans and twenty-six whites had been killed.

With the influx of settler and miners, the Yurok not only lost land but were exposed to fatal diseases. In addition, the government offered a five-dollar bounty for each severed Native head. Although this was intended to eliminate tribes who had been attacking settlers, bounty hunters beheaded many peaceful tribes too. In 1851 and 1852, the new state of California spent $1 million a year on exterminating (killing) Native peoples. The combination of diseases and massacres reduced the Yurok population by almost 75 percent.

Red Cap War

Concerned that Native nations' retaliation for the killings would lead to war, Colonel Redick McKee (1800–1886), a U.S. Indian Agent, negotiated treaties with most tribes in the area. The Yurok signed the Treaty of Peace and Friendship in 1851, which promised them a reservation along the Eel River. McKee gave them food, oxen, and farm implements.

The Yurok Coastal Bluffs at Redwood National Park overlook the Pacific Ocean. The Yurok lived in northwestern California along the Klamath River and the Pacific Coast.
© DAVID MUENCH/CORBIS.

The Yurok kept their part of the bargain. They moved to the reservation and maintained peaceful relations with the settlers in the area. The U.S. Senate, however, failed to ratify the treaty.

Hostilities escalated on both sides. Some tribes wanted revenge and united under a coalition called the Red Caps. The Yurok remained peaceful and even offered to help the government, but settlers murdered the Yurok leader, Patora, after he urged his people to give up their arms. Later, army volunteers rode out to the rancherías, shook hands with the Yurok men, then shot them and took women prisoners. Still, the Yurok did not break the peace treaty they had signed.

Move to reservation

After the Red Caps surrendered, the U.S. government relocated the Yurok to the Klamath River Reserve along with other tribes, including the Tolowa, enemies of the Yurok. Many Tolowa fled, and another reservation was established for them at Smith River. In 1860, the Mad River and Eel River Indians moved onto the Klamath Reservation. The following year floods destroyed the reservation and left two thousand Native Americans starving. The government tried to move the Yurok to Smith River, but they refused to go.

In 1864, the Hoopa Valley Reservation opened, and many Yurok moved there. The Mad and Eel River Indians joined them. In 1874, settlers pressured the government to open the Klamath area for homesteads even though some Yurok still lived there. The U.S. Army investigated and found that, although many Yurok were suffering from disease, they had plenty of salmon to eat. They had built log cabins and were farming potatoes. Many Yurok men also traveled to Humboldt Bay to work on farms. By the 1890s, a large number of Yurok living at Klamath had intermarried with the settlers, and most spoke English.

Reservation life

In 1891, the U.S. government enlarged the reservation to encompass a mile-wide strip down each side of the Klamath River for 40 miles (64 kilometers) to the Pacific Ocean. This piece of land connected the Hoopa and the Klamath Reservations.

About this time, the government opened a school in Hoopa Valley to assimilate Native children; the main goal was to make them more like American citizens. Students were forbidden to use their native language. Girls learned homemaking skills, and boys learned farming or other trades.

The early 1900s were a time of poverty and hunger for the people. The Yurok Tribal Organization formed to reverse this situation. The group worked for the right to use traditional hunting and fishing sites. Although they had some success, in 1934, laws banned Native American commercial fishing and gill netting. Unable to support themselves as they once had done, tribe members worked for commercial fishing companies and fish-packing plants. Others took jobs in the timber industry or on area farms.

Fight for rights

The Yurok continued to fish along the Klamath River. In 1964, however, the Department of Fish and Game began arresting them and taking their nets. The Yurok felt that because their fishing areas were part of the reservation, their right to fish was protected under U.S. law. They took their case to court and won. Nevertheless, throughout the 1970s the people had to fight for fishing rights. In 1979, they were allotted a certain portion of the salmon harvest.

The Yurok also had court battles over their land. Several rancherías were terminated, but a 1983 court ruling overturned that decision. That same year, the Yurok, Karok, and Tolowa won a ten-year legal battle over sacred sites in Six Rivers National Forest in northern California. The tribes claimed that plans by the Forest Service interfered with their use of the high country for religious purposes. The court agreed, and the tribes retained their right to use the mountains for vision quests, ceremonies, and dances.

Five years later, the Yurok were given a separate reservation. During the early 1900s, the U.S. government had combined the Hoopa and Yurok Reservations. The two tribes operated under a joint tribal council until the Hoopa-Yurok Settlement Act of 1988 passed, allowing the Yurok to establish their own tribal government; it also divided the reservation land between the two nations.

Present-day life

The Yurok wrote a constitution on November 24, 1993, and their tribal government took office in 1994. As of 2007, the council is housed in a new office complex constructed in 2002. One of the government's first concerns was stimulating tribal economy.

Timber had been a good source of income for the tribe, but in the early years of twenty-first century, declining amounts and environmental regulations resulted in lower harvests. With changes due to the Hoopa-Yurok Settlement Act, management of timber resources began to provide good harvests. Since the 1980s, the fishing industry also declined. Dams and logging affected the flow of water and the number of fish available. Working with Pacific Coastal Salmon Recovery funds as well as state, local, and tribal money, the Yurok opened fisheries and began working to increase salmon survival (see "Current tribal issues").

At the start of the twenty-first century, the Yurok were preserving their traditions and language. They had revived many cultural practices such as the Jump and Brush Dances (see "Festivals"). In 2004, the Brooklyn Museum of Art responded to the Yurok's request and returned tribal artifacts they had on display; these items are now used during dances.

RELIGION

Traditional beliefs

According to Yurok oral history, the "Immortals" showed humans the correct forms of behavior, dances, and interaction. After the Yurok people arrived, the Immortals departed, except from one place, *Sumeg*, which today is called Patrick's Point. The three main "Beforetime People" were Wohpekumew, the human creator who was also a trickster-hero; Pulekuk-W-erek, who rid the world of bad things; and Coyote (*segep*), also a trickster and the main character of minor origin stories. Pulekuk-W-erek, the most spiritual of the Immortals, was an example of virtue for men. An excellent warrior, he introduced the Yurok to the sweathouse and the wealth quest.

Many Yurok believed that "Indian devils," or sorcerers, caused accidents and evil to befall people. Sometimes, the wealthy (*peyerk*) were accused of causing evil. Because they had been trained in prayers, people believed this also gave them knowledge of "bad prayers." In addition, because the *peyerk* owned the regalia (fancy clothes) for dances, he might also use the special costumes to go abroad at night on evil missions. Sorcerers were not only held responsible for illness and death, they were also blamed for famine or natural events, such as floods.

The central feature of Yurok religion is the recitation of formulas. Before people can access their power, they have to use medicine properly and recite a mythical account of each act before performing it. The purpose of this is to recreate a spiritual pattern.

Men prepared themselves for ten days before dances or other important undertakings. They used the sweathouse, stayed away from women, ate special foods, and bathed twice a day. In addition, they wore grass ankle bracelets to protect them from snakebite, gathered wood, observed certain rituals (such as cutting their legs with white quartz), and recited long formulas. These intense training periods were followed by more relaxed times, because it was important to have a balanced life, to be "in the middle" (*wogi*).

Other religious practices

In the late 1800s, the Ghost Dance spread to the Yurok from the Shasta, Karok, and Tolowa, but it lasted only a short while. The Indian Shaker Church came to some villages during the late 1920s. This religion—with its emphasis on dancing, shaking, ringing bells, and burning candles—combines elements of the Christian faith with traditional Native beliefs. After a few decades, however, the Assemblies of God church replaced it. During the 1970s, along with a revival of traditional tribal dances such as the Brush Dance and Jump Dance (see "Festivals and ceremonies"), the Indian Shaker Church again became popular.

LANGUAGE

In the early days, tribes living near boundary lines often spoke the language of their nearest neighbors. Thus some Yurok spoke their own language as well as Tolowa or Karok. Unlike most Native nations of northern California, the Yurok speak an Algic (Ritwan) language. Yurok is related to Wiyot but not to the other native languages of northern California. Wiyot and Yurok are actually distant relatives of Algonquian languages, such as Ojibway and Cree (see entries).

In addition to being fluent in other languages, the Yurok had several dialects of their own. Common people spoke the "low" language, whereas upper classes spoke the "high" language. The tribe also claimed there were differences between women's and men's speech. Some anthropologists (people who study culture) said that vocabulary for all of these seemed to be the same.

At the time of European contact in the 1800s, the Yurok language had several thousand speakers; in the early twenty-first century, there are about a dozen fluent native speakers, all elderly. In the early 2000s, few people younger than twenty years old could speak the language. Most tribe members who participate in the Jump Dance now speak English rather than Yurok. The tribe, however, has begun an active language revitalization program.

Yurok Words

Aiy-yue-kwee	"Hello."
O' -lo' mo	"Come in."
mullah	"horse"
puuktek	"deer"
wrgrs	"fox"
keget	"cougar"
chir' r' y	"bear"
nekwel	"porcupine"
me' woo	"fish"
leyes	"snake"
krhlkrh	"turtle"
trwrmrs	"bee"
new	"see"
ko' m	"hear"
' e' gah	"eat"

GOVERNMENT

In the past, the position of headman was not hereditary. More often than not, the richest man in the village served as leader. The chief's leadership role was advisory; he gave his opinion, but others did not have to heed it. One of the main functions of a village leader was to organize the dances and provide the regalia for them.

The Yurok developed a system of laws that specified certain penalties for crimes. Each wrongdoing, from stealing to murder, resulted in a monetary payment to the injured party. If the criminals did not pay their debts, their families were held responsible. In rare cases where the penalty

A Yurok fisherman holds a freshly caught salmon. Fishing is a part of the modern Yurok economy. © CATHERINE KARNOW/CORBIS.

remained unpaid, the Yurok who was owed the money might take revenge.

After the U.S. government relocated the tribes, the Hupa and Yurok not only shared a reservation but also a tribal government. Once the Hoopa-Yurok Settlement Act passed, the Yurok wrote their own constitution in 1993 and set up the Yurok Tribal Council.

In the 2000s, the majority of the rancherías are home to many different tribes. They are governed by tribal councils elected by all the residents. Most also have business councils or a tribal administrator to manage tribal programs and oversee economic development. On the Yurok Reservation, the tribal council consists of seven members, one from each of the various districts, as well as a tribal chair and vice chair who are elected to three-year terms. The council usually meets monthly, and district meetings occur quarterly. All regular and special meetings of the council are open to members of the Yurok Tribe.

ECONOMY

Early economy

Most Native nations believed that land belonged to everyone, and they shared their possessions freely. The Yurok, though, not only owned land, they measured wealth by it and sold it to each other. Although all tribal members used some of the land, most hunting and fishing grounds were individually owned. If men wanted to fish at someone else's fishing station, they rented it for a share of their catch.

Traveling by canoe, the Yurok carried on extensive trade with other tribes. They valued woodpecker scalps, obsidian (shiny black or banded volcanic glass), and white deerskin. Their money, called *Ali-cachuck,* was a long, conical shell found in Queen Charlotte Sound. The wealthiest members of Yurok society owned multiple sets of dance regalia and hosted ceremonies. They also displayed their status through their clothing, especially basketry caps, and speech patterns.

Modern economy

Major income producers on the rancherías in the early twenty-first century include casinos, service and retail businesses, and tourism. Some also have forestry, fisheries, farmland, mining, or real estate development. At Elk Valley, proceeds from the tribe's casino and investments fund social and educational programs; by 2003, there were no tribe members on welfare.

On the Yurok Reservation, the government provides almost half of all jobs. Other employment is found in farming, forestry, fishing, tourism, management, and professional occupations. The tribe's goals for the Hoopa-Yurok Settlement Act monies (see "Current tribal issues") were to manage timber resources, develop more recreational sites in the Klamath River Basin, begin a gravel operation, and create a travel center.

DAILY LIFE

Families

In most Yurok households, several generations of men (related on their father's side) lived with their wives, children, unmarried relatives, adopted kin, and daughters who had in-marrying husbands (see "Marriage"). The eldest male owned the house. If the family grew too large, the people built another house nearby with the same name. Residents of the new house shared the sweathouse.

Buildings

The Yurok dug a hole 4 to 5 feet (1 to 2 meters) deep and 12 to 15 feet (3 to 5 meters) in diameter that served as a fire pit and eating area. This formed the center of the 20-foot (6-meter) square cabin built of redwood or cedar planks split from fallen trees or cut from large trees, allowing the tree to heal and remain alive. The single or double pitched roof had moveable planks to let in more air in warm weather. It also had an opening for smoke from the fire pit.

The door was a round hole, just large enough for a person to crawl through on all fours. To reach the center pit, people climbed down a ladder made of a notched log. Logs also served as benches. Mats and furs made the house more comfortable. The Yurok used the space along the walls for storage. Racks hung from the ceiling for drying fish over the fire.

A Yurok sweathouse stands at Patrick's Point State Park in Trinidad, California. © MARILYN ANGEL WYNN/NATIVESTOCK PICTURES/CORBIS.

Outside, the ground was swept clean and often paved with stones. Large rocks on each side of the door allowed women to sit while they wove and talked. Men did not sleep in their family houses, but in sweat-houses, which were 4 feet (about 1 meter) deep and covered with layered boards. A notched stone slab led down to the inside. The sweathouses had an escape tunnel if the room grew too hot or smoky.

At seasonal fishing or gathering spots, families built temporary shelters of branches.

Tools and transportation

Men used stone adzes and elkhorn wedges to carve redwood into stools, storage boxes, cooking implements, and blunt-ended dugout canoes. To make canoes, they spread pitch on a fallen tree trunk and burned out the center, leaving the sides and ends thin and smooth. The process

A Yurok fish trap is a basket-like device used to catch salmon in streams and rivers. © MARILYN ANGEL WYNN/NATIVESTOCK PICTURES/CORBIS.

often took five to six months, because canoes were 20 to 30 feet (6 to 9 meters) long. The Yurok often sold them to other tribes because the canoes worked well for both river and sea traveling.

Men used marten or raccoon skin turned inside out to make quivers to hold their arrows. They sewed it so that the tail fluttered in breeze. Hunters carried the quivers over their shoulders with a thong, head-end down. They stuffed the animal head with grass or moss to cushion the arrowheads.

Clothing and adornment

Women wore knee-length deerskin skirts open in front to show an apron underneath. This fringed apron had pine nut shells strung on grass cords. Skirts for special occasions were adorned with clam or abalone shells.

Yurok men and children rarely wore clothing. Men sometimes wore a deerskin breechcloth (garment with apronlike flaps that covered the front and back). In cold weather, both men and women added leggings, moccasins with elk hide soles, and robes made of deer, coyote, or raccoon.

Both sexes parted their hair in middle and tied it to each side in ropes. Some men had one rope in back. Wealthier women wore basketry caps, and men sometimes used deerskin headbands. For dances or ceremonies, Yurok warriors donned headdresses decorated with woodpecker scalps or sea lion teeth.

Women tattooed lines on their chins; men tattooed their arms. Earrings were large discs of abalone shell or strings of dentalium (shell money) decorated with red woodpecker feathers. Both sexes draped multiple shell necklaces around their necks.

Food

Yurok men caught salmon, sturgeon, eel, and shellfish from their canoes. Along the coast, they collected mussels, clams, sea anemones, and seaweed for salt. Hunters, disguised in bear or deerskins, waited on rocks for sea lions and seals to emerge from the water. They then barked and twisted their bodies to get the animals' attention so they could harpoon them. The Yurok liked whale meat, but they only ate those animals that were stranded; they never hunted them.

Inland people hunted deer, elk, bear, rabbit, and other small game. To catch salmon, they wove nets of grass and stretched them across a stream. They then made fishing booths by sticking poles in the water and lashing branches to make a floor a few feet above water. They covered these with brushwood roofs and slept there with a string attached to their fingers or to an alarm system of sticks and bones (later they used bells). When salmon swam into the net, the string jerked and alerted them. To catch ducks, they sprinkled berries underwater and put a coarse net under the surface. When the ducks dove for the berries, they got tangled in the net and drowned; using this system kept the ducks quiet so they did not warn off other birds.

The Yurok sundried surf-fish whole and hung them in rows over poles. They split salmon and lamprey eel (also prized for its grease) for drying. Most fish was smoked and then packed in baskets. Women gathered acorns and ground them into meal, and they collected wild oats, bulbs, seeds, berries, and roots. Anise, grapes, ferns, chinkapins, hazelnuts, pine nuts, and angelica grew wild and added to their diets.

Education

Boys learned to hunt and fish, whereas girls learned to cook, weave, and care for babies. Wealthy Yurok also traveled, learned other languages, and memorized religious formulas. In explaining traditional Yurok educational practices, Harry Roberts, a white man adopted by the tribe who later became a Yurok leader and medicine man, once told the writer Lee Sannella:

> [A] Yurok child is taught but one lesson at a time. If the child or young person cannot answer the question his teacher asks, then he simply goes off and 'studies' that area until he comes up with a better answer. Until he does, he is not asked another question. His education has come to an end until one thing at a time is mastered.

From the late 1800s until 1932, Yurok children were forced to learn English and various trades at the government school in Hoopa Valley. Today, most students attend public schools or the Yurok Magnet Elementary School in Weitchpec that opened in 2003. The tribe also has various educational programs such as Head Start, vocational training, cultural programs, and tutoring. The Yurok Language Program sets up master/apprentice teams to pass on language skills to the younger generation. The tribe also supports higher education through scholarships.

Healing practices

To become a healer, a person (usually a woman) dreamed about it. She then asked an experienced doctor to teach her. The training was intense and ended with a dance where the teacher "vomited up her pain" and the novice ate it, enabling her to heal others. Doctors also held dances when they dreamed of new cures.

Doctors came to the house to cure the sick or had people brought to them. They were paid in advance, and if a doctor could not heal the patient, she recommended someone else. Healing techniques included using herbal medicines, reciting formulas, and sucking out illness. One of the most important cures was for a patient to confess past wrongs; this could also include wrongs done by his ancestors. The healer then offered positive prayers.

How Thunder and Earthquake Made Ocean

This Yurok tale explains how the oceans were formed and filled with fish. Thunder, Earthquake, and Kingfisher all played important roles in the creation of the earth. The story takes place in the time when animals were like people.

One day Thunder wanted to give people water, so he sent Kingfisher and Earthquake with abalone shells to collect water at Opis. First Earthquake sank the north end of the world.

Then Kingfisher and Earthquake started for Opis. They went to the place at the end of the water. They made the ground sink behind them as they went. At Opis they saw all kinds of seals and salmon. They saw all the kinds of animals and fish that could be eaten there in the water at Opis. Then they took water in the abalone shells.

"Now we will go to the south end of the world," said Earthquake. "We will go there and look at the water. Thunder, who is at Sumig, will help us by breaking down the trees. The water will extend all the way to the South end of the world. There will be salmon and fish of all kinds and seals in the water."

Now Kingfisher and Earthquake came back to Sumig. They saw that Thunder had broken down the trees. Together the three of them went north. As they went together they kept sinking the ground. The Earth quaked and quaked and water flowed over it as Kingfisher and Earthquake poured it from their abalone shells. Kingfisher emptied his shell and it filled the ocean halfway to the north end of the world. Earthquake emptied his shell and it filled the ocean the rest of the way.

As they filled in the ocean, the creatures which would be food swarmed into the water. The seals came as if they were thrown in in handfuls. Into the water they came, swimming toward shore. Earthquake sank the land deeper to make gullies and the whales came swimming through the gullies where the water was deep enough for them to travel. The salmon came running through the water.

Now all the land animals, the deer, and elk, the foxes and mink, the bear and others had gone inland. Now the water creatures were there. Now Thunder and Kingfisher and Earthquake looked at the ocean. "This is enough," they said. "Now the people will have enough to live on. Everything that is needed is in the water."

So it is that the prairie became ocean. It is so because Thunder wished it so. It is so because Earthquake wished it so. All kinds of creatures are in the ocean before us because Thunder and Earthquake wished the people to live.

SOURCE: Bruchac, Joseph. *Native American Stories.* Golden, CO: Fulcrum Publishing, 1991.

Positive prayer also helped babies affected by witchcraft. It removed any influences of "bad prayers." Brush Dances might be held for an ill child. These five-day dances included singing and holding a child near steaming herbs or blazing spruce.

By 1970, most Yurok, especially the younger generation, used the Indian Shaker religion or modern medicine rather than traditional healing techniques. By that time, the tribe had no surviving healers, so those who wanted to participate in healing ceremonies called on two female shamans, or healers, from another tribe.

ARTS

Yurok artists are known for their basketry and woodcarving (see "Tools and transportation"). Women wove willow twigs or pine roots into large round mats to hold acorn flour. They also wove squash-shaped watertight baskets, drinking cups, and hats. They decorated their basketry by weaving black roots among the beige twigs to form patterns of squares, diamonds, or zigzags.

Traditional basketwork gave way in the 1970s to brighter, more colorful patterns. The new baskets were either black and white, or red and yellow. Most basketmakers no longer made mush pots, large regalia storage containers, or Jump Dance baskets; instead, they designed fruit baskets, place mats, and miniature baskets made into earrings or pins.

CUSTOMS

Society

Yurok communities consisted of the aristocrats (the wealthy), commoners, and slaves. Wealthy people had homes at higher elevations. Called *peyerk,* meaning "real man," the wealthy went on sponsored vision quests and were the only ones who performed religious duties. They wore stylish clothes, ate imported foods, practiced special eating etiquette, hosted ceremonies, spoke several languages, and traveled to gain knowledge and prestige.

Puberty

On her first menses, a girl stayed apart from her family, using her own fire. For good luck, she collected fuel. At sunset, she ran from her house down to the river, went into the water, then raced back to the hut, pursued by young boys who made sure that she ran quickly. She repeated this for ten days, each day adding one more run than the previous day. When she reached her house, she stopped near the doorway, raised her hands with palms facing out, then turned and ran back to the river.

She wore a skirt of shredded maple bark and bands of grass on her head, arms, and legs. For ten days, she did not comb her hair or touch herself, except with a bone scratcher hung around her neck on a string. Using this prevented her from absentmindedly touching herself, because she was to pay full attention to her body. She ate acorn mush and salmon only three times during her seclusion. A friend carried her food for her, and the girl sat near the river so she would not hear animal or bird sounds. Whenever she heard one of those sounds, she had to stop eating. This time of being alone was for finding her life's purpose and acquiring spiritual energy.

From then on, during her periods, she lived in a separate, underground hut. Special food was collected and stored there, along with her own utensils. During this ten-day menstrual seclusion, women ate no red meat or fresh fish and followed a program of bathing, wood gathering, and saying long prayers. Their husbands did not hunt during this time, and the women could not participate in ceremonies.

Marriage

Most families valued girls because they received a payment when their daughters married. If the groom did not have enough shells, he paid half of the cost and was "half-married." Instead of taking his bride to his cabin, he lived with her family and became a slave. Their children took the mother's name. Men who paid full price lived with the man's parents, and the children took the father's name. Both spouses kept their personal property when they married.

If a girl became pregnant, the man who was responsible had to purchase and marry her. The birth of a child was celebrated with a dance. In the case of divorce, a man received the bride payment back.

Festivals

Traditional Yurok ceremonies include the Deerskin Dance, Doctor Dance, Jump Dance, Brush Dance, Kick Dance, Flower Dance, and Boat Dance. These draw the Yurok people and neighboring tribes together for renewal, healing, and prayer. An annual Salmon Festival is held in August.

Deerskin dancers wear civet cat or deerskin aprons, many dentalium shells necklaces, and forehead bands of wolf fur. A stick on their heads holds two or four black-and-white eagle or condor feathers with woodpecker scalps attached. They carry poles with stuffed deer heads (usually white) that have fake tongues decorated with woodpecker scalps. The deer hide and legs dangle down.

The Jump Dance is held for world renewal. Two sides form separate camps and engage in heated debate. The dance combines prayers, formulas, and formal speeches, and ends with both sides dancing together—representing the balance in the world being restored. Feasting follows. The dance shows that unity does not always mean that two people or groups must be in perfect agreement; they can be very different, but complementary, like voices that harmonize. As one Hupa participant explained, "The longer one dances, the closer to restoring world balance the dance comes, the more *xoche* each person becomes, the more 'right,' 'clean,' 'real'—the more Indian."

Death rituals

A corpse was carried, feet first, in a complete circle around the room, then out through an opening in the roof or through a hole in the wall made by removing a board. One person sprinkled ashes and said, "I wish you may never return," to prevent the deceased's spirit from returning to the house.

The Yurok buried their dead lying down, with their heads facing upstream. They placed dentalium shells, woodpecker scalps, obsidian blades, ceremonial costumes, and weapons in the grave. All items were broken to make them useless to grave robbers. The tribe burned food and clothes to send them along with the dead into the afterlife. A fire burned for five nights near grave, and the widow or widower stayed to be sure the spirit departed. This also prevented sorcerers from digging up the body to make death-causing medicine.

The people believed the spirits of dead crossed a horizontal, greased pole over the chasm of the "Debatable Land" to reach the "Happy Western Land" beyond the ocean. The spirits needed fire to light their way. Good people moved faster, so the number of nights the fire was lit depended on the person's actions. Dead souls, especially those of the wicked, could return as animals.

Funeral participants went through a purifying ritual for five days afterward. Every morning in the sweathouse, a male or female priest repeated a formula, then gave each person a piece of háiwamás, a plant that they pulverized with water in a small basket. They used this mixture to wash themselves. After inhaling the smoke from a fire kindled with buckbrush, they went to the river to bathe.

Following this two-hour ritual, everyone except the gravedigger went about their usual duties. He prepared and ate his meals at his own fire and carried a staff in his right hand and Douglas fir branches in his left over his head. Relatives cut the ends of their hair, but the widow cut hers short. Family members, including children, wore plaited grass necklaces until they fell off; they never spoke the dead person's name again.

CURRENT TRIBAL ISSUES

Interest in traditional religion, tradition, dances, and language is high. The tribe has been working to restore many of the practices that had been outlawed or lost over the decades of reservation living. One of their missions has been to recover artifacts, sacred objects, and human remains that have been taken by museums, colleges, and individuals.

Dams on the Klamath River have reduced the river flow and killed many salmon, affecting the Yurok's ability to subsist. Although they won the right to fish there, they have restricted fishing until the fish population increases. Pollution, too, is causing many difficulties.

Poverty on the reservation has been severe; more than 70 percent of the homes were without basic phone or electric service in the early 2000s. In 2007, the Yurok received approval to build a casino, and funds from gaming gave the tribe more resources to help their people. With the $90 million settlement they received as part of the Hoopa-Yurok Settlement Act, the Yurok began to install utility services, improve homes and roads, construct public buildings, and fund higher education.

In 2011, the Yurok reservation acquired 22,237 acres of their former homeland. This land, which more than doubles the size of the reservation, will be used as a community forest. The Yurok want to restore the salmon habitats and the meadows that were formerly used for hunting and gathering. They hope this additional land will aid them in bringing back many traditional practices, including hunting, fishing, gathering, and basketmaking.

NOTABLE PEOPLE

Two of the most well-known Yurok women during the late 1800s and early 1900s were Lucy Thompson (1856–1932), who wrote *To the American Indian: Reminiscences of a Yurok Woman* in 1916 to preserve her tribe's culture and heritage, and Fanny Flounder (c. 1870–1945), a famous tribal doctor. Other Yurok who achieved fame include Robert Spott (1888–1953), coauthor of the *Yurok Narratives* published in 1942 and chairman of the Yurok Tribal Council; Leo Carpenter Jr., a Karuk-Hupa-Yurok Indian known for his basket weaving and his contributions to the California Indian Cultural Center and Museum (CICCM); Frank G. Gist Jr. (1954–), a self-taught carver; and Amy Smoker (1897–1989), a weaver who created baskets that continue to be used in ceremonies.

BOOKS

Buckley, Thomas, and Alma Gottlieb, eds. *Blood Magic: The Anthropology of Menstruation.* Berkeley: University of California Press, 1988.

Buckley, Thomas. *Standing Ground: Yurok Indian Spirituality, 1850–1990.* Berkeley: University of California Press, 2002.

Holm, Bill. *Spirit and Ancestor: A Century of Northwest Coast Indian Art in the Burke Museum.* Seattle: Burke Museum; University of Washington Press, 1987.

Gray-Kanatiiosh, Barbara A. *Yurok.* Edina, MN: ABDO, 2007.

Irwin, Lee, ed. *Native American Spirituality: A Critical Reader.* Lincoln: University of Nebraska Press, 2000.

Keeling, Richard. *Cry for Luck: Sacred Song and Speech Among the Yurok, Hupa, and Karok Indians of Northwestern California.* Berkeley: University of California Press, 1993.

O'Neale, Lila M. *Yurok-Karok Basket Weavers.* Berkeley, CA: Phoebe A. Hearst Museum of Anthropology, 2007.

Platt, Tony. *Grave Matters: Excavating California's Buried Past.* Berkeley, CA: Heyday, 2011.

Spott, Robert, and A. L. Kroeber. *Yurok Narratives.* Trinidad, CA: Trinidad Museum Society, 1997.

Thompson, Lucy. *To the American Indian: Reminiscences of a Yurok Woman.* Berkeley: Heyday Books, 1991.

WEB SITES

Edward S. Curtis's The North American Indian, Vol. 13. Northwestern University Digital Library Collections. http://curtis.library.northwestern.edu/curtis/viewPage.cgi?showp=1&size=2&id=nai.13.book.00000064&volume=13 (accessed on August 11, 2011).

Fryer, Francesca. "Sandspit II." *A Redwood Northcoast Notebook.* http://www.sandspitbooks.com/book2.html (accessed on August 11, 2011).

Redish, Laura, and Orrin Lewis. "Native Languages of the Americas: Yurok." *Native Languages of the Americas.* http://www.native-languages.org/yurok.htm (accessed on August 11, 2011).

Sanella, Lee. "Yurok Indians of the Klamath River and Delta Bay." *The Visionary Life.* http://skaggsisland.org/humanistic/sannella/visionarylife.html (accessed on December 1, 2011).

"Yurok." *Four Directions Institute.* http://www.fourdir.com/yurok.htm (accessed on August 11, 2011).

"The Yurok." *California History Online.* http://www.californiahistoricalsociety.org/timeline/chapter2/002d.html# (accessed on August 11, 2011).

"Yurok Language Project." *University of California.* http://linguistics.berkeley.edu/-yurok/ (accessed on August 11, 2011).

The Yurok Tribe. http://www.yuroktribe.org/ (accessed on August 11, 2011).

Plateau

Plateau

Anumber of Native tribal communities of the Plateau region of the Northwest continue to live in their ancestral lands, which once spread across the Columbia River Plateau of eastern Oregon and Washington State. Many years ago, ancestors of the area's tribes migrated south from northern territories in present-day British Columbia, Canada, and eventually moved throughout the northwestern United States.

The various Native nations on the Plateau shared their natural environment as well as an array of cultural traditions. Tribal elders of the Spokane (pronounced *spoh-KAN*), Flathead, Nez Percé (*nez-PURSE* or *nay per-SAY*), Cayuse (*KIE-yoos*), Okanagan (*OAK-uh-NAHG-uhn*), Wishram (*WISH-rum*), and neighboring tribes were united by the belief that their Creator had placed them on the Plateau. They trace their history to when the earth was new. The tribes in the area possess remarkable oral traditions about their origins and their interactions with nature.

For generations the Plateau tribes adapted their lifestyle to the landscape, developing complex cultures around the rich natural environment of the region's salmon-filled rivers. Their land was lush with fertile soil, evergreen forests, and wide varieties of game and vegetation. Inevitably, such natural wealth attracted the attention of U.S. explorers and settlers, especially as Americans began journeying westward at the turn of the nineteenth century.

Encountering outsiders

Many of the Plateau tribes played significant roles in the expedition that American explorers Meriwether Lewis (1774–1809) and William Clark (1770–1838) led through the Plateau and out to the Pacific Ocean between 1804 and 1806. Their Corps of Discovery surveyed the Plateau region and its peoples, while outlining the potential development of the continent for U.S. president Thomas Jefferson (1743–1826; served 1801–09).

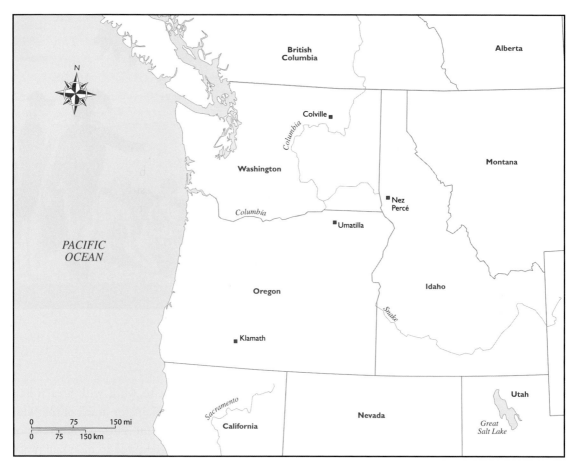

A map showing some contemporary Native American communities in the Plateau region. MAP BY XNR PRODUCTIONS. CENGAGE LEARNING, GALE. REPRODUCED BY PERMISSION OF GALE, A PART OF CENGAGE LEARNING.

Lewis and Clark, the first whites that many Plateau tribes had ever encountered, entered the land of the Nez Percé in October 1805. The tribe offered them food and canoes, enabling the expeditionary force to travel to the Pacific Coast. Other Plateau region tribes—the Wishram, the Walla Walla, and the Cayuse among them—sent diplomatic representatives to meet Lewis and Clark. Goods were exchanged. A special medal bearing the image of two hands shaking and engraved with the words "Peace and Friendship" was presented to tribal chiefs by the U.S. government, and more than fifty Native chiefs accepted an invitation to meet President Jefferson in Washington, D.C.

Explorers Lewis and Clark were the first whites that many Native American people had ever seen. © NORTH WIND PICTURE ARCHIVES/ALAMY.

Impact on Native culture

William Clark later returned to the Plateau to work with area tribes. When he became superintendent of Indian Affairs for much of the West in 1807, he was widely recognized as a fair and effective advocate of Native interests. Clark and others like him attempted to maintain peace and forge satisfactory relationships with the region's Native peoples, but they were not able to prevent the devastating consequences brought about by the development of the West. The transformation of the Plateau region into U.S. territory altered nearly every aspect of life for the tribes who resided there.

The United States eventually staked its claim to the entire Northwest, including the Plateau region, and began encouraging U.S. settlement in the area. Because Lewis and Clark had observed and reported on the numerous furbearing animals of the region, traders and trading companies took an immediate interest in developing the fur industry on the Plateau. Within a matter of years, the animal population was decimated by trappers, and the tribes had lost a valuable natural resource.

Decades before the American development of the West, certain cultural changes began taking place among the tribes of the Plateau. The Shoshone tribe acquired horses—probably through trade with

Spaniards—and as a result travel by horse became popular throughout the Plateau region. Prior to that time, the Plateau tribes engaged solely in hunting, fishing, and gathering activities. Contact with traders, explorers, and missionaries who moved through these tribal territories also brought exposure to non-Native diseases, especially smallpox, which struck the people hard early in the nineteenth century.

In an attempt to "civilize" the tribes, U.S. policymakers failed to see the importance of maintaining traditional Native ways of life. The American reformers had little or no knowledge of the region's Native cultures, their traditional economic practices, or their heavy reliance on natural resources. The tribes ended up being forced onto reservations by the U.S. government. (Reservations are lands set aside for use by tribes.)

Allotment

In 1887, Congress passed the Allotment Act, which divided the reservations into small plots of land that were to be owned by individual tribal members. Prior to that, almost all Native communities owned land communally, and this was a vital part of their traditions. After tribal members received their allotments, the government sold the remaining reservation land to nontribal members who used it for harvesting timber, farming, and ranching. The American government began allotting tribal reservation land in the Plateau region in the 1890s and continued the process until 1914. Conservative Native nations (those who favored the old ways and were opposed to change) rejected the allotment process. Many were worshipers of the Washani religion, a belief system that emphasized the preservation of Native lands and traditions. Still, the government's policy continued.

On June 19, 1902, Congress passed a resolution directing the secretary of the Department of the Interior to allot Spokane tribal land

Other pioneers

Lewis and Clark were the first in a long line of explorers—including American army officer Zebulon Pike (1779–1813), American military and political leader John Charles Frémont (1813–1890), and American geologist John Wesley Powell (1834–1902)—who were sent into the West by the federal government. Their mission was to penetrate the Native territories and prepare the way for U.S. settlers to take over the tribal lands.

In 1843, John Frémont began developing the westward path that had first been explored by Lewis and Clark. He surveyed the Oregon Trail (a route stretching from western Missouri through Nebraska, Wyoming, and Idaho and into Oregon) through Modoc (pronounced MOH-dock; see entry) territory. Within a decade, pioneers moved in great numbers through Modoc hunting grounds, scaring game and depleting the tribal food supply. With rations scarce, the tribe became more vulnerable to disease. Epidemics (uncontrolled outbreaks of disease) started taking their toll on the Native population. In frustration, the Modoc attacked the settlers, who then retaliated with much greater force. Overall, the efforts to "open" the West to U.S. citizens brought disastrous consequences for the Native peoples of the region.

holdings. The Spokane could do nothing to prevent the division and destruction of their territory. Land that was not distributed among the Spokane people was sold to non-Native businesses, farmers, and ranchers.

On the Flathead Reservation, the allotment process yielded similar results. In its original form, the Flathead Reservation consisted of about 1.25 million acres of land. From 1904 until 1908, U.S. policymakers allotted 80 acres each to the Salish (Flathead) they designated as "farmers" (not many Plateau Indians farmed) and 160 acres each to those identified as "ranchers." In all, less than 2,500 Native people were assigned allotments on the Flathead Reservation. The 400,000 acres that remained—a third of the original reservation—were sold, and the state of Montana retained about 60,000 acres for the construction of schools.

Aside from losing significant portions of their lands, the Plateau tribes became victims of treaty violations—violations that robbed them of fishing rights and timber interests. For example, the Nez Percé filed petitions with the Indian Claims Commission in July 1951 for the theft of their original homelands in northeastern Oregon and western Idaho. The claim was not settled until twenty years later, when the victorious Nez Percé received $3.5 million to compensate for the loss.

Termination and beyond

During the 1950s, the U.S. government began to "terminate," or put an end to, the reservation system and the treaty relationships it had established with tribes throughout the United States. The Confederated Tribes of the Colville Reservation in the state of Washington were particular targets of the termination policy. Colville tribal members who were not living on the reservation accepted termination in the hopes that it would bring them individual cash settlements. Those tribal members living on the reservation, however, rejected termination, fearing it would lead to the loss of historically established treaties and the destruction of the Colville tribal culture.

The Colville fought termination for many years. Finally, in the late 1960s, the U.S. government ended the termination policy. The Colville Reservation in the early twenty-first century remains intact and is stronger than ever. Workshops are offered to revitalize tribal culture, and the annual Powwow and Circle Celebration help unite tribal members and enhance community life. A sawmill, a mail-order log cabin sales business, and a trading post aided economic development among the Colville Indians. Casinos, commercial farmland, timber harvesting, and tourism provide income for the tribe as well as jobs for its people into the second decade of the 2000s.

The Flathead Reservation has also undergone vital tribal economic and cultural revitalization over the past two decades. There, the Kootenai (pronounced *COO-ten-eye*), the Kalispel, and the Salish people work hard to preserve tribal languages, oral histories and stories, and traditional ways of life. Financial support for this critical mission comes from business partnerships established between the tribe and the Montana Power Company. The operation of the Kerr Dam on the reservation land and the development of a tourist resort at Blue Bay on Flathead Lake provide key economic support for the reservation's cultural outreach programs, as well as jobs for many Flathead Reservation tribal members. Revenue from forestry and gaming supports health care and other tribal programs.

Freed from the destructive policy of termination, the tribes of the Plateau Region are now focusing their energies on other issues. For example, the Cayuse, Umatilla (pronounced *you-muh-TILL-uh*), and Walla Walla tribes of the Umatilla Reservation in Oregon are trying to cope with the devastating consequences of depression, especially among the younger generations of tribal members. The rates of alcoholism and suicide are statistically much higher among the Native people on the reservations than among the rest of the American population. Tribal leaders are determined to reverse these trends.

Fanning the fires of tradition

Throughout the nineteenth and twentieth centuries, the tribes of the Plateau region sought to retain a measure of tribal identity, control, and uniqueness. U.S. government policy has had a devastating impact on their culture, land, and resources. Nevertheless, the Plateau tribes are working to preserve traditions through education, language training, and social activities. Their respect for old ways, however, has not blinded them to the realities of life in the modern world. They offer scholarship programs for college education, day-care centers to allow more parents to work, and public health programs aimed at treating and preventing alcoholism, depression, and a host of other social ills. Education, both in tribal traditions and in standard college courses and job-training programs, has become the key survival tool of all the Plateau region nations.

By the beginning of the twenty-first century, the Plateau region nations were actively engaged in sharing their own story of the Northwest expansion. They have invested in extremely successful gaming resorts, arts and crafts enterprises, business councils, wildlife and fisheries management, timber processing and protection, and legal claims to tribal land, fishing, and water rights. The conservation of salmon sources, as one example, has been the focus of intense effort on the part of the Nez Percé, Yakama (pronounced *YAYK-uh-muh* or *YAYK-uh-maw*), and Palouse (*puh-LOOS*) over the past decades. Fortunately, an increasing number of U.S. citizens have come to respect the rights of the Native peoples. Tribal fishing rights were a hot political issue in the 1992 campaign for governor of the state of Washington; the state elected a staunch supporter of Native nation treaty rights.

The tribes of the Plateau region have found the means to provide for themselves and control their own destiny. Whether they are seeking renewed rights to old salmon fishing territories, reclaiming ancestral lands, developing new industries, securing political support, or devising tribal educational and public health strategies, the tribal leaders of the Plateau are becoming—like Lewis and Clark—pathfinders in their own terrain. In the early twenty-first century, Native nations were seeking to recapture the West for themselves.

BOOKS

Ackerman, Lillian A. *A Necessary Balance: Gender and Power Among Indians of the Columbia Plateau.* Norman: University of Oklahoma Press, 2003.

Ackerman, Lillian A., ed. *A Song to the Creator: Traditional Arts of Native American Women of the Plateau.* Norman: University of Oklahoma Press, 1996.

Aguilar, George W., Sr. *When the River Ran Wild!: Indian Traditions on the Mid-Columbia and the Warm Springs Reservation.* Portland: Oregon Historical Society Press, 2005.

Brown, John Arthur, and Robert H. Ruby. *Dreamer-Prophets of the Columbia Plateau: Smohalla and Skolaskin.* Norman: University of Oklahoma Press, 2002.

Downey, Roger. *Riddle of the Bones: Politics, Science, Race, and the Story of Kennewick Man.* New York: Copernicus, 2000.

Fitzgerald, Judith, and Michael Oren Fitzgerald, eds. *The Spirit of Indian Women.* Bloomington, IN: World Wisdom, 2005.

Ditchfield, Christin. *Plateau Indians.* Chicago: Heinemann Library, 2012.

Doherty, Craig A., and Katherine M. Doherty. *Plateau Indians.* New York: Chelsea House, 2008.

Indians of the Northwest Coast and Plateau. Chicago: World Book, 2009.

Kuiper, Kathleen, ed. *American Indians of the Plateau and Plains.* New York: Rosen Educational Services, 2012.

Ortega, Simon, ed. *Handbook of North American Indians.* Vol. 12: *The Plateau.* Washington, DC: Smithsonian Institution, 1978.

Simms, Steven R. *Ancient Peoples of the Great Basin and the Colorado Plateau.* Walnut Creek, CA: Left Coast Press, 2008.

Tate, Michael L. *Indians and Emigrants: Encounters on the Overland Trails.* Norman: University of Oklahoma Press, 2006.

Waldman, Carl, ed. *Encyclopedia of Native American Tribes.* New York: Facts on File, 2006.

Wilkinson, Charles F. *Blood Struggle: The Rise of Modern Indian Nations.* New York: W. W. Norton, 2005.

WEB SITES

"Columbia River History: Indian Tribes." *Northwest Power and Conservation Council.* http://www.nwcouncil.org/history/IndianTribes.asp (accessed on August 11, 2011).

Columbia River Inter-Tribal Fish Commission. http://www.critfc.org/ (accessed on August 11, 2010).

"First Nations: People of the Interior." *British Columbia Archives.* http://www.bcarchives.gov.bc.ca/exhibits/timemach/galler07/frames/int_peop.htm (accessed on August 11, 2011).

"Indians of the Northwest—Plateau and Coastal." *St. Joseph School Library.* http://library.stjosephsea.org/plateau.htm (accessed on August 11, 2011).

Monroe, Barbara. "Plateau Indian Ways with Words." *National Council of Teachers of English.* http://www.ncte.org/library/NCTEFiles/Resources/Journals/CCC/0611-sep09/CCC0611Plateau.pdf (accessed on August 11, 2011).

Nesbit, Jack. "Plateau Indians Pit House Information." *Wellpinit School District.* http://www.wellpinit.wednet.edu/pithouses (accessed on August 11, 2011).

"Plateau Indians." *University of Connecticut Libraries.* http://classguides.lib.uconn.edu/content.php?pid=147451&sid=1327191 (accessed on August 11, 2011).

"Questions and Answers about the Plateau Indians." *Wellpinit School District 49 (WA).* http://www.wellpinit.wednet.edu/sal-qa/qa.php (accessed on August 11, 2011).

Redish, Laura, and Orrin Lewis. "Indian Tribes and Languages of the Great Plateau." *Native Languages of the Americas.* http://www.native-languages.org/plateau-culture.htm (accessed on August 11, 2011).

Colville

Name

The Colville (pronounced *COAL-vill*) were known by many names. In 1846, an American coined the term "Basket People," referring to the tall woven baskets the Colville made to snare salmon. The tribe has also been called *Scheulpi* or *Chualpay*. French traders called them *Les Chaudières* ("the kettles"), perhaps because they lived near Kettle Falls. The name by which they are most commonly known, Colville, was that of Governor Eden Colville of the Hudson's Bay Company. They may also have been named for Colonel John Colville of the U.S. Army, the local Indian agent.

Location

The Colville Reservation, about 100 miles (160 kilometers) northwest of Spokane, covers about 1.4 million acres of land in northeastern Washington State, ranging from the Okanagon River in the west, south to the Spokane River, and as far east as the Columbia River. The reservation has four districts: Omak, Nespelem, Keller, and Inchelium. It is located in southeastern Okanogan county and the southern half of Ferry County, but a small piece of off-reservation trust land lies in Chelan County, northwest of the city of Chelan.

Population

In 1806, there were an estimated 2,500 Colville. In 1904, only 321 were left. In the 1990 U.S. Census, 7,057 people identified themselves as Colville. According to the 2000 census, that number had increased to 8,398, and 10,076 people claimed to have some Colville ancestry. Tribal enrollment in 2007 was 8,700. By the time of the 2010 census, 8,114 Colville were counted, with 10,549 people claiming some Colville heritage. According to tribal sources, the total enrollment in 2011 had reached 9,365.

Language family

Salishan.

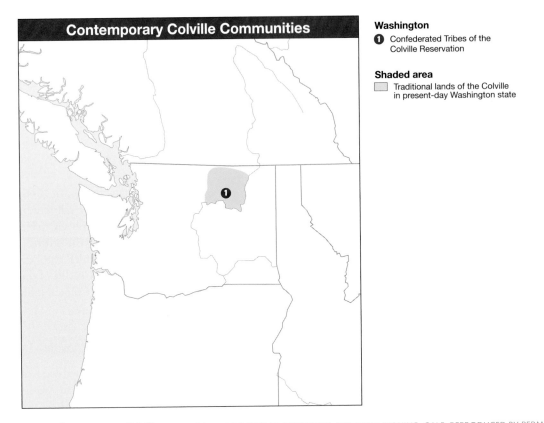

Contemporary Colville Communities

Washington
① Confederated Tribes of the
Colville Reservation

Shaded area
Traditional lands of the Colville
in present-day Washington state

A map of contemporary Colville communities. MAP BY XNR PRODUCTIONS. CENGAGE LEARNING, GALE. REPRODUCED BY PERMISSION OF GALE, A PART OF CENGAGE LEARNING.

Origins and group affiliations

The Colville settled in the Northwest around 1500, migrating from present-day British Columbia, Canada. They were closely related to other Salishan-speaking groups, including the Okanagon, Lake, and Sanpoil tribes. During the eighteenth century, the Colville allied with the Okanagon to fight the Nez Percé and Yakama tribes farther to the south. Conflict with the Shuswap and Blackfoot was common, and the Colville took Blackfoot and Umatilla women as slaves. After the fur trade began, the tribe often intermarried with French Canadians and Iroquois.

The Colville were one of the largest tribes in the Pacific Northwest, inhabiting a land rich in natural resources. Once the Colville Reservation was established, at least ten different tribes lived there together, producing a rich new culture. In modern times, this jointly owned land offers timber and mineral resources, water power for hydroelectric plants (to make electricity), and fish and wildlife preserves.

HISTORY

Early European contact

The first meeting between the Colville and Europeans may have occurred before 1800, but no records of the contact exist. In 1782 and 1783, a smallpox epidemic swept through the area, indicating that Europeans were nearby. Later, other contagious diseases would have killed most of the tribe if Roman Catholic priests had not given the people vaccines.

In addition to diseases, the Europeans also introduced horses. When the Colville obtained horses in the eighteenth century, their territory expanded. By the early 1800s, they had begun trading furs at the Northwest Company. In 1806, the Lewis and Clark expedition, which was exploring the western lands of the United States, visited the tribe.

Settlement of Colville territory

Kettle Falls became the center of Colville activities. There they fished, traded with Europeans, and met with Roman Catholic missionaries. The North West Company and the Pacific Fur Company set up depots for trade in 1811. A little over a decade later in 1825, the Hudson's Bay Company, the powerful British traders, established Fort Colville. It came to be the second largest center for fur trading in the Northwest. In 1845, the Jesuits, a Roman Catholic priestly order, built a log chapel there, and Father Pierre-Jean De Smet (1801–1873) conducted services for the Colville people.

In the mid-1800s, the ever-growing groups of settlers caused problems for the Natives, especially when they brought another smallpox epidemic in 1853. The Colville way of life was further disrupted from 1858 to 1860 by prospectors who crossed their territory on their way to search for gold near the Fraser River.

Members of the U.S. military were stationed at Kettle Falls in 1859 to staff a new fort that had been established there. The Americans built the fort when they discovered the Native peoples in the area excelled at

Important Dates

1782–83: Smallpox epidemic strikes the Colville population.

1825: Fort Colville is established.

1846: Treaty of Washington divides Okanagan territory and gives United States control of the Oregon Territory.

1872: The Colville Reservation is established.

1892: U.S. government takes the northern half of the reservation.

1938: Constitution is approved; Colville Business Council is formed to govern tribe.

1938: Newly opened Grand Coulee Dam floods salmon spawning areas, orchards, and farms.

1956: Federal government returns about 800,000 acres of reservation land to the tribe.

1984: The Colville Tribal Enterprise Corporation (CTEC) is established to improve economic development.

trapping and stalking game and would benefit the fur trade. Father De Smet—a priest well known among other tribes of the Pacific Northwest—soon came to live among the Colville; he had previously established the mission near Kettle Falls. The Saint Francis Regis Mission soon became a favorite site for tribes to meet and visit with one another.

The Colville disliked the fact that large numbers of settlers, miners, and soldiers were crowding their territory, but their chiefs did not join the wars that neighboring tribes, such as the Yakama (see entry), waged against the settlers. Facing superior firepower and greater numbers, the Colville realized that they had little chance of winning such battles.

Reservation life

The three-million-acre Colville Reservation east of the Columbia River was established in 1872 for the Colville and other area tribes, including the Okanagon, Sanpoil, Lake, Kalispel, Spokane, and Coeur d'Alene (*ker-duh-LEEN*). However, American settlers wanted the fertile land of the river valley for themselves and urged the government to move the tribe again. The land also proved to be rich in minerals. Only three months after the reservation was established, the government relocated the tribes to a second reservation west of the Columbia River.

In the 1870s, the reservation was reduced to half its original size. In 1892 Congress took over the northern half of the acreage and allotted a portion of it to tribal members. This meant the government divided the reservation land into small plots and gave one to each household, then invited American colosts to settle on the leftover land. The federal government also purchased 1.5 million acres of unallotted land but allowed the Colville to retain their hunting and fishing rights to this property. In 1900, 1.4 million acres went to homesteaders. The government allotted the southern half of the reservation five years later. By 1916, they opened the remaining 417,841 acres to settlers.

During this time the tribes on the new reservation formed the Confederated Tribes of the Colville Reservation. The newly united group struggled with American settlers and with each other over land rights, a struggle that resulted in several lawsuits. In 1956, the Colville won a case against the federal government, and the United States returned about 800,000 acres of reservation land to the tribe. It was, however, only a small portion of that which had originally been taken. To restore that additional acreage, the Colville Business Council has been buying back any parcels of original reservation land that go up for sale as they can afford it.

In modern times, in addition to the Colville, the Confederation is made up of eleven bands, including the Wenatchee, Entiat, Chelan, Methow, Okanogan, Nespelem, San Poil, Lake, Moses-Columbia, Palus, and Nez Percé (see entry). With a land rich in resources, they have been able to thrive. They are very much a part of modern society, but they also strive to preserve their ancient customs.

RELIGION

The Colville refer to their supreme being by various names. One is "The Chief Above." The people believe that all things found in nature—animals, rocks, plants—contain spirits that can be called on for aid in healing, raising crops, and making war. Young men and women take part in a vision quest—a ceremony in which they undergo a secluded training period in the wilderness to seek out their guardian spirit (see "Puberty"). The guardian spirit protects the individual and guides him or her throughout life.

In the nineteenth century, some Colville adopted the Roman Catholic religion, whereas others became Protestants. The twentieth century saw the Colville people become involved in the Seven Drum religion (which included playing sacred drums), the Native American Church (see Makah entry), and the Indian Shaker religion (see sidebar). Many Christian Colville take part in Native religious practices as well.

Indian Shaker Religion

John Slocum, a member of the Squaxin tribe, founded the Indian Shaker religion in 1881 near Olympia, Washington. Slocum became ill and seemed to have died; he returned to life with a mission to found a new church. About a year later, before starting his missionary work, Slocum fell ill again. As his wife, Mary, approached his sickbed, she trembled uncontrollably. Her shaking was seen as a divine sign and became a part of Slocum's religious services.

Slocum recovered, and word of his religion spread. It came to be known as the Indian Shaker religion, and tribes from California to British Columbia practiced it. Each tribe added its own variations.

The Indian Shaker religion combined elements of Native and Christian beliefs and practices. Members used crucifixes, bells, candles, pictures, dancing, and prayer in their services. Originally they did not read the Bible because they believed God communicated to them directly. Later some "progressives" allowed written materials, but traditionalists did not.

Christian missionaries and government Indian agents objected to their meetings, and the Indian Shakers called a meeting on June 6, 1892, to assert their right to practice the religion. Eventually they were left in peace, and the religion is still practiced today.

LANGUAGE

The Salishan language family includes twenty-three languages divided into three major branches: Coast Salish, Tsamosan Salish, and Interior Salish. The Interior branch spoken by the Colville is the most popular of the three

Colville Words

naks	"one"
usil	"two"
kalis	"three"
mus	"four"
tsilikst	"five"
sqaltumiah	"man"
tłkłamiluh	"woman"
xai'alax	"sun"
sokemm	"moon"
si'ulq	"water"

branches. In the early twenty-first century, more than three thousand people spoke the language. Elders are training young speakers as teachers so the language can be passed on to the next generation.

GOVERNMENT

In the early days, each village was an independent unit headed by a chief. The chief was usually the oldest member of the group. He decided when it was time to move to a new area and was in charge of running ceremonies and keeping the peace within the village. Usually, the chief's younger brother took over the job when the chief died.

In modern times, a fourteen-member business council governs the Colville Reservation from its administrative offices in Nespelem. Members are elected to staggered two-year terms. A chairperson, vice chairperson, and secretary, chosen by the council to serve one-year terms, lead the Colville Business Council. Members receive pay while they are in office. A tribal administrator oversees the administrative department of the reservation and reports directly to the council.

ECONOMY

Early lifestyle

For centuries, the tribe subsisted as hunter-gatherers, living mainly on fish. They gathered roots and berries and hunted deer and small game, first for food and later for furs to trade. Groups of men worked together to drive deer over cliffs or into blinds. The Colville had four main hunts a year: 1) deer and sheep in spring; 2) elk, bear, sheep, and deer in late fall; 3) deer in midwinter; and 4) sheep in late winter. After they acquired horses, they also hunted bison.

Once the Canadian border had been established, the tribe could no longer roam freely. They were further confined on the reservation. Many turned to farming to survive. Others worked as loggers or laborers. When the federal government opened the Grand Coulee Dam in 1938, it flooded many farms and orchards and destroyed salmon spawning grounds. This drastically changed the tribe's economic base and lifestyle.

Modern economy

Today, the tribe's main natural resource is its forests. It owns more than a million acres of valuable timberlands, and timber is processed at a sawmill and wood treatment plant. Its wood products are marketed worldwide. To replenish its forests, a tribal nursery grows and replants trees. In addition, Colville Tribal Enterprise Corporation (CTEC) owns a construction company that uses the lumber. The company builds tribal housing and public facilities on the reservation and has secured construction contracts with the U.S. Army, the Bureau of Indian Affairs, and the U.S. Forest Service. In the early 2000s, CTEC also managed thirteen other enterprises, employed one thousand people, and generated over $120 million in revenue each year.

Other businesses that CTEC oversees include the casinos, retail businesses, and recreation and tourism. Tourist attractions are the Grand Coulee Dam on the reservation and eighteen lakes, including Lake Roosevelt, which backs up for 150 miles (240 kilometers) behind the dam. On the site of the dam is an art gallery and tribal museum with exhibits representing each of the twelve tribes that now live on the Colville Reservation. The nearby luxury houseboat rental operation began in 1988. The Kettle Falls Historical Center features Native American crafts, history, and a retail shop. Small business development and mining also provide income and employment opportunities.

The reservation has extensive ranges for grazing livestock, forested rangelands, and farmlands. The tribe owns cattle and horses. It also runs a profitable meatpacking operation and raises wheat, alfalfa, barley, and apples. The tribal fish hatchery stocks many lakes and streams throughout north-central Washington.

DAILY LIFE

Buildings

Like many tribes who lived in cold climates, the Colville maintained both winter and summer homes. Their early winter dwellings were about 45 feet (14 meters) in diameter and were located almost completely underground. These circular lodgings were entered through a hole in the roof. Later homes were lodges, 20 to 60 feet (6 to 18 meters) long and covered with several layers of tule mats, fir branches, and bark. The Colville dug a few feet into the dirt so their homes were partially underground.

In the summer, the Colville lived in cone-shaped or oblong homes of pole frames wrapped with mats made from rushes. They used portable tents made from animal skins when hunting buffalo farther south.

The Colville also constructed sweathouses, structures used by men and women for religious rites of purification. They filled the building with steam by pouring water over heated rocks. Visiting a sweathouse was part of the ritual in which people sought their guardian spirits. Men also purified themselves in sweathouses before they hunted.

Manufacturing

Because they lived near many rivers and lakes, the Colville often traveled in canoes made of white pine or birch bark. They also used trees to create many useful items—baskets from birch bark, coiled cedar, or spruce roots; bows and arrow shafts of juniper; and snowshoes from a variety of woods. They wove blankets from goat's wool or strips of rabbit's fur and made sacks from bulrushes, bark, and hemp.

The sister and granddaughter of Colville chief Moses pose at the Colville Reservation, circa 1902. UNIVERSITY OF WASHINGTON LIBRARIES. SPECIAL COLLECTIONS DIVISION.

To keep food from spoiling, they inflated animal intestines using a tube made from an elderberry stem. They then filled these flexible sacs with grease, dried meat or fish, nuts, berries, or roots. This kept their food fresh for long periods of time. They also stuffed softened animal skins with down feathers to make pillows.

Clothing and adornment

In the winter, Colville women wore tunics with leggings and moccasins. Men wore leggings, moccasins, and breechcloths (flaps of animal skin that covered the front and back and were suspended from the waist). The Colville fringed, punctured, and embroidered their clothing using porcupine quills and decorated them with seeds, hoofs, shells, elk's teeth, tufts of hair, feathers, and ermine skins. Both men and women added fur robes for warmth. They lined their moccasins with bunchgrass, goat hair, or down to keep out the cold.

During the summer, men and children usually went nude or wore a blanket around their waists. Most people went barefoot. Until the nineteenth century, both men and women wore nose pins. Many people used face and body paint, but tattooing was uncommon. Sometime in the twentieth century, most men opted for very short hair over the traditional long braids, but during the 1990s, some men returned to the earlier style.

Food

Their location near the Northwest Coast provided the Colville with a rich and varied menu. Their staple food was salmon, and they ate the entire fish, including the head. They often retrieved the salmon that died after spawning and ate those, too. Traveling with nearby tribes, the men hunted deer, elk, bear, and beaver as well as buffalo. Following a hunt or large catch, the tribe held a feast. The leftovers were dried or frozen for later consumption. The stored food supplied their nutritional needs during the winter.

As soon as spring arrived, the Colville replenished their food supplies. Food hunts were extremely well organized. Special camps were set up for fishing and collecting nuts, roots, and berries. Camas, an edible root, along with other roots and huckleberries were particularly favored. In the early spring, before the salmon camps were established, the Colville sought out suckerfish and steelhead trout.

Education

Colville children learned how to do the duties of men and women by observing their elders. Mission schools operated during the nineteenth century, but in modern times, most students attend public schools on the reservation or the nearby Paschel Sherman Indian School. A number of tribal members seek higher education in fields that will make them useful to the reservation, such as natural resource management, law, business, social work, and health policy. The Colville Tribal Enterprise Corporation set up a scholarship fund to assist students in paying for college.

In conjunction with the University of Washington, the Colville and Yakama tribes received a $500,000 grant to set up community technology centers in each tribal community. The Colville also began programs to

Chipmunk and the Owl Sisters

This Colville tale is part of a much longer tale that tells how Coyote tricks the Owl Sisters to save Chipmunk. It is set during the time animals had human characteristics, so the Owl Sisters have hands. This selection from the story explains why chipmunks have stripes on their backs. Grandmother sends Chipmunk to pick berries but warns her not to stay too long because the Owl Sisters will eat her.

"I will do as you say, Grandmother," Chipmunk said and she went into the forest with her berry basket. Soon she reached the berry bushes. She climbed up into them and began to pick. Before long she had picked eleven berries. But just as she picked the twelfth berry, she dropped it. When she reached down to pick it up, she brushed against some berries which were so ripe that the sweet juice covered her arm.

"Ah," Chipmunk said, "I must clean myself off." She licked off the berry juice. It was so sweet! "This is good," Chipmunk said. "I must have more." Then she put down her basket and climbed higher into the berry bushes and began to eat berries. She ate and she ate and the sun moved further toward the west. Now it was dark and the forest was filled with shadows, but still Chipmunk did not stop eating.

Suddenly Chipmunk heard a sound.... Chipmunk looked down and what she saw was so frightening that she almost screamed. There was the oldest of the Owl Sisters right below her.

"Little One," the Owl Sister said, "come down to me." She lifted her arms up toward Chipmunk. There were long sharp claws on the Owl Sister's hands and on her back was a basket full of the little ones she had caught. She was taking them home to eat them with her sisters. She wanted to put Chipmunk in her basket, too, but Chipmunk was too high up in the bushes for Owl to reach her. Chipmunk did not move....

"Come down," Owl said. "Your grand-mother wants you to come home."

Now Chipmunk did not know what to do. Perhaps her grandmother had called her. "I will come down," she said to Owl, "but you must cover your eyes."

"I will cover my eyes," Owl said and raised her arms over her face, but she peeked between her fingers.

Chipmunk did not climb down, though. Instead she took a great leap, right over Owl's head! Owl grabbed at her as she went by and scraped Chip-munk's back with three of her long claws. Ever since then, all Chipmunks bear those scars on their backs.

SOURCE: Caduto, Michael J., and Joseph Bruchac. *Keepers of the Night: Native American Stories and Nocturnal Activities for Children.* Golden, CO: Fulcrum Publishing, 1994.

teach the three languages spoken on the reservation. Tribal elders instruct young people who plan to become language teachers.

Healing practices

Male and female healers called shamans (pronounced *SHAH-munz* or *SHAY-munz*) were responsible for curing the sick, with the assistance of guardian spirits. They underwent a difficult training period to learn how to remove evil spirits from the afflicted. They cured by singing sacred songs and chants to drive the evil from the body. They practiced preventive medicine by warding off evil spirits before they could enter the body. Being a shaman was a risky business; it was common for a patient's family to kill one who failed to heal.

In modern times, the Indian Health Service provides health-care services on the reservation, and the people use hospitals in nearby towns. Programs instituted by the tribe include infant care, family planning, dental health, and substance-abuse counseling.

CUSTOMS

Birth and naming

During the last month of pregnancy, the mother stayed in a birth hut. Midwives assisted at the birth; a female shaman might be called in for difficult births. Afterward they washed the newborn in cool water, wrapped him or her in buckskin, and burned the afterbirth. Babies' noses and mouths were massaged daily to shape them properly. The mother and baby remained in the hut for a month.

When they returned home, a feast was held. The baby received a name chosen by elderly relatives. Such nicknames lasted until the child was nine years old; he or she then received another name at a feast and giveaway. Colville babies received ancestor names at birth. Later names referred to a war honor, special feat, or spiritual power.

Puberty

Before puberty, both boys and girls were sent to a secluded spot to train for a guardian spirit. They did physical activities, used the sweat lodge, took baths in herbs, and observed nature. With their faces marked with red paint or charcoal, they prayed at dawn and sunset. At night, they danced and begged the spirits to protect them. After a guardian spirit

Riders from the Colville Reservation take part in the annual Suicide Race in Omak, Washington. © RON WURZER/ GETTY IMAGES.

appeared and the child received a song, the child might carve or burn the spirit's face into wood or paint it on a rock.

Marriage

The parents of a couple exchanged gifts, but there was no real ceremony. In the early 1900s, a young couple walked together under an arch of saplings and wished for unity.

Funerals

The Colville flexed their dead, wrapped them in robes or mats, and either buried them on their sides in the ground or placed them in canoes. They marked the graves with a pile or circle of stones and placed a long stick at the head of the grave; three sticks stood for a shaman. The souls of the dead traveled to the land of the beyond, somewhere in the West or the South. After the death of a loved one, widows and widowers showed their grief by cutting off their hair and wearing old, tattered clothing.

Festivals

In times past, the Colville scheduled celebrations and ceremonies throughout the year. They performed puberty rites for girls, held a festival when the trees bore their first fruits, and conducted various dances on the occasions of going into battle, scalping enemies, summoning guardian spirits, getting married, and honoring the sun.

In modern times, the tribe holds a number of annual events, including the Omak Stampede and the world-famous Suicide Race, which take place in August and feature horse-related activities and Native food. The Suicide Race is a 225-foot (68.5-meter) downhill sprint, followed by an Okanogan River crossing and a 500-yard (457-meter) dash to the finish line. The Fourth of July Powwow at Nespelem attracts visitors from several states, many of whom come in Native dress to dance, play stick games, participate in parades, and enjoy rodeo events. Memorial giveaways are held in honor of deceased tribal members.

CURRENT TRIBAL ISSUES

Improving conditions on the reservation

The Confederated Tribes is working to improve conditions on the Colville reservation, but the people struggle with high unemployment rates. Many live below the national poverty level and lack adequate housing. Some have no water or electricity. The reservation also needs better roads, more youth shelters, and modernized health clinics. Other major problems include domestic violence, drug and alcohol abuse, and a high crime rate.

Since the middle of the twentieth century, the Colville have won a number of claims against the U.S. government for the past illegal takeover of land and for purchasing the land at unusually low prices.

Principles of Holistic Management

The Colville are trying to maintain their way of life as their resources decrease. The problems they face involve forest fires, inadequate road-ways, heavy use of pesticides, and clear-cutting (the removal of all the trees in an area). For years, they have used crisis management, that is, dealing with problems as they occur.

In recent years, the tribe's Natural Resources Department introduced holistic management. (Holism is a theory that nature works as a whole or complete unit, rather than as separate parts.) The Colville method of holistic management combines respecting both human values and the environment, rather than setting them against one another.

For example, not long ago elders were taken to an area on the reservation where timber is har-vested. They and the forest resource managers sat quietly there for hours. The elders then described their feelings about the condition of the land. They all expressed very deep sorrow.

After that, they were asked to offer suggestions about what would restore their pride in the land.

A conservationist in attendance explained: "They [the elders] talked about open, grassy parkland, pine forests, diversity of wildlife, diversity of cultural species, clean water, stable soils. That became part of the goal for that watershed plan."

The project planning team examined whether the proposed actions would lead toward or away from the goal. It took two years to convince the various specialists working on the project of the value and workability of the holistic decision-making process.

A conservationist noted that, because the new process fits with the tribe's traditional values, the people follow through and make better decisions. Council member and former Colville tribal chairperson Matthew Dick said: "Holistic management is getting all the people involved. That's the way our chiefs did it a long time ago."

The tribe also won a case that accused the federal government of mis-managing tribal resources. The lawsuit involved salmon runs that were destroyed by hydroelectric projects such as the Grand Coulee Dam. The money awarded as a result of these cases provided funds for a long-term program to repurchase former tribal lands.

Environmental concerns and successes

In 2004, tribal executives sued a Canadian business, Teck Cominco, because of pollution the company emits from its lead smelter at the Columbia River and Lake Victoria. The state of Washington joined the Colville in the lawsuit. The lead-zinc smelter, about 10 miles (16 kilometers) north of the U.S.-Canada border, has sent as much as 20 million tons of heavy metals from the smelter downriver to Lake Roosevelt. Because the firm does not operate within U.S. borders, the company tried to have the case dismissed. They were not successful, and the judge ordered the company to come up with a solution to reverse the damages.

In recent years, the Colville have begun using a new method for making decisions called holistic management. Holistic management considers the feelings and values of the people involved, not only the opinions of experts. The Colville are determined to manage their tribe wisely, to use its resources effectively, and to implement a plan for balanced economic and social development.

The Colville concern for the environment has been gaining them notice in many ways. In 2011, the Natural Resources Conservation Service awarded the Colville Confederated Tribes a grant for a little over one million dollars to demonstrate how to lower greenhouse gases. These Conservation Innovation Grants are given to environmental programs that have the possibility of being adopted on a nationwide scale. Other groups are also studying the Colville's fish hatchery and salmon management plans, hoping to have the same success. With salmon returning in greater numbers due to the Colville's excellent oversight of natural resources, the tribe has now begun a program to catch and freeze fish that will help feed the elderly and needy. Surplus fish have been distributed to other tribes in Washington State and Canada.

NOTABLE PEOPLE

Mourning Dove (c. 1885–1936; born Christine Quintasket) was a Colville/Okanagon writer and activist who fought for American Indian rights throughout her life. She helped found the Colville Indian Association and was the first woman elected to the Colville Tribal Council. She is considered the first female Native American novelist. Her first novel, *Cogewea, the Half Blood: A Depiction of the Great Montana Cattle Range,* was published in 1927. She then wrote traditional stories of her tribe, and her second book, *Coyote Stories,* was published in 1933. Her autobiography was published in 1990, long after her death.

BOOKS

Chatters, James C. *Ancient Encounters: Kennewick Man and the First Americans.* New York: Simon and Schuster, 2001.

De Smet, Pierre-Jean. *New Indian Sketches.* Ann Arbor: Scholarly Publishing Office, University of Michigan Library, 2006.

Dunn, Jacob Piatt. *Massacres of the Mountains: A History of the Indian Wars of the Far West 1815–1875.* Whitefish, MT: Kessinger Publishing, 2006.

Waldman, Carl. "Colville Reservation." In *Encyclopedia of Native American Tribes.* New York: Facts on File, 2006.

Smith, Jerry. *Boom Towns & Relic Hunters of Washington State.* Bellevue, WA: Elfin Cove Press, 2011.

PERIODICALS

Gooding, Susan S. *Imagined Spaces, Storied Places: A Case Study of the Colville Tribes and the Evolution of Treaty Fishing Rights.* Madison: Land Tenure Center, University of Wisconsin, 1998. Reprinted from *Revue Droit et Cultures* no. 33 (1997): 53–95.

WEB SITES

"Ancient One: Kennewick Man." *Confederated Tribes of the Umatilla Reservation.* http://www.umatilla.nsn.us/ancient.html (accessed on August 11, 2011).

"Colville Indian Reservation Chronology and Avery Project Bibliography." *Washington State University Libraries.* http://www.wsulibs.wsu.edu/holland/masc/xaverytime.html (accessed on August 11, 2011).

Colville Tribal Enterprise Corporation. http://ctecorp.org/enterprises/default.htm (accessed on August 11, 2011).

Confederated Tribes of the Colville Reservation. http://www.colvilletribes.com/ (accessed on August 11, 2011).

"Dams of the Columbia Basin and Their Effects on the Native Fishery." *Center for Columbia River History.* http://www.ccrh.org/comm/river/dams6.htm (accessed on August 11, 2011).

Donovan, Peter. "The Colville Tribe Blazes the Trail." *Managing Wholes: Creating a Future That Works.* http://managingwholes.com/cct6.htm (accessed on August 11, 2011).

Okanagan Nation Alliance. http://www.syilx.org/ (accessed on August 11, 2011).

Flathead

Name

The Flatheads called themselves *Séliš* (pronounced *SEH-lish*), *Se'lic, Salish,* or *Selish,* which means "people" or "we the people." They were sometimes referred to as *Sčhífsuhétŭqi* ("Red Willow River") after the stream where they made their home. Theories vary as to how the people acquired the name Flathead. Some say it was because they practiced head-flattening (strapping a board to a baby's forehead to shape the skull into a rounded point at the top of the head). Others say it was the opposite: the Flathead were one of the few tribes in that area who did not flatten their heads, so their skulls were flat on top rather than rounded. Pictures of the Flathead people from the 1800s show no signs of head-flattening. Another theory is that their name came from the Native custom of calling lakes "flat water." Because they were located near the headwaters, they called their waters "Flathead Lake," and the term was later used for the tribe itself.

Location

The Flatheads' original territory encompassed more than 20 million acres in what is now western Montana, parts of Idaho, Wyoming, and British Columbia, Canada. Later, they made their home in the valleys of Clark's Fork on the Columbia River and along its tributaries in present-day Montana. In the late 1800s, the Flathead began moving to the reservation they now occupy in northwestern Montana.

Population

At the time of the first European contact, about 400 Flatheads lived in thirty-three lodges, according to the explorers Meriwether Lewis (1774–1809) and William Clark (1770–1838). Other sources place the population between 600 and 3,000 during the 1800s. By 1875, 81 people had moved to Jocko Valley, and 304 remained at Bitterroot Valley. Because the Flathead intermarried and accepted members of refugee tribes, most were of mixed blood by the end of the nineteenth century. The 1990 U.S. Census showed 4,455 Flathead, living both on and off the reservation. By 2011, the Confederated Salish and Kootenai Tribes had a tribal enrollment of 7,753, of which about 65 percent lived on the reservation.

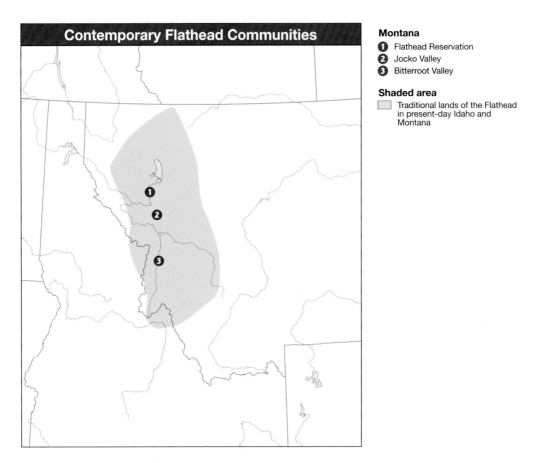

Contemporary Flathead Communities

Montana
1. Flathead Reservation
2. Jocko Valley
3. Bitterroot Valley

Shaded area
Traditional lands of the Flathead in present-day Idaho and Montana

A map of contemporary Flathead communities. MAP BY XNR PRODUCTIONS. CENGAGE LEARNING, GALE. REPRODUCED BY PERMISSION OF GALE, A PART OF CENGAGE LEARNING.

Language family

Salishan.

Origins and group affiliations

According to Flathead oral tradition, their people have always lived in Montana, but some anthropologists suggest they may have originated in the west, possibly Oregon. The Salish were living around the Columbia River in Montana when the American explorer William Clark recorded the names of four bands of Flatheads. He placed the "Oate-lash-schute Tribe of the Tush-she-pah Nation" in the Bitterroot (St. Mary's) Valley. This was the main group of Flatheads. The others that Clark named may have been the Kalispel, Colville (see entry), and Pend d'Oreille. These tribes had close relations and similar customs to the Flathead, and the Pend d'Oreille regularly made their summer camp with the Flathead. Intermarriage was common among the Flathead, so they incorporated into their tribe the Spokane, Delaware, Iroquois, Shoshone, Nez Percé (see entries), Tunàha, and many others. As for enemies, the Blackfoot, Shoshone (see entries) Sioux (see Dakota, Lakota, Nakota entries), Kutenai, Apsaroke, Piegan, Coeur d'Alene, and Bannock raided and stole horses from the Flatheads' large herds. In the twenty-first century, the Bitterroot Salish (Flathead), the Pend d'Oreille, and the Kootenai tribes live together on the Flathead Reservation as the Confederated Salish and Kootenai Tribes.

A peaceful people who negotiated for their rights rather than fighting, the Flathead welcomed refugees from other tribes and often intermarried, until by the 1900s few, if any, full-bloods remained. Although the people once roamed the northern plateau from Idaho and Montana to British Columbia, the government later confined them to a reservation in northwestern Montana that they share with the Kootenai and Pend d'Oreille. Now part of the Confederated Salish and Kootenai Tribes, a federally recognized nation, the people's philosophy and vision for the future is best expressed in this motto posted on their Web site by the Salish Culture Committee:

> Our stories teach us that we must always work for a time when there will be no evil, no racial prejudice, no pollution, when once again everything will be clean and beautiful for the eye to behold—a time when spiritual, physical, mental and social values are interconnected to form a complete circle.

Important Dates

1760–70; 1781: The Flathead and Blackfoot engage in war.

1805: American explorers Meriwether Lewis and William Clark arrive in Flathead territory.

1840: Father Pierre-Jean De Smet arrives. St. Mary's Mission is established the following year.

1855: Hell's Gate Treaty is signed. The Flathead cede their land and move to Bitterroot Valley.

1890–91: The Flathead move to Jocko Reservation.

1935: Under the Indian Reorganization Act, the bands living on the Flathead Reservation form a tribal government.

1960: The U.S. government pays more than $4 million for land taken in the 1855 treaty.

1977: Salish Kootenai College is founded.

HISTORY

Early tribal history

The Flathead and other closely connected tribes of Interior Salish once had as their homeland more than 20 million acres in present-day Montana, Idaho, Wyoming, and Canada. The people migrated from their buffalo hunting grounds on the northern plains to the Bitterroot Valley along the Columbia River, where they fished and gathered wild plants and berries. With the exception of skirmishes when other tribes raided their horses (see "Origins and group affiliations"), the Flathead got along well with neighboring tribes and shared their summer camp with the Pend d'Oreille.

Life began to change in the 1700s. Smallpox epidemics decimated the people, and although the Flathead possessed many horses and were excellent riders, they could not compete with the Blackfoot, who now owned muskets. As the Flathead moved farther into the Plains territory to hunt buffalo, conflict erupted with the Blackfoot, twice escalating into war. The first battles lasted from 1760 to 1770; another raged in 1781. With their superior firepower, the Blackfoot defeated the Flathead both times.

The Flathead population declined sharply throughout the century. After the head chief of the Tunàha was murdered, his people, already decimated by smallpox, joined the Flatheads. One member of that group, Big Hawk, later became a Flathead leader. When he was murdered by the Piegan, the people selected Three Eagles as their new chief, and he still headed the tribe when the first American explorers reached the area.

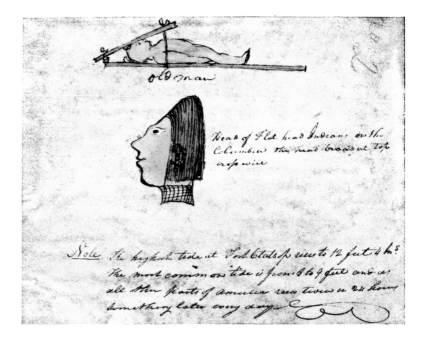

Explorer William Clark included a sketch of the Flathead Indians in the diary he kept during his expedition through the West. © NORTH WIND PICTURE ARCHIVES/ALAMY.

Americans and Europeans arrive

The first contact the Flathead had with Americans occurred when Meri-wether Lewis (1774–1809) and William Clark (1770–1838) arrived in their territory along the Columbia River in 1805. The people supplied Lewis and Clark with buffalo skins when the explorers complained that some Indians had stolen their blankets. The Flathead also fed the explorers from their store of berries and sold the Americans some horses from the tribe's large herd of about five hundred.

Around this time, the tribe came into contact with European traders, accompanied by Iroquois (see entry) who later made their home with the Flathead. Catholic missionaries also arrived in Flathead territory and began visiting the tribe. Another major influence on Flathead religious belief was Ignace La Mousse, an Iroquois, who had been baptized. He encouraged the people to turn to Catholicism, and by 1831, the Flathead and their neighbors, the Nez Percé (see entry), wanted their own priest. Four Native delegates set out for St. Louis to request a priest, but none returned; two died of illness in St. Louis, but the fate of the others is unknown. Another party set out in 1837, and everyone in it died at the hands of the Sioux. The messengers sent in 1839 finally got through and received assurance that a priest would come.

In 1840, Father Pierre-Jean De Smet (1801–1873) arrived to work among them. He was joined by five assistants, and St. Mary's Mission was built along the Bitterroot River at present-day Stevensville, Montana. Although the people accepted Catholicism, they did not agree with the many restrictions the faith imposed on them and continued to live their traditional lifestyles. The missionaries closed the mission from 1850 to 1866, but when it reopened, they found the people had remained faithful in the interim.

Treaties with the United States

In 1855, Governor Isaac Stevens (1818–1862) reached the summer camp that the Flatheads were sharing with the Pend d'Oreille and Kutenai. His objective was to move all three tribes to one reservation along with other bands. The Pend d'Oreille agreed to cede the land around Flathead Lake and the river, but the territory was not theirs to give. The Flathead, whose homeland it was, objected. After long negotiations, Stevens promised the Flathead better land than where they currently dwelled.

On July 16, 1855, the tribes signed away all the land in Montana that reached to the mountains and a small piece of Idaho. In exchange, they received land surrounded by the Mission mountain range; their reservation ran northwest from what is now Evaro, Montana, to the Flathead Lake. Some people turned to farming in their new valley, but their fertile fields attracted U.S. settlers, who began to set up homesteads in the area. The settlers soon pressed the government to remove the Flathead from this rich agricultural land.

Changes to treaty

The government decided to send the Flathead to the Jocko Reservation in northwestern Montana. Because the Flathead treaty stipulated that the tribe must be moved to land that was better than that which they inhabited, President Ulysses Grant (1822–1855; served 1869–77) stated that a survey had been completed. His executive order said that the two properties—the present Flathead home of Bitter Root Valley and the new reservation—were equivalent, so the Indians were to be removed to the reservation. Congressman James A. Garfield (1831–1881; later president, 1881) was sent to secure the tribe's agreement.

The tribe's attitude toward the Americans had changed, though. Victor, the chief who had signed the original treaty, had died of a leg wound. His son Grizzlybear Claws (Charlo; c. 1830–1910) blamed his father's Catholic baptism for the death, believing that it had interfered with Victor's traditional healing powers. Charlo refused to negotiate with Garfield when they met in 1872. Two subchiefs agreed to sign, but when the document was printed, Charlo's name appeared as signer, although it was misspelled as Charlot. In a letter, Garfield wrote that he thought Charlot would cooperate if the subchiefs and the rest of the people moved. Charlo protested that he never signed the treaty, and when the original agreement on file with the Department of the Interior was examined, Charlo's signature does not appear. That did not stop the federal government plans to move the Flathead.

Removal to reservation

It took the U.S. government more than a year to build the promised housing on the reservation. Arlee, one of the subchiefs who had signed the treaty, moved to the reservation. Other than his family, few others followed him. By 1875, only twenty families lived on the

Chief Charlo poses on the Flathead Reservation in Montana in 1908. © NORMAN A. FORSYTH/BUYENLARGE/GETTY IMAGES.

reservation. The rest of the Flatheads, totaling 304 people, remained with Charlo in Bitterroot Valley.

In 1889, Charlo agreed to move to the Jocko Valley reservation in exchange for $27,000 for the Flathead's present lands. In 1891, he and his people settled on the new reservation. Most people became farmers, a lifestyle that was foreign to this hunting-gathering people.

Little more than a decade later, the federal government allotted the reservation land by dividing it into individual plots and giving one parcel to each head of a household. The land not given to the Flathead was opened for U.S. settlers. Over the next few decades, many Flathead lost their land to taxes or sold it to survive. By the mid-1900s, only one farm in seven on reservation land was owned by a Flathead.

Life in the twentieth century and beyond

When the federal government passed the Indian Reorganization Act, Native nations had to set up tribal governments, which U.S. officials needed to approve. The Flathead, who were now officially called Salish, were chartered in 1934. The Flathead/Salish, along with the Kootenai and Kalispel tribes who shared the reservation, formed a tribal council and organized as the Confederated Salish and Kootenai Tribes.

The federal government tried to close the Flathead Reservation in 1953, but the tribes negotiated for better treaty terms. In 1960, the government repaid the tribes more than $4 million for the land taken in the 1855 treaty. They continue to receive additional revenue from the Kerr Dam hydroelectric power plant, which they initially leased to the Montana Power Company; the agreement was set up so the operating license would return to the tribe in 2015. The tribes also opened Salish Kootenai College in 1977 and took charge of their own law enforcement in 1993. As the tribe moved into the twenty-first century, they were well on their way to achieving self-sufficiency as a sovereign (self-governing) nation.

RELIGION

Traditional beliefs

The Flathead believed the sun, Amo'tken, created the world, and Coyote came from the sun. Coyote's role was as creator of the Flathead people, and he was responsible for driving away evil. The people called themselves *skeligu,* which means "human beings," but it also indicated their status as angels and Indians.

To the people, everything in the world possesses power, including rocks and trees. Because of this, the Flathead take responsibility for caring for the earth, which provides them with food and shelter. Their beliefs led to a rich ceremonial life that they maintained even after they accepted Christianity. Some of the traditions they continued to observe were the Hunting Dance, First Fruit Dance, Praying Dance, and Sun Dance.

Honor for all living things extended particularly to the beavers, whom they believed had formerly been people. Because beavers had been evil, the Good Spirit turned them into animals, but someday their power to speak would return.

Catholicism

Long before the arrival of the Europeans, a Salish prophet, Shining Shirt, predicted that fair-skinned men with long, black robes would come. He said these men would enslave the people, who should not resist. He promised that later the people would rise again, so when the Flathead met the Catholic priests, they were open to their teachings and even went so far as to send several messengers to request a priest for their people (see "History").

Father Pierre-Jean De Smet and other priests arrived and established St. Mary's Mission in 1841. Many Flathead were baptized into the Catholic faith, but they often combined Christian beliefs and celebrations with their traditional religion. The missionaries closed the mission from 1850 to 1866. Throughout the next centuries, Catholicism was the predominant religion on the reservations.

In 2011, some tribal members supported the construction of Ewam, a Buddhist center and garden, on reservation land, because they saw a parallel between the treatment of Native nations and the political oppression of the Tibetan peoples. Some traditionalists, however, objected, saying that Buddhism, like Catholicism, could contribute to the loss of their Native religion and culture.

LANGUAGE

When the explorers and traders arrived, Salish was the main language spoken on the Plateau. The Spokane (see entry) and Kalispel (Pend d'Oreille) spoke similar languages to the Flathead. Many of the words were so close that some experts considered them dialects, or variations, of the same language.

Flathead Words

The Flathead and Kalispel dialects were quite close. For example, all the words listed here are the same in both languages, with the exception of the word for water. In Kalispel, it is *se'uliq,* and in Spokane, it is *se'ulq,* which makes all three dialects quite similar to each other, but not identical.

Because the people were dependent on horses for their livelihoods, many of their words are related to horses. For example, many Salish color names actually describe the shades of horses' coats. The word for "brunette" translates as "sorrel horse," and "orange" is "light yellow horse."

simmu'en	"woman"
skaltamiax	"man"
spukani	"sun"
saka'am	"moon"
se'ulku	"water"

The Salish on the Flathead reservation spoke two dialects: Flathead and Kalispel. Over time the younger generations learned to use English at government-run schools, and by the 2000s, few fluent speakers of the language remained. To prevent their languages from dying out, schools began teaching it to the students.

GOVERNMENT

In the early days, the Flathead had a principal chief, a position that was hereditary. They also selected a war chief by his bravery, strength, and wisdom. The war chief only led during battles and hunting expeditions, where everyone followed his commands, but in the day-to-day matters of governing the tribe, he had no authority. War chiefs could change from battle to battle, and former leaders served as warriors under a new war chief. As a sign of power, the war chief carried a whip adorned with scalps and feathers as he rode in the lead (see "War and hunting rituals"). When the company returned, he always brought up the rear. Two of the bravest warriors served as his aides.

After the federal government passed the Indian Reorganization Act in 1934, the Flathead became one of the first tribes to set up a tribal government. They were now called the Salish, and together with the Kootenai and Kalispel tribes with whom they shared the reservation, they formally organized as the Confederated Salish and Kootenai Tribes (CSKT), governed by an elected, ten-person tribal council with a chair, vice chair, secretary, and treasurer.

During the 1970s and 1980s, the CSKT struggled with their relationship to the Bureau of Indian Affairs (BIA). They tried switching agencies from Billings, Montana, to Portland, Oregon, but eventually returned to Billings. The CSKT government was determined to provide its own services for the people on the reservation rather than relying on the BIA. After some political upheaval and protests among the non-Natives living on the reservation, the CSKT moved ahead with their self-government plans. The CSKT later instituted reforms to their government in the 1990s after difficulties arose between the tribal government and the court system. Since that time the CSKT has taken over many functions and facilities that were once under BIA control. For example, rather than relying on the U.S. government for health care, the tribes now run their own facility. This has allowed them more self-determination and strengthened their own government.

ECONOMY

Forested valleys nestled between mountains with a rushing river and many lakes supplied the Flathead with an abundance of fish, small game, and plants to gather for subsistence. The Flathead along with other Interior Salish tribes migrated in a cycle that began with an autumn spent on the northern plains hunting buffalo. As invaders of other tribes' territory, the Flathead kept constant watch as they gathered their winter stores of meat. They returned to their villages and, in the spring, built weirs (traps made of sticks) to catch the salmon in the nearby Clearwater River.

The move to the reservation in the late 1800s forced the people to give up their hunting and gathering lifestyle. Most became farmers. Soon ranching, logging, and general wage work employed many of the people.

Eventually the establishment of the Kerr Dam for hydropower brought in revenue; the tribe leased the dam to Montana Power Company until 2015. In addition to the millions they receive from the dam, the Confederated Salish and Kootenai Tribes gain income from the timber industry, tourism, a casino and resort, and a tribal corporation that runs several businesses and provides loans to Native entrepreneurs.

DAILY LIFE

Family life

Families were the most important social unit. The Flathead had a strong moral code that valued attention to parents, affection for spouses and children, and obedience to their chiefs. People also believed that honesty and bravery were important. Following these codes meant happiness in the afterlife (see "Death and burial").

Buildings

The Flathead dug a foot or two into the ground to build their lodges. They sank poles into the ground, made frames of branches, and covered them with mats woven from cattails. The lodges housed several families.

After the Flathead had horses and traveled to the Great Plains to hunt, they began constructing tepees. They could easily transport these homes as they journeyed to hunting camps far from home. They covered the cone-shaped wooden frames with skins or mats. Later, canvas took the place of the animal skins.

After the move to the Jocko Reservation, most people built their own houses of wood with shingled roofs. Although some cabins were small and poorly put together, the Indian agent who reported on reservation conditions in the late 1800s said the majority were neat and well-built. He also mentioned that the homes had curtains at the windows and fenced-in enclosures. The community had a gristmill, sawmill, shingle machine, and irrigation system, which the people had constructed themselves.

Clothing and adornment

Like the Plains tribes, the Flathead wore clothing made from buffalo hides or deerskin. The men wore loincloths, fabric that hung from the waist with apronlike flaps in the back and front. In cooler weather, men wore leggings that went from their ankles to their hips. Strings tied to a leather belt around the waist held up the leggings. Knee-length shirts were made from two deerskins and had loose sleeves. Women had long dresses that reached their ankles. Dresses, leggings, and shirts all had fringe. Clothing was cleaned with pipe clay. Both sexes kept warm and dry with buffalo robes. Moccasins and headbands or hats completed their outfits. The Flathead wore many necklaces, decorative hair ties, and beaded belts. Feathered headdresses were sometimes used.

In the early days, women adorned clothing with hawkbills and dyed porcupine quills. Later, they added beaded designs after contact with the traders. Trading changed their traditional clothing as the people began to use wool and calico rather than hides.

Food

The early Flathead lived by hunting and gathering. They hunted buffalo on the Great Plains and tracked smaller game, such as deer and elk, closer to home. With the lake and a river nearby, the people had access to fish; they caught salmon, sturgeon, sucker, whitefish, and trout that they dried for winter use.

The women collected bitterroot, wild onions and potatoes, carrots, moss, and a variety of berries (hawthorne berries, servis or serviceberries, huckleberries, and strawberries). Camas, a bulb from the lily, became a staple food that was baked and dried so it could be stored.

It was roasted in a pit on hot rocks covered with wet grasses or leaves. Onions were sometimes baked with the camas. Cooks covered the bulbs with bark and dirt, and built a fire on top. The camas roasted for half a day or as long as three days. When it was done, the women dried some of it for about a week, which preserved it. The people could then keep it for years.

Education

Children learned from an early age to do adult duties. A young boy received a small bow, and his father taught him how to hunt small animals and birds. He learned to walk quietly so animals did not sense his presence and the best places to find prey. Girls learned cooking, childcare, sewing, and gathering.

The Sisters of Providence of Charity in St. Ignatius started the first school on the Flathead Reservation in 1864. In 1888, the Jesuits opened a trade school for boys. Some children attended these religious boarding schools, whereas others were sent to government boarding schools in other states. At the boarding schools, students did most of the work. Farming, carpentry, housekeeping, laundry, cooking, sewing, and other domestic jobs were part of the curriculum, and students did these chores daily in addition to their schoolwork. In the late 1800s, an Indian agent noted that the Flathead students excelled in drawing, music, and handwriting.

One of the problems with the boarding schools, in addition to reports of cruel treatment and rapid spread of diseases, was that students were forbidden to speak their native language or practice their customs. Many students grew up not knowing their culture or traditions. Beginning in the 1960s and 1970s, the tribes on the reservation determined to restore their traditions and languages. They set up culture committees that later became departments overseen by the tribal government. One of the initiatives was to collect stories from the elders so children could learn oral history. The Two Eagles School opened to teach tribal culture, and Salish Kootenai College, founded in 1977, offers many educational and cultural activities for the community.

The Salish also organized special hunting camps so youth could see what life was like for their people long ago. The participants say prayers and follow traditional hunting rituals. During the camp, an elder gives an inspirational speech that helps the youth become more connected with their culture.

Origin of Spokane Falls

Like many tribes, the Flathead tell stories of Coyote, who came to Earth with his brother Fox to save the world from evil (see "Religion"). Coyote and Fox gave the people special knowledge and skills in addition to creating many of the natural landforms. This short story tells how Spokane Falls was created.

> Coyote and Fox were travelling together. They were coming up the river. When they got to where Spokane Falls now are, Coyote said to Fox: "I believe I'll get married. I'll take a woman of the Pend d'Orielles for my wife."
>
> So Coyote went to visit the chief of the Pend d'Orielles. He said he wanted a wife.
>
> Chief said, "No." Chief said that Pend d'Orielle women could not intermarry with other tribes.
>
> Coyote said, "Then I will make a falls here in the river. I will make falls so that the salmon cannot get past them." This is how Spokane Falls were made.

SOURCE: Judson, Katharine Berry. "Origin of Spokane Falls." In *Myths and Legends of the Pacific Northwest: Especially of Washington and Oregon.* Cambridge, MA: A.C. McClurg, 1910, p. 118.

Healing practices

The Flathead used herbs and other natural remedies along with spiritual healing practices. Most shamans (pronounced *SHAH-munz* or *SHAY-munz*), or healers, knew how to use herbs, but they often concentrated on the supernatural side of the healing process.

The tribal doctors administered medicines or potions made from plant products. Some of the common remedies were fir-needle tea for coughs, They treated broken bones by tightly bandaging the broken limb to a piece of wood to hold it in place until it healed. For bumps, they used an arrowhead or sharp piece of flint to pierce the skin of the temples, ankles, or wrists to let out some blood.

One writer who stayed with the Flathead complained of rheumatism. The tribal doctor recommended a treatment that included jumping into the frozen river. The doctor broke the ice and went into the river with the patient. While the patient soaked, the doctor rubbed the man's aching limbs. When they got out, the man was wrapped in a blanket and laid near the fire in his house. After twenty-five days of treatment, the man never again had rheumatic pains.

ARTS

Clothing was decorated with geometric designs using dyed porcupine quills. After traders brought glass, metal, and cloth, the women added these to their traditional crafts to create floral beadwork designs. Some people on the reservation still make a living by selling traditional crafts.

The main musical instruments were the drum and flageolet, a type of flute. The people also used various bells. Dancing and singing were an important part of the culture.

CUSTOMS

Birth and childrearing

Many rituals were followed prior to childbirth to ensure a healthy baby. Once infants were born, mothers placed them in cradleboards. Children received their names during a ceremony when they were about one year old. Everyone in the family, including grandparents, aunts, and uncles, participated in rearing a child. Grandparents supervised the child's bathing, both in cold water to toughen the child and in sweat baths. Family friends, or sometimes relatives, did the whipping when it was needed.

Puberty

Boys, and occasionally girls, went on vision quests. Once they acquired a spirit guide, young men were considered adults. After horses became a common means of transportation, stealing horses became another rite of passage for young men.

Girls were sent to menstrual lodges when they had their first menses. They could not touch their bodies, except with scratching sticks, and had to drink from a tube. They were painted and dressed, and they had their hair bound up to signify their move into womanhood.

Couples could have premarital sex, but members of the tribe looked down upon girls who became pregnant before marriage.

Marriage

Usually, mothers arranged the marriages for their children. Some young couples eloped if they were unhappy with the choices their mothers made. Rather than paying a bride price, which was the custom in many tribes, the families exchanged presents. Men could have more than one wife, but that was rare. If a spouse died, the widow or widower usually married someone from his spouse's family.

A trader who married a Flathead woman described the ceremony, which began with his gifts of cloth, weapons, and ornaments to the family. In the chief's lodge, the chief, the bride's mother, and some of the elders lectured the woman as to her wifely duties. These responsibilities included being moral, hardworking, obedient, and silent.

Next, an old woman took the bride to another hut, where she changed from her deerskin dress into a calico one. Back at the lodge,

Salish Marriage Blessing

Now for you there is no rain, for one is shelter to the other.

Now for you the sun shall not burn, for one is shelter to the other.

Now for you nothing is hard or bad, for the hardness and badness is taken by one for the other.

Now for you there is no night, for one is light to the other.

Now for you the snow has ended always, for one is protection for the other.

It is that way, from now on, from now on. And now there is comfort.

Now there is no loneliness. Now forever, forever, there is no loneliness.

after more lectures, the wedding procession escorted the couple, led by the chiefs and warriors holding torches of pitch pine. The men went first, singing war songs. The women, some crying, some joyful, followed. Everyone then formed a circle and danced and sang. The calumet, or peace pipe, was passed around. Then the bride accompanied her husband to his home.

Death and burial

When someone died, the body was watched constantly for days before it was buried. After a grave was dug, the Flathead wrapped the corpse in a fine robe or blanket before burial. Most bodies were placed in pits dug in the sand or gravel near riverbanks. Each family marked the spot with piles of stones and sticks.

The funeral concluded with a Feast for the Dead, particularly if it was a person of importance. A giveaway was held to dispose of a person's belongings; the person conducting the feast distributed the possessions. Spouses cut their hair and dressed in old clothes as a sign of mourning. After a year or more, they could remarry.

Because the Flatheads believed in a Supreme Being as well as an evil spirit, they believed in an afterlife that rewarded the good and punished the bad. Those who had lived a proper life went to a place of eternal summertime. Fish and buffalo were plentiful, and war did not exist. There, the person was reunited with any family members who had already died.

Evildoers ended up in a snow-covered land, seeing fires far off that they could never reach. They could also see water and game but had no way to take advantage of them. Separating the two worlds was a woods filled with snakes, panthers, and wolves that they could not get past. They were confined to this world for as long as it took to pay off the crimes or bad deeds they had done on Earth. Then they could join their friends in the land of summer.

War and hunting rituals

Battle leaders The war chief who led the party carried a long whip (see "Government"). He used this to keep everyone in order as they marched. Those who fell out of line or disobeyed orders received a lashing. The war chief was the absolute authority during battle, and he rode at the tail end of the party on the way home. Once the warriors returned to their village, they voted on a new war chief. Sometimes the same man was reelected, but often power changed hands.

Prisoners of war, including women, were usually tortured. One early writer described a Blackfoot warrior being slowly dismembered. After the priests and Indian agents arrived, they tried to stop this practice by promising government help and goods for returning captives to their own tribes.

Buffalo hunting Before the Flathead had guns and horses, the people worked together to trap buffalo, usually by driving them over a cliff. After they had horses, they began to use pens. Prior to leaving on a hunt, the people consulted the medicine men. They then departed for the Great Plains, where they set up a hunting camp. Guards were appointed to be sure that no one startled the buffalo herds. Penalties for disobeying this rule applied not only to members of the tribe, but also to strangers who happened to pass by. The guards broke an offender's bow and arrows or destroyed his gun, killed his dogs, and took all food and hides the person carried. Resistors were beaten with sticks or clubs.

The people all worked together to build a pen about an acre in size. They drove stakes into the ground, and filled the areas in between with logs and stones, leaving only one opening facing a slope. The Flathead then selected a leader, or grand master, usually a medicine man and elder, whose duty was to start the hunt. The grand master placed a pole in the

Flathead warrior Heo-a-h-co-a-h-cotes-min, circa 1848. ©THE PRINT COLLECTOR/ALAMY.

center of the pen. Attached to the post were a red cloth banner, a buffalo horn, and tobacco. At dawn, he played the drum, chanted songs, and consulted his guardian spirit to choose the correct timing for the chase. Four runners, who traveled as far as 50 miles (80 kilometers), headed off in different directions to locate the best herds. The grand master fasted until they returned with the wak-kon ball he had given them. The runner who had found a promising herd presented the ball to the leader.

Hunters on horseback then lined up on either side of the pen opening, stretching in a long line out to the plain. Women and children filled in any gaps. One rider approached the buffalo, staying downwind. When he neared the herd, he covered himself and his horse with a buffalo skin and cried like a buffalo calf. When the herd began to follow, he headed toward the pen.

As they neared the hunters, the buffalo shied away, but they could not go far because they were enclosed on both sides. They had no choice but to run toward the pen opening. As the herd rushed by, the hunters

Dancers wear traditional costumes at a powwow at the Flathead Reservation in Montana. © DANITA DELIMONT/ALAMY.

shot them. Those that got past ended up in the pen where they were trapped, making them easy targets.

Men, women, and children worked together to skin and butcher the animals. Many of them ate the still-warm meat, especially the kidneys, brains, and livers. Hides and meat were divided among the families, who then dried the meat. The people also extracted the grease from the bones. Once all the work was completed, they spent several days dancing and celebrating.

CURRENT TRIBAL ISSUES

The Consolidated Salish and Kootenai Tribes strive to apply their traditional values to their present-day lives. They have worked to become self-sufficient, restore their natural resources, care for their homeland, preserve their culture, create a strong community, and maintain their values while incorporating the advances and innovations of modern society.

During the 1940s and 1950s, under the direction of the Bureau of Indian Affairs, much of the timber on the reservation was logged. This caused soil degradation and road problems. In 1962, the people began to reclaim the forest and to view it as more valuable than just a resource for timber products. In 2000, the Confederated Salish and Kootenai Tribes (CSKT) developed a Forest Management Plan that left approximately half of the acreage as treed wilderness areas, even though it meant a loss of logging revenue. Several years later, they adopted a community-based ecosystem management system. Tribal elders now give their input on planned projects for forestland. The CSKT have been finding that this new management system is helping them maintain a sustainable forest for the future.

A study by the Montana government is assessing the impact of proposed changes to the highway system in the reservation area. The Salish and Kootenai have concerns about safety, impact on the environment and endangered species habitats, water quality, and other problems that the roadway plan will bring. At the same time, the reservation needs additional roads to accommodate their growing community and businesses.

As with many tribes in the West and Midwest, water rights are of great importance. The Confederated Salish and Kootenai Tribes began working to secure the water they need for the future by gathering testimony and supporting evidence for the 2015 water rights determination hearings with the state of Montana.

NOTABLE PEOPLE

Chief Charlo (also known as Charlot, Charlos, Siemhakkah, or Grizzlybear Claws; c. 1830–1910), son of the famous chief Victor, refused to sign an order removing his people from Bitterroot Valley to the Jocko reservation. After his signature was forged, he and several other Flatheads went to Washington, D.C., to discuss the matter. He refused all monetary offers and eventually gained the right to stay in the territory of his ancestors. This land was later taken from him, and Charlo was forced onto the reservation in 1891.

Although D'Arcy McNickle (1904–1977) was of Cree and Scottish ancestry, he and his siblings were adopted by the Flathead. Educated at several colleges, including Oxford, McNickle went on to hold posts at the Bureau of Indian Affairs and to become one of the founders of the National Congress of American Indians. When his novel *The Surrounded* came out in 1936, it was hailed as a masterpiece in Native literature. The book focuses on how the losses of land and culture resulted in the breakdown of traditional tribal values and religion. McNickle wrote many other books, which earned him literary awards, including a Guggenheim fellowship (1963–64). The D'Arcy McNickle Center at Chicago's Newberry Library is now one of the leading facilities for Native historiography (study of historical writing).

Other noted authors include Salish-Dakota artist and author Philip H. Red Eagle (1945–); spiritual leader and author Johnny Arlee (1940–), who was honored in the Indian Hall of Fame; and author/educator Shirley Sterling (died 2005).

BOOKS

Arlee, Johnny. *Over a Century of Moving to the Drum: Salish Indian Celebrations on the Flathead Reservation.* Helena: Montana Historical Society Press, 1998. Available online from http://www.archive.org/stream/historicalsketch00ronarich/historicalsketch00ronarich_djvu.txt (accessed on August 11, 2011).

Challenge to Survive: History of the Salish Tribes of the Flathead Indian Reservation. Pablo, MT: Salish Kootenai College Tribal History Project, 2008. Available online from http://www.archive.org/stream/challengetosurvi20081salirich/challengetosurvi20081salirich_djvu.txt (accessed on August 11, 2011).

Confederated Salish and Kootenai Tribes. *Bull Trout's Gift: A Salish Story about the Value of Reciprocity.* Lincoln: University of Nebraska Press, 2011.

Hungrywolf, Adolf. *Tribal Childhood: Growing Up in Traditional Native America.* Summertown, TN: Native Voices, 2008.

Ketcham, William Henry. *Report upon the Conditions on the Flathead Indian Reservation.* Reprint. Charleston, SC: BiblioBazaar, 2009.

Merriam, Alan P. *Ethnomusicology of the Flathead Indians.* Reprint. New Brunswick, NJ: AldineTransaction, 2011.

Plummer, Maggie. *Passing It On: Voices from the Flathead Indian Reservation.* Pablo, MT: Salish Kootenai College Tribal History Project, 2008.

Ronan, Peter. *Historical Sketch of the Flathead Indian Nation from the Year 1813 to 1890.* Reprint. Charleston, SC: Nabu Press, 2010.

Whealdon, Bon I. *I Will Be Meat for My Salish.* Edited by Robert Bigart. Helena: Montana Historical Society Press, 2002.

PERIODICALS

Durglo, Jim. "Ecosystem Management and Tribal Self-Government on the Flathead Indian Reservation, Montana."*Evergreen,* Winter 2005–06. Available online from http://evergreenmagazine.com/magazine/article/ Ecosystem_Management_and_Tribal_Self_Government_on_the_Flathead_ Indian_Reservation_Montana.html (accessed on August 11, 2011).

WEB SITES

Baumler, Ellen. "St. Mary's Mission: Statement of Significance, 1841–1954." *Montana Historical Society.* http://bloximages.chicago2.vip.townnews.com/ ravallirepublic.com/content/tncms/assets/editorial/2/02/750/202750a0- bf95-11df-b231-001cc4c03286-revisions/4c8ebe8d0a96d.pdf.pdf (accessed on August 11, 2011).

The Confederated Salish and Kootenai Tribes. http://www.cskt.org/ (accessed on August 11, 2011).

Curtis, Lori S. "Flathead Watershed Sourcebook: A Guide to an Extraordinary Place." *Thomas Printing Company.* http://www.flatheadwatershed.org/index. shtml (accessed on August 11, 2011).

"The Fabulous Flathead and Beyond." *University of Montana.* http://www.umt. edu/ling/ICSNL44/flatheadlakebook.pdf (accessed on August 11, 2011).

"Flathead Indian Agency and Flathead and Jocko Reservations." *Access Genealogy.* http://www.accessgenealogy.com/native/census/condition/ flathead_indian_agency_flathead-jocko_reservation.htm (accessed on August 11, 2011).

"Flathead Indians." *FamilySearch.* https://wiki.familysearch.org/en/Flathead_ Indians (accessed on August 11, 2011).

"Flathead Indians (Salish)." *National Geographic.* http://www.nationalgeo graphic.com/lewisandclark/record_tribes_022_12_16.html (accessed on August 11, 2011).

"Flathead Reservation." *Montana Tribes Digital Archives.* http://www. montanatribes.org/links_&_resources/tribes/Flathead_Reservation.pdf (accessed on August 11, 2011).

Hammer, Keith J. "The Lineage of Chief Aeneas." *Swan View Coalition.* http:// www.swanview.org/reports/Lineage_of_Chief_Aeneas.pdf (accessed on August 11, 2011).

Montana Arts Council. "From the Heart and Hand: Salish Songs and Dances: Johnny Arlee, Arlee/John T., Big Crane, Pablo." *Montana Official State Website.* http://art.mt.gov/folklife/hearthand/songs.asp (accessed on August 11, 2011).

"The People of the Flathead Nation." *Lake County Directory.* http://www.lakecodirect.com/archives/The_Flathead_Nation.html (accessed on August 11, 2011).

Redish, Laura, and Orrin Lewis. "Flathead Salish Culture and History." *Native Languages of the Americas.* http://www.native-languages.org/flathead_culture.htm (accessed on August 11, 2011).

Redish, Laura, and Orrin Lewis. "Spokane/Kalispel/Flathead Salish Language." *Native Languages of the Americas.* http://www.native-languages.org/salish.htm (accessed on August 11, 2011).

"The Rez We Live On" (videos). *The Confederated Salish and Kootenai Tribes.* http://therezweliveon.com/13/video.html (accessed on August 11, 2011).

"S'elish-Ktunaxa: Flathead." *Montana Office of Tourism.* http://visitmt.com/places_to_go/indian_nations/selish-Ktunaxa-flathead/ (accessed on August 11, 2011).

"Time Line: Flathead Indian Reservation." *Flathead Indian Historical Society.* http://www.flatheadreservation.org/timeline/precontact.html (accessed on August 11, 2011).

Modoc

Name

The name Modoc (pronounced *MO-dock*) may mean "southerners." Some Sahaptian speakers called the people on the Klamath Reservation, including the Modoc, *aígspaluma*, "people of the chipmunks." The Modoc called themselves *Mqlaqs* or *Ma Klaks* ("the people").

Location

The Modoc formerly occupied about 5,000 square miles (13,000 square kilometers) on the California-Oregon border. Their tribal headquarters is located in Miami, Oklahoma. Most of the people live in California, Oregon, and Oklahoma. The present separation of the tribe is a result of the Modoc War of 1872–73.

Population

Before contact with Europeans, there were about 2,000 Modoc. In the 1990 U.S. Census 521 people identified themselves as Modoc. In the 2000 census, 573 people said they were Modoc, and 1,585 claimed to have some Modoc background.

Language family

Penutian.

Origins and group affiliations

The modern Modoc are descendants of the Modoc group that was forcibly removed to Oklahoma in 1873. The tribe was divided into three groups: the Gumbatwas or "people of the west," the Kokiwas or "people of the far country," and the Paskanwas or "river people." The Modoc traded with the Shasta and Achomawi. Their major enemies were the Klamath and the Paiute, with whom they were forced to live.

The Modoc were an optimistic people who saw the world as a friendly place. They first lived in the Lakes District of Oregon and California, where they hunted, fished, and gathered food. Modoc land was fertile,

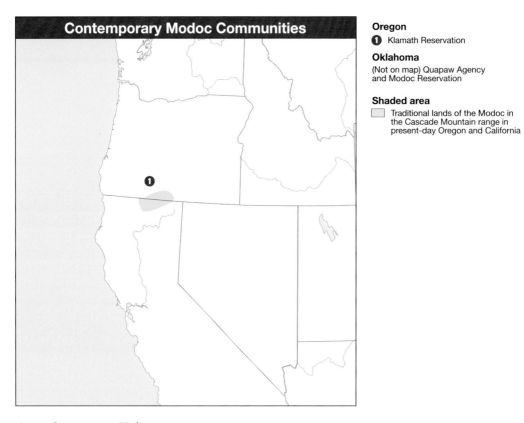

Contemporary Modoc Communities

Oregon
❶ Klamath Reservation

Oklahoma
(Not on map) Quapaw Agency
and Modoc Reservation

Shaded area
☐ Traditional lands of the Modoc in
the Cascade Mountain range in
present-day Oregon and California

A map of contemporary Modoc communities. MAP BY XNR PRODUCTIONS. CENGAGE LEARNING, GALE. REPRODUCED BY PERMISSION OF GALE, A PART OF CENGAGE LEARNING.

and the people believed that if they worked hard, it would provide them with the things they needed. Their history has been a harsh one, however, and only in recent years have they been able to reclaim a part of their heritage.

HISTORY

Arrival of Europeans

For centuries before the coming of Europeans, the Modoc people roamed the land around Lost River, Tule Lake, Willow Creek, and Ness Lake in what is now northern California and southern Oregon. They hunted and gathered food and harvested reeds and grasses to weave clothing and baskets. They traded with some neighboring tribes and raided others. As a result of these interactions, they heard about white explorers, and they acquired European goods. They were quick to adopt any goods they considered superior to their own. Their use of steel knives, hatchets, iron pots, mirrors, and cloth soon changed their way of life.

By the mid-1830s, the Modoc owned guns and horses, which brought further changes. They could now hunt deer, and they began to wear buckskin clothing in place of grass or fur garments. Copying the Plains Indians, they applied war paint to their faces when they went on raids. In time, they even took non-Native American names.

Conflict with settlers

In 1843, the American explorer John Charles Frémont (1813–1890) brought a team of survey-ors and explorers into Modoc territory. The party went about their business without incident, but when Frémont returned with another team three years later, nearby Klamath Indians attacked and killed four men. The Americans burned a Klamath village in retaliation. Thereafter, both the Klamath and the Modoc feared Americans.

By 1847, the Applegate Trail was heavily traveled by settlers on their way to the Oregon Territory. The settlers frightened away game on Modoc hunting grounds, making food scarce. Tragedy struck when diseases brought by the settlers killed more than one-third of the Modoc tribe. During the summer of 1847, a group of Natives, possibly Modoc, attacked a wagon train and stole the horses; several dozen settlers were killed during the raid.

In 1852, a wagon train of settlers again entered Modoc territory. The tribe killed sixty-two of the sixty-five people at Bloody Point, along the shore of Tule Lake. They took two girls prisoner, and one man escaped. He reached California, and when he told his tale, the settlers organized to bury the dead and avenge the deaths. The group, under the leadership of Jim Crosby, had one skirmish with the Modoc. Later Ben Wright, a Native fighter, ambushed the tribe and killed about eighty Modocs.

Important Dates

1843: John Charles Frémont arrives in Modoc territory, heading a survey and exploring party.

1847: Travel on the Applegate Trail disrupts Modoc game hunting. The tribe attacks wagon trains in retaliation.

1848: Modoc population falls to about 900 after epidemics.

1864: In October, the Council Grove Treaty concludes. Modoc, Klamath, and Paiute tribes are relocated to a single reservation in Oregon.

1872: The Modoc War begins. Captain Jack (Kintpuash) refuses to return to the reserva-tion and leads a group of Modoc in revolt.

1978: The Modoc tribe gains federal recognition.

1983: The Modoc Tribal Complex, the tribe's headquarters, is completed.

1986: The tribes on Klamath Reservation regain federal recognition.

The discovery of gold in the West brought even more settlers, and clashes with the Modoc became more frequent. The Modoc were sometimes blamed for attacks carried out by neighboring tribes, and Americans retaliated against the Modoc, increasing the conflicts. Estimates indicate that the Modocs killed approximately three hundred settlers between 1846 and 1873. Settlers probably killed a similar number of Modoc.

Council Grove Treaty

During the fierce winter of 1861–62, heavy snows killed plants and drove away wild game, causing starvation among the Modoc. The U.S. government offered to help the tribe if they signed a treaty giving up their lands. Modoc tribal chief Old Schonchin urged his people to agree, but younger warriors, including Captain Jack (Kintpuash; c. 1837–73), strongly resisted such a move. For a few more years, the Modoc continued their struggle to survive, and some men had to take jobs in a nearby mining town.

After continued pressure from the U.S. government, Old Schonchin signed the Council Grove Treaty at Fort Klamath in 1864. The treaty stated that the Modoc tribe would give up most of its land to the federal government and move to the Klamath Reservation in southern Oregon to live with their enemies, the Paiute (see entry) and the Klamath. In turn, the government agreed to send them food and supplies every year.

Problems with the Klamath

Once the three enemy tribes arrived on the reservation, problems arose. The reservation was located on former Klamath hunting grounds, and the Klamath felt this gave them special rights. They insisted that the Modoc give them a certain amount of their cut timber. They put obstacles in the way of Modoc fishermen, and they bothered Modoc women who were gathering seeds at the lake. To add to these hardships, U.S. government agents failed to provide the food and supplies that they had promised. It was not long before the Modoc on the reservation suffered from almost constant hunger.

In an attempt to reconcile the tribes, an Indian agent suggested a "democratic" self-government be adopted on the reservation. This would require electing leaders for a council similar to that of the U.S. Congress. This effort failed, and the Modoc requested a reservation of their own in California. The government turned them down.

Modoc War begins

An unhappy group of Modoc, led by Captain Jack, decided to take matters into their own hands. They left the reservation in 1870 and returned to Lost River, only to find it overrun by settlers. Nevertheless, they set up camp and began to hunt, fish, and visit in the nearby town of Eureka. Because they remained apart from the settlers, the Superintendent of Indian Affairs at first ignored their presence. Before long, though, the U.S. settlers demanded that the "renegades" be removed, and army troops tried to force them to return to the reservation.

Just before the outbreak of hostilities with American soldiers, Captain Jack declared: "I am not a dog! I am a man, if I am an Indian.... I and my men shall not be slaves for a race of people that is not any better than my people. I shall not live here. If the government refuses to protect my people, who shall I look to for protection?"

Captain Jack refused to obey the order of federal troops to return to the reservation. Instead, he and his group fled south to the rugged lava beds of northeastern California, the place the Native peoples called "Land of Burnt-out Fires." For nearly a year, he and his small group avoided capture. Despite being outnumbered, they won at least one battle and blocked all military attempts to flush them out.

Move to Oklahoma

Captain Jack finally agreed to a meeting to discuss peace. His followers were angry and called him a coward, and Captain Jack changed his plan. Convinced that if he killed the leaders of the army, U.S. troops would retreat, Captain Jack shot several army officers.

His act sealed the Modocs' fate. The army pursued them relentlessly. In the end, Captain Jack was betrayed by a comrade. He and three other leaders of the revolt were caught, tried, and hanged. The remaining Modocs were exiled to Oklahoma to live with the Wyandotte (see Wyandot entry), Peoria, and Ottawa (see entry) tribes at the Quapaw Agency.

The Modoc War was the single most costly Indian war in American history in terms of both money and the loss of human life. It was later estimated that the total cost to the U.S. government for the military campaign was about $1 million. If the government had simply bought land and established a reservation where Captain Jack suggested, the cost would have been about $20,000.

I Have Said Yes, and Thrown Away My Country

Captain Jack and his small band of Modocs resisted the army but ended up surrendering. Jack was hanged on October 3, 1873. His sister, Mary, delivered a written copy of this speech to the peace commission on March 6, 1873, before the warfare began.

> I am very sad…. I don't want my people shot. I don't want my men to go with guns any more. I have quit forever. I have buried the past, and don't want to be mad for the past…. I don't want to shoot or be shot. I don't want anyone to get mad as quick as they did before. I want to live in peace….
>
> Let everything be wiped out, washed out, and let there be no more blood. I have got a bad heart about those murderers. I have got but a few men and I don't see how I can give them up. Will they give up their people who murdered my people while they were asleep? I never asked for the people who murdered my people….
>
> There must be no more bad talk. I will not. I have spoken forever. I want soldiers all to go home. I have given up now and want no more fuss. I have said yes, and thrown away my country….
>
> I don't want to live here any more, because I can't live here any more in peace. I wish to go to southern country and live in peace….
>
> I talk with my mouth. They have paper men to write down what I say…. I want and hope Mary will come back with message and say yes, just as I have said.

SOURCE: Vanderwerth, W. C. *Indian Oratory: Famous Speeches by Noted Indian Chieftains.* Norman: University of Oklahoma Press, 1971.

A new beginning

More than 4,000 acres of land were set aside in Oklahoma for the Modoc tribe. The people continued to suffer because of lack of food and clothing. Meanwhile, the government adopted a new policy called allotment, and in 1891, reservation lands were divided into small plots for farming and given to the sixty-eight tribal members who remained there. Leftover land was sold to U.S. settlers. The government believed the Native peoples would assimilate faster—become more like other Americans—if they owned individual pieces of land.

During the half-century following allotment, many Modoc became successful farmers in northeastern Oklahoma, but over time, they lost many of their Native ways. In 1967, the Oklahoma Modoc once again banded together to form a tribal government, and they are now called the Modoc Tribe of Oklahoma. The tribe was recognized by the federal government in 1978. Federally recognized tribes are those with which the U.S. government maintains official relations. Without federal recognition, a tribe does not exist as far as the government is concerned and is not entitled to any financial or other help.

The tribe has headquarters in Miami, Oklahoma. The Modoc Tribal Complex, completed in 1983, houses the tribal office, library, and historical archives. In recent times, the Modoc have been trying to reestablish a land base and preserve their culture.

Life with the Klamath

The Modoc who remained on the Klamath Reservation in Oregon retained their rights to unallotted land, which enabled them to keep valuable timberland, an important source of income. By the 1950s, they had become the second wealthiest tribe in the country.

Under the Termination Act of 1954, however, the federal government officially terminated the tribe's federal recognition. Tribe members had to choose whether to withdraw from the tribe and receive their share of the assets or to have their land taken and placed in a private trust. Most voted to withdraw from the tribe. To pay their claims, the government sold most of the 880,000 acres of land.

In 1971, members who had left their land in trust asked to have the private trustee removed. The trustee decided this meant they wanted to sell the land and gave the title to the U.S. Forest Service. Until that time, the tribe had continued to hunt, gather, and fish there—rights they had been promised in the treaty. The state of Oregon, however, did not recognize their rights, and they were often harassed or arrested.

Five tribe members filed a lawsuit against the state in 1972 and won. The court upheld their treaty rights. In 1986, the tribe regained federal recognition. It is now eligible for government funds and services. The tribe is also trying to revitalize its culture by translating books into Penutian and by returning to its traditional crafts, ceremonies, and religion.

RELIGION

According to Modoc beliefs, after the creator made human beings and provided the food they needed, he and the other gods departed. In their place, the creator left animals who were inhabited by spirits, including

Klamath-Modoc Words and Phrases

waq lis?i	"How are you?"
sepk'eec'a	"thank you"
balaq hak	"hurry up"
dwaa dal hoot	"What is that?"
waq dal?i seesetk'ip	"What is your name?"
kani dal hoot	"Who is that?"
hiswaqs	"man"
sn'eweets	"woman"
watc	"dog"
s'aba	"sun"
s'aba	"moon"
'ambo	"water"

Frog, Mole, Fish, Rattlesnake, Coyote, and Hawk. With their help, human beings could influence events in their world.

The Modoc prayed to the spirits of the moon, stars, and sky. Most religious ceremonies took place in the sweathouse, a tiny, airtight hut where people could pour water over heated rocks to produce steam. The Modoc thought that sweating purified the body and prepared a person to request good health, hunting, or fortune from the spirits.

In the late 1800s, some Modoc embraced the Ghost Dance religion. A Paiute (see entry) named Wovoka (c. 1856–1932) started the religion after he had a vision. Wovoka predicted that one day the Americans would disappear and Native people would rise from the dead if everyone performed the Ghost Dance. Modoc dancers painted their faces red and drew two horizontal black lines on each cheek. They held hands and formed a circle around the fire, chanting and dancing. Government agents on many reservations forbid the religion, forcing the people to practice in secret.

During the 1870s, many of the Modoc living in Indian Territory became members of the Society of Friends, also known as Quakers. Today, Modoc religion combines elements of Christianity and traditional Native rituals.

LANGUAGE

The Modoc were closely related to the Klamath tribe, and together they formed an independent language family called Penutian. The Modoc spoke the Lituami dialect. Originally, the Klamath and Modoc had separate dialects, but it was easy for the speakers to understand each other.

By the early twenty-first century, only one truly fluent Klamath speaker was alive, but several dozen elders remembered the language. Many linguists (people who study languages) now label the two languages as one—Klamath-Modoc—and consider it endangered. Many books, though, have been written in the language, so they have been used to reconstruct the language. Textbooks are being translated into Penutian to help keep the language vital and strengthen the community. Some young people are also working to keep their language alive.

GOVERNMENT

The chief of each village, always a male, gained his position through his public speaking skills, good judgment, friendliness, tact, and ability to handle himself in a crisis. The best way to get people to follow was by effective argument and persuasion. Chiefs were not elected by a vote; instead everyone in the entire village had to agree on their leader. A single village might have more than one leader who ruled with a council. The chief of the tribe was called *la gi* (leader).

In modern times, the Oklahoma tribe is governed by the Modoc Tribal Council, made up of a chief, second chief, secretary-treasurer, and two council members who serve four-year terms. Members of the council, the governing body for the tribe, serve four-year terms. Every enrolled tribal member over age eighteen is part of the council.

On the Klamath Reservation, the government is organized according to the 1953 constitution. All enrolled members of the tribe make up the general council. They elect a ten-member tribal council, which is composed of a chairperson, vice chairperson, secretary, treasurer, and six council members, who serve three-year terms.

ECONOMY

For centuries, the Modoc were hunters, fishermen, and gatherers who moved from place to place depending on the season. In the spring, they left their winter homes. The men fished. The women built drying racks to hold the day's catch and gathered parsley roots. Later in the spring, the group moved so the women could harvest a vegetable root called epos. During the summer, the men traveled into the mountains to hunt deer and mountain sheep, leaving the women behind to harvest camas roots. Hunting trips continued until late summer, when full-time fishing resumed.

Men made canoes, built winter homes, and protected the tribe as needed. Women tended the children, gathered nuts and berries, dug for roots and bulbs, made baskets and clothing, and prepared and stored food. The tribe also traded with neighboring tribes and later with fur companies. Instead of money, the Modoc used dentalium shells harvested on Vancouver Island that they received from the Shasta. They traded it to the Achomawi for shell beads, baskets, and skirts made of grass or pine nut string. They exchanged slaves with the Klamath for baskets, blankets, fishhooks, beads, clothing, axes, and spears.

In modern times, Modoc people work in ranching, teaching, small businesses, and other professions. Casinos bring profits to both reservations; both also depend on tourism and recreation. Forestry still provides the Oregon Modoc with a significant portion of their income. In Oklahoma farming, livestock, pecan groves, and a variety of service and retail businesses help to support the people. The Oklahoma Modoc have also reintroduced bison to the area; they raise them and sell bison products. In spite of these businesses, unemployment rates remain high on both reservations. Many people who need work are unable to find it.

DAILY LIFE

Buildings

In the winter, the Modoc lived in pit houses—earth-covered, circular dwellings with an entrance ladder sticking out the top. They dug a pit, ranging from 15 to 40 feet (5 to 12 meters) in diameter and 3 to 4 feet (about 1 meter) deep. They sank timbers into the pit to support the rafters and to form a roof and walls. Woven mats of dried grass covered the roof and walls, which they topped with sheets of bark. They piled dirt from the pit on top as a final layer.

One entered by crawling across the roof and climbing down the ladder. The entrance also provided fresh air and light. Two or three families shared each pit house, and a central fire provided warmth. The people slept on mats made of rushes, and their fur blankets were stored at the outer edges of the house along the walls. They used a separate building made of grass mats for cooking.

The framework of Modoc summer homes was made of willow poles stuck into the ground and tied together at the top. Mats of woven grass covered the poles. Later, winter homes were also made of mats, but these homes were longer and were erected over a shallow pit.

Clothing and adornment

In the winter, the Modoc wore moccasins, leggings, shirts, skirts, and robes made from deer or coyote skin. Fur or woven-grass robes were tied together and worn on top to provide added warmth. Woven rabbit skin, feather strips, or bird skins were also used for robes. Wealthier people wore elk skin, puma, or bobcat robes with a fur hat. For added warmth, the Modoc stuffed their moccasins with shredded sagebrush bark. They greased their faces to prevent chapping and applied charcoal around their eyes to prevent snow blindness.

In the summer, the people wore loincloths (flaps of material that covered the front and back and were suspended from the waist) or skirts made of tule or other plentiful grasses. Grass clothing did not last long, but it was easily woven and replaced. Both genders wore these skirts.

Men and women wore waterproof, basket-shaped hats woven from tule or rushes. The men's hats were usually plain but had a visor. The women's often had decorative designs. In the winter, they sometimes wore fur hats with earflaps.

Men and women had long braids; men had two, and women had one. They painted their faces red. Black paint signaled mourning, whereas white was used for dances. Men wore nose pins of bone, shells, or pine nuts. They pulled out their facial hair, and they carved designs into their chests and arms, then filled them with charcoal. Women tattooed their chins with two or three lines.

Food

During fishing season, the men caught trout, perch, and suckerfish. Women dried extra fish and stored it in baskets of woven grasses for later use. The men hunted rabbit, squirrel, duck, geese, prairie chickens, deer, elk, antelope, and sheep for both food and clothing. Women prepared the meat and dried some for winter. The tribe camped near streams so the men could more easily fish or hunt.

They later moved on to another camp where the women dug for desert parsley, camas bulbs, the root vegetable epos, and wild potatoes. They consumed some of these fresh, and they dried others for winter use. Some camas bulbs were poisonous; these needed to be soaked before they were used. Women often baked camas in earth ovens and then sun-dried it for storage. They also ground the seeds of the pond lily between stones and made that into a variety of dishes.

Families who did not gather and store sufficient food during the rest of the year could starve in the winter. Those who did gather food buried it, covered the spot with grass mats and baskets, and kept its location secret.

Education

Early teachings Until age six, boys and girls played together and competed in foot races, swimming, tops, and sometimes target shooting. Before sunrise, an elder man in the household would wake the children for a swim and a run.

Older children watched younger ones. They also learned to perform their adult duties by observing and assisting their elders. Girls learned to dig roots, get wood and water, cook, and care for babies. Boys learned to hunt, fish, and fight. When a boy killed his first game, his mother gave it away to someone who was not a relative, and the boy was praised for his generosity.

Lessons in manners, culture, and proper behavior came from elders who told stories around the fire. Stories of the Owl were used to scare naughty children. Parents sometimes scolded or whipped youngsters who did not behave.

Education from the 1800s on Unlike many other tribes, the Modoc were eager to send their children to school. Twenty-five children were sent to boarding school soon after the people were removed to the reservation. Reports indicated that they learned English quickly; their parents, too, also learned to read and write. After a student death at the Carlisle Indian School in Pennsylvania, however, the Modoc became hesitant to send their children there.

During the late 1870s, Modoc children attended a school run by the Society of Friends, also known as Quakers. They studied reading, writing, mathematics, and geography, and they learned about the Bible and the importance of not drinking alcohol. Girls learned practical skills such as cooking, sewing, and caring for a house, and boys learned carpentry and farming.

In modern times, Modoc children attend public schools. Culture and language classes are now available so children can learn Modoc traditions.

Healing practices

Men or women who felt a calling to become shamans (pronounced *SHAH-munz* or *SHAY-munz*), or healers, went on a quest for spiritual guidance and spent five days fasting alone in the woods. In time, spirits would appear and teach them special healing songs and dances. The shamans also learned how to influence the weather. Some knew of ways to inflict disease or death on a victim.

A new shaman put up a pole laden with symbols outside his home. He painted the interior posts and put images of his guardian spirit on the roof and indoors. He sent out invitations and gathered enough food for five days, then danced for everyone at night and performed magic tricks, such as producing fish or blood in a basket far from him.

Shamans usually cured by singing and sucking objects out of the body. They were also expected to find lost objects. For minor ailments, shamans administered herbs. Puffball fungus was used on sores and skin swellings, rabbitbrush leaves and stems were steamed to produce a cough medicine, and sagebrush leaves relieved headaches and rheumatism. Shamans were paid for their services and could become very wealthy. However, they could be killed if their patients did not recover.

ARTS

Men hollowed out shovel-nosed canoes with fire and elkhorn picks. They made bows of juniper or yew, and they fashioned arrows, spears, and digging sticks from mountain mahogany. Women sometimes made canoes, but most often, they spent their time weaving baskets of nettle fiber and Indian hemp. They worked designs into them with cattail (white), porcupine quills (yellow), and dyed tule (black). They created trays, bowls, and caps. Burden baskets, cradles, and seed beaters were made of willow. Both sexes tanned hides using animal brains, and women sewed them into clothing.

CUSTOMS

Festivals

On the Klamath Reservation, the tribes host the annual Restoration Celebration in August to remember receiving federal recognition in 1986. They hold a powwow (Native singing and dancing), a rodeo, a parade, arts and crafts displays, and sporting events. Several other celebrations are held yearly: the New Year's Eve Powwow, which they now call the New Year's Eve Sobriety Celebration to encourage no drinking or drugs on the holiday; the Captain Jack Memorial Day Rodeo and Powwow; and the Return of the C'waam Ceremony in March.

The c'waam, or lost river sucker, swims up the Sprague River in Chiloquin, Oregon, to spawn after the first March snow. Long ago, the tribe stationed watchmen on the riverbanks to alert the people when the fish arrived. A shaman then offered thanks. Today, tribal leaders or members perform this tradition. Present-day celebrations include drumming and dancing, feasting, and releasing a pair of fish from the Klamath aquatic center into the river.

Courtship and marriage

Marriages were arranged by the families. A boy's parents chose a mate for him, then visited her family together with relatives, bringing presents of food. The women from both families prepared the food and everyone feasted. If the girl's parents favored the match, they soon returned the visit. The boy's parents then assembled gifts such as baskets, beads, skins, furs, robes, weapons, and canoes. Relatives took the items to the girl's family. If they liked the gifts, her family gave a favorable response. If they did not, the gifts were returned.

A wedding took place soon after the bride's family agreed to the match. More gifts were exchanged, and the bride's family escorted her to the groom's house, marking the beginning of the marriage. For four days the bride sat facing a wall, eating very little and speaking in whispers. During that time, the groom appeared only in the late evening.

After four days, the bride began to take part in the activities of the household. The couple moved in with the bride's family, where they stayed until the birth of their first child. They could then choose whether to live with the bride's parents or the groom's parents.

Birth and naming

Babies were born in wickiups (domed wigwams) with a midwife in attendance. The baby was washed after birth and received a steam bath the next day. An infant's head and face were massaged to shape it. To recover from childbirth, mothers laid for two days on sand that was spread over hot rocks.

The father stayed home or went running in the mountains, seeking power. He gave away his first kill after the birth, just as he had done as a boy. When the mother returned, they both took a sweat bath, swam, and changed into fresh clothes. Fathers made a wooden cradleboard for the child to use the first year.

At age one, the child received a name, usually an animal name or one based on a personal characteristic. Other nicknames might later be given.

War and hunting rituals

War chiefs, who were not the same as village chiefs, accompanied warriors into battle. Any man who could attract enough followers could become a war chief, but it was usually a man who had proven he was a successful raider. Raiding parties consisted of ten to twenty men. They raided for goods, such as weapons or skins, and to capture slaves. The usual targets of raids were the neighboring Pit River Indians (see entry), Paiute, or Shasta.

Warriors sought the help of shamans if they wanted to kill an enemy through magic or if they wished to influence the outcome of a battle.

Gambling

A very popular pastime among the Modoc was gambling. Women enjoyed a game played with dice made of beaver teeth. Men played a complicated game in which they tried to guess how others had arranged their playing pieces. They had to study the faces and body language of their opponents for clues. Players bet large amounts of goods during the game, and a man might gamble away all of his possessions. Because of the risk of losing everything and starving, gambling did not take place in winter.

Funerals

The Modoc believed that after death, a person's soul went to the "land of the dead" somewhere in the west. They also believed that the soul could leave the body during sleep. For that reason, they slept with their heads facing east so their soul would not mistakenly go to the land of the dead. They always cremated bodies with their heads facing west. After the flames consumed the corpse, the living tried to forget the dead.

CURRENT TRIBAL ISSUES

The Modoc are trying to establish a land base so they can work together to restore their culture. Meanwhile, members live in different places, mainly in Oregon and California. At their Oklahoma headquarters, some Modoc are involved in efforts to keep the language and oral histories alive. Elders are compiling family photographs and letters. Many Modoc travel to the Klamath Reservation in Oregon to participate in ceremonies.

Concern about the decrease in salmon due to dam construction prompted the tribes on the Klamath Reservation to sue PacifiCorp.

Owned by the British company ScottishPower, PacifiCorp has built hydroelectric plants on the Klamath River. These plants produce electricity through waterpower, but the dams that provide power to the plants also prevent salmon from reaching their spawning grounds, so the fish cannot reproduce. The dams also reduce the flow of water. The tribes want the company to create special passages so the salmon can get through. PacifiCorp claimed it would cost $100 million to add ladders and screens to its four dams. In 2009, after protests, civil disobedience, and lawsuits, the parties compromised. The hydroelectric company agreed to remove its dams by 2020, after being allowed to add a surcharge to customers' bills for a decade. Those fees will cover the costs the company will incur, and additional funds may come from the state of California.

NOTABLE PEOPLE

Michael Dorris (1945–1997) was a novelist and anthropologist who taught Native American Studies at Dartmouth College. He published many scholarly works, including some on Native peoples. In his later years, Dorris gained fame as a novelist. He wrote *Yellow Raft in Blue Water* in 1989 and a best-selling novel titled *The Crown of Columbus* (1992) with his wife Louise Erdrich, a well-known fiction writer. Together, Dorris and Erdrich also wrote a prize-winning nonfiction book, *The Broken Cord: A Family's Ongoing Struggle with Fetal Alcohol Syndrome* (1989). The book describes their adopted son, who had been damaged by his birth mother's alcohol consumption while pregnant. Michael Dorris committed suicide in April 1997.

Kintpuash (c. 1837–1873), the son of a Modoc chief, was called Captain Jack because he liked to wear a U.S. military jacket with brass buttons. Kintpuash is best known for protesting conditions on the Klamath reservation in Oregon and leading the Modocs in the Modoc War. He was hanged in 1873 for the shooting of American General Edward Canby.

Other notable Modoc include the last chief of the Modoc, Bogus Charley (d. 1881); Kintpuash's adviser, Schonchin John (1797–1892); Winema Riddle (c. 1850–1920), an interpreter during the Modoc War; and the shaman Curly-headed Doctor (1828–1890), who served as the Modoc spiritual adviser during the Modoc War.

BOOKS

Barrett, Samuel A. *The Material Culture of the Klamath Lake and Modoc Indians of Northeastern California and Southern Oregon (1910)*. Reprint. Whitefish, MT: Kessinger Publishing, 2010.

Cozzens, Peter. *The Army and the Indian*. Mechanicsburg, PA: Stackpole Books, 2005.

Curtin, Jeremiah. *Myths of the Modocs*. Whitefish, MT: Kessinger Publishing, 2006.

DuBois, Cora. *The 1870 Ghost Dance*. Reprint. Lincoln: University of Nebraska, 2007.

James, Cheewa. *Modoc: The Tribe That Wouldn't Die*. Happy Camp, CA: Naturegraph, 2008.

Gray-Kanatiiosh, Barbara A. *Modoc*. Edina, MN: ABDO, 2007.

Gunther, Vanessa. *Chief Joseph*. Santa Barbara, CA: ABC-Clio, 2010.

Meacham, A. B. *Wi-ne-ma (The Woman Chief) and Her People*. Reprint. Charleston, SC: BiblioBazaar, 2009.

Miller, Joaquin. *Life amongst the Modocs: Unwritten History*. Reprint (1873). Charleston, SC: BiblioBazaar, 2009.

Riddle, Jeff C. *The Indian History of the Modoc War*. Reprint. Charleston, SC: Nabu Press, 2011.

Williams, Jack S. *The Modoc of California and Oregon*. New York: PowerKids Press, 2004.

PERIODICALS

Bales, Rebecca. "Winema and the Modoc War: One Woman's Struggle for Peace." *Prologue Magazine* 37, no. 1 (Spring 2005). Available online from the National Archives. http://www.archives.gov/publications/prologue/2005/spring/winema.html (accessed on August 15, 2011).

McLeod, Christopher. "Mount Shasta: A Thousand Years of Ceremony." *Earth Island Journal* 10 (January 1995).

"The Surrender: Bogus Charley and His Companions in Camp Appearance of the Prisoners." *New York Times,* June 2, 1873: 1. Available online from http://query.nytimes.com/mem/archive-free/pdf?res=F50611FF3F5E137B93C0A9178DD85F478784F9 (accessed on August 15, 2011).

WEB SITES

Allen, Cain. "The Oregon History Project: Toby Winema Riddle." *Oregon Historical Society.* http://www.ohs.org/education/oregonhistory/historical_records/dspDocument.cfm?doc_ID=000A9FE3-B226-1EE8-827980B05272FE9F (accessed on August 11, 2011).

"The Gathering Spot for Klamath, Modoc, and Yahooskin Snake Paiute Peoples." *Maqlaqs Hemcunga (People Talking).* http://www.maqlaqshemcunga.com/ (accessed on August 11, 2011).

The Klamath Tribes. http://www.klamathtribes.org/ (accessed on August 11, 2011).

"The Long Struggle Home: The Klamath Tribes; Fight to Restore Their Land, People and Economic Self-Sufficiency." *The Klamath Tribes.* http://www.klamathtribes.org/information/background/home.html (accessed on August 11, 2011).

"Modoc." *Four Directions Institute.* http://www.fourdir.com/modoc.htm (accessed on August 11, 2011).

"Modoc." *College of the Siskiyous.* http://www.siskiyous.edu/shasta/nat/mod.htm (accessed on August 11, 2011).

"Modoc Indian Chiefs and Leaders." *Access Genealogy.* http://www.accessgenealogy.com/native/tribes/modoc/modocindianchiefs.htm (accessed on August 11, 2011).

Modoc Tribe of Oklahoma. http://www.modoctribe.net/ (accessed on August 11, 2011).

"The Modocs—History and Culture of the Modocs." *History Rhymes.* http://www.historyrhymes.info/category/multi-part-series/the-modocs/ (accessed on August 11, 2011).

The Oregon History Project. "Modoc." *Oregon Historical Society.* http://www.ohs.org/education/oregonhistory/search/dspResults.cfm?keyword=Modoc&type=&theme=&timePeriod=&region= (accessed on August 11, 2011).

Redish, Laura, and Orrin Lewis. "Klamath-Modoc Indian Language." *Native Languages of the Americas.* http://www.native-languages.org/klamath-modoc.htm (accessed on August 11, 2011).

Weiser, Kathy. "The Modoc—Fighting in the Lava Beds." *Legends of America.* http://www.legendsofamerica.com/na-modoc.html (accessed on August 11, 2011).

Weiser, Kathy. "Old Schonchin—Modoc Chief and Warrior." *Legends of America.* http://www.legendsofamerica.com/na-schonchin.html (accessed on August 11, 2011).

Nez Percé

Name

Nez Percé (pronounced *nez PURSE* or *nay per-SAY*). Before it had horses, the tribe called itself *Cuupn'itpel'uu,* meaning "we walked out of the woods" or "we walked out of the mountains." Neighboring tribes called the Nez Percé "people under the tule," referring to the way they built their houses, or "khouse eaters" after their favorite root. The name *Nez Percé* means "pierced nose" in French and was applied to the tribe by early fur traders, even though the tribe did not traditionally practice nose piercing. The Nez Percé now call themselves *Nimi'ipuu* (also spelled *Nee-Me-Poo*), which means "real people" or "we the people."

Location

The Nez Percé lived on lands in present-day central Idaho, northeastern Oregon, and southeastern Washington. At one time, their territory also extended into western Montana and Wyoming. In modern times, most of the descendants of the tribe live on the Nez Percé Reservation near Lapwai, Idaho, or on the Colville Reservation in the state of Washington. Some still live in Oklahoma, where they were removed for a time, and others remained in Canada.

Population

There were approximately 6,000 Nez Percé in 1800, and 1,500 in 1900. In the 1990 U.S. census, 4,003 people identified themselves as members of the Nez Percé tribe. The 2000 census showed that 4,082 Nez Percé lived in the United States, and 6,857 people claimed to be of Nez Percé heritage.

Language family

Penutian.

Origins and group affiliations

Before the Europeans arrived, the Nez Percé lived for centuries in small villages along the Clearwater, Salmon, and Snake Rivers in the Pacific Northwest. They are linked culturally and by language to other tribes in that region,

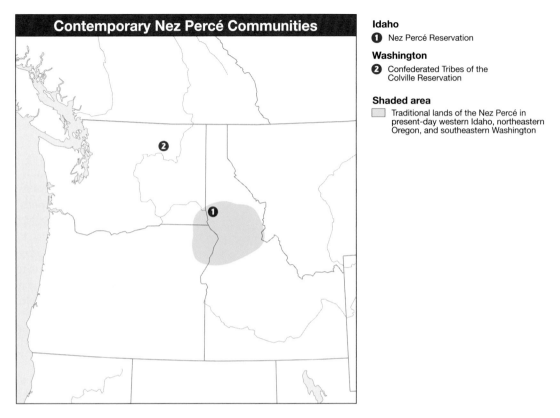

Contemporary Nez Percé Communities

Idaho
❶ Nez Percé Reservation

Washington
❷ Confederated Tribes of the Colville Reservation

Shaded area
Traditional lands of the Nez Percé in present-day western Idaho, northeastern Oregon, and southeastern Washington

A map of contemporary Nez Percé communities. MAP BY XNR PRODUCTIONS. CENGAGE LEARNING, GALE. REPRODUCED BY PERMISSION OF GALE, A PART OF CENGAGE LEARNING.

including the Yakama, Umatilla (see entries), Klickitat, and Walla Walla. They allied with the Cayuse and Flatheads (see entry) to defend themselves against the Blackfoot, Northern Paiute, Shoshone (see entries), and Bannock. In the early twenty-first century, some Nez Percé live on a reservation with the Colville (see entry).

The Nez Percé were once one of the largest and most powerful tribes of the Northwest, controlling a swath of territory along the Clearwater and Snake Rivers in present-day Idaho and lands in Oregon and Washington. They traveled the area each season as fishermen, hunters, and gatherers. Chief Joseph (1840–1904), their leader during the 1800s, is famous for his resistance to U.S. expansion into Nez Percé territory and his role in the tribe's final surrender. The dramatic "Flight of the Nez Percé" was front-page news in the United States when it occurred and is still studied by military historians.

HISTORY

Horses bring changes

Before the Nez Percé acquired horses in the early 1700s, they spent most of their time fishing, hunting on foot, or gathering wild plants for food. Within a generation of acquiring horses, however, their lifestyle changed. They started trading with neighboring tribes and began annual trips to the Great Plains to hunt buffalo. Their rich grasslands enabled the Nez Percé to raise some of the largest herds of horses of any Native group. They became skilled horse breeders and trainers, particularly of the sturdy, spotted horses now called Appaloosas.

The Nez Percé maintained friendly relations with most neighboring tribes, except those to the south—the Shoshone, Northern Paiute (see entries), and Bannock. Every summer, however, the Nez Percé called a truce with their enemies in order to trade with them at a large gathering.

Important Dates

1805: The Nez Percé assist American explorers Meriwether Lewis and William Clark during their expedition to the Pacific Coast.

1855: The Nez Percé enter into a treaty with the U.S. government.

1863: The 1855 treaty is amended by trickery, and the document becomes known as the Thief Treaty.

1877: During the Nez Percé War, Chief Joseph and his people try fleeing to Canada, but are captured by U.S. Army troops.

1951: The Nez Percé receive $3.5 million from the U.S. government to compensate for the loss of their homelands.

1996: The Nez Percé are invited back to the Wallowa Valley.

American explorers enter tribal lands

The first contact between the Nez Percé and non-Native people took place in 1805 when the Lewis and Clark expedition, led by Meriwether Lewis (1774–1809) and William Clark (1770–1838), wandered into the Wallowa Valley in western Idaho. At that time, the American explorers were cold, tired, and running out of food. The Nez Percé aided the members of the expedition and may have kept them from starving. Later, the Nez Percé helped them build boats and guided them to the Pacific Coast. Over the next few decades, the Nez Percé established friendly relations with French-Canadian and American fur traders, missionaries, and settlers.

Through the mid-1800s, the number of settlers in the Northwest greatly increased. For the most part, the Nez Percé avoided the conflicts that plagued other tribes. They signed the Walla Walla Council of 1855, a treaty giving some of their ancestral territory to the government in exchange for money and a guarantee that the rest of their lands—13 million acres—would remain intact.

The Nez Percé face the U.S. Army at the Battle of Birch Creek during the Nez Percé War in 1877. © NORTH WIND PICTURE ARCHIVES/ALAMY.

Many of the Plateau tribes felt double-crossed when, shortly thereafter, the governor of Washington Territory, Isaac Ingalls Stevens (1818–1862), wrote a letter to an eastern newspaper proclaiming that the Northwest was open for settlement. His trickery, which resulted in a flood of settlers, caused several area tribes to react with violence. The Nez Percé, however, remained neutral and did not participate in any wars waged by neighboring tribes against the United States military.

In the early 1860s, gold was discovered on Nez Percé lands, and fortune seekers ignored the 1855 treaty. In 1863, reacting to pressure from the new settlers, Nez Percé leaders tried but failed to reach a new treaty agreement. Governor Stevens then collected the signatures of a few members of the tribe on a deed ceding (giving away) another 7 million acres of Native land. This document, which came to be known as the Thief Treaty, cost the Nez Percé their claim to Wallowa Valley. Upon hearing the news, Old Chief Joseph (c. 1785–1871), the peaceful leader of the Wallowa band and a Christian convert, tore up his Bible. Despite their anger and resentment, however, the Nez Percé remained peaceful in their relations with whites. They expressed their discontent by refusing to abide by the treaty.

Nez Percé War

When Old Chief Joseph died in 1871, his son Young Chief Joseph (1840–1904) took over leadership of the Wallowa group. In 1876, the young chief represented the Nez Percé in a meeting with the U.S. government. He informed them that he would not honor the 1863 Thief Treaty, nor would he give up the tribe's ancestral valley. The government gave the tribe thirty days to vacate Wallowa Valley and move to a reservation near Lapwai, Idaho. When it became clear that war was the only other alternative, Chief Joseph agreed to move. He said sadly: "I would give up everything rather than have the blood of my people on my hands."

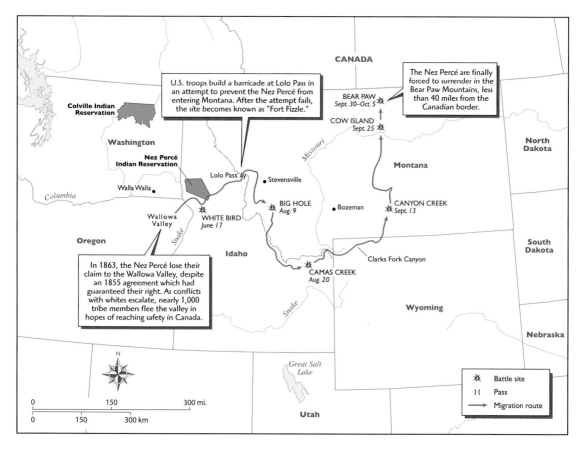

A map showing the flight of the Nez Percé in 1863. MAP BY XNR PRODUCTIONS. CENGAGE LEARNING, GALE. REPRODUCED BY PERMISSION OF GALE, A PART OF CENGAGE LEARNING.

Before the move began, young rebels from the tribe attacked a group of settlers who had mistreated them, killing three men and wounding another. Chief Joseph, along with 250 warriors and 500 women, children, and elderly members of the tribe, reluctantly joined the rebels as they fled the valley, hoping to find safety in Canada. Nearly 2,000 U.S. Army troops set out in pursuit, thus beginning the Nez Percé War of 1877.

Over the next four months, the Nez Percé traveled 1,600 miles (2,575 kilometers). They crossed the rugged wilderness of Idaho, Wyoming, and Montana, trekking over mountains, through canyons, and across rivers. In all, they fought fourteen battles against a better-equipped enemy. Until the last battle, they consistently outsmarted the larger military forces.

Chief Joseph's Surrender Speech, October 5, 1877

Tell General Howard I know his heart. What he told me before I have in my heart. I am tired of fighting. Our chiefs are killed. Looking Glass is dead. Toohoolhoolzote is dead. The old men are all dead. It is the young men who say yes or no. He who led on the young men [Ollikut] is dead. It is cold and we have no blankets. The little children are freezing to death. My people, some of them, have run away to the hills, and have no blankets, no food. No one knows where they are—perhaps freezing to death. I want to have time to look for my children and see how many of them I can find. Maybe I shall find them among the dead. Hear me, my chiefs, I am tired. My heart is sick and sad. From where the sun now stands, I will fight no more forever.

SOURCE: Chief Joseph. "Chief Joseph Surrenders." *The History Place.* http://www.historyplace.com/speeches/joseph.htm (accessed on August 11, 2010).

Nez Percé surrender

In their final battle, which took place just thirty miles from the Canadian border and lasted for six days, the Nez Percé fought off one army unit but were finally surrounded by another. To save the wounded and the women and children, Chief Joseph surrendered along with four hundred Nez Percé in 1877. It was then that he gave his famous surrender speech. Although some people question whether the words are his, others say it is much like his other speeches.

Not everyone surrendered with Chief Joseph, though. Chief White Bird (d. 1892) and between fourteen and one hundred followers escaped to Canada and joined Sioux leader Sitting Bull (c. 1831–1890). The people who surrendered were sent to reservations in Kansas, then Oklahoma. They later ended up sharing the Colville Reservation near Nespelem, Washington. Another part of the tribe was placed on the Nez Percé Reservation near Lapwai, Idaho.

In 1895, the reservation was divided into small individual plots for farming, and leftover property went to U.S. settlers. Much of the land from the treaty of 1863 was lost. Taxation reduced Nez Percé landholdings even more. The tribe's land base was reduced from 13 million acres in 1800 to less than 80,000 acres by 1975. Since 1980, though, the people have been reacquiring land and now have about 110,000 acres.

RELIGION

The Nez Percé felt a deep spiritual connection with the earth and lived in harmony with nature. For the Nez Percé, all living things were closely related to each other and to people. Each member of the tribe had a guardian spirit, or *wyakin,* that protected him or her from harm and provided help when needed. For example, people might pray to their wyakins for help in conquering an enemy or in crossing a dangerous river. The Nez Percé often carried small medicine bundles containing materials that represented their wyakins.

Many modern Nez Percé have adopted Christianity, but combine it with elements of the Dreamer religion. Followers of this traditional Nez Percé religion say that in past times their prophets dreamed about and accurately predicted events such as the arrival of Lewis and Clark and an earthquake near the present-day town of Whitebird.

LANGUAGE

The Nez Percé spoke a Sahaptin dialect (variety) of the Penutian language family, one of the oldest known language stocks in North America. The Nez Percé language is closely related to that of the Walla Walla, Palus, and other tribes of the region. By the late 1990s, only some older members of the tribe could speak the language.

Nez Percé Words

Manaawees?	"How are you?"
Ta'cmeeywi	"Good morning."
T'ckuleewit	"Good evening."
i s	"mother"
t'o t	"father"
s'ik'em	"a horse"
hiy'u m	"bear"
cú-y'em	"fish"
sác'as	"porcupine"
páyos	"snake"
'á-cix	"turtle"
qa-sí'	"bee"

GOVERNMENT

Prior to meeting white missionaries in the 1840s, the seventy small communities that made up the Nez Percé people did not have a formal governing system. Each village had a council of three or four respected men, one of whom was called chief. The job generally went to the person who had the most relatives in the village. Upon the death of a chief, his son usually replaced him. The chief resolved disputes and disciplined unruly children.

Each independent village or group had a headman who spoke for his own followers. When a major decision was needed, the headmen and other respected people would meet in a tribal council to reach an agreement. The Nez Percé had few laws; order was maintained by social pressure. Meetings to discuss problems took place when people gathered to fish or harvest crops. Even then, no tribe member had to obey any group decision.

The Nez Percé rejected U.S. government attempts to reorganize them. Instead, in 1948, they established their own tribal constitution and government. On the Idaho reservation, the Nez Percé Tribal Executive Committee is made up of nine elected officers who serve three-year terms. The committee oversees economic development, tribal social service programs, natural resources, and tribal investments. A fourteen-member business council, whose members serve two-year terms, governs the Colville Reservation from its administrative offices in Nespelem, Washington.

ECONOMY

Early livelihoods

Before American settlers moved into their lands, the Nez Percé provided for their needs by digging roots, picking berries, and killing small animals for food. In May and June, they caught salmon, which they preserved by drying so that it could be eaten throughout the year. The people, along with many neighboring tribes, moved seasonally to different hunting, gathering, and fishing grounds.

When the Nez Percé acquired horses in the 1700s, they found them valuable for trading and for traveling long distances. Horses also enabled them to hunt buffalo. The tribe became skilled at horse breeding and training. They were known for their large herds of Appaloosa (horses with spotted coats).

Many tribes from the Plains and Plateau met to barter goods. The Nez Percé traded dried berries and dried cakes made of sweet-tasting camas lily bulbs and corn-like roots called khouse, as well as salmon oil and dried salmon. They traded horns from mountain sheep, bowls and other objects made from the sheep horns, cedar-root baskets, eagle feathers, and the hunting tools for which they were famous.

Modern economy

By the early 2000s, the tribe was cultivating nearly 38,000 acres of reservation land. Wheat was the primary crop; other crops included barley, dry peas, lentils, canola, bluegrass seed, alfalfa, and hay. The Nez Percé also began breeding an Appaloosa-Akahal Teke cross. They hope to reestablish the horses that were an important part of their herds before the arrival of Lewis and Clark in 1806. They were also raising cattle.

Some Nez Percé work at farming and lumbering, while others have jobs in the medical, legal, and engineering professions, among many others. The Nez Percé Reservation operates a tribal store, limestone quarrying, and a logging business. The tribe is also developing small businesses and expanding their economic base. Tribal casinos generate millions of dollars a year in revenues.

Tourism and gaming are also important sources of income for the Nez Percé on the Colville Reservation. They operate fisheries and engage in forestry. Agriculture and livestock as well as construction and manufacturing are important to the economy.

In spite of the many new economic opportunities, unemployment remains high on the reservation. During the mid-1990s, the tribe's unemployment rate stood at 26 percent. By the early 2000s, that figure had jumped to 39 percent. Some tribal sources indicate unemployment could possibly be as high as 64 percent. Even into the second decade of the 2000s, in spite of economic growth, many Nez Percé who sought employment could not find jobs.

A Nez Percé infant is tucked inside a cradleboard, a device for holding babies that was used among many Native American tribes. © EVERETT COLLECTION INC./ALAMY.

DAILY LIFE

Families

Large families were common among the Nez Percé. Although it was primarily the mother's job to raise the children, the responsibility was shared by uncles, aunts, cousins, and older siblings. Most jobs in a family were assigned by gender. Women generally picked berries, dug up camas bulbs, and made pottery. Men did the hunting and fishing.

Buildings

During the summer, when the Nez Percé moved in search of food, they lived in quickly built lean-tos consisting of a pole framework covered with mats woven of plant fibers. Their winter shelters were pole-framed structures covered with layers of cedar bark, sagebrush, packed grass, and earth. Each winter dwelling, which usually housed several families, contained a small door and a smoke hole in the roof. Five or six houses made up a village.

After horses were introduced, the tribe moved around more and saw the lifestyles of other tribes. Nez Percé buildings then grew larger and more sophisticated. Their winter houses sometimes extended to 100 feet (30 meters) in length and housed many families. They also adopted the

A Nez Percé man in traditional regalia attends the Chief Joseph Days Festival. © NIK WHEELER/ALAMY.

Plains method of covering their portable dwellings with buffalo skins. Hide-covered tepees were used during summer fishing and hunting trips. Tepee coverings were later made of canvas.

Clothing and adornment

In early times, the Nez Percé used shredded cedar bark, deerskin, or rabbit skin to make clothing. In the summer, men usually wore capes and breechcloths (flaps of material that cover the front and back and are suspended from the waist), adding fur robes and leggings when it turned cold. The women were known for the large basket hats they wove out of dried leaves and plant fibers.

By the early 1800s, as the Nez Percé came into contact with tribes of the Pacific Coast and Great Plains, they imitated their tailored skin garments decorated with shells, elk teeth, and beads. Men wore their hair arranged in a high mound that stood straight up from the forehead. The remaining hair was braided and hung down the chest. They also adopted feathered war bonnets. Women wore long, belted dresses of buckskin that had fringe at the hem and knee length moccasins. Both men and women painted their faces.

Food

Food gathering was a time-consuming task for the Nez Percé, who lived in dry, rugged high country. The people lived mainly by fishing, hunting, and gathering fruit and vegetables from spring through fall, and storing surplus food for winter use.

During the spring, they caught large numbers of salmon that swam upstream to spawn. They fished with spears, hand-held and weighted nets, small brush traps, and large, fenced enclosures. The Nez Percé used bows and arrows to hunt elk, deer, and mountain sheep, although hunting was often difficult on the hot, open plateaus of their homeland. To approach their prey and kill them more easily, they sometimes disguised themselves in animal furs and worked together to surround an animal herd. After they started using horses, the Nez Percé sent a hunting party to the Great Plains to hunt buffalo each year.

In the spring, Nez Percé women went out to the hillsides and used sharp digging sticks to turn up khouse, a root. The khouse was ground up and boiled to make soup or was shaped into cakes and dried for later use. Other plants found in summer included wild onions and carrots, bitterroot, blackberries, strawberries, currants, huckleberries, and nuts. Pine nuts, sunflower seeds, and black moss supplemented the vegetables, fruits, and roots they stored for winter. In the late summer, several Nez Percé bands came together to gather camas bulbs. These were steamed and then made into dough or gruel (a thin, watery substance).

Women stored food in coiled baskets inside bark- and grass-lined pits or in parfleche bags, decorated rawhide sacks. They also used baskets to boil food by dropping hot stones into water. They baked other foods in large earthen ovens or broiled them over an open fire using a wooden frame or sticks inserted into the ground.

Education

Grandparents provided much of a child's education. From their grandmothers, girls learned food-gathering techniques and household management. Boys learned from their grandfathers to fish and to hunt with small bows and arrows. By age three, all children participated in food gathering. Their parents tied them to the saddles of horses and gave them miniature tools. Around age six, each child received a lecture about proper morals and behavior from a respected elder.

Children also learned rules of conduct and tribal history from their grandparents. The tradition continues in modern times as children at Nez Percé summer camps learn the importance of preserving their culture through the teachings of tribal elders.

Fruit Leather

The Nez Percé gathered a great variety of berries. Some were eaten fresh; others were dried for winter. This recipe from the Nez Percé National Historic Trail is a way to sun-dry fruit so it can be enjoyed later as a snack. Many people buy these rolled fruit treats at the store, but they are easy to make at home.

> 2 cups of ripe fruit (berries, cherries, plums, apricots, peaches, apples, or a mixture of these)

Wash the fruit and let it drain on a clean towel. Wash your hands well, then carefully cut the fruit into small chunks. Leave the peels on—they are chewy and nutritious.

Put the fruit into a blender or food processor and blend on high for 15 seconds. Cover a large flat cookie sheet with plastic wrap or wax paper, then pour the fruit mixture onto it. Let it dry in a warm place for a day or so.

To eat the fruit leather, peel the fruit off the plastic wrap. You can also roll it up in the plastic wrap and keep it in a covered container (like a cookie jar or refrigerator box) if you want to store it.

SOURCE: *Nez Percé National Historic Trail.* http://www.fs.fed.us/npnht/life/index.shtml#fruitleather (accessed on August 11, 2007).

Healing practices

Nez Percé doctors called shamans (pronounced *SHAH-munz* or *SHAY-munz*), who could be male or female, had miraculous powers. They could change the weather, find lost or stolen items, cause bad people to have misfortunes, remove curses, and cure the sick by singing sacred songs and prescribing herbal remedies. Sometimes, the shamans held cleansing ceremonies to purify spirits before special events or to cure illness.

During healing ceremonies, assistants often sang and beat on a log placed near the shaman and the patient. Some shaman used a leaf funnel or bone whistle to suck out the curse that had caused the illness. Skilled shaman did not need to touch the patient's body; they made gathering motions with their arms and hands to concentrate the evil in one place. Those who had a woodpecker as their guardian spirit, or *wyakin* (see "Religion") used an index finger much as the woodpecker used its bill. They only had to tap on the spot to draw the curse out.

ARTS

Dances

In modern times, dances involving members of several tribes are held at the reservation. Both adults and children are encouraged to display their own personal interpretation of traditional Nez Percé dances to the beat of a drum. During men's traditional dances, the dancers remain upright as they move to a drumbeat, looking down as though to examine the tracks of wild game or the enemy. In the Men's Fancy Dance, they wear outfits adorned with feathers and ribbons and perform fast, spinning movements to a quick beat. During the Grass Dance, they use graceful, swaying motions that resemble prairie grass bending before the wind.

For their traditional dance, women wear dresses decorated with beadwork, porcupine quills, elk's teeth, and ribbons. They gently bounce, dip, and sway to the slow beat of the drum. During the Jingle Dance, they move in dresses adorned with cones made by rolling the lids from metal cans.

Oral literature

Nez Percé families often gathered to tell stories, especially during the winter months. Many of the tales they shared spoke of the interrelated nature of all things. Legends often explained how natural landmarks came to be or how animals received their physical characteristics. Some stories also taught children proper behavior.

CUSTOMS

Festivals

The Nez Percé hold festivals several times a year in celebration of their heritage. These special events feature drumming, singing, and sharing traditional foods. Feasts are held to mark the arrival of edible plants and the major salmon runs. Older members tell stories that pass along the traditional dances, religion, and language.

Finding a guardian spirit

Traditionally, an important task for a Nez Percé youngster was finding his or her personal guardian spirit, known as the *wyakin*. Between the ages of nine and thirteen, boys and girls were instructed by an older tribe member who had a very strong wyakin. After being tutored for several years, the boy or girl went on a solitary journey to find this personal spirit-helper. The individual was not allowed to take food, water, or weapons on the journey.

Sometimes, the wyakin came to the young person through dreams that could be peaceful or agitated. Occasionally, the adolescent returned home, frightened or homesick, without having acquired the wyakin. In the winter, young people who had succeeded would dance and sing in ways designed to make them one with their guardian spirits. By watching and participating, other members of the tribe could often discover the identity of the young people's wyakins. The ceremony sometimes involved contests to see who had received the greatest powers from their wyakin.

Modern celebrations

The Nez Percé people have taken steps to remember their unique and tragic tribal history. In 1996, descendants of the Wallowa band held their twentieth annual ceremony commemorating the members of the tribe who died in the Bear Paw Mountains during the Nez Percé War of 1877. They gathered to smoke pipes, sing, and pray. They also conducted an empty saddle ceremony, in which they lead horses around without riders to appease the spirits of the dead.

Other events that continued into the early decades of the 2000s are the annual Tamkaliks Celebration held in Wallowa, Oregon, that consists of a friendship feast with the surrounding community and a powwow with traditional dances. In Kamiah, Idaho, the Nez Percé hold the annual Chief Looking Glass Days and Pow Wow with namegiving and memorials, dancing contests, and a parade; and Lapwai Days with arts and crafts, a film festival, a community feast, contests, and a parade. Other powwows are held throughout the year.

Hunting and war rituals

When a young boy had his first successful hunt or caught his first fish, a ceremony took place in which the meat or fish was served to the tribe's best hunter. The people believed that this ceremony would make the young boy a good provider. A similar ceremony was held in which a skilled gatherer from the tribe would consume the roots or berries that a girl had collected for the first time.

As part of their war preparations, Nez Percé men stripped to breechcloths and moccasins. They applied brightly colored paint to their faces and bodies. Red paint was placed on the part in a warrior's hair and across his forehead. A variety of colors were applied to his body in special, individual patterns. The warriors also decorated themselves with animal feathers, fur, teeth, and claws representing their connection to their guardian spirits.

CURRENT TRIBAL ISSUES

Modern Nez Percé have been involved in several legal cases; in some instances, rights to hunt and fish on their ancestral lands have been restored. Other cases involve water rights and fights against environmental damage inflicted by outside companies. For example, the Nez Percé, along with the Confederated Salish and Kootenai Tribes, filed a motion in 2011 to stop highway improvement projects they say will damage cultural areas and hunting grounds, destroy archaeological sites, and block their own access routes. The Nez Percé also sued the U.S. government for mismanagement of tribal funds held in trust.

In the early twenty-first century, the Nez Percé were purchasing property to enlarge their landholdings and to restore tribal land lost during the 1800s. They have increased their landholdings, but still only hold title to a tiny portion of the vast homeland they once owned. As members of the Columbia River Inter-Tribal Fish Commission, the Nez Percé, along with the Umatilla, Yakama (see entries), and the Warm Springs nations, work together to promote policies that will restore salmon to the river and ensure that this valuable natural resource is available for future generations.

In the mid-1990s, declines in the timber and cattle markets brought hard economic times to non-Native residents of Wallowa Valley. Valley residents invited the Nez Percé to return to the area. A boom in tourism resulted. The Nee-Me-Poo Trail, the Nez Percé National Historical Park, and the burial site of Old Chief Joseph have become major tourist attractions. Valley residents raised money to build an interpretive center and purchase 160 acres of land for the tribe to use for cultural events. Many members of the tribe were pleased to recover some of their ancestral territory. "The whites may look at it as an economic plus, but we look at it as a homecoming," said tribal member Soy Redthunder.

NOTABLE PEOPLE

Chief Joseph (1840–1904), the son of Old Chief Joseph (c. 1785–1871), assumed leadership of the tribe after his father's death. When the U.S. Army attacked his people who were fleeing the move to a reservation, Chief Joseph led his followers at the Battle of White Bird Canyon. His forces defeated the U.S. Army, killed thirty-three soldiers, and suffered no casualities. They fought valiantly and cleverly against U.S. forces until their final defeat four months later. His people were removed to sites in Washington and Idaho, and Joseph was never allowed to return to his homelands in Oregon and Idaho. He died in 1904, but his words live on. He told *North American Review* in 1879:

> Whenever the white man treats the Indian as they treat each other then we shall have no more wars. We shall be all alike—brothers of one father and mother, with one sky above us and one country around us and one government for all. Then the Great Spirit Chief who rules above will smile upon this land and send rain to wash out the bloody spots made by brothers' hands upon the face of the earth. For this time the Indian race is waiting and praying. I hope no more groans of wounded men and women will ever go to the ear of the Great Spirit Chief above, and that all people may be one people.

Chief Joseph led the Nez Percé against the U.S. Army in the 1870s. © NORTH WIND PICTURE ARCHIVES/ALAMY.

BOOKS

Baird, Dennis W., and Lynn Baird, eds. *In Nez Percé Country: Accounts of the Bitterroots and the Clearwater after Lewis and Clark.* Moscow: University of Idaho Library, 2003.

Biskup, Agnieszka. *Thunder Rolling Down the Mountain: The Story of Chief Joseph and the Nez Percé.* Mankato, MN: Capstone Press, 2011.

Bonvillain, Nancy. *The Nez Percé.* New York: Chelsea House, 2011.

Dwyer, Helen, and Mary A. Stout. *Nez Percé History and Culture.* New York: Gareth Stevens, 2012.

Forczyk, Robert. *Nez Percé 1877: The Last Fight.* Long Island City, NY: Osprey, 2011.

Greene, Jerome A. *Beyond Bear's Paw: The Nez Percé Indians in Canada.* Norman: University of Oklahoma Press, 2010.

Haines, Aubrey L. *Battle of the Big Hole: The Story of the Landmark Battle of the 1877 Nez Percé War.* Guilford, CT: TwoDot, 2007.

Hopping, Lorraine Jean. *Chief Joseph: The Voice for Peace.* New York: Sterling, 2010.

Josephy, Alvin M., Jr. *Nez Percé Country.* Lincoln: University of Nebraska Press, 2007.

King, David C. *The Nez Percé.* New York: Benchmark Books, 2008.

McCoy, Robert R. *Chief Joseph, Yellow Wolf and the Creation of Nez Percé History in the Pacific Northwest.* New York: Routledge, 2004.

Pearson, J. Diane. *The Nez Percés in the Indian Territory: Nimiipuu Survival.* Norman: University of Oklahoma Press, 2008.

Schofield, Brian. Selling *Your Father's Bones: America's 140-Year War against the Nez Percé Tribe.* New York: Simon & Schuster, 2009.

Sneve, Virginia Driving Hawk. *The Nez Percé.* New York: Holiday House, 1994.

West, Elliott. *The Last Indian War: The Nez Percé Story.* Oxford, UK: Oxford University Press, 2009.

Wilfong, Cheryl. *Following the Nez Percé Trail: A Guide to the Nee-Me-Poo National Historic Trail with Eyewitness Accounts.* Corvallis: Oregon State University Press, 2006.

PERIODICALS

Chief Joseph. "An Indian's View of Indian Affairs." *North American Review* 128, no. 269 (April 1879): 412–33.

WEB SITES

"Chief Joseph." *PBS.* http://www.pbs.org/weta/thewest/people/a_c/chiefjoseph.htm (accessed on August 11, 2011).

"Chief Joseph Surrenders." *The History Place.* http://www.historyplace.com/speeches/joseph.htm (accessed on August 11, 2011).

Columbia River Inter-Tribal Fish Commission. http://www.critfc.org/ (accessed on August 11, 2011).

"The Journals of the Lewis and Clark Expedition: Nez Percé." *University of Nebraska.* http://www.nationalgeographic.com/lewisandclark/record_tribes_013_12_17.html (accessed on August 11, 2011).

"Nez Percé." *Countries and Their Culture.* http://www.everyculture.com/multi/Le-Pa/Nez-Perc.html (accessed on August 11, 2011).

"Nez Percé Indians." *Valley Vision.* http://www.lewis-clarkvalley.com/indian.html (accessed on August 11, 2011).

"Nez Percé National Historical Park." *National Park Service.* http://www.nps.gov/nepe/ (accessed on August 11, 2011).

"Nez Percé (Nee-Me-Poo) National Historic Trail." *USDA Forest Service.* http://www.fs.fed.us/npnht/ (accessed on August 11, 2011).

"Nez Percé (Nimiipuu) Tribe." *Wisdom of the Elders.* http://www.wisdomoftheelders.org/program303.html (accessed on August 11, 2011).

"The Nez Percé Tribe." *Columbia River Inter-Tribal Fish Commission.* http://www.critfc.org/text/nezperce.html (accessed on August 11, 2011).

Nez Percé Tribe. http://www.nezperce.org/ (accessed on August 11, 2011).

"Opening the Door to the Trail Home." *Wallowa Band Nez Percé Trail Interpretive Center, Inc.* http://www.wallowanezperce.org/ (accessed on August 11, 2011).

Peterson, Keith C. "Dams of the Columbia Basin and Their Effects of the Native Fishery." *Center for Columbia River History.* http://www.ccrh.org/comm/river/dams7.htm (accessed on August 11, 2011).

Weiser, Kathy. "Chief Joseph—Leader of the Nez Percé." *Legends of America.* http://www.legendsofamerica.com/na-chiefjoseph.html (accessed on August 11, 2011).

Weiser, Kathy. "Nez Percé—A Hard Fight for Their Homeland." *Legends of America.* http://www.legendsofamerica.com/na-nezperce.html (accessed on August 11, 2011).

Spokane

Name

Several stories are told of the origin of the Spokane (pronounced *spo-KAN*) name, which is also spelled Spokan. The people say that one of their early chiefs beat on a hollow tree that contained a serpent. From within the tree came a noise that sounded like "spukane." As he thought about that sound, vibrations came from his head, and the word came to be translated as "power from the brain." For a long time, the people had called themselves *Spukanees,* which meant "sun people" or "children of the sun." Other sources state that the name came from an important chief or from *Spoq'ind* ("round head"), which distinguished them from the Flatheads. The Upper Spokane called themselves *Sintutuuli,* or "Muddy Creek People." The Middle Spokane referred to themselves as *Sinhomene,* or "Salmon-Trout People," and the Lower Spokane went by *Tskaistsihlini,* a name similar to the people's name for the Spokane Falls.

Location

The Spokane once occupied about three million acres of land in what is now northeastern Washington, northern Idaho, and western Montana. At the time of the first European contact, their homeland stretched along the Spokane River in the present-day state of Washington. The three main bands—the Upper, Lower, and Middle—occupied land from the present-day Idaho border to the Columbia River. Upper Spokane territory, which was the farthest east, ran from the Washington-Idaho border west to Spokane Falls, north of what is now the city of Spokane. The Middle Spokane lived west of the falls in the area around the Little Spokane River, and Lower Spokane land extended to where the Spokane and Columbia Rivers meet at present-day Wellpinit, where the nation's reservation is now located.

Population

Prior to European contact, the Spokane population was estimated to be between 1,400 and 2,500. It fell rapidly after that, and by 1827, only 704 Spokane were counted. The 1910 U.S. Census showed 643. Their numbers increased during the later 1900s, and in 1985, tribal enrollment had reached 1,961. The 1990 census indicated the population had risen to 2,118; the

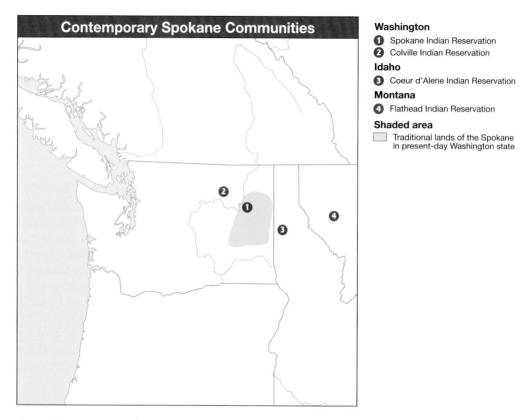

Contemporary Spokane Communities

Washington
1. Spokane Indian Reservation
2. Colville Indian Reservation

Idaho
3. Coeur d'Alene Indian Reservation

Montana
4. Flathead Indian Reservation

Shaded area
  Traditional lands of the Spokane in present-day Washington state

A map of contemporary Spokane communities. MAP BY XNR PRODUCTIONS. CENGAGE LEARNING, GALE. REPRODUCED BY PERMISSION OF GALE, A PART OF CENGAGE LEARNING.

2000 census showed 2,886 Spokane, with 2,004 of those people living on the reservation.

Language family

Salishan.

Origins and group affiliations

For the most part, the Spokane lived in peace. They had close ties with the Flathead, Nez Percé (see entries), and Kalispel, with whom they traded. Once they acquired horses in 1730, these tribes hunted buffalo together. When they did, they came into conflict with the Plains tribes, especially the Blackfoot (see entry), Piegan, and Apsaroke, who considered the Spokane and their allies as poachers in their territory. The Middle Spokane fought with the Coeur d'Alene before U.S. settlement began, but they later moved onto the Coeur d'Alene reservation.

A migrating people, the Spokane dispersed in March from their winter camps into small groups that fished for salmon, dug for roots, and hunting small game. By late summer, those activities also included berry picking. The bands socialized as they gathered and prepared stores of food for the coming winter. The coming of the Europeans and, later, American settlers disrupted their lifestyles, and the forced move to the reservation changed their culture forever. Like the Colville (see entry), the Spokane assimilated (adopted the ways of mainstream American society), a trend they later reversed.

HISTORY

Relations with neighboring tribes

The Spokane, as did most of the Plateau tribes, moved into the area from the north sometime before the 1800s. The Spokane generally got along well with the neighboring Interior Salish tribes, such as the Flathead (see entry) and Kalispel, although the groups occasionally fought amongst themselves.

By 1730, the Spokane and other Interior Salish tribes had acquired horses. With the ability to range farther afield, the bands began to hunt buffalo. The Upper Spokane, who lived the farthest east, were the main participants; the Middle and Lower Spokane continued to hunt small game in their own territories. Buffalo hunting brought the Spokane into conflict with the Plains dwellers, who resented what they considered to be poachers on their land. This led to skirmishes between the Spokane and the Blackfoot, Crow (see entries), Apsaroke, and Piegan nations.

Other battles occurred among the Interior Salish tribes. The Coeur d'Alene and Middle Spokane clashed, as did the Nez Percé (see entry) and the Upper and Middle Spokane. The Yakama (see entry) to the south called the Spokane "robbers," because Spokane raiding parties stole horses, food, and weapons, and took women as slaves. Later, all these groups would unite against a common enemy: U.S. settlers encroaching on their land.

Important Dates

1807: David Thompson, a Canadian trapper, first arrives in Spokane territory.

1855: The Spokane meet withterritorial governor Isaac Stevens, who opens their land to U.S. settlers a short while later.

1881: Spokane Reservation is established.

1940: Coulee Dam floods Spokane land and stops the salmon from running.

1951: Spokane tribal constitution is ratified.

1976: U.S. government returns half of Lake Roosevelt to the Spokane and Colville tribes.

2000: Midnight Mine becomes Superfund cleanup site.

Arrival of the first Europeans

The first Spokane contact with Europeans occurred in 1807, when British fur agent and trapper David Thompson (1770–1857) arrived in their territory. Thompson (who gave the people the name "Spokane") and his party soon established trading posts in the area, and by 1810, the Spokane had begun to trade furs for American goods. Both Fort Spokane and the Spokane House conducted business on Spokane lands until these trading posts were moved to Fort Colville in 1826.

Additional influences from outsiders came through religion. In the 1830s, Spokane Garry (later Chief Garry; c. 1811–1892) returned from the Red River Settlement's missionary school in Canada. He encouraged people to convert to Protestantism. Over the next decades, two missionaries brought the Anglican religion to the people. By 1858, the Catholics had established a mission at Coeur d'Alene, and the priest there visited the Spokane. Later, a Presbyterian church was built. These new religions caused discord among the Spokane, who split into Catholic and Protestant factions. Not until the end of the century did the people find a way to live together in peace.

Trouble with settlers

The mid-1800s were also marked by another brewing conflict. Congress had passed the Donation Act in 1850. This law opened to settlement the Oregon Territory, which included land belonging to the Spokane and many other Native nations. Any U.S. citizen could claim up to 320 acres of land. Native peoples had to give up their tribal affiliation and become citizens if they wanted to own land. Most Natives did not understand the law. They defended their homelands against the invasion of settlers.

When Washington became a territory in 1853, Governor Isaac Stevens (1818–1862) met with various Native nations to make treaties. His treaty commission reached the Spokane in 1855, but they did not come to an agreement. Tensions increased as miners and settlers continued taking over tribal land and food supplies decreased. Several Native nations—Coeur d'Alene, Palouse, Kalispel, Yakima (see Yakama entry), and Northern Paiute (see entry)—formed an alliance to protect themselves from the invasion of these newcomers. In May 1858, when U.S. troops were sent to investigate the murders of two miners in their territory, the Native alliance warned them not to cross the Palouse River.

Battles against the United States

The U.S. military did not heed the warning. The Spokane and their allies defeated U.S. Army troops under the command of Lieutenant Colonel Edward Steptoe (1816–1865). Following this victory at the Battle of Pine Creek, the Americans retaliated. On September 1, additional forces under Colonel George Wright (1803–1865) overtook the Native allies at the Battle of Four Lakes. The Americans imprisoned some of the Native warriors that they captured and hanged others, giving the nearby creek the name of Hangman Creek. These battles, considered part of the second Yakima War (see Yakama entry), are usually called the Coeur d'Alene War. The conflict ended with the Spokane being forced to give up land and to accept the construction of a road through their territory.

Wright held the Spokane chief and four other families hostage for a year to ensure the tribe's cooperation. He also slaughtered horses and destroyed food supplies, leaving the Spokane and their allies to starve that winter. Because Spokane Garry could speak English, the tribe designated him to negotiate a formal treaty. Chief Garry tried unsuccessfully for more than a decade to come to terms with the United States.

When the Nez Percé tried to recruit the Spokane as allies in a war against the United States in 1877, both the Spokane and the Coeur d'Alene stayed neutral. That did not win them any favor with the U.S. government, which later that year negotiated terms that gave the Spokane a reservation in exchange for their traditional homelands.

Loss of traditional territory

In the pact the people signed with the United States in 1877, the Lower Spokane had to move to land that in 1881 became the Spokane Reservation. A decade later, the Upper and Middle Spokane were given the option of moving to one of three reservations—Flathead, Colville (see entries), or Coeur d'Alene. They were promised benefits if they relocated. Most of the Uppers went to the Coeur d'Alene Reservation; others chose the Flathead Reservation. The majority of the Middles joined the Lowers on their reservation.

The Spokane who, like Chief Garry, refused to relocate to the reservation continued to fight for their land, but they eventually lost to the citizens of the growing city of Spokane. Those on the reservation did not fare much better. In 1902, the government divided reservation land into individual parcels and gave one plot to each head of household. The

A Spokane man sits atop his horse in the early 1900s. © MICHAEL MASLAN HISTORIC PHOTOGRAPHS/CORBIS.

United States then sold the leftover land to settlers. The landholdings of the Spokane, once about 3 million acres, was reduced to 64,750 acres.

Dealings with United States

Unlike many tribes, the Spokane welcomed a government school for their children. They believed it was important for the next generation to adopt American ways so that they could part of the society around them. The people kept some of their traditional ways but remained open to the technology and strengths of mainstream American life.

In the 1930s, the Spokane began buying back reservation land. A decade later, the U.S. government took over land along the Spokane

River to build the Grand Coulee Dam. The dam flooded their former lands, but an even greater loss was the salmon runs. No longer could the salmon swim upstream to spawn. The Spokane lost a valuable part of their culture as well as their main food source. To compensate, the government promised them access to Lake Roosevelt, the reservoir created by the dam.

By 1951, the people had a written constitution that had been approved by the federal government. That same year, they filed a petition to get paid what their original homeland was worth. They also questioned the management of the funds the government had been holding in trust for them. In the 1960s, they won $6.7 million, of which half was divided among the tribal members. The other half funded many tribal programs. Another judgment in 1981 awarded the Spokane more than $270,000. These successful lawsuits have enabled the tribe to expand their land holdings and fund projects that benefit the people.

RELIGION

The Spokane believed that the world was divided into three parts that were layered on top of each other. The upper part was ruled by a Superior Being, the middle section was Earth, and the lower portion was under the control of an evil being. Good events, such as rain or a good harvest, came from above. Times of drought or scarce prey were sent by the Black One, who represents the forces of evil. The most important figure in the Spokane religion is the giver of life, Amotkan, portrayed as a bearded white man associated with the sun.

The people also believe that animals became guardian spirits. During the Winter Spirit Dance, the Spokane interacted with these guardians.

Shamans (pronounced *SHAH-munz* or *SHAY-munz*) acted as both healers and religious leaders. They were expected to predict the future. It was also their duty to find animals when hunters returned empty-handed.

Protestants and Catholics

In the 1830s, Spokane Garry (see "History"), who had been schooled at an Anglican mission in Canada, returned to the tribe. His influence, as well as that of missionaries over the next two decades, encouraged many people to become Anglicans. Later in the 1800s, Chief Enoch, a Catholic convert, was removed to the reservation. His larger following and the presence of priests caused divisions between Protestants and Catholics. These conflicts were not settled until the end of the century.

Spokane Words

pus	"cat"
st'ma	"cow"
t'en'w'ey'e?	"bat"
snine?	"owl"
lipul	"chicken"
t'may'oy'e?	"snail"

The Assembly of God built churches on the reservation during the twentieth century. Because of the influence of the Christian faith, the movements adopted by many other reservations in the Northwest—the Native American Church and the Shaker religion—did not take hold on the Spokane reservation. Most present-day Spokane belong to Presbyterian or Catholic churches. Some also combine their Christian faiths with their traditional religion and a belief in Amotkan.

LANGUAGE

The Spokane, along with the Kalispel and Flathead, speak the Salish language, which is considered endangered. Only two hundred people, mostly elders, still speak the language in the twenty-first century. The Salish people are teaching their children to speak Salish, so that their culture gets passed along to future generations.

GOVERNMENT

Each of the three Spokane bands had a chief and several sub-chiefs, but no leader oversaw the whole group. The chief of the Upper Spokane usually filled that position; he met with the other chiefs and announced their mutual decisions. Tribal leaders moved into their positions because of their wisdom, battle skills, wealth, dignity, and good looks. When a chief died, one of the sub-chiefs was picked to take his place. Subchiefs oversaw the smaller groups that were hunting or gathering; some took care of the horses or divided up food.

The Spokane Tribe passed a constitution in 1951. They set up a Business Council to govern the reservation. In 1972, an amendment to the constitution increased the number of tribal council members from three to five. Council decisions are approved by the General Membership, which consists of every tribal member over the age of eighteen.

ECONOMY

Early livelihood

The early economy of the Spokane depended on hunting, fishing, and gathering. Their camps were situated near water, giving them access to abundant plant and aquatic life. Everyone in the village—men, women, and children—participated in the hunts in the early days. The people formed a large circle around their prey and then moved in closer until those with bows could shoot the animals. Later, after the introduction of horses, some Spokane expanded their hunting territory to include buffalo on the Plains.

With the arrival of the trading posts in the 1800s, the people's lifestyle changed. They acquired guns, and European goods began replacing traditional items. The people used iron cooking pots rather than baskets, wool blankets instead of furs. As the Spokane became dependent on these products, they increased their trapping of beaver.

The move to the reservation in the late 1800s left many without livelihoods. The U.S. government encouraged the people to become farmers instead of hunter-gatherers. Many fought to retain their land, but in the end, the Spokane land holdings decreased to small individual plots.

Economic improvement

The Spokane economy began to turn around after they won two settlements from the federal government totaling almost $7 million. The discovery of uranium on the reservation in 1954 brought in additional revenue. The construction of the Grand Coulee Dam in 1940 had flooded Spokane land and destroyed the salmon runs. Several decades later the Spokane received $6 million in compensation that allowed them to install an irrigation system, which benefited the farmers on the reservation. Other important occupations of the Spokane people included cattle-raising and logging.

An Indian Action program run by the Bureau of Indian Affairs provided training in various professions. Some Spokane learned skills such as electrical installation, heavy-equipment operation, carpentry, and clerical work. In 1995, the Spokane government passed the Tribal Employment Rights Ordinance (TERO), which, according to tribal sources, "provides for Indian Preference in any employment, contract and subcontract conducted on or near the Spokane Indian Reservation." Casinos also bring in income and help fund various projects.

DAILY LIFE

Families

Women had most of the daily responsibilities in the camp: they cooked, made clothes, tanned hides, built the tepees, gathered fuel and plants,

helped with hunts, and wove mats and baskets. Men fished, hunted, created tools and weapons, cared for the horses, and went to war.

Buildings

Most Spokane built tepees from a circle of poles that leaned into the center. In the early days, they used tule mats to cover the frame. After the people began hunting buffalo, hides replaced the mats. These portable homes allowed the Spokane to move from place to place so they could hunt and gather.

During the winter, the people built long, rectangular lodges that could hold several families. By digging down into the ground several feet and using earthen walls, they could keep warm in winter. The larger home of the chief, which could be up to 60 feet (20 meters) long, served as a meeting room for ceremonies, festivals, and other gatherings when it was cold. Other important buildings in every village were the sweat lodges and menstrual huts.

Clothing and adornment

Because of their contact with the Plains Indians, the Spokane used buckskin for their clothing. Men wore breechcloths (flaps of material that hung down in the front and back and tucked over a belt). Buckskin shirts, hats, headbands, belts, and sometimes long aprons were often added to their outfits. Leggings along with fur parkas, cloaks, or buffalo robes kept them warm in winter as did fur-lined moccasins and hats. Warriors attached scalps to their war shirts.

Women's long dresses were made of deer or elk skin. They too donned leggings, belts, moccasins, and headbands or caps. Early caps were woven from grass. The Spokane used bear claws, elk teeth, beads, fringe, shells, and feathers for decoration.

Food

In March, the Spokane moved from their winter camps to take advantage of the abundant plants and wildlife in their summer camps, which were situated along rivers or creeks. The men fished for salmon, trout, codfish, devilfish, and whitefish, and they hunted for deer, elk, caribou, antelope, mountain goat and sheep, bear, and cougar. Small game, such as beaver, wolverine, and rabbit, along with duck, geese, and other fowl made up a large portion of the meat in the Spokane diet. Swan eggs and those of other birds provided additional protein.

A Spokane man wears traditional regalia at a tribal powwow at the Spokane Reservation. © SUPERSTOCK/ ALAMY.

Later, some of the people, particularly the Upper Spokane, occasionally traveled to the Plains to hunt buffalo. Women and children accompanied the hunters. Their job was to prepare the meat for the trip home.

Gathered foods formed an important part of Spokane meals. Women collected berries, nuts, roots, and bulbs. Camas (bulb of the lily), cattail shoots, and bitterroot were staple foods. The Spokane layered brown camas, an onion-like bulb, with moss to dry it in fire pits. It was either eaten whole or used to spice meat. Cooks also boiled and mashed it like potatoes. White camas bulbs were ground into flour and baked into cakes.

Wild onions and carrots seasoned stews. Dessert might be black moss, which was boiled and pressed and tasted like licorice. Wild peppermint was used for tea.

Education

At the end of the 1800s, the government opened a boarding school in the abandoned Fort Spokane, which had once been a trading post. One of the main goals of the school was to teach Spokane children to fit into American society. This meant they had to learn English and stop speaking their own languages and practicing their traditions. Many Native nations opposed this, but the Spokane encouraged their children to learn American ways. As recorded by photographer and author Edward S. Curtis in the early 1900s, Spokane Chief Lot said that "money would do the people little good, for when it was spent, it was gone; but a school they would always have, and what their children learned there, they would always know."

Healing practices

The Spokane used many herbal remedies to treat illness. Some of the common cures were enghanchason for toothaches, cascara bark as a laxative, and marijuana as an anesthetic to reduce pain. Red willow bark cleared eye infections, and elderberry leaves worked on skin infections. Balsam, a fir tree, had many healing properties. The people made balsam tea as a cough syrup, bathed with balsam branches to relieve achy joints, and used balsam oil to get rid of blisters.

In addition to herbs and plants, the people relied on spiritual healers called shamans (see "Religion"). These medicine people, who could be men or women, warded off evil spirits before they could harm a victim. To help those who already had evil spirits in their bodies, the shamans removed the invisible darts these spirits had inserted. This was done by sucking or blowing them out or through incantations. Shamans who did not heal their patients were often killed.

During the 1970s, health-care facilities expanded on the reservation. One major concern is the impact of uranium mines, which cause cancer and other health problems. Drug and alcohol abuse programs, along with dietary programs to decrease the high rates of diabetes, were added to deal with these ongoing problems.

ARTS

Spokane art differed little from that of other neighboring Plateau tribes. The people who lived farther west adopted the styles of the Northwest tribes, whereas the eastern peoples used the Plains Indian styles of decoration. The Plains nations were known for their decorative beadwork.

Women created intricate floral and geometric designs on soft animal skins. Clothing, particularly vests, as well as cradle covers, sashes, and bags, were woven in a variety colors; many also incorporated beading and fringe. The Northwest nations also used beadwork, but their designs contained abstract symbols representing important animals; they were created from dentalium and abalone shells and porcupine quills.

As did the other Plateau peoples, the Spokane passed their oral history on to the next generation through stories. Coyote, often a part of many Spokane tales, came from the world above (see "Religion"). He gave people knowledge and abilities. In most stories, Coyote is a trickster who beats his rivals or enemies.

CUSTOMS

Family life

Extended families—usually consisting of grandparents, aunts, uncles, cousins, mothers, fathers, and children—lived close together. The word for female cousin was the same as for sister, so children considered their cousins as part of the family. That also meant that cousins could not marry.

Puberty

Once boys reached puberty, they went to an isolated place to fast and watch for a *sumesh,* or guardian spirit. After a few days, or sometimes many days, the sumesh appeared, most often as an animal, and taught the teen a song. This song and spirit later became part of the symbols in the man's medicine pouch.

At her first menstruation, a girl went to the menstrual lodge, located a distance from the community. Her face was painted yellow or red, her hair was bound into rolls, and she wore plain clothing. She could only use a small comb and had to drink from a drinking tube rather than directly from the well. After her flow ended, she went to the sweathouse to cleanse herself. Following a few months of seclusion, she said evening prayers on a hill and then returned to the village.

Marriage

Before a man could marry the woman of his choice, he had to get her consent as well as her parents' and the chief's approval. If a couple eloped, the men in the tribe treated the woman like a prostitute, and her parents were entitled to take all of her husband's property. If a man married a woman from another tribe, they lived with the wife's tribe, because the Spokane believed the wife would work harder among her own people.

Husbands who abused their wives were looked down on, and if his wife died because of his harsh treatment, her husband had to give gifts to her parents. If the wife died of natural causes, however, the husband could demand the bride price back. Husbands were free to discard their wives for any cause, and men could have more than one wife.

Death and mourning

Before people died, they usually decided how their possessions would be divided up. After someone died, the body was bathed, and the face was painted red. The Spokane then sewed the corpse into skins or robes, or wrapped it in mats. They put the body on a scaffold (a ladder-like structure) or in a tree while they dug the grave, usually in a sandy area parallel to the river. Bodies were placed upright or seated. After the body had been buried, a shaman led a ceremony and pushed a wooden marker into the stones covering the grave. People tied offerings to the marker. Feasts and speeches followed the burial.

Mourners cried loudly and beat themselves on their chests, faces, and arms. Face painting was forbidden for several days. Families of the deceased cut their hair and their horses' tails. No one spoke the dead person's name again, and widows changed their names.

Because they believe every part of the body must buried or the spirit will become a ghost, the Spokane wiped up any spilled blood and buried the cloth with the corpse. This is why present-day Spokane do not participate in organ donation and are opposed to autopsies if any parts or tissues need to be removed for testing. Patients who have their gall bladder or appendix removed often request to keep it afterward.

Games and festivities

For centuries, men celebrated the Salmon Ceremony for four days of the salmon run, a time when salmon swim upstream to spawn. They divided the first salmon they caught into seven pieces and cooked it in a special manner. The people believed that if they held this ceremony the salmon would return each year.

A popular game among the Spokane is the hand game, which is now known as the stick game. Teams take turns singing and beating out

Young people from the Spokane tribe learn traditional dancing and drumming. © ED KASHI/CORBIS.

rhythms with drumstick, while a bead is passed from hand to hand. Players on the opposite team must guess who is holding the bead. Sticks pushed into the ground keep tally of the score. People often bet on the outcome of the game. In earlier centuries, people wagered beaded jewelry, moccasins, or other items of clothing. Modern betting is done with money.

Present-day festivities include rodeos and powwows, which feature games, dancing, and contests. The people also hold a Reservation Day Celebration and the Spokane Indian Days Celebration, with exhibits, games, dances, and handicrafts to sell or trade.

CURRENT TRIBAL ISSUES

Over the past decades, the Spokane Reservation has been the site of some major environmental disasters that require ongoing cleanup and have affected air, soil, and water quality. In 1980, the volcanic eruption of Mount St. Helens left a residue of ash behind. In 2000, the Midnight

Mine was declared a Superfund Site for cleanup. Uranium mining in Spokane territory has been the cause of environmental pollution as well as health problems for the tribe.

The Spokane are still seeking additional compensation for the construction of the Grand Coulee Dam in the 1940s, which took tribal land and destroyed the salmon runs. They also want compensation for the water that is no longer flowing into their territory but instead is backed up behind the dams. The government had promised the Spokane and Colville tribes a portion of the revenue from the hydroelectric power the dams generated and compensation for their losses. In 2011, a bill was introduced in Congress to provide the "fair and equitable compensation" the tribes had been waiting for.

Archaeological sites along Lake Roosevelt have been the target of looters since the Coulee Dam was constructed. Visitors to area beaches take home souvenirs, sometimes not realizing their historic value. Other times, they accidentally destroy important cultural information. Not all thefts are innocent, however. Some people steal the artifacts to resell at a profit. Although laws provide penalties for theft or destruction, most thieves are never caught, and the pieces of history and culture they take are lost to the tribe forever.

In 2011, the Spokane Tribe began working on the development of a $400 million casino. Although local authorities supported the plan, the Kalispel have expressed concern that another casino opening only a few miles from their Northern Quest Casino will cause too much competition and result in layoffs and loss of revenue at Northern Quest.

NOTABLE PEOPLE

Spokane Garry (Ilumhu-spukani, or Chief Sun; c. 1811–1892) led the Spokane during the mid- to late 1800s. He was known for bringing Christianity to the tribe. Spokane Garry was educated at an Anglican school in Manitoba, Canada. He requested schools and churches and urged his people to attend them and become more like mainstream American society. The town that Garry built, Spokane Falls, became the U.S. city of Spokane in 1881. U.S. settlers who wanted the land forced Garry from his home, and he died in poverty in 1892.

The Spokane/Coeur d'Alene poet, novelist, and filmmaker Sherman Alexie (1966–) has won many awards for his work, including the National Book Award for Young People's Literature, a PEN/Hemingway award, a PEN/Faulkner award, and a PEN/Malamud award. His books include the young-adult novel *The Absolutely True Diary of a Part-Time Indian* (2007) and the short-story collection *The Lone Ranger and Tonto Fistfight in Heaven* (1994), and his movies include *The Business of Fancydancing* (2002) and *Smoke Signals* (1998).

BOOKS

Alexie, Sherman. *The Absolutely True Diary of a Part-Time Indian.* Waterville, ME: Thorndike Press, 2008.

Curtis, Edward S. "Salishan Tribes." In *The North American Indian.* Vol. 7. Edited by Frederick Webb Hodge. Norwood, MA: The Plimpton Press, 1911. Available online from http://curtis.library.northwestern.edu/curtis/viewPage.cgi?showp=1&size=2&id=nai.07.book.00000075&volume=7 (accessed on August 11, 2011).

Drury, Clifford M., ed. *Nine Years with the Spokane Indians: The Diary, 1838–1848, of Elkanah Walker.* Glendale, CA: Arthur H. Clark Company, 1976.

Hill, George, Robert H. Ruby, and John A. Brown. *The Spokane Indians: Children of the Sun.* Norman: University of Oklahoma Press, 2006.

Manring, Benjamin Franklin. *The Conquest of the Coeur d'Alenes, Spokanes and Palouses; The Expeditions of Colonel E. J. Steptoe.* Reprint. Charleston, SC: BiblioBazaar, 2009.

Popejoy, Don, and Penny Hutten. *Early Spokane.* Mt. Pleasant, SC: Arcadia Publishing, 2010.

Wynecoop, David C. *Children of the Sun: A History of the Spokane Indians.* Wellpinit, WA, 1969. Available online from http://www.wellpinit.wednet.edu/shorthistory (accessed on August 11, 2011).

Wynecoop, Robert. *The Way It Was According to Chick: Growing Up on the Spokane Indian Reservation.* Spokane, WA: Tornado Creek Publications, 2003.

PERIODICALS

Roy, Prodipto, and Della M. Walker. "Assimilation of the Spokane Indians." *Washington Agricultural Experiment Station Bulletin.* No. 628. Pullman: Washington State University, Institute of Agricultural Science, 1961.

WEB SITES

Fletcher, Alice. "Guessing Games: Hand Games." *Science Views.* http://www.scienceviews.com/indian/indiangames14.html (accessed on August 11, 2011).

"Native American Literature: The Spokane." *Reed College.* http://academic.reed.edu/english/courses/english201nal/spokane.html (accessed on August 11, 2011).

Nisbet, Jack. "David Thompson among the Kalispels, 1800–1812." *Diggings,* Spring 2011. http://diggings.org/thompsonkal.html (accessed on August 11, 2011).

"Questions and Answers about the Spokane Indians." *Wellpinit School District.* http://wellpinit.org/q%2526a (accessed on August 11, 2011).

Redish, Laura, and Orrin, Lewis. "Spokane/Kalispel/Flathead Salish Language." *Native Languages of the Americas.* http://www.native-languages.org/salish.htm (accessed on August 11, 2011).

"A Short History of the Spokane Indians." *Wellpinit School District.* http://www.wellpinit.wednet.edu/shorthistory (accessed on August 11, 2011).

"Spokane Indian Tribe." *Access Genealogy.* http://www.accessgenealogy.com/native/tribes/salish/spokanhist.htm (accessed on August 11, 2011).

"Spokane Indian Tribe." *United States History.* http://www.u-s-history.com/pages/h1570.html (accessed on August 11, 2011).

"Spokane Indians." *The Church of Jesus Christ of Latter-Day Saints.* https://wiki.familysearch.org/en/Spokane_Indians (accessed on August 11, 2011).

"Spokane Tribe." *Governors Office of Affairs.* http://www.goia.wa.gov/Tribal-Information/Tribes/spokane.htm (accessed on August 11, 2011).

Spokane Tribe of Indians. http://www.spokanetribe.com/ (accessed on August 11, 2011).

Spokane Tribe of Indians Language Program. http://spokanelanguage.com/ (accessed on August 11, 2011).

"Tribal History." *Spokane Tribe Economic Project.* http://www.stepspokane.com/?page_id=18 (accessed on August 11, 2011).

Umatilla

Name

The name Umatilla (pronounced *you-muh-TILL-uh*) comes from the name of the tribe's winter village, *imatilam,* and means "many rocks." Other possible translations are "rocky bottom" or "water rippling over sand."

Location

The Umatilla hunted, gathered, and fished the area ranging from the site of present-day Arlington, Oregon, east to the Walla Walla River. Traditional tribal territory included land in what is now northern Oregon and southern Washington State. Along with other Plateau tribes, the Umatilla settled along the banks of the Umatilla and Columbia Rivers. In the early twenty-first century, most Umatilla live with members of the Cayuse, Walla Walla, Warm Springs, Nez Percé, and other tribes on or near the Umatilla Reservation in northeastern Oregon.

Population

In 1780, there were about 1,500 Umatilla. When the explorers Meriwether Lewis (1774–1809) and William Clark (1770–1838) arrived in 1805, the population was estimated to be 2,500. By 1910, only 272 had survived, following epidemics of diseases brought by outsiders, warfare, and attacks by other tribes, including the Pauite. In the 1990 U.S. Census, 1,285 people identified themselves as Umatilla. The 2000 census showed 1,608 Umatilla and 2,169 people with some Umatilla heritage. In 2011, tribal sources noted that more than 2,800 members were enrolled as members of the Confederated Tribes of the Umatilla Indian Reservation, but those numbers also include the Cayuse and Walla Walla.

Language family

Penutian-Sahaptian.

Origins and group affiliations

The Umatilla say they have lived in their homeland since the beginning of time. They reject scientists' theories that they migrated from Asia. Objects from their homeland that have been dug up and studied indicate that the

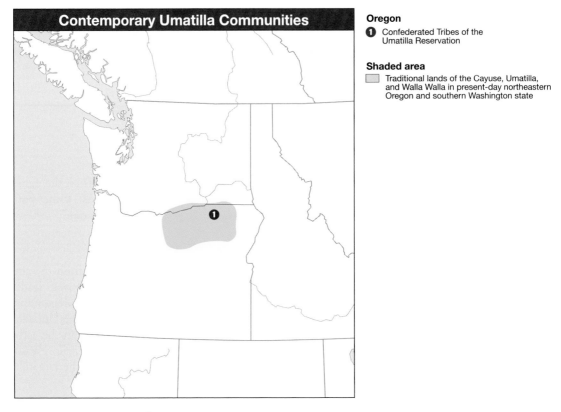

Contemporary Umatilla Communities

Oregon

❶ Confederated Tribes of the Umatilla Reservation

Shaded area

Traditional lands of the Cayuse, Umatilla, and Walla Walla in present-day northeastern Oregon and southern Washington state

A map of contemporary Umatilla communities. MAP BY XNR PRODUCTIONS. CENGAGE LEARNING, GALE. REPRODUCED BY PERMISSION OF GALE, A PART OF CENGAGE LEARNING.

Umatilla culture may have begun there 10,000 years ago. The Umatilla inter-married with and were related to the Nez Percé, Yakama, Modoc, Cayuse, Palus, and Walla Walla tribes of the Columbia Plateau region of Oregon and Washington. The neighboring Paiute often raided Umatilla villages; other enemies included the Shoshone, Blackfoot, and Bannock. In 1855, the Umatilla, the Cayuse, and the Walla Walla joined as the Confederated Tribes of the Umatilla Reservation.

The Umatilla prospered in a barren, dry landscape of sand and gravel in the Columbia Plateau, where the most attractive features were the warm winters and the abundant salmon in the crystal-clear waters of the Columbia River. They moved from the river to the plains and mountains in a cycle that included hunting, fishing, celebrating, and trading. The tribe gave its name to a county, a town, and a river. The people found prosperity during the twentieth century through running casinos and are using those profits to revitalize their ancient culture.

HISTORY

Contact with Americans

Although explorers Meriwether Lewis (1774–1809) and William Clark (1770–1838) were the first European Americans to meet the Umatilla in 1805, smallpox had already been introduced to the region. An epidemic (uncontrolled outbreak of disease) swept through the tribe as early as 1775, brought by other tribes already in contact with outsiders. Smallpox greatly reduced the Umatilla population.

The Umatilla had never seen guns before, so they hid rather than encounter Lewis and Clark. They had seen Clark shoot a crane and believed the whites were sky gods who had come to kill them. Clark described this meeting in his journal: "They said we came from the clouds and were not men." The Umatilla overcame their fears when they saw Sacajawea (pronounced *sak-a-ja-WEE-a*; c. 1786–1812), the young Shoshone (see entry) woman who accompanied Lewis and Clark on their expedition.

Lewis and Clark found the people of the Columbia Plateau region to be rich in horses and dogs. Like their neighbors, the Nez Percé and the Yakama (see entries), the Umatilla acquired horses through trade with other tribes in the early 1700s and became skilled horse breeders and trainers. Using the horse for transportation, the Umatilla could cover a larger territory in the search for food. They ventured all the way to the Great Plains east of the Rocky Mountains and hunted buffalo.

Soon after Lewis and Clark left, traders took their place. An American trading company set up a post in Oregon in 1812, and the North West Company, a huge fur-trading enterprise, built a fort on the Walla Walla River in 1818. Most of the tribes in the area traded horses for European goods such as guns and ammunition, iron pots, blankets, cloth, beads, and cattle. Rivalry over trade added to the hostilities that already raged among the tribes in the region, which were fueled in part by the custom of raiding other tribes for horses and slaves. The Umatilla could not avoid becoming involved in the conflicts.

Important Dates

Early 1700s: The Umatilla acquire horses.

1805: Lewis and Clark are the first explorers to make contact with the Umatilla.

1848–50: The Cayuse War takes place.

1855: Under the Walla Walla Treaty, the Umatilla, the Cayuse, and the Walla Walla join as the Confederated Tribes of the Umatilla Reservation.

1949: The Confederated Tribes organize a tribal government.

1965: The Umatilla are awarded more than $2 million for land lost in the 1855 treaty.

American missionary Dr. Marcus Whitman is attacked by a Cayuse Indian at his home at Walla Walla. His wife and twelve associates were killed in what became known as the Whitman Massacre.
© MPI/GETTY IMAGES.

Battles and land losses

In the 1840s, the Umatilla joined the Nez Percé in a fight against their Paiute enemies (see entries). To add to the already tense situation, settlers and missionaries began arriving in the 1840s. The missionaries were especially active among the Cayuse. When a measles epidemic struck the Cayuse in 1847, the Native peoples blamed the missionaries for it and killed several of them. Those killings (called the Whitman Massacre after one of the missionaries) and concern over the flood of American settlers led to the Cayuse War (1847–50) between the Cayuse and Americans. In 1848, a number of Umatilla warriors joined the Cayuse in that battle. The tribes, however, could not stand up to the superior numbers and fire power of the Americans, and they finally gave up in 1850.

U.S. settlers wanted land, so Congress passed the Donation Land Law of 1851. It granted settlers permission to build homesteads on any Oregon lands, even those that belonged to Native nations. The Native peoples reacted with violence to this unjust new law. To keep peace, the federal government established the Umatilla Agency on the Umatilla River near present-day Echo, Oregon, in 1851. The new agency provided area tribes with food and supplies, and re-established the Saint Anne Mission that had been abandoned after the Whitman Massacre.

Signing of first treaty

Conflicts between the Americans and Native nations escalated, and on May 28, 1855, Washington Territory governor Isaac Ingalls Stevens (1818–1862) called the Walla Walla Treaty Council. Stevens convinced some chiefs to sign a treaty giving up their lands to the United States. The treaty formally combined the Umatilla, Walla Walla, and Cayuse in one group as the Confederated Tribes of the Umatilla Indian Reservation. The treaty reduced the tribes' 6.4 million acres of land to a 250,000-acre reservation along the banks of the Umatilla River near present-day Pendleton, Oregon.

Like all the tribes that signed treaties in 1855, the Umatilla were distrustful of the U.S. government and reacted violently to further trespassing by American settlers on lands they considered their own. It took more than four years for Congress to ratify the Walla Walla Treaty. The fact that it was illegal did not stop Governor Stevens from announcing that American settlers could come and build homesteads on the land.

Another war

Increasing numbers of immigrants trespassed on tribal lands and farms. When gold was discovered in the area, miners and settlers flooded the area. The Yakama tribe was the first to repel the settlers in the Yakama War of 1855–56. The Umatilla joined the Yakama in their war against the Americans while still defending themselves against Paiute raiders. The Umatilla were forced to flee several times during the Yakama War when the Paiutes attacked. The war went badly for the Native warriors. As the U.S. Army gradually took control of the territory, the Umatilla surrendered, along with many of the Yakama, during the second Walla Walla peace council in 1856.

Although the Umatilla agreed to peace, other tribes still fought the Americans for several years. Meanwhile, many of the tribe members on the reservation were unwilling to give in to government agents' urging to settle down and become farmers. Soon, U.S. settlers realized that the Native grazing land was prime wheat-growing land. They decided they wanted it, and the government obliged them by passing the Slater Act in 1885, which established an allotment system for reservation land.

Lands allotted

Under allotment, reservation land was divided into 160-acre plots that were assigned to individual tribe members. Any land left over was opened up to American settlement. By the end of the allotment period, the 250,000-acre Umatilla reservation had shrunk to 82,742 acres for 1,118 Indians.

Allotment affected the Native peoples in many ways. Owning plots of land went against their traditional values of using land in common. Conflicts arose when Indians who owned large herds of horses could no longer graze them on land now used for farming. People whose families had lived in an area for ages were barred from their homelands because someone else held title to the property.

The Walla Walla Regale Lewis & Clark

In 1806, the explorers Meriwether Lewis and William Clark visited a Walla Walla village on the return trip of their Corps of Discovery expedition. Walla Walla Chief Yellept was delighted to see them, and he presented them with gifts of firewood, fish, and a white horse. Yellept received Clark's sword in exchange for his generosity. One of the Corps of Discovery members brought out his fiddle and the treated the Walla Walla villagers and their Yakama guests to an hour of dancing. Lewis reported that in turn, 550 Indian men, women, and children had then "sung and danced at the same time," and were pleased to have some of their guests join in the dance with them. Lewis later recorded in his journal: "I think we can justly affirm to the honor of these people that they are the most hospitable, honest, and sincere people that we have met with in our voyage."

Twentieth-century successes

The Umatilla found it hard to adjust to reservation life, and many left, moving to urban areas to look for work. Those who remained behind faced unrelenting poverty. Conditions only began to improve in the 1960s, when money from land claims and from new federal programs enabled the tribe to start development projects. The land claim issue was first raised in 1951, when the Umatilla filed lawsuits against the United States, demanding payment for four million acres of land taken in the 1855 treaty. In 1965, they were finally awarded more than $2 million. The Umatilla won other claims after their fishing sites were destroyed by the construction of a dam.

The Confederated Tribes of the Umatilla Indian Reservation took advantage of these funds and other monies from the government to improve their living conditions and to develop an economic base. In the 1980s, the government agreed to allow gaming on reservations. After the tribe built casinos, more money flowed into the reservation. The Confederated Tribes are using this money to fund programs to revive their culture.

RELIGION

Like many tribes of the West, the Umatilla did not have a supreme being. They believe that an Old Chief, who had great power, created the seasons. He is invisible but good; unlike some of the gods of other tribes, he demanded no sacrifices. After him come animals in human form as well as giants, elves, and other mythical beings. Signs of all these creatures can be found in nature.

People have guardian spirits who give them a specific power. By way of a ceremony called a vision quest, an individual gets in touch with his or her guardian spirit. No one can control the type of powers received from the spirits. A person might receive the power to cure illnesses or to be successful in hunting or war. Tribe members communicate with their guardian spirits through songs and drumming. Each Umatilla "owns" rhythmic and hypnotic personal songs that are their most important possessions.

The most powerful guardian spirits are the heavenly ones: the sun, moon, and stars. Other spirits come from animals, thunder, wind, and other forces of nature. Umatilla who receive powers from these spirits are directly connected to nature and can hear the whispers and songs of the trees and the messages of beasts of all kinds.

The Umatilla express religious feelings through a ritual called the Washat Dance. The dance marks changes in the seasons and rites of passage. It features male and female dancers, seven drummers, and feasts of salmon and roots. The Washat Dance religion flourished in ancient times, went through changes under the influence of Christian missionaries in the mid-1800s, and then was restored to its original meaning by Dream Prophets in the late 1800s. Umatilla Dream Prophets named Luls and Pinapuyuset helped people in the Columbia Plateau stay in touch with their old religion when it came under attack by Christian missionaries. The Washat Dance religion remains a major form of religious expression in the Northwest.

LANGUAGE

The Umatilla version of the Northern Sahaptian language is related to the languages spoken by the Yakama (see entry), Palus, and Walla Walla, among others. After the establishment of the reservation in the late nineteenth century, all the people there adopted the language of the Nez Percé (see entry). By the 1990s, only a handful of people could speak or even understand the languages of the Umatilla, Walla Walla, and Cayuse Indians. Furthermore, the languages formerly spoken by the people on the reservation had never been written down.

By the end of the twentieth century, tribal elders realized that unless they wrote their languages down and taught them to young people, they would be lost forever. Edith McCloud (1924–2010), who taught the Walla Walla language prior to her death, explained why she was at first unwilling to pass on her knowledge of the language:

> When I first started, I would have preferred never to have the language written down, never documented. What our elders used to say was that the white man is taking everything from us except our language. We didn't want to give it away. But today, in today's world, children are conditioned to learn from documents, tape recorders and now computers. If we keep the language to ourselves and try to teach it only verbally, it really is going to get lost.

Umatilla Words

There are many similarities between the three languages spoken on the reservation. A few simple Umatilla expressions and words are below:

Niix pačway	"Good day."
Wayaninamwa?	"How are you?"
wapayatat	"to learn or teach"
ispilyay	"coyote"

McCloud was one of several tribal elders who began teaching weekly classes in Umatilla, Walla Walla, and other languages. Using elders who are fluent in their languages to assist the youth in learning to speak their traditional languages is part of an ambitious program to revive and preserve them; it is funded by profits from tribal gaming operations.

GOVERNMENT

Each Umatilla group who shared a winter camp had its own chief or headman. Long ago, the position was hereditary (passed down from father to son), but when the people began to hunt buffalo, they adopted the Plains custom of electing chiefs for their skills. The primary duties of a chief were to keep the peace and to promote good behavior among his people. He could not force people to obey him but rather had to convince them that his way was best.

The chief represented his group in meetings with other chiefs. A chief's authority was limited, so when only a few chiefs signed the 1855 treaty with the U.S. government, most tribe members did not believe that all tribal members should be forced to move to the reservation. They soon realized, however, that if they did not comply, they would be destroyed.

After they moved to the reservation, government agents selected and paid the chiefs. In 1949, the Confederated Tribes of the Umatilla Indian Reservation formed their own government. In modern times, a nine-member Board of Trustees, elected every two years, is responsible for overseeing the reservation. The general council (consisting of all tribal members age eighteen and older) elects the board and makes decisions about life on the reservation. Four officers lead the general council: a chair, vice chair, secretary, and interpreter.

ECONOMY

The Umatilla depended on fishing before they acquired horses in the early 1700s. Their economy then expanded to include buffalo hunting. Every year, tribes from all over the Northwest and from as far away as the Great Plains came to the Columbia River to trade for dried fish.

The early days on the reservation were difficult. The people were not allowed to leave without a permit, so they could not gather their traditional foods. They came to depend on government handouts and grew so dispirited that observers predicted the culture would perish. After allotment went into effect (see "History"), most Umatilla found they could not afford to farm their land, so they leased or sold it to U.S. farmers. Some people continued to fish in the old way, but their fishing spots flooded and became unusable once dams were built on the Columbia River in the early and mid-1900s.

After suffering through years of struggle and limited opportunities, the Umatilla people are experiencing a turnaround. The tribal economy that once depended heavily on farming and forestry has expanded, and today, the Confederated Tribes are a major economic force in northeastern Oregon. The tribal government and tribally owned businesses employ more than eleven thousand people. In addition to leasing land, the people also have acreage for agriculture, livestock, and forestry. Fisheries are restoring the salmon to area rivers. Mining, construction, real estate development, service-retail operations, and an industrial park all generate income. The Wánapa Energy Center, Wildhorse Resort and Casino, and Tamástslikt Cultural Institute provide revenue for the Wildhorse Foundation (a charitable organization) and for tribal programs.

DAILY LIFE

Families

In traditional times, extended Umatilla families—parents, children, grandparents, and other close relatives—all lived together in small groups called bands. Families were large, and everyone had an assigned job. If anyone failed to do a job, the family might starve or freeze when winter came. Grandmothers stayed in the camp and watched the children while their mothers were digging roots.

Education

Children began their training in adult skills at age ten. Boys watched as older men hunted and fished but did not participate until they were teens because an untrained person was an insult to the prey. Girls helped with household chores. From ages twelve to sixteen, they lived together in a separate house where they were closely guarded and kept away from boys. There, older women taught them to cook and to make baskets and clothing. They also learned about personal hygiene.

Christian missionaries began their work in Oregon as early as 1836, introducing their concept of formal education. In addition to gaining converts, the missionaries hoped to guide the Umatilla into becoming like mainstream American society. They believed the best way to do that was to educate the Umatilla children. The Presbyterian missionary Dr. Marcus Whitman (1802–1847) and others taught American domestic skills to the youth. As the Umatilla saw it, Whitman was turning their children into servants for whites. This was one of the misunderstandings that led to the Whitman Massacre (see "History").

Roman Catholic missionaries set up a school on the reservation in the 1870s, and the Presbyterians opened their school in 1871. Some children were educated at those schools, whereas others were sent to a government-run boarding school in Forest Grove, Oregon. This style of education weakened traditional Native culture and language.

In modern times, young children attend Head Start classes on the reservation; then most of them attend public schools in Pendleton. Along with casino proceeds, money won in land claims helps to fund scholarships, language and tutoring programs, and adult education.

Buildings

The Umatilla favored winter homes called longhouses, which they built along the Columbia River. The homes, sometimes as long as 80 feet (24 meters), were made of dried mats arranged over a pole frame. Winter lodges could house many families, and a village might contain five or six of them.

The Umatilla devised portable mat tepees to take along on buffalo hunting or gathering trips. They did not use buffalo skins for tepees because their supply of buffalo skins was not as large as that of the Plains tribes. Today, they use tepees covered with canvas for celebrations and for camping in the mountains.

Food

The Umatilla ate fish—salmon, steelhead trout, eel, and sturgeon—as their primary food source. The tribes of the region gathered along the Columbia River in spring and fall for salmon runs. In late summer, men hunted wild game such as deer, elk, mountain sheep, bear, antelope, wolf, fox, and cougar. Later, the Umatilla also hunted buffalo on the Great Plains.

While the men hunted and fished, women gathered camas roots, onions, potatoes, carrots, acorns, and a variety of nuts and berries. One root, called biscuitroot, was mashed and shaped into small cakes that they dried in the sun and stored for later use. Black moss from pine and fir trees was baked to form a cheese-like food.

In modern times, because of dams on the Columbia River, salmon is no longer as plentiful, but it is still caught. The people on the reservation continue to rely on salmon and other traditional foods such as roots, berries, deer, and elk.

Clothing and adornment

Umatilla dressed in robes, vests, and aprons, all made from skins and furs. Women wore basket-shaped hats woven from dried leaves. After they began to hunt buffalo, their clothing styles changed to resemble the buckskin shirts, leggings, and dresses of the Plains Indians. They tied their side-stitched, beaded moccasins around their ankles with thongs.

After cloth became more widely available, women made "wing" dresses. These T-shaped dresses had wide, full sleeves that looked like wings. They decorated them with dentalia (shells), elk teeth, and beads. Men had pictures of their war exploits painted on their elkskin

Umatilla chief Raymond Burke wears a traditional feather bonnet. © JOSE AZEL/ AURORA PHOTOS.

robes. They often decorated their shirts with tallies of war and painted symbols on their faces.

Healing practices

The Umatilla used herbal remedies to treat a variety of illnesses. Conditions caused by evil spirits required a medicine man, or shaman (pronounced *SHAH-mun* or *SHAY-mun*). The shaman either expelled the evil spirits or filled the afflicted person with a powerful spirit to drive out the sickness. Most healing rituals involved singing, chanting, and drumming and could get very loud. Shamans used rattles, smoke, and face-painting as part of the healing ritual. The shaman's job was a dangerous one because those who failed to cure their patients were often killed.

ARTS

Oral literature

Tribal elders say their oral tradition dates back ten thousand years. Men and women were encouraged to display their oral skills by reciting tribal myths and tales, especially during the winter when cold weather kept everyone inside at night. A favorite character in their stories was Coyote, who sometimes played a fool and sometimes a wise man. An often-told tale describes how Coyote made the world safe for the first people by ridding the world of dangerous monsters.

Decorative arts

Women were known for their beadwork; they still decorate bags, baskets, and children's dancing costumes with beautiful geometric designs. Men painted their robes and war shields with pictures of their brave deeds. Basket twining, beadwork, and regalia (fancy clothing or other symbols of high rank) sewing are some of the local arts that were revived at Crow's Shadow Institute on the Umatilla Indian Reservation. The institute brings artists, teachers, and arts professionals from around the world to the reservation to help local artists develop careers in the arts.

The work of artists affiliated with Crow's Shadow Institute and of other local craftspeople is shown at the Tamástslikt Cultural Institute, which opened in 1998. The institute has displays that tell the story of the Cayuse, Umatilla, and Walla Walla tribes. Special exhibits feature the work of established artists as well as children.

CUSTOMS

Rites of passage

When a boy felt he was ready to be a man, he went through a period of training to test his strength, courage, and endurance. He was sent to a spot far from the village, which was marked by a special stone. This spot was located close to tribal enemies, and the boy was required to spend a day and a night there without being detected.

The Umatilla had no ceremony to mark a girl's first menstruation, but she remained in a separate hut for the duration of her period. She then bathed, put on fresh clothes, and resumed her daily chores.

Courtship and marriage

Because girls were so closely watched, boys had to seize opportunities to catch them alone. A boy might court a girl by singing to her from the shadows or waylaying her on the way to a water source. At about age sixteen, boys and girls were ready for marriage. The boy's parents sent a relative to speak to the parents of the girl he chose.

If the girl's parents agreed to the marriage, the boy's parents presented the family with horses. Much feasting and gift exchanging followed. Givers competed to offer the best presents. Afterward the couple was considered married. The newlyweds usually moved in with the groom's parents for a while before establishing their own home.

Divorce happened frequently in the early years of marriage. Children went to live with the parent of the same sex. Husbands could kill unfaithful wives. Wealthy men could have more than one wife; usually they chose their wives' sisters.

Babies

Pregnant women hoped to keep their babies small by swimming frequently. They avoided unpleasantness that might upset them and affect the child. Mothers stayed secluded for ten days after the birth; the new parents then sweated and bathed. The woman destroyed any clothing or dishes she had used during her pregnancy.

Newborns were bound tightly to cradleboards. Girls had their foreheads compressed so that their heads would grow flat. This was considered an attractive feature, but the custom was given up soon after the settlers came.

Childhood

Children had many toys, including stilts, buzzers, bull roarers, popguns, and tops. They played cat's cradle with string, making shapes of animals, such as the porcupine or elk. Tug-of-war and hide-and-seek were popular. Most children also practiced adult skills. Girls played with dolls, rode on stick horses, and practiced setting up tepees and moving camp.

Elders lectured youngsters and told stories to teach them proper behavior. Disobedient children would be threatened with the "whipper," a man whose job was to discipline village youngsters. If boys fought, they had to lie on a blanket on the ground. The whipper gave them a spanking with a willow whip and then lectured them. Afterward, the whipper took the blanket as payment. A child who got into trouble frequently might be sent out alone to seek a guardian spirit. Children who were too young to have a guardian spirit were rarely punished.

War rituals

Entire tribes seldom fought together as a unit. Instead, they recruited warriors from other tribes who lived nearby. This is how the Umatilla came to participate in the Cayuse War. Horse-stealing raids were a form of warfare, a manly pursuit, and a way to demonstrate bravery. Raiding parties usually consisted of five or six people.

War parties attacked in the early morning and took women and children as slaves. Sometimes, slain enemy warriors were scalped, or their hearts were eaten (to ingest the strength of the fallen warrior). Upon returning to the village, successful warriors held a scalp dance and then purified themselves in a sweat bath. Warriors from other tribes who were taken captive had their fingers, hands, or limbs cut off.

Burial

A shaman supervised the washing and dressing of the corpse and then fumigated the house and family with rosebushes. The family held a wake during the night. Friends and relatives visited, but children, especially those who did not have a guardian spirit, were kept away. The next day the community took the corpse to the cemetery.

The Umatilla wrapped the dead in animal skins and tule mats and buried the body in a shallow grave in rocky ledges. They laid the body on its back heading west and surrounded it with farewell gifts and personal possessions. Graves were enclosed by cedar poles and stones. Often, the Umatilla killed horses and left the corpses near the grave. Mourners stopped eating for a while and cut off their hair to show their grief. Those who had touched the body purified themselves in the sweat lodge.

Early observers claimed that death by suicide was quite common and often came about after a person's feelings had been hurt. Sometimes, grieving relatives decided to be buried alive with their loved ones. A memorial feast was held five days after the burial. The dead person was praised, then his or her name was never mentioned again so the soul could rest.

Festivals and ceremonies

Ceremonies were held before raiders or war parties set off and later to welcome them home. The most important ceremonies, however, concerned food, which was considered a sacred substance. In a custom known as "first food observances," the people thanked the first salmon of the season and the first roots before they ate them.

Drumming and singing have always been an important part of the culture, and every important occasion featured performances that took years to learn. The Umatilla beat two types of drums: the big drum and the smaller hand drum. The music they make is not only intended for entertainment; most songs have religious significance. Some songs are prayers; they may honor certain foods, the seasons, or birth and death. Drumming and singing are important parts of dances and celebrations throughout the year.

In the early twenty-first century, many tribal festivities took place on the reservation's July Grounds. In the late 1800s, the federal government tried to discourage traditional celebrations. The Confederated Tribes gathered at the July Grounds and pretended to celebrate Independence Day (July 4). Instead, they were actually celebrating their own heritage through horse and foot races, spear throwing, dancing, singing, and drumming.

CURRENT TRIBAL ISSUES

Reburial of ancient remains

Two major tribal issues concern the reburial of the remains of the individual known as Kennewick Man and the struggle for salmon recovery in the Columbia River.

The 1995 discovery of a 9,300-year-old skeleton near Kennewick, Washington, ignited a controversy that still continued into the 2000s. Kennewick Man is the oldest skeleton ever found in the Pacific Northwest. Scientists wanted to study it, but the tribe contended that their religious and cultural beliefs required the immediate reburial of the remains of what is likely one of their ancestors.

In 2005, the U.S. Army Corps of Engineers, which controls the land on which Kennewick Man was discovered, decided to turn the bones over to the tribes. Scientists sued; they wanted time to examine the bones. They won their case, and by 2007, a team of experts was studying the skeleton. One startling discovery they made is that the bones more closely resemble those of a Japanese Ainu (an ethnic group indigenous to Japan). Some researchers speculate that the body may be from the Pacific Rim.

Environmental concerns

Technology has had a devastating impact on the Umatilla Reservation. The U.S. Department of Energy's Hanford Nuclear Reservation, the U.S. Department of Defense's Umatilla Army Depot, nearby coal-fired plants, and hydroelectric projects and dams on the rivers have disturbed the environmental balance of the area and destroyed parts of the ecosystem, in addition to causing health concerns. At one time, the people gathered about sixty-four roots and plants for food and medicine. Only six of those still remain. The animals and fish that once were abundant in Umatilla territory have, in some cases, almost disappeared. The beaver had to be reintroduced, and the Umatilla have been working with other groups to recover the dwindling salmon population.

In 1998, the Confederated Tribes of the Umatilla Indian Reservation announced a campaign to restore natural salmon runs in the Columbia River Basin. The campaign is called *Waykaanashmiyay Nishaycht* ("Home for the Salmon"). The tribe and its supporters claim that dams on Columbia and Snake River tributaries have destroyed the wild salmon runs on the rivers. By 2011, the Umatilla's efforts had paid off: enough spring and coho salmon had returned to support a tribal and a sports fishery. Now the Umatilla want to see the salmon restored throughout the Northwest. The Campaign Mission Statement declares: "We believe that a Pacific Northwest without salmon is unacceptable. For our children, we must again make the Columbia River and all of its tributaries Home for the Salmon."

BOOKS

Burke, Heather, et al, eds. *Kennewick Man: Perspectives on the Ancient One.* Walnut Creek, CA: Left Coast Press, 2008.

Chatters, James C. *Ancient Encounters: Kennewick Man and the First Americans.* New York: Simon and Schuster, 2001.

Curtis, Edward S. "Umatilla." In *The North American Indian,* edited by Fredrick Webb Hodge. Vol. 8. 1911. Available online from http://curtis.library.northwestern.edu/curtis/viewPage.cgi?showp=1&size=2&id=nai.08.book.00000129.p&volume=8#nav (accessed on August 11, 2011).

Fisher, Andrew H. *Shadow Tribe: The Making of Columbia River Indian Identity.* Seattle: University of Washington Press, 2010.

Karson, Jennifer, ed. *Wiyaxayxt/ Wiyaakaa'awn: As Days Go By: Our History, Our Land, Our People—the Cayuse, Umatilla, and Walla Walla.* Portland: University of Washington Press, 2006.

Kirkpatrick, Katherine. *Mysterious Bones: The Story of Kennewick Man.* New York: Holiday House, 2011.

McKenzie, Michael. "Washat Religion (Drummer-Dreamer Faith)." In *The Encyclopedia of Religion and Nature.* London: Thoemmes Continuum, 2005: 1713–14.

Rubalcaba, Jill, and Peter Robertshaw. *Every Bone Tells a Story: Hominin Discoveries, Deductions, and Debates.* Watertown, MA: Charlesbridge Publishing, 2010.

PERIODICALS

Et-twaii-lish, Marjorie Waheneka. "Indian Perspectives on Food and Culture." *Oregon Historical Quarterly,* Fall 2005.

"Q: Should Scientists Be Allowed to 'Study' the Skeletons of Ancient American Indians?" (Symposium: U.S. Representative Doc Hastings; Confederated Tribes of the Umatilla Indian Reservation Spokesman Donald Sampson). *Insight on the News* 13, no. 47 (December 22, 1997): 24.

WEB SITES

"Ancient One: Kennewick Man." *Confederated Tribes of the Umatilla Reservation.* http://www.umatilla.nsn.us/ancient.html (accessed on August 11, 2011).

Columbia River Inter-Tribal Fish Commission. http://www.critfc.org/ (accessed on July 27, 2007).

Confederated Tribes of the Umatilla Indian Reservation. http://www.umatilla.nsn.us/ (accessed on August 11, 2011).

"Confederated Tribes of the Umatilla Indians." *Wisdom of the Elders.* http://www.wisdomoftheelders.org/program305.html (accessed on August 11, 2011).

Crow's Shadow Institute of the Arts. http://www.crowsshadow.org/ (accessed on August 11, 2011).

McManamon, F. P. "Kennewick Man." *Archaeology Program, National Park Service, U.S. Department of the Interior.* http://www.nps.gov/archeology/kennewick/index.htm (accessed on August 11, 2011).

Peterson, Keith C. "Dams of the Columbia Basin and Their Effect on the Native Fishery." *Center for Columbia River History.* http://www.ccrh.org/comm/river/dams7.htm (accessed on August 11, 2011).

"Picturing the Cayuse, Walla Walla, and Umatilla Tribes." *University of Oregon Libraries.* http://oregondigital.org/digcol/mh/ (accessed on August 11, 2011).

Redish, Laura, and Orrin Lewis. "Umatilla-Tenino (Warm Springs, Celilo)." *Native Languages of the Americas.* http://www.native-languages.org/umatilla.htm (accessed on August 11, 2011).

Swan, Daniel C. "Native American Church." *Oklahoma Historical Society.* http://digital.library.okstate.edu/encyclopedia/entries/N/NA015.html (accessed on August 11, 2011).

"Umatilla." *Columbia River Inter-Tribal Fish Commission (CRITFC).* http://www.critfc.org/text/tribes.html (accessed on August 11, 2011).

"Umatilla Indian Agency and Reservation, Oregon." *Access Genealogy.* http://www.accessgenealogy.com/native/census/condition/umatilla_indian_agency_reservation_oregon.htm (accessed on August 11, 2011).

"Umatilla, Walla Walla, and Cayuse." *TrailTribes.org: Traditional and Contemporary Native Culture.* http://www.trailtribes.org/umatilla/home.htm (accessed on August 11, 2011).

Wolf, Ashleigh W. "The Confederated Tribes of the Umatilla Indian Reservation: Culture, Renewable Energy, and the Hanford Nuclear Reservation." *International Institute for Indigenous Resource Management.* http://www.iiirm.org/publications/Articles%20Reports%20Papers/energy/DOSE-IIIRM_Final%20Draft_071107.pdf (accessed on August 11, 2011).

Yakama

Name

Yakama (pronounced *YAYK-uh-muh* or *YAYK-uh-maw*). Some sources say the tribe's name originated from *E-yak-ma,* meaning "a growing family," or from the Sahaptin word *iyakima,* which translates to "pregnant ones." Others say the name may have come from *yákama* ("black bear") or *Ya-ki-ná* ("runaway"). The Yakama were also called *Waptailnsim,* meaning "people of the narrow river," or *Pa'kiut'lĕma,* which means "people of the gap." Both of these names refer to the narrows in the Yakima River at Union Gap, the site of the Yakama's main village at one time. The Yakama called themselves *Mamachatpam.* In 1994, the tribe changed its name from Yakima to Yakama to reflect the native pronunciation. The official name of the tribe is Confederated Tribes and Bands of the Yakama Nation.

Location

Originally, the Yakama occupied the area on both sides of the Columbia River and on the northern branches of the Yakima (formerly Tapteal) and Wenatchee Rivers in the state of Washington. In the early twenty-first century, their 1,377,034-acre reservation is located on the western part of the Columbia Plateau in south-central Washington, along the eastern slopes of the Cascade Mountain Range.

Population

Some sources believe that prior to 1805, approximately 7,000 Yakama lived in the area around the Columbia River. That number dropped to 3,500 in 1805. In 1806, the explorers Meriwether Lewis (1774–1809) and William Clark (1770–1838) estimated the Yakama population to be 1,200. The number of people living on the Yakama Reservation in 1909 was 1,900, but that included all the various tribes, not just the Yakama. According to a 1990 estimate, about 8,000 Yakama lived in the United States. In 2000, the U.S. Bureau of the Census noted that the Yakama population was 8,337; of those, 5,125 lived on the reservation. The 2010 census counted 8,786 Yakama, with a total of 11,527 people claiming some Yakama ancestry.

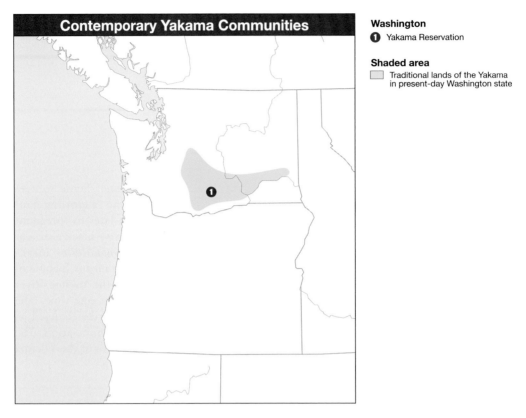

Contemporary Yakama Communities

Washington
❶ Yakama Reservation

Shaded area
Traditional lands of the Yakama in present-day Washington state

❶

A map of contemporary Yakama communities. MAP BY XNR PRODUCTIONS. CENGAGE LEARNING, GALE. REPRODUCED BY PERMISSION OF GALE, A PART OF CENGAGE LEARNING.

Language family
Penutian.

Origins and group affiliations
The Confederated Tribes and Bands of the Yakama Nation, or simply the Yakama Nation (formerly Yakima), was a consolidation of fourteen bands, or tribes: Kah-milt-pah, Klickitat, Klinquit, Kow-was-say-ee, Li-ay-was, Oche-chotes, Palouse (Palus), Pisquose, Se-ap-cat, Shyiks, Skin-pah, Wenat-shapam, Wish-ham, and Yakama. During their wars with the United States in the 1800s, the Yakama allied with the Nez Percé, Umatilla, Walla Walla, Pala, Cayuse, Spokane, and Coeur d'Alene.

The isolation of the Columbia Plateau enabled the Yakama to live undisturbed by outsiders for almost twelve thousand years. As the climate and environment changed over time, the people adapted but maintained most of their traditions, some of which they still practice today. The arrival of horses in the 1730s and of the Northern Pacific Railroad in 1883 greatly changed the lives of the people. When the government took over Yakama territory in the mid-1800s, they consolidated the fourteen bands and relocated them to a reservation. At the start of the twenty-first century, their reservation along the Yakima River covers approximately 1.4 million acres, only a small portion of the area the tribe once roamed.

HISTORY

Prehistory

According to Yakama oral history, they dwelt in the area of the Columbia Plateau for centuries. Archaeologists found evidence dating back twelve thousand years, which supports the Yakama account of their ancestors. Cave dwellings, rock shelters, and camps from thousands of years ago are scattered throughout the area. Artifacts such as ancient tools and stone carvings have also been discovered.

Important Dates

1730: The introduction of the horse changes the Yakama lifestyle.

1805: Lewis and Clark expedition arrives in Yakama territory.

1811: First trading post is established.

1855: The Yakama sign a treaty with the U.S. government.

1855–58: The tribe and its allies fight the U.S. Army in the Yakima Wars.

1883: The Northern Pacific Railroad is built through Yakama land.

1972: The U.S. government returns 21,000 acres to the Yakama Nation.

1990s: The Yakama spend almost $54 million to repurchase reservation land.

Early tribal life

The Yakama lived in sixty or seventy villages of about fifty to two hundred people. The bands lived in their own areas of the Yakima River Valley during the winter, but the rest of the year, they met and shared hunting grounds and fishing areas. In addition to gathering food, they bartered goods, held horse races, played sports, and spent time visiting.

During the 1700s, a Yakama leader named We-ow-wicht united a large part of the territory. When he died, the land was divided between his eight sons. Around this time, the tribe acquired horses, enabling them to increase its food supplies and barter for new goods. The need for horse pastures led the Yakama to explore the area east of the Cascade Mountains, which spread their language and led to intermarriage with other tribes.

Contact with outsiders

Long before any settlers arrived, the Yakama who traded with the Plains Indians brought Euro-American illnesses back to the tribe. In the late

1700s, many Yakama died from smallpox. Later, outbreaks of disease killed more people; the tribe's population dropped from an estimated 7,000 to 3,500.

The first non-Native Americans to enter the tribe's territory were members of the Lewis and Clark expedition, who arrived in 1805. Fur trappers and traders soon followed. In 1811, the Pacific Fur Company opened the first trading post on the Columbia River. After the Hudson's Bay Company established Fort Vancouver in 1825, the Yakama traded there. When Chief Kamiakin (died 1877) traded horses for cattle, the people began raising livestock.

As more U.S. settlers entered their lands, the Yakama unified their villages into two territories under the leadership of We-ow-wicht's descendants. Wenas Creek served as the dividing line. The Lower Yakama lived south of the creek; Chief Kamiakin and his brothers, Skloom and Showaway, led them. Their uncles, Teias and Owhi, became headmen of the Upper Yakama, or Kittitas, who settled north of the creek.

Fort Walla Walla is where a tribal council met with Governor Stevens and signed a treaty giving up more than 10 million acres.
© BETTMANN/CORBIS.

Treaty at Walla Walla

Isaac Ingalls Stevens (1818–1862), governor of the Washington Territory, called a council at Fort Walla Walla in 1855. Along with the Yakama, the Umatilla, Nez Percé (see entries), Cayuse, Walla Walla, and other bands attended. The tribes signed a treaty giving up more than 10 million acres, but they kept their hunting, fishing, and gathering rights. They agreed to move to Simcoe Reservation, an area of 1.2 million acres.

The treaty consolidated the fourteen different Yakama bands and tribes into one nation. Treaty terms ensured that no settlers would live on reservation lands. The U.S. government also agreed to supply two schools, a hospital, a sawmill, a flourmill, and craftspeople to teach the Yakama trades. The Yakama would receive two cents for every acre they turned over to the government. They were also to get yearly payments for twenty years and money to help them relocate and build homes on the reservation.

Yakima Wars

Although the treaty guaranteed the tribes two years to relocate, Governor Stevens opened the land to settlers two weeks later. Chief Kamiakin organized several tribes to oppose this violation. They fought U.S. soldiers for almost three years in the Yakima Wars (1855–58). Other tribes in the territory rose up as well. In September 1858, the U.S. Army defeated the Native warriors at the Battle of Four Lakes near Spokane. Chief Kamiakin escaped to Canada, but two dozen other leaders were executed.

The Yakama then moved to the reservation. When Kamiakin refused to return, a Klikitat named Spencer was appointed chief. In 1867, the people elected White Swan (Joe Stwire) as head chief. He served until he died in 1910.

Pressure from whites

The federal agents who ran the reservation tried to make the Yakama more like mainstream Americans. They established a boarding school at Fort Simcoe to educate the Yakama children. Students were forced to speak English, dress in American clothes, and learn non-Native ways.

In the late 1800s, a new government policy called allotment divided the reservation into eighty-acre plots for each person. The Yakama who had always relied on fishing, hunting, and gathering now had to grow crops instead. Reverend James H. Wilbur (1811–1887), an Indian agent,

Crowds gather to celebrate the completion of the Northern Pacific Railroad. To the Yakama, however, the coming of the railroad meant the loss of their fishing, hunting, and gathering grounds. © MPI/GETTY IMAGES.

fought for the tribe's rights in Washington, D.C., but he enforced strict rules on the reservation. The Yakama who complied with government policy and those who converted to Christianity received clothing, food, and farm supplies. Wilbur also rewarded Natives who cut their hair because he felt they were less likely to follow traditional Native practices.

With the opening of the Northern Pacific Railroad, which ran through Yakama fields and orchards and brought homesteaders to the area, the tribe gradually lost their fishing, hunting, and gathering areas. Some Yakama still struggled to maintain their old ways, but settlers' livestock fed on roots and berries, and their plowing ruined plant and animal habitats. Irrigation projects and dams destroyed salmon runs.

By the 1900s, much of the best farmland had been purchased from the Yakama. Towns were established on former Native American allotments. Landowners blocked the tribe's access to the Columbia Plateau and the rivers, claiming they were trespassing. Even county and state officials opposed Native fishing privileges. Time and again the Yakama went to court to establish their treaty rights.

Legal battles

Beginning in 1900, when the tribe won a court case that redrew the reservation boundary to add 357,879 acres that rightfully belonged to them, the Yakima fought many successful cases. Over the years, they reasserted their rights to hunt and fish according the terms of the 1855 treaty.

In the 1950s, the Yakama received more than $15 million for the Celilo Falls fishery, which flooded when the Dalles Dam was built. That dam was one of nineteen that the government constructed on the Columbia and Snake Rivers. All of the dams caused the death of many young salmon. From 14 million salmon yearly, the runs dropped to 2.5 million in 1980. The Yakima Nation and several other Plateau tribes formed the Columbia River Intertribal Fish Commission and convinced Congress to write new legislation to protect fish and wildlife. They also lobbied for funds to start fish hatcheries and to build fish ladders and screens, so salmon fingerlings do not remain trapped in irrigation ditches.

Two court cases, one in 1969 and one in 1974, reaffirmed Yakama fishing rights and gave the tribe a 50percent share of the fish in tribal fishing grounds. The Boldt decision of 1974 also led to the federal government and the tribe cooperating in the management of the Columbia River waterways. In the early 2000s, the Yakama prevented nuclear waste disposal from the Hanford Nuclear Plant on tribal land.

Aerial view of the Hanford Nuclear Plant. The Yakama have worked to help protect the environment from nuclear waste generated by the plant.
© ROGER RESSMEYER/CORBIS.

RELIGION

Guardian spirits

The Yakama went on vision quests as children to get a guardian spirit. Children went alone to a remote spot and stayed overnight or for several days until they had a vision. Those who received a spirit never talked about it but would later experience "spirit sickness," whereupon a twáti (medicine doctor; see "Healing practices") would explain how to use the power.

Yakama who had guardian spirits participated in winter spirit dances, or *wáanpsha* ("medicine sings"). These were sponsored by the family of a person who had been cured. Wáanpsha lasted five days, and those with guardian spirits sang and danced, accompanied by drummers who pounded on planks with sticks or canes.

Longhouse religion

The traditional Yakama religion has several different names: Wáashat, Longhouse or Seven Drum religion, and Native American worship. The term *Wáashat* comes from the Sahaptin word for "dance." Derived from ideas of early Native prophets, it focuses on ancient rituals such as the First Foods Feast (see "Festivals").

Services were held in a longhouse, where participants were separated by gender. Males stood along the northern wall; females stood along the southern one. Everyone dressed up and painted their faces red and yellow. Drummers, led by a bell ringer, sat or stood on the west side.

Participants sang and danced in sets of seven (a sacred number) on a hard-packed earthen floor. At the end of each song, everyone turned in place to get rid of their troubles. Between song series, elders spoke to the youngsters to remind them of their grandparents' teachings. Children sometimes performed using rapid, hopping steps.

Water was important to the ceremony. Before the ritual feast, a bell rang, and everyone sang a prayer. The second time it rang, they all said *chiish* ("water") and then sipped from their cups. They repeated this at the end of the meal.

Although the Native American Church and many of its practices were forbidden over the years, some Yakama remained faithful to thoserituals, and the religion thrived in spite of suppression and persecution. The Native American Church gained a stronghold among the Yakama tribe; even those who practice other faiths on the reservation adhere to its emphasis on respect for the environment. Many traditional beliefs are incorporated into the religion, which is sometimes called Seven Drum or Longhouse religion.

Outside influences

In 1847, Pascal Richard and Eugene Casimir Chirouse established the first Christian mission, but they abandoned it later that year during the

Cayuse War (1847–55; a conflict between the Cayuse tribe and the U.S. government). Other denominations set up missions over the next few years. In the early twenty-first century, many Catholic and Protestant churches offer services on the reservation.

The Indian Shaker Church is also a strong influence in Yakama religious life. Founded by John Slocum in 1881, this combination of Christian and Native American beliefs was introduced to the tribe in 1890. Participants use bellringing, foot stomping, shaking, and Native prayers to communicate with God and to heal illness.

Yakama prophets

During the 1850s, the Wanapum prophet Smohalla (c. 1815–1895) called for a return to Native ways. He told his followers to avoid white ideas and goods, never cut their braids, eat traditional foods, and go on vision quests. He also urged people not to move to reservations or become farmers. Although he preached nonviolence and peaceful coexistence, his teachings were influential in organizing the confederacy of tribes that fought the Yakima Wars.

Jake Hunt, a Klikitat, started Waptashi, or the Feather religion, in about 1904. Whereas traditional religions revered God and Mother Earth, the Waptashi believed the Eagle to be the supreme being. Messages came from the Eagle through Jake Hunt. Although he had been raised in the Washani ways, Hunt cut his hair and wore typical American clothing.

Modern religious beliefs

In modern times, the Yakama worship in various ways. Three longhouses on the reservation serve as traditional places of worship. Some tribe members participate in the Washani or Feather religions. Others attend Christian churches or the Indian Shaker Church. Many Yakama, however, see no conflict in combining both native and Christian practices.

LANGUAGE

Most Yakama on the reservation speak Ten-tumpt, a northwestern Sahaptin dialect (variety) of the Plateau Penutian family. Yakama and Klickitat speakers have trouble understanding Umatilla or Walla Walla speakers, but the languages are similar enough that speakers can communicate with each other.

Yakama Words

á'a	"crow"
átmupil	"car"
áay	"hello"
mishcosk	"red"
kúpi	"coffee"
likúk	"chicken"
lkw'í	"day"
k'usík'usi	"dog"
iníit	"house"
p'úus	"cat"
tíin	"person"
tkwátat	"food"
wásiis	"canoe"
xítway	"friend"

Only a few dozen Yakama elders use their language exclusively, but many people can speak it. Some Yakama elders believe that their language should not be written anywhere until the afterlife.

In spite of this opposition, the reservation holds language classes for middle school students that incorporate both speaking and sign language. These classes, which meet two days a week, are intended to keep the Yakama language and culture alive. Signing (using hand signals to communicate) is an important part of the Yakama language, and sign language is used in certain ceremonies where talking is forbidden. Because of this, the students also learn to use signs.

GOVERNMENT

The small independent village was the main political unit among the early Yakama. The headman of each group had to be wise and generous, have good morals, and be a good speaker. Rarely, a chief led a larger band or several groups, usually during war. He often inherited his position, but the people also had to respect him.

Several men served on a council to settle disputes and oversee activities. Elderly women also had a say in tribal decisions. Men and women earned leadership positions through their skills in special activities such as digging, hunting, or leading ceremonies. To keep people informed, the headman's assistant walked through the village every evening announcing news and repeating speeches.

In 1933, the people set up a tribal government. When Congress passed the Indian Reorganization Act in 1934, the Yakama refused to comply with the U.S. guidelines for creating a government and a constitution, because they already had a government. In 1946, the tribe set new rules for the tribal government. They also made all tribal members over eighteen years of age automatic voting members of the tribe.

The Yakama Nation Tribal Council consists of one representative from each of the fourteen tribes and bands, a chairperson, a vice chairperson, and a secretary. Originally, the tribe elected council members by a show of hands, and representatives served for life. In the early 2000s, the tribe elected half of the tribal council members every two years for four-year terms.

ECONOMY

Traditional economy

Early Yakima economy depended on trapping, fishing, hunting, and gath.ering. Later, the tribe traded fish products, baskets, mats, furs, jewelry, artwork, dogs, and horses with other tribes. Other trade goods included food, canoes, feathers, mountain goat wool, and even slaves. Most tribes used dentalia, shells harvested on Vancouver Island, in place of money. Later, horses replaced dentalia as currency. The acquisition of horses allowed the tribe to travel greater distances, giving them access to more food supplies, which improved their economy.

When the tribe ceded their land to the U.S. government in 1855, they kept their rights to hunt and fish on the land as well as to graze livestock, gather traditional foods and medicinal herbs, and have sufficient water.

Modern economy

Many Yakama still engage in ceremonial, subsistence, and commercial fishing for salmon, steelhead, and sturgeon. The tribe supervises the Columbia and eight other rivers in conjunction with the state of Washington. Another project, cosponsored by the U.S. Department of Energy, established radiation-free settling ponds at the Hanford Nuclear Reservation for young Chinook salmon to be released into the Columbia River.

The tribe manages 600,000 acres of timber and 15,000 acres of cultivated land. In addition, it irrigates 90,000 acres from the Wapato Project and leases farming and grazing acreage. On tribal land, it raises alfalfa hay, wheat, hops, sugar beets, grapes, asparagus, spearmint, and sweet corn. Orchards produce apples, including the tribe's own Yakama apple, which it packages in its warehouse. Grazing land supports livestock and a buffalo herd.

Yakama Industries and Yakama Forest Products employ many people. Other tribal businesses include a restaurant, sawmill, furniture factory, manufacturing plant, and real estate development office. Many tourists visit the Yakama Nation Cultural Center, Legends Casino,

Mount Adams Recreation Area, and the recreational vehicle park. The tribe is also known for its professional basketball team, the Yakama Sun Kings of the Continental Basketball Association.

DAILY LIFE

Families

Most villages consisted of extended families. They contained five to fifteen lodges; each house usually had three generations living together. Families took the name of the villages where they lived; a tradition that continues today.

Buildings

The earliest Yakama houses were small underground pits with domed roofs. They were about 3 or 4 feet (1 meter) deep and 12 to 18 feet (4 or 5 meters) around. The Yakama laid poles over the hole to hold up mats. An opening in the roof allowed smoke to escape and light to enter. It also served as a door. To exit, people climbed a notched log.

In later years, the Yakama lashed up to ten pairs of cottonwood poles together at the top to make their winter lodges. Workers held these 12- to 15-foot (4- to 5-meter) poles upright while others used thatch made of willows to connect them. They draped several layers of rush matting over the structure, leaving an opening for a door, and often banked dirt against the lower part of the house to keep it warmer. Up to ten families shared these 40- to 60-foot (12- to 18-meter) homes; each one had its own central fire. At the back of the lodge, they hung fish on racks to dry. Mats served as floor coverings, bedding, partitions, and doors; smaller ones were used for plates and platters.

In the summer, the Yakama used tepees covered with tule mats. After the arrival of horses, the tribe hunted buffalo, so later tepees were often covered with hide. For beds, they spread mats over a layer of dried grasses and used blankets of jack rabbit fur.

Clothing and adornment

In the early days, men wore only a breechcloth (a piece of fabric attached at the waist that covered the front and back) and moccasins. Moccasins were one piece of deerskin sewed in the front from toe to ankle and held around the ankles by thongs or cords.

Women had two different styles of dress, depending on where they lived. Women who lived near the Snake River wore long leather skirts decorated with beads and shells, whereas those near the Columbia River tied a piece of leather around their waists and used cord to draw and tighten it between and against their legs almost like pants. They painted their shoes and faces red.

Before the Yakama acquired horses in the 1700s, most of their clothing was made of sagebrush, willow bark, and cedar. After they began riding and had more contact with the Plains Indians, their clothing changed. They used buckskin, and men wore leggings and shirts with their breechcloths. Women sewed buckskins together at the shoulders and laced them or sewed them along the sides. Porcupine quills, elk teeth, and fringe adorned the people's clothing.

The men also adopted feathered war bonnets. For dances, they wore roaches (tufts of animal hair, often dyed bright colors) on their heads, hair and bone breastplates, and feather bustles. During ceremonies, women wore flat-topped, cone-shaped hats of mountain grass with dyed designs. In the twentieth century, they tied colorful scarves over their hair for everyday wear.

A Yakama woman wears traditional dress. © THE ART ARCHIVE/ BUFFALO BILL HISTORICAL CENTER, CODY, WYOMING/ THE PICTURE DESK, INC.

Food

The seasons determined the tribe's activities and locations. In March, when the first wild plants (*khásiya,* or "first celery") appeared, the Yakama camped with neighboring tribes in areas where they could gather roots and plants. In May or June, when salmon swam up the Columbia River, they moved to the riverbanks to catch and preserve fish. They prepared these by splitting them and spreading them in the sun to dry. They then wrapped them in rush mats. In the fall, the people traveled to the Cascade Mountains, where they hunted and picked berries. During the winter, they moved into their lodges along the streams and ate dried foods.

The river provided the mainstay of their diet. Men waited for their leader's permission before fishing for salmon, then seven men caught a few fish for a tribal feast. This religious practice ensured that some salmon escaped upstream to reproduce for other years. In addition to salmon, men caught steelhead trout, sturgeon, suckers, and eel. Fish was roasted or boiled with roots.

In the spring, women gathered more than twenty kinds of roots using a root digger (a curved, pointed stick with a bone handle). Camas, carrots, and bitterroot were the most common. Roots were eaten or dried; some were ground into flour to make bread.

In August, the Yakama picked berries. Huckleberry was a favorite, and they celebrated after gathering it (see "Festivals"). They dried whatever they did not eat by placing it on a smoldering log, then packed it into bags, and sewed it into cedar bark containers for winter. Men hunted for mountain sheep and goats, elk, bear, wolf, fox, and birds. Deer provided meat, clothing, tepee covers, and household items. The Yakama made antlers into tools, and sheep horns into spoons, ladles, and utensils. They carved mountain goat horns into bowls.

During the mid-1800s, the Yakama traded horses for cattle, and beef became an important part of their diet. They also bartered for seeds from the Hudson's Bay Company and planted gardens. They dug their gardens near the streams and irrigated the land, where they raised potatoes, melons, squash, barley, and corn.

Games

When the various tribes and bands gathered on the hunting or fishing grounds in warmer weather, they enjoyed competing in sports. Men held wrestling matches and foot races, and they played shinny, a sport similar to field hockey. Horseracing was also popular. A less active game was *paalyút*, the bone and stick game, which could last all night. This game consisted of a thin, pointed bone attached by a leather thong to a round, hollow bone. Players swung the hollow bone into the air and tried to catch it on the pointed bone. Women liked to play games as well; especially one in which they used dice made from beaver teeth.

Education

Learning of long ago While the parents worked, grandparents taught the children. Lessons included appreciation for the tribe's way of life, respect for others, and proper behavior. Children were respected and allowed to express their individuality.

To learn their adult roles, children imitated their parents. When a child performed an important feat (for example, if a boy killed his first animal or a girl gathered her first basket of berries), the parents invited the whole community to a feast. The family gave gifts to the guests and praise to the child.

Childhood was also a time to seek a guardian spirit (see "Religion"). A youngster went alone overnight or for several days and left a token to mark where he or she had been. The spirit gave the child special powers and instructions on taboos, dress, face painting, songs, and dance.

Modern schooling The Yakama have always encouraged academic achievement. Outstanding students receive scholarships, and the tribe sponsors Camp Chaparral to teach traditions and to encourage students to stay in school. The Yakama Nation Tribal School operates on the reservation and offers Sahaptin language classes. Adult education classes also teach the Yakama dialect. The Yakama Nation Cultural Center provides opportunities to learn traditional arts and crafts, history, language, and literature.

In 1981, the tribe opened Heritage College to offer higher education to multicultural students. In the early 2000s, it offers four-year programs in many disciplines as well as master's degrees through many satellite campuses. The school changed its name to Heritage University in 2004 to reflect its growth.

Healing practices

The Yakama believed supernatural powers caused some illnesses. These needed to be treated by a medicine person. The healer, or *twáti*, wore a coyote or wolf headdress, a bear claw necklace, and a rattle of deer dewclaws. The doctor sang, massaged the body, or sucked out the illness. Sometimes patients drank a special herbal tea. Women healers were especially gifted in using herbs to cure.

Doctors were asked to change the weather, foresee the future, and find lost objects. A powerful guardian spirit, T'amánws, gave them all these skills. Doctors also received power from the sweat lodge, which served as a place for healing.

The Yakama built sweat lodges alongside streams. These dome-shaped buildings had a fire inside for heating rocks. After users sealed the doorway, they piled the hot rocks into a shallow pit and poured water over them to create steam. They sang or chanted; afterward they jumped into the cold water of the nearby stream. They repeated this several times to clean their bodies but also to purify their minds and spirits from evil.

Both the Indian Shaker Church and Feather religion offered healing in the past and still do so in the present-day. Many Yakama rely on traditional forms of healing as well as modern medicine.

The Indian Health Service operates the Yakama Nation Tribal Health Facility. The tribe also owns the White Swan Health Clinic and a mother-child health center. Other offerings include community health and nutrition programs, WIC (Women, Infants and Children), and alcoholism programs.

ARTS

Crafts

The Yakama were known for their basketry, which they often traded with other tribes. They made baskets of many sizes; some were for carrying water or for cooking. These baskets were woven so tightly that water did not drip out. They had tapered bottoms so they could be wedged into the ground. To cook in them, women dropped hot stones into water until it boiled.

Most baskets were made of coiled cedar roots that they stitched together and decorated with beargrass. The beargrass was left white or dyed black by dipping it in blue clay or colored yellow by boiling it in berries. Women also made softer bags of hemp for gathering roots. They often decorated these with human or animal figures made from beargrass or cornhusks.

Small, flat, flexible baskets shaped like wallets held personal items or could be used to store dried roots and berries. These were made of hemp with cornhusk, twine, or colored yarn designs.

To make dishes and spoons, men carved cottonwood with elk-horn chisels, then they burned out the hollows. Knives and arrowheads were made of flint.

Storytelling

In the cold northern winters, families gathered around the fire for storytelling. Grandparents passed down tales of the people to their grandchildren. Stories began when the elder said, *Awacha nay!,* which meant, "This is the way it was in the legendary days of the animal world." Children let their grandparents know they were listening by saying, *Eeee!*

All legends of ancient times had animal characters, because oral tradition indicated that long ago animals had been like humans. Many stories were about the trickster Speelyáy, or Coyote, who did things to help the world. Other tales told how natural features were formed or taught children proper behavior.

CUSTOMS

Birth and naming

Babies were born in a small, cone-shaped hut set apart from the main lodge. Older female relatives assisted at the birth. Afterward, the mother and child stayed isolated for five days and then returned home.

Babies were placed in cradleboards made of wood and buckskin. A hoop of wood protected the baby's head. Parents hung a buckskin bag containing the infant's umbilical cord (the cord attaching a baby to its mother before birth) on the hoop.

After a couple's first child was born, the wife's family invited the husband's relatives to a feast. They gave gifts of baskets, food, and strings of beads wrapped in tule mats. Later, the man's family hosted a meal and gave blankets and hides in a rawhide container. Wealthier grooms might give saddles, horses, and cattle. Following the ceremony, the guests took home the plates, pots, and mats used at the feast. This gift exchange was the first public recognition of a marriage.

Childrearing

Children learned cooperation and sharing. Parents praised and honored youngsters with feasts when they took on adult responsibilities (see "Education"). Each town also had a "whipper" to discipline children who did not listen during ceremonies. If children misbehaved, parents would threaten to call the whipper, and that threat usually worked to make children obey.

Puberty

When a boy turned thirteen, he began to do men's work. A girl became a woman after her first menses; she was then ready to marry. She started an *ititamat,* or counting ball, by winding a string of hemp into a ball. For each important event in her life, she tied a knot in the string or added a shell. She recorded her courtship, her marriage, and the birth of her children. When she died, the ball was buried with her.

Marriage

Families arranged marriages, but only with the couple's consent. The bride and groom went to live with either his or her family until their first child was born. At that point, the wedding was formally recognized. Men who could afford it might have more than one wife.

Death rituals

When someone died, the whole family gathered around to help the mourners. Relatives brought and prepared food. Services lasted five days and nights. Family circled the body, sang, and beat a drum to help the spirit move on to the afterlife. Afterward, they held a givea-way and burned the deceased's lodge. One year later, the family held a memorial parade and dinner. Those who had received the deceased's clothes and accessories wore them and gave gifts in honor of the dead. The family then could once again participate in ceremonies and other tribal events.

Festivals

First Fruits Feasts are the most important ceremonies for the tribe. They are held before hunting, fishing, or gathering. Along with dancing shoul-der-to-shoulder in separate men's and women's circles, the ceremony also includes drumming, bell ringing, and prayers. According to tradition, when the creator made people, he asked the animals to care for them by sacrificing their lives. The salmon agreed first to be food for the people, then the deer and elk, next the roots, and finally the berries; during the feast, the food is set out and eaten in that order.

Once a year, between the full moons of December and March, the Yakama hold a winter dance. To honor the ancestors and give strength and guidance to the tribe, medicine songs are presented. Singers place homemade objects on the floor. When they are finished their songs, members of the audience can take the items.

CURRENT TRIBAL ISSUES

Buying back land

The Yakama Reservation, like that of many other tribes, is a checkerboard area of Native and non-Native land. After the U.S. government allocated land during the early 1900s, many tribe members could not afford to keep their land because of taxation (see "History"). Much of the land was also subject to different municipal laws and taxes, so people who could not pay these fees lost their land or had to sell it. Yakama land holdings dwindled as more and more property ended up in American settlers' hands. This caused difficulties in governing, grazing, and overall tribal unity.

In 1950, the tribe formed the Yakama Nation Land Enterprise to buy back former reservation land. They repurchase parcels inside their original Nation boundaries. In 2001, they added 27,939 acres of forestland to their holdings. They develop the parcels they buy to produce income, thereby generating funding for additional land purchases.

Environmental concerns and risks

In the late twentieth century, nuclear waste, dams, and water diverted to irrigation destroyed many traditional foods. In the early decades of the twenty-first century, the Yakama have been working to reverse that damage. In 1986, they fought to prevent nuclear waste from being stored on the site of the Hanford Nuclear Plant, but prior to that, a great deal of radioactive and chemical waste had been discharged into the Columbia River and into the air. In addition, during the 1950s and 1960s, liquid waste containing plutonium, uranium, and other radioactive materials was kept in a large storage crib on the property. The area was declared a Superfund site in 1989; this designation allows the U.S. Environmental Protection Agency to assess and clean up the hazardous waste in the area. In 2007, a crawling camera was designed; it is lowered into the crib and sends pictures to a computer screen so scientists can safely assess what is in the pit without exposing themselves to the danger. That was the first step in an ongoing cleanup process. The Yakama have been participating in health studies to assess their exposure.

The Yakama also had concerns that pesticides used by farmers were polluting the rivers and killing the salmon. Working with the state of Washington, the tribe developed new laws to prevent chemical runoff and dumping in the rivers. They are also working to restore fish runs on the Yakima River. They hope to convince authorities to breach four Snake River dams to reclaim salmon habitats. Lewiston, Idaho, however, would lose its seaport if that happens. At first many people were against the idea, but as of the early 2000s, it had gained some support from environmentalists, scientists, and anglers.

Improvements to the environment

In addition to lobbying for policy change, the Yakama continue to improve their own practices. They invented a unique system called winter logging. Crews wait until the ground is snow-covered and has frozen eighteen inches under the surface before cutting trees. This prevents the soil and plants from being crushed by trucks and workers. It also protects any artifacts buried on the site.

Another ongoing environmental project is wetland restoration. Every year, the Yakama restore about 1,000 to 3,000 acres of habitat. They have completed more than 21,000 acres since 1994. Before 2013, they intended to have 27,000 acres restored along the Satus and Toppenish Creeks and the Yakima River. The Yakama are careful not to disturb archaeological or cultural sites, and they only plant on land that has previously been disturbed, so as not to spoil any original growth.

The tribe is guarding and preserving sacred sites, including petroglyphs, which have been vandalized. They are restoring these rock paintings for future generations.

Conflicts over rights

In 2011, the Yakama Nation sued the U.S. government over a treaty rights violation. As a sovereign (self-governing) nation, the Yakama said the FBI violated their rights when they raided a cigarette plant on their reservation. The federal agents, who did not notify the Yakama until the raid was in progress, seized records and computer equipment without explanation. The lawsuit seeks damages and an order that the tribe must receive notification before federal officials enter the reservation.

NOTABLE PEOPLE

Russell Jim, a Yakama elder, has worked for decades to protect tribal land, his people, and the Columbia River from the damaging effects of the Hanford Nuclear Plant. During the 1970s, he suspected a connection between high rates of rheumatoid arthritis among his people and radioactive waste disposal nearby. In the 1980s, he helped convince the government not to store more nuclear waste in the area. As manager of the tribe's Environmental Restoration/Waste Management Program into the early 2000s, he instituted projectsto clean up the site. In 2002, he received the Paul Beeson Peace Awardfrom the Washington Physicians for Social Responsibility for his efforts.

Chief Yowlachie (Daniel Simmons; 1891–1966) started out as an opera singer but switched to films in the 1920s. Over the next twenty-five years, he played many different characters in more than eighty-seven movies and television shows. Two of his well-known roles include Quo in *Red River* (1948) and Geronimo in *Son of Geronimo: Apache Avenger* (1952).

BOOKS

Alexander, Annie Lou. *Blood Is Red…So Am I.* New York: Vantage Press, 2007.

Brown, John Arthur, and Robert H. Ruby. *Dreamer-Prophets of the Columbia Plateau: Smohalla and Skolaskin.* Norman: University of Oklahoma Press, 2002.

Cardozo, Christopher, Edward S. Curtis, and Joseph D. Horse Capture. *Sacred Legacy: Edward S. Curtis and the North American Indian.* New York: Simon and Schuster, 2000.

Fisher, Andrew H. *Shadow Tribe: The Making of Columbia River Indian Identity.* Seattle: University of Washington Press, 2010.

Hines, Donald M. *Magic in the Mountains, the Yakima Shaman: Power & Practice.* Issaquah, WA: Great Eagle Publishing, 1993.

McWhorter, Lucullus Virgil. *Tragedy of the Wahk-Shum: Prelude to the Yakima Indian War, 1855–6.* Yakima, WA: L. V. McWhorter, 1937.

Scheuerman, Richard D., and Michael O. Finley. *Finding Chief Kamiakin: The Life and Legacy of a Northwest Patriot.* Pullman, WA: Washington State University Press, 2008.

Trafzer, Clifford E., and Robert R. McCoy. *Forgotten Voices: Death Records of the Yakama, 1888–1964.* Lanham, MD: Scarecrow Press, 2009.

Wilkinson, Charles F. *Messages from Franks Landing: A Story of Salmon, Treaties, and the Indian Way.* Seattle: University of Washington Press, 2006.

WEB SITES

"Ancient One: Kennewick Man." *Confederated Tribes of the Umatilla Reservation.* http://www.umatilla.nsn.us/ancient.html (accessed on August 11, 2011).

Confederated Tribes and Bands of the Yakama Nation. http://www.yakamana tion-nsn.gov/ (accessed on August 11, 2011).

"The Confederated Tribes and Bands of the Yakama Nation." *Columbia River Inter-Tribal Fish Commission (CRITFC).* http://www.critfc.org/text/yakama. html (accessed on August 11, 2011).

"Confederated Tribes of the Yakama Nation." *Wisdom of the Elders.* http://www.wisdomoftheelders.org/program304.html (accessed on August 11, 2011).

"Dams of the Columbia Basin and Their Effects on the Native Fishery." *Center for Columbia River History.* http://www.ccrh.org/comm/river/dams7.htm (accessed on August 11, 2011).

Redish, Laura, and Orrin Lewis. "Yakama Indian Language (Yakima, Klicki-tat)." *Native Languages of the Americas.* http://www.native-languages.org/yakama.htm (accessed on August 11, 2011).

Splawn, A. J. *Ka-mi-akin, the Last Hero of the Yakimas.* Portland, OR: Kilham Stationary and Printing, 1917. Reproduced by Washington Secretary of State. http://www.secstate.wa.gov/history/publications_detail.aspx?p=24 (accessed on August 11, 2011).

"Treaty with the Yakama, 1855." *Governors Office of Indian Affairs.* http://www.goia.wa.gov/Treaties/Treaties/yakima.htm (accessed on August 11, 2011).

"Welcome to the Yakama Reservation." *KNDO/KNDU Tri-Cities, Yakima, WA.* http://www.kndu.com/Global/story.asp?S=4737077 (accessed on August 11, 2011).

Yakama Nation Cultural Heritage Center. http://www.yakamamuseum.com/ (accessed on August 11, 2011).

"Yakima Indian Tribe History." *Access Genealogy.* http://www.accessgenealogy.com/native/tribes/yakimaindianhist.htm (accessed on August 11, 2011).

Where to Learn More

Books

Abel, Kerry. *Drum Songs: Glimpses of Dene History.* Montreal, Quebec: McGill–Queen's University Press, 1993.

Adams, Richard C. *A Delaware Indian Legend and the Story of Their Troubles.* Whitefish, MT: Kessinger Publishing, LLC, 2006.

Adamson, Thelma, ed. *Folk-tales of the Coast Salish.* Lincoln: Bison Books, 2009.

Aderkas, Elizabeth, and Christa Hook. *American Indians of the Pacific Northwest.* Oxford: Osprey Publishing, 2005.

Adil, Janeen R. *The Northeast Indians: Daily Life in the 1500s.* Mankato, MN: Capstone Press, 2006.

Agonito, Joseph. *Lakota Portraits: Lives of the Legendary Plains People.* Guilford, CT: TwoDot, 2011.

Agoyo, Herman, and Joe S. Sando, eds. *Po'pay: Leader of the First American Revolution.* Santa Fe, NM: Clear Light Publishing, 2005.

Akers, Donna L. *Culture and Customs of the Choctaw Indians.* Santa Barbara, CA: Greenwood, 2012.

The Aleut Relocation and Internment during World War II: A Preliminary Examination. Anchorage, AK: Aleutian/Pribilof Islands Association, 1981.

Alexander, Annie Lou. *Blood Is Red…So Am I.* New York: Vantage Press, 2007.

Alexie, Sherman. *The Absolutely True Diary of a Part-Time Indian.* Waterville, ME: Thorndike Press, 2008.

Alfred, Agnes. *Paddling to Where I Stand: Agnes Alfred, Kwakwaka'wakw Noblewoman.* Seattle: University of Washington Press, 2005.

Alger, Abby L. *In Indian Tents: Stories Told by Penobscot, Passamaquoddy and Micmac Indians.* Park Forest, IL: University Press of the Pacific, 2006.

Allen, John W. *Legends and Lore of Southern Illinois.* Carbondale: Southern Illinois University Press, 2010.

Andersen, Raoul R., and John K. Crellin. *Miʹsel Joe: An Aboriginal Chief's Journey.* St. John's, Newfoundland: Flanker Press, 2009.

Anderson, Jeffrey D. *One Hundred Years of Old Man Sage: An Arapaho Life.* Lincoln: University of Nebraska Press, 2003.

Andersson, Rani-Henrik. *The Lakota Ghost Dance of 1890.* Lincoln: University of Nebraska Press, 2008.

Angell, Tony, and John M. Marzluff. *In the Company of Crows and Ravens.* New Haven, CT: Yale University Press, 2007.

Anthony, Alexander E., Jr., David Neil Sr., and J. Brent Ricks. *Kachinas: Spirit Beings of the Hopi.* Albuquerque, NM: Avanyu Publishing, 2006.

Archer, Jane. *The First Fire: Stories of the Cherokee, Kickapoo, Kiowa, and Tigua.* Dallas, TX: Taylor Trade, 2005.

Arnold, Caroline, and Richard R. Hewett. *The Ancient Cliff Dwellers of Mesa Verde.* New York: Clarion Books, 2000.

Aron Crowell, ed. *Living Our Cultures, Sharing Our Heritage: The First Peoples of Alaska.* Washington, DC: Smithsonian Institution, 2010.

Augaitis, Daina, Lucille Bell, and Nika Collison. *Raven Travelling: Two Centuries of Haida Art.* Seattle: University of Washington Press, 2008.

Ayagalria, Moses K. *Yupik Eskimo Fairy Tales and More.* New York: Vantage Press, 2006.

Bahti, Mark. *Pueblo Stories and Storytellers.* 3rd ed. Tucson, AZ: Rio Nuevo Publishers, 2010.

Bahti, Mark, and Eugene Baatsoslanii Joe. *Navajo Sandpaintings.* 3rd ed. Tucson, AZ: Rio Nuevo Publishers, 2009.

Bailey, Garrick, ed. *Traditions of the Osage: Stories Collected and Translated by Francis la Flesche.* Albuquerque: University of New Mexico Press, 2010.

Baker, Wendy Beth. *Healing Power of Horses: Lessons from the Lakota Indians.* Irvine, CA: BowTie Press, 2004.

Ball, Eve, Nora Henn, and Lynda A. Sánchez. *Indeh: An Apache Odyssey.* Reprint. Norman: University of Oklahoma Press, 1988.

Ballantine, Betty, and Ian Ballantine, eds. *The Native Americans: An Illustrated History.* Atlanta: Turner Publishing, 1993.

Bancroft-Hunt, Norman. *People of the Totem: The Indians of the Pacific Northwest.* Photographs by Werner Forman. New York: Putnam, 1979.

Barbeau, Marius. *Huron and Wyandot Mythology.* Ottawa, Ontario: Government Printing Bureau, 1915.

Barbour, Jeannie, Amanda J. Cobb, and Linda Hogan. *Chickasaw: Unconquered and Unconquerable.* Ada, OK: Chickasaw Press, 2006.

Barker, James H., and Ann Fienup-Riordan. *Yupiit Yuraryarait = Yup'ik Ways of Dancing.* Fairbanks: University of Alaska Press, 2010.

Barkwell, Lawrence J. *Women of the Metis Nation.* Winnipeg, Manitoba: Louis Riel Institute, 2009.

Barnett, James F., Jr. *The Natchez Indians: A History to 1735.* Jackson: University Press of Mississippi, 2007.

Barrett, Samuel Alfred. *Ceremonies of the Pomo Indians and Pomo Bear Doctors.* University of California Publications in American Archeology and Ethnology. 1917. Reprint. Whitefish, MT: Kessinger Publishing, 2010.

— — —. *The Washo Indians.* 1917. Reprint. Charleston, SC: Kessinger Publishing, 2010.

Barron, Donna Gentle Spirit. *The Long Island Indians and their New England Ancestors: Narragansett, Mohegan, Pequot and Wampanoag Tribes.* Bloomington, IN: AuthorHouse, 2006.

Bartram, William, and Gregory A. Waselkov. *William Bartram on the Southeastern Indians.* Lincoln: University of Nebraska Press, 2002.

Basel, Roberta. *Sequoyah: Inventor of Written Cherokee.* Minneapolis, MN: Compass Point Books, 2007.

Bastedo, Jamie. *Reaching North: A Celebration of the Subarctic.* Markham, Ontario: Red Deer Press, 2002.

Bauerle, Phenocia, ed. *The Way of the Warrior: Stories of the Crow People.* Lincoln: University of Nebraska Press, 2003.

Bean, Lowell John, ed. "Introduction." In *The Ohlone Past and Present: Native Americans of the San Francisco Bay Region.* Menlo Park, CA: Ballena Press, 1994.

Bean, Lowell John, and Florence C. Shipek. "Luiseño." In *Handbook of North American Indians.* Vol. 8: *California,* edited by Robert F. Heizer. Washington, DC: Smithsonian Institution, 1978.

Bean, Lowell, Frank Porter, and Lisa Bourgeault. *The Cahuilla.* New York: Chelsea House, 1989.

Beasley, Richard A. *How to Carve a Tlingit Mask.* Juneau: Sealaska Heritage Institute, 2009.

Becenti, Karyth. *One Nation, One Year: A Navajo Photographer's 365-Day Journey into a World of Discovery, Life and Hope.* Los Ranchos, NM: Rio Grande Books, 2010.

Beck, Mary G. *Heroes and Heroines: Tlingit-Haida Legend.* Anchorage: Alaska Northwest Books, 2003.

Beckwourth, James. *The Life and Adventures of James P. Beckwourth, Mountaineer, Scout, and Pioneer, and Chief of the Crow Nation of Indians.* Paris, France: Adamant Media Corporation, 2005.

Behnke, Alison. *The Apaches.* Minneapolis, MN: Lerner Publications, 2006.

Behrman, Carol H. *The Indian Wars.* Minneapolis, MN: Lerner Publications, 2005.

Belting, Natalia. *Whirlwind Is a Spirit Dancing: Poems Based on Traditional American Indian Songs and Stories.* New York: Milk and Cookies Press, 2006.

Bergon, Frank. *Shoshone Mike.* New York: Viking Penguin, 1987.

Berleth, Richard. *Bloody Mohawk: The French and Indian War and American Revolution on New York's Frontier.* Hensonville, NY: Black Dome, 2009.

Betty, Gerald. *Comanche Society: Before the Reservation.* College Station: Texas A&M University Press, 2005.

Bial, Raymond. *The Chumash.* New York: Benchmark Books, 2004.

— — —. *The Cree.* New York: Benchmark Books, 2006.

— — —. *The Delaware.* New York: Benchmark Books, 2006.

— — —. *The Menominee.* New York: Marshall Cavendish Benchmark, 2006.

— — —. *The Tlingit.* New York: Benchmark Books, 2003.

Bibby, Brian. *Deeper than Gold: A Guide to Indian Life in the Sierra Foothills.* Berkeley: Heyday Books, 2004.

Bielawski, Ellen. *In Search of Ancient Alaska: Solving the Mysteries of the Past.* Anchorage: Alaska Northwest Books, 2007.

Birchfield, D.L., and Helen Dwyer. *Apache History and Culture.* New York: Gareth Stevens, 2012.

Biskup, Agnieszka. *Thunder Rolling Down the Mountain: The Story of Chief Joseph and the Nez Percé.* Mankato, MN: Capstone Press, 2011.

Bjorklund, Ruth. *The Cree.* Tarrytown, NY: Marshall Cavendish, 2009.

— — —. *The Hopi.* Tarrytown, NY: Marshall Cavendish Benchmark, c. 2009.

Blackbird, Andrew J. *History of the Ottawa and Chippewa Indians of Michigan.* Charleston, SC: Nabu Press, 2010.

Bodine, John. "Taos Pueblo." *Handbook of North American Indians,* Vol. 9: *Southwest.* Ed. Alfonso Ortiz. Washington DC: Smithsonian Institution, 1979.

— — —. *Taos Pueblo: A Walk Through Time.* Tucson, AZ: Rio Nuevo, 2006.

Bodinger de Uriarte, John J. *Casino and Museum: Representing Mashantucket Pequot Identity.* Tucson: University of Arizona Press, 2007.

Bogan, Phebe M. *Yaqui Indian Dances of Tucson Arizona: An Account of the Ceremonial Dances of the Yaqui Indians at Pascua.* Whitefish, MT: Kessinger Publishing, 2011.

Bonvillain, Nancy, and Ada Deer. *The Hopi.* Minneapolis, MN: Chelsea House Publications, 2005.

— — —. *The Nez Percé.* New York: Chelsea House, 2011.

— — —. *The Zuñi.* New York: Chelsea House Publishers, 2011.

Boule, Mary Null. *Mohave Tribe.* Vashon, WV: Merryant Publishers Inc., 2000.

Bourque, Bruce J., and Laureen A. LaBar. *Uncommon Threads: Wabanaki Textiles, Clothing, and Costume.* Augusta: Maine State Museum in association with University of Washington Press, 2009.

Bowes, John P. *The Choctaw.* New York: Chelsea House, 2010.

Bradley, Donna. *Native Americans of San Diego County, CA.* Mt. Pleasant, SC: Arcadia, 2009.

Bragdon, Kathleen J. *The Columbia Guide to American Indians of the Northeast.* New York: Columbia University Press, 2005.

Braje, Todd J., and Torben C. Rick, eds.*Human Impacts on Seals, Sea Lions, and Sea Otters: Integrating Archaeology and Ecology in the Northeast Pacific.* Berkeley: University of California Press, 2011.

Bray, Kingsley M. *Crazy Horse: A Lakota Life.* Norman: University of Oklahoma Press, 2006.

Breen, Betty, and Earl Mills, Sr. *Cape Cod Wampanoag Cookbook: Wampanoag Indian Recipes, Images & Lore.* Santa Fe, NM: Clear Light Books, 2001.

Brehm, Victoria. *Star Songs and Water Spirits: A Great Lakes Native Reader.* Tustin, MI: Ladyslipper Press, 2010.

Brimner, Larry Dane. *Pocahontas: Bridging Two Worlds.* New York: Marshall Cavendish Benchmark, 2009.

Bringhurst, Robert. *A Story as Sharp as a Knife: The Classical Haida Mythtellers and Their World.* 2nd ed. Vancouver, BC: Douglas & McIntyre, 2011.

Bringing the Story of the Cheyenne People to the Children of Today. Northern Cheyenne Curriculum Committee. Helena, MT: Office of Public Instruction, 2009.

Broker, Ignatia, *Night Flying Woman: An Ojibway Narrative.* St. Paul: Minnesota Historical Society Press, 1983.

Brown, Dee. *Bury My Heart at Wounded Knee: An Indian History of the American West.* New York: Holt, Rinehart, and Winston, 1970.

Brown, James W., and Rita T. Kohn, ed. *Long Journey Home: Oral Histories of Contemporary Delaware Indians.* Bloomington: Indiana University Press, 2008.

Brown, John A., and Robert H. Ruby. *The Chinook Indians: Traders of the Lower Columbia River.* Norman: University of Oklahoma Press, 1988.

Brown, Joseph. *The Spiritual Legacy of the American Indian: Commemorative Edition with Letters while Living with Black Elk.* Bloomington, IN: World Wisdom, 2007.

Brown, Tricia, and Roy Corral. *Children of the Midnight Sun: Young Native Voices of Alaska.* Anchorage: Alaska Northwest Books, 2006.

— — —. *Silent Storytellers of Totem Bight State Historical Park.* Anchorage: Alaska Geographic Association, 2009.

Brown, Virginia Pounds, Laurella Owens and Nathan Glick. *The World of the Southern Indians: Tribes, Leaders, and Customs from Prehistoric Times to the Present.* Montgomery, AL: NewSouth Books, 2011.

Browner, Tara, ed. *Music of the First Nations: Tradition and Innovation in Native North America.* Urbana: University of Illinois Press, 2009.

Bruchac, Joseph. *Flying with the Eagle, Racing the Great Bear: Tales from Native North America.* Golden, CO: Fulcrum, 2011.

Bruemmer, Fred. *Arctic Visions: Pictures from a Vanished World.* Toronto, Ontario: Key Porter Books, 2008.

Brugge, Doug, Timothy Benally, and Esther Yazzie-Lewis. *The Navajo People and Uranium Mining.* Albuquerque: University of New Mexico Press, 2006.

Bullchild, Percy. *The Sun Came Down: The History of the World as My Blackfeet Elders Told It.* Lincoln: University of Nebraska Press, 2005.

Burgan, Michael. *The Arapaho.* Tarrytown, NY: Marshall Cavendish Benchmark, 2009.

— — —. *Inuit History and Culture.* New York: Gareth Stevens, 2011.

Burke, Heather, et al, eds. *Kennewick Man: Perspectives on the Ancient One.* Walnut Creek, CA: Left Coast Press, 2008.

Burns, Louis F. *A History of the Osage People.* Tuscaloosa: University of Alabama Press, 2004.

— — —. *Osage Indian Customs and Myths.* Tuscaloosa: University of Alabama Press, 2005.

Button, Bertha P. *Friendly People: The Zuñi Indians.* Santa Fe, NM: Museum of New Mexico Press, 1963.

Calloway, Colin G. *The Shawnees and the War for America.* New York: Viking, 2007.

Carbone, Elisa. *Blood on the River: James Town 1607.* New York: Viking, 2006.

Carlos, Ann M. *Commerce by a Frozen Sea: Native Americans and the European Fur Trade.* Philadelphia: University of Pennsylvania Press, 2010.

Carlson, Paul H., and Tom Crum. *Myth, Memory, and Massacre: The Pease River Capture of Cynthia Ann Parker.* Lubbock: Texas Tech University Press, 2010.

Carlson, Richard G., ed. *Rooted Like the Ash Trees: New England Indians and the Land.* Naugatuck, CT: Eagle Wing Press, 1987.

Carpenter, Cecelia Svinth, Maria Victoria Pascualy, and Trisha Hunter. *Nisqually Indian Tribe.* Charleston, SC: Arcadia, 2008.

Carter, John G. *The Northern Arapaho Flat Pipe and the Ceremony of Covering the Pipe.* Whitefish, MT: Kessinger Publishing, 2007.

Cashin, Edward J. *Guardians of the Valley: Chickasaws in Colonial South Carolina and Georgia.* Columbia, SC: University of South Carolina Press, 2009.

Cassidy, James J., Jr., ed. *Through Indian Eyes: The Untold Story of Native American Peoples.* Pleasantville, NY: Reader's Digest Association, 1995.

Cassinelli, Dennis. *Preserving Traces of the Great Basin Indians.* Reno, NV: Jack Bacon & Company, 2006.

Castillo, Edward D. *The Pomo.* Austin: RaintreeSteck-Vaughn, 1999.

Chalcraft, Edwin L. *Assimilation's Agent: My Life as a Superintendent in the Indian Boarding School System.* Lincoln: University of Nebraska Press, 2007.

Champagne, Duane, ed. *The Native North American Almanac.* Detroit: Gale, 1994.

Charles, Nicholas and Maria. *Messenger Spirits: Yup'ik Masks and Stories.* Anchorage, AK: N & M, 2009.

Chatters, James C. *Ancient Encounters: Kennewick Man and the First Americans.* New York: Simon and Schuster, 2001.

Chaussonnet, Valerie, ed. *Crossroads Alaska: Native Cultures of Alaska and Siberia.* Washington, DC: Arctic Studies Center, National Museum of Natural History, Smithsonian Institution, 1995.

Chehak, Gail, and Jan Halliday. *Native Peoples of the Northwest: A Traveler's Guide to Land, Art, and Culture.* Seattle: Sasquatch Books, 2002.

Chenoweth, Avery, and Robert Llewellyn. *Empires in the Forest: Jamestown and the Making of America.* Earlysville, VA: Rivanna Foundation, 2010.

Childs, Craig. *House of Rain: Tracking a Vanished Civilization across the American Southwest.* 2nd ed. New York: Back Bay Books, 2008.

Clark, Cora, and Texa Bowen Williams. *Pomo Indians: Myths and Some of Their Sacred Meanings.* Reprint. Charleston, SC: Literary Licensing, 2011.

Clark, Ella E. *Indian Legends of the Pacific Northwest.* Berkeley: University of California Press, 2003.

Clark, Jerry E. *The Shawnee.* Lexington: University Press of Kentucky, 2007.

Clow, Richmond L., ed. *The Sioux in South Dakota History: A Twentieth-Century Reader.* Pierre, SD: South Dakota State Historical Society Press, 2007.

Cobb, Amanda J. *Listening to Our Grandmothers' Stories: The Bloomfield Academy for Chickasaw Females, 1852–1949.* Lincoln: University of Nebraska Press, 2007.

— — —. *Massacre at Camp Grant: Forgetting and Remembering Apache History.* Tucson: University of Arizona Press, 2007.

Cone, Marla. *Silent Snow: The Slow Poisoning of the Arctic.* New York: Grove Press, 2005.

Confederated Salish and Kootenai Tribes. *Bull Trout's Gift: A Salish Story about the Value of Reciprocity.* Lincoln: University of Nebraska Press, 2011.

Cook, Franklin A. "Nunapitchuk, Alaska: A Yup'ik Eskimo Village in Western Alaska." *Anna Tobeluk Memorial School, Nunapitchuk, Alaska.* Lincoln: University of Nebraska Press, 2005.

Cook, R. Michael, Eli Gifford, and Warren Jefferson, eds. *How Can One Sell the Air?: Chief Seattle's Vision.* Summertown, TN: Native Voices, 2005.

Corwin, Judith Hoffman. *Native American Crafts of the Northwest Coast, the Arctic, and the Subarctic.* New York: Franklin Watts, 2002.

Costa, David J. *Narratives and Winter Stories.* Oxford, OH: Myaamia Publications, 2010.

Coté, Charlotte. *Spirits of Our Whaling Ancestors: Revitalizing Makah, and Nuu-chah-nulth Traditions.* Seattle: University of Washington Press, 2010.

Coyote, Bertha Little, and Virginia Giglio. *Leaving Everything Behind: The Songs and Memories of a Cheyenne Woman.* Norman: University of Oklahoma Press, 1997.

Cozzens, Peter. *The Army and the Indian.* Mechanicsburg, PA: Stackpole Books, 2005.

Crediford, Gene J. *Those Who Remain.* Tuscaloosa: University of Alabama Press, 2009.

Crompton, Samuel Willard. *The Mohawk.* Edited by Paul C. Rosier. New York: Chelsea House Publishers, 2010.

Medicine Crow, Joseph. *Counting Coup: Becoming a Crow Chief on the Reservation and Beyond.* Washingon, DC: National Geographic, 2006.

———. *From the Heart of the Crow Country: The Crow Indians' Own Stories.* Lincoln: University of Nebraska Press, 2000.

Crowell, Aron L. *Living Our Cultures, Sharing Our Heritage: The First Peoples of Alaska.* Washington, DC: Smithsonian Books, 2010.

Croy, Anita. *Ancient Pueblo: Archaeology Unlocks the Secrets of America's Past.* Washington, DC: National Geographic, 2007.

Cunningham, Kevin, and Peter Benoit. *The Wampanoag.* New York: Children's Press, 2011.

Curtin, Jeremiah. *Myths of the Modocs.* Whitefish, MT: Kessinger Publishing, 2006.

———. "The Yanas." In *Creation Myths of Primitive America.* Boston, MA: Little, Brown, and Company, 1903.

Curtain, Jeremiah, and Roland B. Dixon, eds. *Achomawi and Atsugewi Myths and Tales.* Reprint.Sandhurst, UK: Abela Publishing, 2009.

———. *The Plains Indian Photographs of Edward S. Curtis.* Lincoln: University of Nebraska Press, 2001.

———. "Salishan Tribes." In *The North American Indian.* Vol. 7. Edited by Frederick Webb Hodge. Norwood, MA: The Plimpton Press, 1911. Available online from http://curtis.library.northwestern.edu/curtis/viewPage.cgi?showp=1&size=2&id=nai.07.book.00000075&volume=7 (accessed on August 11, 2011).

——— "Taos." In *The North American Indian (1907–1930).* Vol. 26. Reprint. New York: Johnson Reprint Corporation, 1970.

———. "Umatilla." In *The North American Indian,* edited by Fredrick Webb Hodge. Vol. 8. 1911. Available online from http://curtis.library.northwestern.edu/curtis/viewPage.cgi?showp=1&size=2&id=nai.08.book.00000129.p&volume=8#nav (accessed on August 11, 2011).

———. "The Washoe." In *The North American Indian*. Vol. 15. Edited by Frederick Webb Hodge. Norwood, MA: The Plimpton Press, 1926: 89–98. Available online from Northwestern University. http://curtis. library.northwestern.edu/curtis/viewPage.cgi?showp=1&size=2&id=nai.15. book.00000141&volume=15 (accessed on August 15, 2011).

Cushing, Frank H. *Zuñi Folk Tales*. Charleston, SC: Kessinger Publishing, 2011)

Cwiklik, Robert. *King Philip and the War with the Colonists*. Englewood Cliffs, NJ: Silver Burdette Press, 1989.

Dahlin, Curtis A., and Alan R. Woolworth. *The Dakota Uprising: A Pictorial History*. Edina, MN: Beaver's Pond Press, 2009.

Damas, David, ed. *Handbook of North American Indians,* Vol. 5: *Arctic*. Washington, DC: Smithsonian Institution, 1984.

Dangberg, Grace, translator. *Washo Tales*. Reprint. Carson City: Nevada State Museum, 1968.

De Angulo, Jaime. *Indian Tales*. Santa Clara, CA: Heyday Books, 2003.

De Capua, Sarah. *The Shawnee*. New York: Marshall Cavendish Benchmark, 2008.

De Laguna, Fredericæ. "Tlingit." In *Handbook of North American Indians: Northwest Coast*. Vol. 7, edited by Wayne Suttles. Washington, DC: Smithsonian Institution, 1990, pp. 203–28.

Decker, Carol Paradise. *Pecos Pueblo People through the Ages: "—And We're Still Here": Stories of Time and Place*. Santa Fe, NM: Sunstone Press, 2011.

Decker, Peter R. *"The Utes Must Go!": American Expansion and the Removal of a People*. Golden, CO: Fulcrum Publishing, 2004.

DeJong, David H. *Forced to Abandon Our Fields: The 1914 Clay Southworth Gila River Pima Interviews*. Salt Lake City: University of Utah Press, 2011.

Deloria, Vine, Jr. *Red Earth, White Lies: Native Americans and the Myth of Scientific Fact*. New York: Scribner, 1995.

Dempsey, L. James. *Blackfoot War Art: Pictographs of the Reservation Period, 1880–2000*. Norman: University of Oklahoma Press, 2007.

Denetdale, Jennifer. *The Long Walk: The Forced Navajo Exile*. New York: Chelsea House, 2008.

———. *The Navajo*. New York: Chelsea House, 2011.

Densmore, Frances. *American Indians and Their Music*. Kila, MN: Kessinger Publishing, 2010.

DeRose, Cat. *Little Raven: Chief of the Southern Arapaho*. Palmer Lake, CO: Filter Press, 2010.

Dial, Adolph L., and David K. Eliades. *The Only Land I Know: A History of the Lumbee Indians*. Syracuse: Syracuse University Press, 1996.

Dickey, Michael E. *The People of the River's Mouth: In Search of the Missouria Indians*. Columbia: University of Missouri, 2011.

Ditchfield, Christin. *Northeast Indians.* Chicago: Heinemann Library, 2012.

— — —. *Plateau Indians.* Chicago: Heinemann Library, 2012.

Doak, Robin S. *Arctic Peoples.* Chicago: Heinemann Library, 2012.

— — —. *Subarctic Peoples.* Mankato, MN: Heinemann-Raintree, 2011.

Doherty, Craig A. *California Indians.* New York: Chelsea House Publications, 2007.

— — —. *Northeast Indians.* Broomall, PA: Chelsea House Publications, March 2008.

— — —. *Southeast Indians.* Minneapolis, MN: Chelsea House, 2007.

Doherty, Craig A., and Katherine M. Doherty. *Arctic Peoples.* New York: Chelsea House, 2008.

— — —. *Great Basin Indians.* Minneapolis, MN: Chelsea House, 2010.

— — —. *Plains Indians.* New York: Chelsea House, 2008.

— — —. *Plateau Indians.* New York: Chelsea House, 2008.

— — —. *Southwest Indians.* Minneapolis, MN: Chelsea House, 2007.

Dolan, Edward F. *The American Indian Wars.* Brookfield, CT: Millbrook Press, 2003.

Donlan, Leni. *Cherokee Rose: The Trail of Tears.* Chicago, IL: Raintree, 2007.

Downum, Christian E. Hisatsinom: *Ancient Peoples in a Land without Water.* Santa Fe: School for Advanced Research Press, 2011.

Dresser, Thomas. *The Wampanoag Tribe of Martha's Vineyard: Colonization to Recognition.* Charleston, SC: History Press, 2011.

Driver, Harold E., and Walter R. Goldschmidt. *The Hupa White Deerskin Dance.* Whitefish, MT: Kessinger Publishing, 2007.

Drury, Clifford M., ed. *Nine Years with the Spokane Indians: The Diary, 1838–1848, of Elkanah Walker.* Glendale, CA: Arthur H. Clark Company, 1976.

DuBois, Cora. *The 1870 Ghost Dance.* Reprint. Lincoln: University of Nebraska, 2007.

Duncan, Kate C. *Northern Athapaskan Art: A Beadwork Tradition.* Seattle: University of Washington Press, 1989.

Dunn, Jacob Piatt. *Massacres of the Mountains: A History of the Indian Wars of the Far West 1815–1875.* Whitefish, MT: Kessinger Publishing, 2006.

Dutton, Bertha P. *Indians of the American Southwest.* Englewood Cliffs, NJ: Prentice-Hall, 1975.

Duval, Kathleen. *The Native Ground: Indians and Colonists in the Heart of the Continent.* Philadelphia: University of Pennsylvania Press, 2006.

Dwyer, Helen, ed. *Peoples of the Southwest, West, and North.* Redding, CT: Brown Bear Books, 2009.

Dwyer, Helen, and D. L. Birchfield. *Cheyenne History and Culture.* New York: Gareth Stevens, 2012.

Dwyer, Helen, and Mary A. Stout. *Nez Percé History and Culture.* New York: Gareth Stevens, 2012.

Eastman, Charles A. *The Essential Charles Eastman (Ohiyesa), Revised and Updated Edition: Light on the Indian World.* Michael Oren Fitzgerald, ed. Bloomington, IN: World Wisdom, 2007.

— — —. *From the Deep Woods to Civilization.* Whitefish, MT: Kessinger Publishing, 2006.

— — —. *The Soul of the Indian.* New York: Dodo Press, 2007.

Eaton, William M. *Odyssey of the Pueblo Indians: An Introduction to Pueblo Indian Petroglyphs, Pictographs and Kiva Art Murals in the Southwest.* Paducah, KY: Turner Publishing Company, 2001.

Ember, Melvin, and Peter N. Peregrine, eds. *Encyclopedia of Prehistory,* Vol. 2: *Arctic and Subarctic.* New York: Kluwer Academic/Plenum Publishers, 2001.

Englar, Mary. *The Iroquois: The Six Nations Confederacy.* Mankato, MN: Capstone Press, 2006.

Erb, Gene, and Ann DeWolf Erb. *Voices in Our Souls: The DeWolfs, Dakota Sioux and the Little Bighorn.* Santa Fe: Sunstone Press, 2010.

Erdoes, Richard. *The Sun Dance People: The Plains Indians, Their Past and Present.* New York: Random House, 1972.

Erickson, Kirstin C. *Yaqui Homeland and Homeplace.* Tucson: University of Arizona Press, 2008.

Erickson, Winston P. *Sharing the Desert: The Tohono O'Odham in History.* Tucson: University of Arizona Press, 2003.

Erikson, Patricia Pierce. *Voices of a Thousand People: The Makah Cultural and Research Center.* Lincoln: University of Nebraska Press, 2005.

Ezell, Paul H. "History of the Pima." In *Handbook of North American Indians,* Volume 10: *Southwest,* edited by Alfonso Ortiz. Washington, DC: Smithsonian Institution Press, 1983.

Falconer, Shelley, and Shawna White. *Stones, Bones, and Stitches: Storytelling through Inuit Art.* Toronto, Ontario: Tundra Books, 2007.

Fariello, Anna. *Cherokee Basketry: From the Hands of Our Elders.* Charleston, SC: History Press, 2009.

Field, Ron. *The Seminole Wars, 1818–58.* New York: Osprey, 2009.

Fitzgerald, Judith, and Michael Oren Fitzgerald, eds. *The Spirit of Indian Women.* Bloomington, IN: World Wisdom, 2005.

Forczyk, Robert. *Nez Percé 1877: The Last Fight.* Long Island City, NY: Osprey, 2011.

Foreman, Grant. *Indian Removal.* Norman: University of Oklahoma Press, 1972.

Foster, Martha Harroun. *We Know Who We Are: Métis Identity in a Montana Community.* Norman: University of Oklahoma Press, 2006.

Foster, Sharon Ewell. *Abraham's Well: A Novel.* Minneapolis, MN: Bethany House, 2006.

Fowler, Loretta. *The Columbia Guide to American Indians of the Great Plains.* New York: Columbia University Press, 2005.

Fradin, Dennis B. *The Pawnee.* Chicago: Childrens Press, 1988.

Frank, Andrew. *The Seminole.* New York: Chelsea House, 2011.

Freedman, Russell. *The Life and Death of Crazy Horse.* New York: Holiday House, 1996.

Gagnon, Gregory O. *Culture and Customs of the Sioux Indians.* Westport, CT: Greenwood, 2011.

Garfinkel, Alan P., and Harold Williams. *Handbook of the Kawaiisu.* Kern Valley, CA: Wa-hi Sina'avi, 2011.

Geake, Robert A. *A History of the Narragansett Tribe of Rhode Island: Keepers of the Bay.* Charleston, SC: History Press, 2011.

Geronimo. *The Autobiography of Geronimo.* St. Petersburg, FL: Red and Black Publishers, 2011.

Giago, Tim A. *Children Left Behind: Dark Legacy of Indian Mission Boarding Schools.* Santa Fe, NM: Clear Light Publishing, 2006.

Gibson, Karen Bush. *The Chumash: Seafarers of the Pacific Coast.* Mankato, MN: Bridgestone Books, 2004.

———. *The Great Basin Indians: Daily Life in the 1700s.* Mankato, MN: Capstone Press, 2006.

———. *New Netherland: The Dutch Settle the Hudson Valley.* Elkton, IN: Mitchell Lane Publishers, 2006.

Giddings, Ruth Warner. *Yaqui Myths and Legends.* Charleston, SC: BiblioBazaar, 2009.

Gipson, Lawrence Henry. *The Moravian Indian Mission on White River: Diaries and Letters, May 5, 1799, to November 12, 1806.* Indianapolis: Indiana Historical Bureau, 1938.

Girdner, Alwin J. *Diné Tah: My Reservation Days 1923–1938.* Tucson: Rio Nuevo Publishers, c2011.

Glancy, Diane. *Pushing the Bear: After the Trail of Tears.* Norman: University of Oklahoma Press, 2009.

Goddard, Pliny Earle. *Hupa Texts.* Reprint. Charleston, SC: BiblioBazaar, 2009.

———. *Life and Culture of the Hupa.* Reprint. Charleston, SC: Nabu Press, 2011.

———. *Myths and Tales from the San Carlos Apache.* Whitefish, MT: Kessinger Publishing, 2006.

— — —. *Myths and Tales of the White Mountain Apache*. Whitefish, MT: Kessinger Publishing, 2011.

Goodman, Linda J. *Singing the Songs of My Ancestors: The Life and Music of Helma Swan, Makah Elder*. Norman: University of Oklahoma Press, 2003.

Goodwin, Grenville. *Myths and Tales of the White Mountain Apache*. Whitefish, MT: Kessinger Publishing, 2011.

Gordon, Irene Ternier. *A People on the Move: The Métis of the Western Plains*. Surry, British Columbia: Heritage House, 2009.

Grafe, Steven L. ed. *Lanterns on the Prairie: The Blackfeet Photographs of Walter McClintock*. Norman: University of Oklahoma Press, 2009.

Grant, Blanche Chloe. *Taos Indians*. 1925 ed. Santa Fe: Sunstone Press, 2007.

Grant, Campbell. *Rock Paintings of the Chumash: A Study of a California Indian Culture*. Reprint. Santa Barbara, CA: Santa Barbara Museum of Natural History/EZ Nature Books, 1993.

Gray-Kanatiiosh, Barbara A. *Cahuilla*. Edina, MN: ABDO, 2007.

— — —. *Modoc*. Edina, MN: ABDO, 2007.

— — —. *Paiute*. Edina, MN: ABDO Publishing, 2007.

— — —. *Yurok*. Edina, MN: ABDO, 2007.

Graymont, Barbara. *The Iroquois*. New York: Chelsea House, 1988.

Green, Michael D., and Theda Perdue. *The Cherokee Nation and the Trail of Tears*. New York: Viking, 2007.

— — —. *The Columbia Guide to American Indians of the Southeast*. New York: Columbia University Press, 2001.

Grinnell, George Bird. *Blackfeet Indians Stories*. Whitefish, MT: Kessinger Publishing, 2006.

— — —. *The Cheyenne Indians: Their History and Lifeways*. Bloomington, IN: World Wisdom, 2008.

Guigon, Catherine, Francis Latreille, and Fredric Malenfer. *The Arctic*. New York: Abrams Books for Young Readers, 2007.

Gunther, Vanessa. *Chief Joseph*. Greenwood, 2010.

Guthridge, George. *The Kids from Nowhere: The Story behind the Arctic Education Miracle*. Anchorage: Alaska Northwest Books, 2006.

Hagan, William T. *The Sac and Fox Indians*. Norman: University of Oklahoma Press, 2008.

Hahn, Elizabeth. *The Pawnee*. Vero Beach, FL: Rourke Publications, Inc., 1992.

Haig-Brown, Roderick. *The Whale People*. Madeira Park, BC: Harbour Publishing, 2003.

Hancock, David A. *Tlingit: Their Art and Culture*. Blaine, WA: Hancock House Publishers, 2003.

Handbook of North American Indians, Vol. 6: *Subarctic.* Ed. June Helm. Washington, DC: Smithsonian Institution, 1981.

Harpster, Jack, and Ken Stalter. *Captive!: The Story of David Ogden and the Iroquois.* Santa Barbara, CA: Praeger, 2010.

Harrington, Mark Raymond. *Certain Caddo Sites in Arkansas.* Charleston, SC: Johnson Press, 2011.

Hayes, Allan, and Carol Hayes. *The Desert Southwest: Four Thousand Years of Life And Art.* Berkeley, CA: Ten Speed Press, 2006.

Hearth, Amy Hill. *"Strong Medicine Speaks": A Native American Elder Has Her Say: An Oral History.* New York: Atria Books, 2008.

Hebner, William Logan. *Southern Paiute: A Portrait.* Logan: Utah State University Press, 2010.

Heinämäki, Leena. *The Right to Be a Part of Nature: Indigenous Peoples and the Environment.* Rovaniemi, Finland: Lapland University Press, 2010.

Heizer, R. F., ed. *Handbook of North American Indians.* Vol. 8: *California.* Washington, DC: Smithsonian Institution, 1978.

Hessel, Ingo. *Inuit Art: An Introduction.* Vancouver, British Columbia: Douglas & McIntyre, 2002.

Hicks, Terry Allan. *The Chumash.* New York: Marshall Cavendish Benchmark, 2008.

— — —. *The Zuñi.* New York: Marshall Cavendish Benchmark, 2010.

Hill, George, Robert H. Ruby, and John A. Brown. *The Spokane Indians: Children of the Sun.* Norman: University of Oklahoma Press, 2006.

Himsl, Sharon M. *The Shoshone.* San Diego, CA: Lucent Books, 2005.

Hirst, Stephen. *I Am the Grand Canyon: The Story of the Havasupai People.* Grand Canyon, AZ: Grand Canyon Association, 2006.

Hobson, Geary. *Plain of Jars and Other Stories.* East Lansing: Michigan State University Press, 2011.

Hodge, Frederick Webb. "Dwamish." *Handbook of American Indians North of Mexico.* New York: Pageant Books, 1959.

Hogeland, Kim, and L. Frank Hogeland. *First Families: Photographic History of California Indians.* Berkeley: Heyday Books, 2007.

Holm, Bill. *Spirit and Ancestor: A Century of Northwest Coast Indian Art in the Burke Museum.* Seattle: Burke Museum; University of Washington Press, 1987.

Hooper, Lucile. *The Cahuilla Indians.* Kila, MN: Kessinger Publishing, 2011.

Hoover, Alan L. *Nuu-chah-nulth Voices, Histories, Objects, and Journeys.* Victoria: Royal British Columbia Museum, 2000.

Hopping, Lorraine Jean. *Chief Joseph: The Voice for Peace.* New York: Sterling, 2010.

Houston, James A. *James Houston's Treasury of Inuit Legends.* Orlando, FL: Harcourt, 2006.

Hungrywolf, Adolf. *Tribal Childhood: Growing Up in Traditional Native America.* Summertown, TN:Native Voices, 2008.

Hyde, Dayton O. *The Last Free Man: The True Story behind the Massacre of Shoshone Mike and His Band of Indians in 1911.* New York: Dial Press, 1973.

Hyde, George E. *Indians of the Woodlands: From Prehistoric Times to 1725.* Norman: University of Oklahoma Press, 1962.

Indians of the Northwest Coast and Plateau. Chicago: World Book, 2009.

Indians of the Southwest. Chicago: World Book, 2009.

Inupiaq and Yupik People of Alaska. Anchorage: Alaska Geographic Society, 2004.

Jacknis, Ira. *The Storage Box of Tradition: Kwakiutl Art, Anthropologists, and Museums, 1881–1981.* Washington, DC: Smithsonian Institution Press, 2002.

Jackson, Helen Hunt. *The Indian Reform Letters of Helen Hunt Jackson, 1879–1885.*Edited by Valerie ShererMathes. Norman: University of Oklahoma Press, 1998.

— — —. *Ramona.* New York: Signet, 1988.

James, Cheewa. *Modoc: The Tribe That Wouldn't Die.* Happy Camp, CA: Naturegraph, 2008.

Jastrzembski, Joseph C. *The Apache.* Minneapolis: Chelsea House, 2011.

— — —. *The Apache Wars: The Final Resistance.* Minneapolis: Chelsea House, 2007.

Jenness, Aylette, and Alice Rivers. *In Two Worlds: A Yu'pik Eskimo Family.* New York: Houghton Mifflin, 1989.

Jennys, Susan. *19th Century Plains Indian Dresses.* Pottsboro, TX: Crazy Crow, 2004.

Jensen, Richard E., ed. *The Pawnee Mission Letters, 1834-1851.* Lincoln: University of Nebraska Press, 2010.

Jeter, Marvin D. *Edward Palmer's Arkansaw Mounds.* Tuscaloosa: University of Alabama Press, 2010.

Johansen, Bruce E. *The Iroquois.* New York, NY: Chelsea House, 2010.

Johnsgard, Paul A. *Wind through the Buffalo Grass: A Lakota Story Cycle.* Lincoln, NE: Plains Chronicles Press, 2008.

Johnson, Jerald Jay. "Yana." In *Handbook of North American Indians.* Vol. 10: *Southwest,* edited by Alfonso Ortiz. Washington, DC: Smithsonian Institution, 1983.

Johnson, Michael. *American Indians of the Southeast.* Oxford: Osprey Publishing, 1995.

— — —. "Duwamish." *The Native Tribes of North America*. New York: Macmillan, 1992.

— — —. *Native Tribes of the Northeast*. Milwaukee, WI: World Almanac Library, 2004.

Johnson, Michael, and Jonathan Smith. *Indian Tribes of the New England Frontier*. Oxford: Osprey Publishing, 2006.

Johnson, Thomas H., and Helen S. Johnson. *Also Called Sacajawea: Chief Woman's Stolen Identity*. Long Grove, IL: Waveland Press, 2008.

— — —. *Two Toms: Lessons from a Shoshone Doctor*. Salt Lake City: University of Utah Press, 2010.

Jonaitis, Aldona. *Art of the Northwest Coast*. Seattle: University of Washington Press, 2006.

Joseph, Frank. *Advanced Civilizations of Prehistoric America: The Lost Kingdoms of the Adena, Hopewell, Mississippians, and Anasazi*. Rochester, VT: Bear & Company, December 21, 2009.

Josephson, Judith Pinkerton. *Why Did Cherokees Move West? And Other Questions about the Trail of Tears*. Minneapolis: Lerner Publications, 2011.

Josephy, Alvin M., Jr. *500 Nations: An Illustrated History of North American Indians*. New York: Knopf, 1994.

— — —. *Nez Percé Country*. Lincoln: University of Nebraska Press, 2007.

Kallen, Stuart A. *The Pawnee*. San Diego: Lucent Books, 2001.

Kaneuketat. *I Dreamed the Animals: Kaneuketat: the Life of an Innu Hunter*. New York: Berghahn Books, 2008.

Kavasch, E. Barrie. *Enduring Harvests: Native American Foods and Festivals for Every Season*. Old Saybrook, CT: The Globe Pequot Press, 1995.

Keegan, Marcia. *Pueblo People: Ancient Tradition, Modern Lives*. Santa Fe, NM: Clear Light Publishers, 1999.

— — —. *Taos Pueblo and Its Sacred Blue Lake*. Santa Fe: Clear Light Publishers, 2010.

Keegan, Marcia, and Regis Pecos. *Pueblo People: Ancient Traditions, Modern Lives*. Santa Fe, NM: Clear Light Publishers, 1999.

Kegg, Maude. *Portage Lake: Memories of an Ojibwe Childhood*. Edmonton: University of Alberta Press, 1991.

Kennedy, J. Gerald. *Life of Black Hawk, or Ma-ka-tai-me-she-kia-kiak. Dictated by Himself*. New York: Penguin Books, 2008.

King, David C. *The Blackfeet*. New York: Marshall Cavendish Benchmark, 2010.

— — —. *First People*. New York: DK Children, 2008.

— — —. *The Inuit*. New York: Marshall Cavendish Benchmark, 2008.

— — —. *The Nez Percé*. New York: Benchmark Books, 2008.

— — —. *Seminole*. New York: Benchmark Books, 2007.

Kiowa and Pueblo Art: Watercolor Paintings by Native American Artists. Mineola, NY: Dover Publications, 2009.

Kirkpatrick, Katherine. *Mysterious Bones: The Story of Kennewick Man.* New York: Holiday House, 2011.

Kissock,Heather, and Jordan McGill. *Apache: American Indian Art and Culture.* New York: Weigl Publishers, 2011.

Kissock, Heather, and Rachel Small. *Caddo: American Indian Art and Culture.* New York: Weigl Publishers, 2011.

Koyiyumptewa, Stewart B., Carolyn O'Bagy Davis, and the Hopi Cultural Preservation Office. *The Hopi People.* Charleston, SC: Arcadia Publishing, 2009.

Kristofic, Jim. *Navajos Wear Nikes: A Reservation Life.* Albuquerque: University of New Mexico Press, 2011.

Kroeber, Theodora. *Ishi in Two Worlds: A Biography of the Last Wild Indian in North America.* Berkeley: University of California Press, 2004.

Krupnik, Igor, and Dyanna Jolly, eds. *The Earth Is Faster Now: Indigenous Observations of Arctic Environmental Change.* Fairbanks, Alaska: Arctic Research Consortium of the United States, 2002.

Kuiper, Kathleen, ed. *American Indians of California, the Great Basin, and the Southwest.* New York: Rosen Educational Services, 2012.

— — —. *American Indians of the Northeast and Southeast.* New York: Rosen Educational Services, 2012.

— — —. *American Indians of the Plateau and Plains.* New York: Rosen Educational Services, 2012.

— — —. *Indigenous Peoples of the Arctic, Subarctic, and Northwest Coast.* New York: Rosen Educational Services, 2012.

Lacey, T. Jensen. *The Blackfeet.* New York: Chelsea House, 2011.

— — —. *The Comanche.* New York: Chelsea House, 2011.

Lankford, George E., ed. *Native American Legends of the Southeast: Tales from the Natchez, Caddo, Biloxi, Chickasaw, and Other Nations.* 5th ed. Tuscaloosa: University of Alabama Press, 2011.

Lanmon, Dwight P. and Francis H. Harlow. *The Pottery of Zuñi Pueblo.* Santa Fe: Museum of New Mexico Press, 2008.

Larsen, Mike, Martha Larsen, and Jeannie Barbour. *Proud to Be Chickasaw.* Ada, OK: Chickasaw Press, 2010.

Lenik, Edward J. *Making Pictures in Stone: American Indian Rock Art of the Northeast.* Tuscaloosa: University of Alabama Press, 2009.

Levine, Michelle. *The Delaware.* Minneapolis, MN: Lerner Publications, 2006.

— — —. *The Ojibway.* Minneapolis, MN: Lerner Publications, 2006.

Levy, Janey. *The Wampanoag of Massachusetts and Rhode Island.* New York: PowerKids Press, 2005.

Liebert, Robert. *Osage Life and Legends: Earth People/Sky People.* Happy Camp, California: Naturegraph Publishers, 1987.

Life Stories of Our Native People: Shoshone, Paiute, Washo. Reno, NV: Inter-tribal Council of Nevada, 1974.

Liptak, Karen. *North American Indian Ceremonies.* New York: Franklin Watts, 1992.

Little, Kimberley Griffiths. *The Last Snake Runner.* New York: Alfred A. Knopf, 2002.

Lloyd, J. William. *Aw-aw-tam Indian Nights: The Myths and Legends of the Pimas.* Westfield, NJ: The Lloyd Group, 1911. Available online from http://www.sacred-texts.com/nam/sw/ain/index.htm (accessed on July 20, 2011).

Lobo, Susan, Steve Talbot, and Traci L. Morris, compilers. *Native American Voices: A Reader.* 3rd ed. Upper Saddle River, NJ: Prentice Hall, 2010.

Lourie, Peter. *The Lost World of the Anasazi: Exploring the Mysteries of Chaco Canyon.* Honesdale, PA: Boyds Mills Press, 2007.

Macdougall, Brenda. *One of the Family: Metis Culture in Nineteenth-Century Northwestern Saskatchewan.* Vancouver, British Columbia: UBC Press, 2010.

Mann, John W.W. *Sacajawea's People: The Lemhi Shoshones and the Salmon River Country.* Lincoln, NE: Bison Books, 2011.

Margolin, Malcolm. *The Ohlone Way.* Berkeley, CA: Heyday Books, 1981.

— — —. *The Way We Lived: California Indian Stories, Songs, and Reminiscences.* Reprint. Heyday Books, Berkeley, California, 2001.

Marriott, Alice, and Carol K. Rachlin. *Plains Indian Mythology.* New York, NY: Thomas Y. Crowell, 1975.

Marshall, Ann, ed. *Home: Native People in the Southwest.* Phoenix, AZ: Heard Museum, 2005.

Marshall, Bonnie. *Far North Tales: Stories from the Peoples of the Arctic Circle.* Edited by Kira Van Deusen. Santa Barbara, CA: Libraries Unlimited, 2011.

Marsi, Katie. *The Trail of Tears: The Tragedy of the American Indians.* New York: Marshall Cavendish Benchmark, 2010.

McDaniel, Melissa. *Great Basin Indians.* Des Plaines, IL: Heinemann, 2011.

— — —. *The Sac and Fox Indians.* New York: Chelsea Juniors, 1995.

— — —. *Southwest Indians.* Chicago: Heinemann Library, 2012.

Mcmullen, John William. *Ge Wisnemen! (Let's Eat!): A Potawatomi Family Dinner Manual.* Charleston, SC: CreateSpace, 2011.

Melody, Michael E., and Paul Rosier. *The Apache.* Minneapolis: Chelsea House, 2005.

Merriam, C. Hart. *The Dawn of the World: Myths and Tales of the Miwok Indians of California.*Kila, MN: Kessinger Publishing, 2010.

Michael, Hauser. *Traditional Inuit Songs from the Thule Area.* Copenhagen: Museum Tusculanum Press, 2010.

Miles, Ray. "Wichita." *Native America in the Twentieth Century, An Encyclopedia.* Ed. Mary B. Davis. New York: Garland Publishing, 1994.

Miller, Debbie S., and Jon Van Dyle. *Arctic Lights, Arctic Nights.* New York: Walker Books for Young Readers, 2007.

Miller, Frederic P., Agnes F. Vandome, and John McBrewster, eds. *Nuu-chah-nulth People.* Beau Bassin, Mauritius: Alphascript Publishing, 2011.

Miller, Raymond H. *North American Indians: The Apache.* San Diego: KidHaven Press, 2005.

Milner, George R. *The Moundbuilders: Ancient Peoples of Eastern North America.* New York: Thames & Hudson, 2005.

Mooney, James. *Calendar History of the Kiowa Indians.* Whitefish, MT: Kessinger Publishing, 2006.

— — —. *Myths of the Cherokee.* New York: Dover Publications, 1996.

Mosqueda, Frank, and Vickie Leigh Krudwig. *The Hinono'ei Way of Life: An Introduction to the Arapaho People.* Edited by Susan Scott Hill. Concho, OK: Cheyenne and Arapaho Tribes of Oklahoma, 2008.

— — —. *The Prairie Thunder People: A Brief History of the Arapaho People.* Edited by Susan Scott Hill. Concho, OK: Cheyenne and Arapaho Tribes of Oklahoma, 2008.

Mossiker, Frances. *Pocahontas: The Life and the Legend.* New York: Alfred A. Knopf, 1976.

Mundell, Kathleen. *North by Northeast: Wabanaki, Akwesasne Mohawk, and Tuscarora Traditional Arts.* Gardiner, ME: Tilbury House, Publishers, 2008.

Myers, Albert Cook, ed. *William Penn's Own Account of the Lenni Lenape or Delaware Indians.* Somerset, NJ: Middle Atlantic Press, 1970.

Myers, Arthur. *The Pawnee.* New York: Franklin Watts, 1993.

Myers, James E. "Cahto." In *Handbook of North American Indians.* Vol. 8: *California,* edited by R. F. Heizer. Washington, D.C.: Smithsonian Institution, 1978: 244–48.

Neeley, Bill. *The Last Comanche Chief: The Life and Times of Quanah Parker.* New York: Wiley, 1996.

Nelson, Sharlene, and Ted W. Nelson. *The Makah.* New York: Franklin Watts, 2003.

Nez, Chester, and Judith Schiess Avila. *Code Talker.* New York: Berkley Caliber, 2011.

Nichols, Richard. *A Story to Tell: Traditions of a Tlingit Community.* Minneapolis: Lerner Publications Company, 1998.

Nowell, Charles James. *Smoke from their Fires: The Life of a Kwakiutl Chief.* Hamdon, CT: Archon Books, 1968.

O'Neale, Lila M. *Yurok-Karok Basket Weavers.* Berkeley, CA: Phoebe A. Hearst Museum of Anthropology, 2007.

Opler, Morris Edward. *Myths and Tales of the Chiricahua Apache Indians.* Charleston, SC: Kessinger Publishing, 2011.

Ortega, Simon, ed. *Handbook of North American Indians.* Vol. 12: *The Plateau.* Washington, DC: Smithsonian Institution, 1978.

Ortiz, Alfonso, ed. *Handbook of American Indians.* Vols. 9–10. *The Southwest.* Washington, DC: Smithsonian Institution, 1978–83.

Owings, Alison. *Indian Voices: Listening to Native Americans.* New Brunswick, N.J.: Rutgers University Press, 2011.

Page, Jake, and Susanne Page. *Indian Arts of the Southwest.* Tucson, AZ: Rio Nuevo Publishers, 2008.

Page, Susanne and Jake. *Navajo.* Tucson, AZ: Rio Nuevo Publishers, 2010.

Paige, Amanda L., Fuller L. Bumpers, and Daniel F. Littlefield, Jr. *Chickasaw Removal.* Ada, OK: Chickasaw Press, 2010.

Palazzo-Craig, Janet. *The Ojibwe of Michigan, Wisconsin, Minnesota, and North Dakota.* New York: PowerKids Press, 2005.

Peltier, Leonard. *Prison Writings: My Life Is My Sun Dance.* New York: St. Martin's, 2000.

Penny, Josie. *So Few on Earth: A Labrador Métis Woman Remembers.* Toronto, Ontario: Dundurn Press, 2010.

Peoples of the Arctic and Subarctic. Chicago: World Book, 2009.

Perritano, John. *Spanish Missions.* New York: Children's Press, 2010.

Philip, Neil, ed. *A Braid of Lives: Native American Childhood.* New York: Clarion Books, 2000.

Pierson, George. *The Kansa, or Kaw Indians, and Their History, and the Story of Padilla.* Charleston, SC: Nabu Press, 2010.

Pijoan, Teresa. *Pueblo Indian Wisdom: Native American Legends and Mythology.* Santa Fe: Sunstone Press, 2000.

Pritzker, Barry, and Paul C. Rosier. *The Hopi.* New York: Chelsea House, c. 2011.

Riddell, Francis A. "Maidu and Concow." *Handbook of North American Indians.* Vol. 8: *California.* Edited by Robert F. Heizer. Washington DC: Smithsonian Institution, 1978.

Rielly, Edward J. *Legends of American Indian Resistance.* Westport, CT: Greenwood, 2011.

Riordan, Robert. *Medicine for Wildcat: A Story of the Friendship between a Menominee Indian and Frontier Priest Samuel Mazzuchelli.* Revised by

Marilyn Bowers Gorun and the Sinsinawa Dominican Sisters. Sinsinawa, WI: Sinsinawa Dominican Sisters, 2006.

Rollings, Willard H. *The Comanche.* New York: Chelsea House Publications, 2004.

Rosoff, Nancy B., and Susan Kennedy Zeller. *Tipi: Heritage of the Great Plains.* Seattle: Brooklyn Museum in association with University of Washington Press, 2011.

Ruby, Robert H., John A. Brown, and Cary C. Collins. *A Guide to the Indian Tribes of the Pacific Northwest.* Norman: University of Oklahoma Press, 2010.

Russell, Frank. *The Pima Indians.* Whitefish, MT: Kessinger Publishing, 2010.

Ryan, Marla Felkins, and Linda Schmittroth. *Tribes of Native America: Zuñi Pueblo.* San Diego: Blackbirch Press, 2002.

— — —. *Ute.* San Diego: Blackbirch Press, 2003.

Rzeczkowski, Frank. *The Lakota Sioux.* New York: Chelsea House, 2011.

Seton, Ernest Thompson. *Sign Talk of the Cheyenne Indians.* Mineola, NY: Dover Publications, 2000.

Sherrow, Victoria. *The Iroquois Indians.* New York: Chelsea House, 1992.

Shipek, Florence Connolly. "Luiseño." In *Native America in the Twentieth Century: An Encyclopedia,* edited by Mary B. Davis. New York: Garland Publishing, 1994.

Shipley, William. *The Maidu Indian Myths and Stories of Hanc'Ibyjim.* Berkeley: Heyday Books, 1991.

Shull, Jodie A. *Voice of the Paiutes: A Story About Sarah Winnemucca.* Minneapolis, MN: Millbrook Press, 2007.

Simermeyer, Genevieve. *Meet Christopher: An Osage Indian Boy from Oklahoma.* Tulsa, OK: National Museum of the American Indian, Smithsonian Institution, in association with Council Oak Books, 2008.

Simmons, Marc. *Friday, the Arapaho Boy: A Story from History.* Albuquerque: University of New Mexico Press, 2004.

Sita, Lisa. *Indians of the Northeast: Traditions, History, Legends, and Life.* Milwaukee, WI: Gareth Stevens, 2000.

— — —. *Pocahontas: The Powhatan Culture and the Jamestown Colony.* New York: PowerPlus Books, 2005.

Slater, Eva. *Panamint Shoshone Basketry: An American Art Form.* Berkeley: Heyday Books, 2004.

Smith, White Mountain. *Indian Tribes of the Southwest.* Kila, MN: Kessinger Publishing, 2005.

Snell, Alma Hogan. *A Taste of Heritage: Crow Indian Recipes & Herbal Medicines.* Lincoln: University of Nebraska Press, 2006.

Sneve, Virginia Driving Hawk. *The Cherokee*. New York: Holiday House, 1996.

— — —. *The Cheyenne*. New York: Holiday House, 1996.

— — —. *The Iroquois*. New York: Holiday House, 1995.

— — —. *The Nez Percé*. New York: Holiday House, 1994.

— — —. *The Seminoles*. New York: Holiday House, 1994.

Snyder, Clifford Gene. *Ghost Trails: Mythology and Folklore of the Chickasaw, Choctaw, Creeks and Other Muskoghean Indian Tribes*. North Hollywood, CA: JES, 2009.

— — —. *The Muskogee Chronicles: Accounts of the Early Muskogee/Creek Indians*. N. Hollywood, CA: JES, 2008.

Solomon, Madeline. *Koyukon Athabaskan Songs*. Homer, AK: Wizard Works, 2003.

Sonneborn, Liz. *The Choctaws*. Minneapolis, MN: Lerner Publications, 2007.

— — —. *The Creek*. Minneapolis: Lerner Publications, 2007.

— — —. *The Chumash*. Minneapolis, MN: Lerner Publications, 2007.

— — —. *The Navajos*. Minneapolis, MN: Lerner Publications, 2007.

— — —. *Northwest Coast Indians*. Chicago: Heinemann Library, 2012.

— — —. *The Shoshones*. Minneapolis, MN: Lerner Publications, 2006.

— — —. *Wilma Mankiller*. New York: Marshall Cavendish Benchmark, 2010.

Spalding, Andrea. *Secret of the Dance*. Orca, WA: Orca Book Publishers, 2006.

Spence, Lewis. *Myths and Legends of the North American Indians*. Whitefish, MT: Kessinger Publishing, 1997.

Spragg-Braude, Stacia. *To Walk in Beauty: A Navajo Family's Journey Home*. Santa Fe: Museum of New Mexico Press, 2009.

Sprague, DonovinArleigh. *American Indian Stories*. West Stockbridge, CT: Hard Press, 2006.

— — —. *Choctaw Nation of Oklahoma*. Chicago, IL: Arcadia, 2007.

— — —. *Old Indian Legends: Retold by Zitkala--Sa*. Paris: Adamant Media Corporation, 2006.

— — —. *Standing Rock Sioux*. Charleston, SC: Arcadia, 2004.

St. Lawrence, Genevieve. *The Pueblo And Their History*. Minneapolis, MN: Compass Point Books, 2006.

Stanley, George E. *Sitting Bull: Great Sioux Hero*. New York: Sterling, 2010.

Stern, Pamela R. *Daily Life of the Inuit*. Santa Barbara, CA: Greenwood, 2010.

Sterngass, Jon. *Geronimo*. New York: Chelsea House, 2010.

Stevenson, Matilda Coxe. *The Zuñi Indians and Their Uses of Plants.* Charleston, SC: Kessinger Publishing, 2011.

Stevenson, Tilly E. *The Religious Life of the Zuñi Child.* Charleston, SC: Kessinger Publishing, 2011.

Stewart, Philip. *Osage.* Philadelphia, PA: Mason Crest Publishers, 2004.

Stirling, M.W. *Snake Bites and the Hopi Snake Dance.* Whitefish, MT: Kessinger Publishing, 2011.

Stone, Amy M. *Creek History and Culture.* Milwaukee: Gareth Stevens Publishing, 2011.

Stout, Mary. *Blackfoot History and Culture.* New York: Gareth Stevens, 2012.

———. *Hopi History and Culture.* New York: Gareth Stevens, 2011.

———. *Shoshone History and Culture.* New York: Gareth Stevens, 2011.

Strack, Andrew J. *How the Miami People Live.* Edited by Mary Tippman, Meghan Dorey and Daryl Baldwin. Oxford, OH: Myaamia Publications, 2010.

Straub, Patrick. *It Happened in South Dakota: Remarkable Events That Shaped History.* New York: Globe Pequot, 2009.

Sullivan, Cathie, and Gordon Sullivan. *Roadside Guide to Indian Ruins & Rock Art of the Southwest.* Englewood, CO: Westcliffe Publishers, 2006.

Sullivan, George. *Geronimo: Apache Renegade.* New York: Sterling, 2010.

Suttles, Wayne, and Barbara Lane. "Southern Coast Salish." *Handbook of North American Indians.* Vol. 7: *Northwest Coast.* Edited by Wayne Suttles. Washington, DC: Smithsonian Institution, 1990.

Swanton, John R., and Franz Boas. *Haida Songs; Tsimshian Texts (1912).* Vol. 3. Whitefish, MT: Kessinger Publishing, 2010.

Sweet, Jill Drayson, and Nancy Hunter Warren. *Pueblo Dancing.* Atglen, PA: Schiffer Publishing, 2011.

Tenenbaum, Joan M., and Mary Jane McGary, eds. *Denaina Sukdua: Traditional Stories of the Tanaina Athabaskans.* Fairbanks: Alaska Native Language Center, 2006.

Tiller, Veronica E. Velarde. *Culture and Customs of the Apache Indians.* Santa Barbara, CA: ABC-CLIO, 2011.

Underhill, Ruth. *The Papago Indians of Arizona and their Relatives the Pima.* Whitefish, MT: Kessinger Publishing, 2010.

Van Deusen, Kira. *Kiviuq: An Inuit Hero and His Siberian Cousins.* Montreal: McGill-Queen's University Press, 2009.

Vanderwerth, W. C. *Indian Oratory: Famous Speeches by Noted Indian Chieftains.* Norman: University of Oklahoma Press, 1979.

Vaudrin, Bill. *Tanaina Tales from Alaska.* Norman: University of Oklahoma Press, 1969.

Viola, Herman J. *Trail to Wounded Knee: The Last Stand of the Plains Indians 1860–1890.* Washington, DC: National Geographic, 2004.

Von Ahnen, Katherine. *Charlie Young Bear.* Minot, CO: Roberts Rinehart Publishers, 1994.

Wade, Mary Dodson. *Amazing Cherokee Writer Sequoyah.* Berkeley Heights, NJ: Enslow, 2009.

Wagner, Frederic C. III. *Participants in the Battle of the Little Big Horn: A Biographical Dictionary of Sioux, Cheyenne and United States Military Personnel.* Jefferson, NC: McFarland, 2011.

Waldman, Carl. "Colville Reservation." In *Encyclopedia of Native American Tribes.* New York: Facts on File, 2006.

— — —. *Encyclopedia of Native American Tribes.* New York: Facts on File, 2006.

Wallace, Mary. *The Inuksuk Book.* Toronto, Ontario: Maple Tree Press, 2004.

— — —. *Make Your Own Inuksuk.* Toronto, Ontario: Maple Tree Press, 2004.

Wallace, Susan E. *The Land of the Pueblos.* Santa Fe, NM: Sunstone Press, 2006.

Ward, Jill. *The Cherokees.* Hamilton, GA: State Standards, 2010.

— — —. *Creeks and Cherokees Today.* Hamilton, GA: State Standards, 2010.

Warm Day, Jonathan. *Taos Pueblo: Painted Stories.* Santa Fe, NM: Clear Light Publishing, 2004.

Waters, Frank. *Book of the Hopi.* New York: Viking Press, 1963.

White, Bruce. *We Are at Home: Pictures of the Ojibwe People.* St. Paul, MN: Minnesota Historical Society Press, 2007.

White, Tekla N. *San Francisco Bay Area Missions.* Minneapolis, MN: Lerner, 2007.

Whitehead, Ruth Holmes. *The Micmac: How Their Ancestors Lived Five Hundred Years Ago.* Halifax, Nova Scotia: Nimbus, 1983.

Whiteman, Funston, Michael Bell, and Vickie Leigh Krudwig. *The Cheyenne Journey: An Introduction to the Cheyenne People.* Edited by Susan Scott-Hill. Concho, OK: Cheyenne and Arapaho Tribes of Oklahoma, 2008.

— — —. *The Tsististas: People of the Plains.* Edited by Susan Scott-Hill. Concho, OK: Cheyenne and Arapaho Tribes of Oklahoma, 2008.

Wiggins, Linda E., ed. *Dena—The People: The Way of Life of the Alaskan Athabaskans Described in Nonfiction Stories, Biographies, and Impressions from All Over the Interior of Alaska.* Fairbanks: Theata Magazine, University of Alaska, 1978.

Wilcox, Charlotte. *The Iroquois.* Minneapolis, MN: Lerner Publishing Company, 2007.

— — —. *The Seminoles.* Minneapolis: Lerner Publications, 2007.

Wilds, Mary C. *The Creek.* San Diego, CA: Lucent Books, 2005.

Wiles, Sara. *Arapaho Journeys: Photographs and Stories from the Wind River Reservation.* Norman: University of Oklahoma Press, 2011.

Williams, Jack S. *The Luiseno of California.* New York: PowerKids Press, 2003.

— — —. *The Modoc of California and Oregon.* New York: PowerKids Press, 2004.

— — —. *The Mojave of California and Arizona.* New York: PowerKids Press, 2004.

Wilson, Darryl J. *The Morning the Sun Went Down.* Berkeley, CA: Heyday, 1998.

Wilson, Elijah Nicholas. *The White Indian Boy: The Story of Uncle Nick among the Shoshones.* Kila, MN: Kessinger Publishing, 2004.

Wilson, Frazer Ells. *The Peace of Mad Anthony: An Account of the Subjugation of the Northwestern Indian Tribes and the Treaty of Greeneville.* Kila, MN: Kessinger Publishing, 2005.

Wilson, Norman L., and Arlean H. Towne. "Nisenan." In *Handbook of North American Indians.* Vol. 8: *California.* Edited by Robert F. Heizer. Washington DC: Smithsonian Institution, 1978.

Winnemucca, Sarah. *Life among the Paiutes: Their Wrongs and Claims.* Privately printed, 1883. Reprint. Reno: University of Nevada Press, 1994.

Wolcott, Harry F. *A Kwakiutl Village and School.* Walnut Creek, CA: AltaMira Press, 2003.

Wolfson, Evelyn. *The Iroquois: People of the Northeast.* Brookfield, CT: The Millbrook Press, 1992.

Woolworth, Alan R. *Santee Dakota Indian Tales.* Saint Paul, MN: Prairie Smoke Press, 2003.

Worl, Rosita. *Celebration: Tlingit, Haida, Tsimshian Dancing on the Land.* Edited by Kathy Dye. Seattle: University of Washington Press, 2008.

Wright, Muriel H. *A Guide to the Indian Tribes of Oklahoma.* Norman: University of Oklahoma Press, 1951.

Wyborny, Sheila. *North American Indians: Native Americans of the Southwest.* San Diego: KidHaven Press, 2004.

Wynecoop, David C. *Children of the Sun: A History of the Spokane Indians.* Wellpinit, WA, 1969. Available online from http://www.wellpinit.wednet.edu/shorthistory (accessed on August 11, 2011).

Wyss, Thelma Hatch. *Bear Dancer: The Story of a Ute Girl.* Chicago: Margaret K. McElderry Books, 2010.

Zepeda, Ofelia. *Where Clouds Are Formed: Poems.* Tucson: University of Arizona Press, 2008.

Zigmond, Maurice L. *Kawaiisu Mythology: An Oral Tradition of South-Central California.* Banning, CA: Malki-Ballena Press, 1980.

———. "Kawaiisu." In *Handbook of North American Indians, Great Basin.* Vol. 11. Edited by Warren L. D'Azavedo. Washington, DC: Smithsonian Institution, 1981, pp. 398–411.

Zimmerman, Dwight Jon. *Tecumseh: Shooting Star of the Shawnee.* New York: Sterling, 2010.

Zitkala-Sa, Cathy N. Davidson, and Ada Norris. *American Indian Stories, Legends, and Other Writings.* New York: Penguin, 2003.

Periodicals

Barrett, Samuel Alfred, and Edward Winslow Gifford. "Miwok Material Culture: Indian Life of the Yosemite Region" *Bulletin of Milwaukee Public Museum* 2, no. 4 (March 1933).

Barringer, Felicity. "Indians Join Fight for an Oklahoma Lake's Flow." *New York Times.* April 12, 2011, A1. Available online from http://www.nytimes.com/2011/04/12/science/earth/12water.html (accessed on June 18, 2011).

Beck, Melinda. "The Lost Worlds of Ancient America." *Newsweek* 118 (Fall–Winter 1991): 24.

Bourke, John Gregory. "General Crook in the Indian Country." *The Century Magazine,* March 1891. Available online from http://www.discoverseaz.com/History/General_Crook.html (accessed on July 20, 2011).

Bruchac, Joseph. "Otstango: A Mohawk Village in 1491," *National Geographic* 180, no. 4 (October 1991): 68–83.

Carroll, Susan. "Tribe Fights Kitt Peak Project." *The Arizona Republic.* March 24, 2005. Available online at http://www.nathpo.org/News/Sacred_Sites/News-Sacred_Sites109.htm (accessed on July 20, 2011).

Chief Joseph. "An Indian's View of Indian Affairs." *North American Review* 128, no. 269 (April 1879): 412–33.

Collins, Cary C., ed. "Henry Sicade's History of Puyallup Indian School, 1860 to 1920." *Columbia* 14, no. 4 (Winter 2001–02).

Dalsbø, E.T., "'We Were Told We Were Going to Live in Houses': Relocation and Housing of the Mushuau Innu of Natuashish from 1948 to 2003." *University of Tromsø,* May 28, 2010. Available from http://www.ub.uit.no/munin/bitstream/handle/10037/2739/thesis.pdf?sequence=3 (accessed on May 26, 2011).

Dixon, Roland B. "Achomawi and Atsugewi Tales." *Journal of American Folklore* 21. (1908): 159–77.

Dold, Catherine. "American Cannibal." *Discover* 19, no. 2 (February 1998): 64.

Duara, Nigel. "Descendants Make Amends to Chinook for Lewis and Clark Canoe Theft." *Missourian.* (September 23, 2011). Available online from http://www.columbiamissourian.com/stories/2011/09/23/descendants-make-amends-chinook-lewis-clark-canoe-theft/ (accessed on November 2, 2011).

Elliott, Jack. "Dawn, Nov. 28, 1729: Gunfire Heralds Natchez Massacre." *Concordia Sentinel.* November 5, 2009. Available from http://www.concordiasentinel.com/news.php?id=4321 (accessed on June 27, 2011).

Eskin, Leah. "Teens Take Charge. (Suicide Epidemic at Wind River Reservation)." *Scholastic Update,* May 26, 1989: 26.

Et-twaii-lish, Marjorie Waheneka. "Indian Perspectives on Food and Culture." *Oregon Historical Quarterly,* Fall 2005.

Griswold, Eliza. "A Teen's Third-World America." *Newsweek.* December 26, 2010. Available online from http://www.thedailybeast.com/articles/2010/12/26/a-boys-third-world-america.html (accessed on July 20, 2011).

ICTMN Staff. "Washoe Tribe's Cave Rock a No-go for Bike Path" *Indian Country Today Media Network,* February 10, 2011. Available online at http://indiancountrytodaymedianetwork.com/2011/02/washoe-tribes-cave-rock-a-no-go-for-bike-path/ (accessed on August 15, 2011).

Johnston, Moira. "Canada's Queen Charlotte Islands: Homeland of the Haida." *National Geographic,* July 1987: 102–27.

Jones, Malcolm Jr., with Ray Sawhill. "Just Too Good to Be True: Another Reason to Beware False Eco-Prophets." *Newsweek.* (May 4, 1992). Available online at http://www.synaptic.bc.ca/ejournal/newsweek.htm (accessed on November 2, 2011).

June-Friesen, Katy. "An Ancestry of African-Native Americans." *Smithsonian.* February 17, 2010. Available online from http://www.smithsonianmag.com/history-archaeology/An-Ancestry-of-African-Native-Americans.html#ixzz1RN1pyiD1 (accessed on June 21, 2011).

Kowinski, William Severini. "Giving New Life to Haida Art and the Culture It Expresses." *Smithsonian,* January 1995: 38.

Kroeber, A. L. "Two Myths of the Mission Indians." *Journal of the American Folk-Lore Society* 19, no. 75 (1906): 309–21. Available online at http://www.sacred-texts.com/nam/ca/tmmi/index.htm (accessed on August 11, 2011).

Lake, Robert, Jr. "The Chilula Indians of California." *Indian Historian* 12, no. 3 (1979): 14–26. Available online from http://www.eric.ed.gov/ERICWebPortal/search/detailmini.jsp?_nfpb=true&_&ERICExtSearch_SearchValue_0=EJ214907&ERICExtSearch_SearchType_0=no&accno=EJ214907

Parks, Ron. "Selecting a Suitable Country for the Kanza." *The Kansas Free Press.* June 1, 2011. Available online from http://www.kansasfreepress.com/2011/06/selecting-a-suitable-country-for-the-kanza.html (accessed on June 17, 2011).

Rezendes, Michael. "Few Tribes Share Casino Windfall." *Globe.* December 11, 2000. Available online from http://indianfiles.serveftp.com/TribalIssues/Few%20tribes%20share%20casino%20windfall.pdf (accessed on July 4, 2011).

Roy, Prodipto, and Della M. Walker. "Assimilation of the Spokane Indians." *Washington Agricultural Experiment Station Bulletin.* No. 628.

Pullman: Washington State University, Institute of Agricultural Science, 1961.

Shaffrey, Mary M. "Lumbee Get a Win, But Not without Stipulation." *Winston-Salem Journal* (April 26, 2007).

Shapley, Thomas. "Historical Revision Rights a Wrong." *Seattle Post-Intelligencer.* (December 18, 2004). Available online from http://www.seattlepi.com/local/opinion/article/Historical-revision-rights-a-wrong-1162234.php#ixzz1WBFxoNiw (accessed on August 15, 2011).

"Q: Should Scientists Be Allowed to 'Study' the Skeletons of Ancient American Indians?" (Symposium: U.S. Representative Doc Hastings; Confederated Tribes of the Umatilla Indian Reservation Spokesman Donald Sampson). *Insight on the News* 13, no. 47 (December 22, 1997): 24.

Siegel, Lee. "Mummies Might Have Been Made by Anasazi." *Salt Lake Tribune,* April 2, 1998.

Stewart, Kenneth M. "Mohave Warfare." *Southwestern Journal of Anthropology* 3, no. 3 (Autumn 1947): 257–78.

Trivedi, Bijal P. "Ancient Timbers Reveal Secrets of Anasazi Builders." *National Geographic Today,* September 28, 2001. Available online at http://news.nationalgeographic.com/news/2001/09/0928_TVchaco.html (accessed on June 29, 2007).

Trumbauer, Sophie. "Northwest Tribes Canoe to Lummi Island." *The Daily.* (August 1, 2007). Available online at http://thedaily.washington.edu/article/2007/8/1/northwestTribesCanoeToLumm (accessed on November 2, 2011).

Van Meter, David. "Energy Efficient." *University of Texas at Arlington,* Fall 2006.

Wagner, Dennis. "Stolen Artifacts Shatter Ancient Culture." *The Arizona Republic,* November 12, 2006.

Warshall, Peter. "The Heart of Genuine Sadness: Astronomers, Politicians, and Federal Employees Desecrate the Holiest Mountain of the San Carlos Apache." *Whole Earth* 91 (Winter 1997): 30.

Win, WambliSina. "The Ultimate Expression of Faith, the Lakota Sun Dance." *Native American Times.* July 4, 2011. Available online from http://www.nativetimes.com/index.php?option=com_content&view=article&id=5657:the-ultimate-expression-of-faith-the-lakota-sun-dance&catid=46&Itemid=22 (accessed on July 4, 2011).

Web Sites

"Aboriginal Fisheries Strategy." *Fisheries and Oceans Canada.* http://www.dfo-mpo.gc.ca/fm-gp/aboriginal-autochtones/afs-srapa-eng.htm (accessed on August 15, 2011).

"Aboriginal Peoples: The Métis." *Newfoundland and Labrador Heritage.* http://www.heritage.nf.ca/aboriginal/metis.html (accessed on August 4, 2011).

"About the Hopi." Restoration. http://hopi.org/about-the-hopi/ (accessed on July 20, 2011).

"Acoma Pueblo." *ClayHound Web.* http://www.clayhound.us/sites/acoma.htm (accessed on July 20, 2011).

"Acoma Pueblo." *New Mexico Magazine.* http://www.nmmagazine.com/native_american/acoma.php (accessed on July 20, 2011).

"Acoma 'Sky City'" *National Trust for Historic Preservation.* http://www.acomaskycity.org/ (accessed on July 20, 2011).

"Address of Tarhe, Grand Sachem of the Wyandot Nation, to the Assemblage at the Treaty of Greeneville, July 22, 1795." *Wyandotte Nation of Oklahoma.* http://www.wyandotte-nation.org/history/tarhe_greenville_address.html (accessed May 12, 2011).

"The Adena Mounds." *Grave Creek Mound State Park.* http://www.adena.com/adena/ad/ad01.htm (accessed June 7, 2011).

Adley-SantaMaria, Bernadette. "White Mountain Apache Language Issues." *Northern Arizona University.* http://www2.nau.edu/jar/TIL_12.html (accessed on July 20, 2011).

Akimoff, Tim. "Snowshoe Builders Display Their Craft at the Anchorage Museum." *KTUU.* May 5, 2011. http://www.ktuu.com/news/ktuu-snowshoe-builders-display-their-craft-at-the-anchorage-museum-20110505,0,7760220.story (accessed on June 6, 2011).

Alamo Chapter. http://alamo.nndes.org/ (accessed on July 20, 2011).

Alaska Native Collections. *Smithsonian Institution.* http://alaska.si.edu/cultures.asp (accessed on August 15, 2011).

— — —. "Unangan." *Smithsonian Institution.* http://alaska.si.edu/culture_unangan.asp (accessed on August 15, 2011).

"Alaska Native Language Center." *University of Alaska Fairbanks.* http://www.uaf.edu/anlc//anlc/languages/ (accessed on June 4, 2011).

Alaska Yup'ik Eskimo. http://www.yupik.com (accessed on August 15, 2011).

All Indian Pueblo Council. http://www.20pueblos.org/ (accessed on July 20, 2011).

Allen, Cain. "The Oregon History Project: Toby Winema Riddle." *Oregon Historical Society.* http://www.ohs.org/education/oregonhistory/historical_records/dspDocument.cfm?doc_ID=000A9FE3-B226-1EE8-827980B05272FE9F (accessed on August 11, 2011).

"Alutiiq and Aleut/Unangan History and Culture." *Anchorage Museum.* http://www.anchoragemuseum.org/galleries/alaska_gallery/aleut.aspx (accessed on August 15, 2011).

Aluttiq Museum. http://alutiiqmuseum.org/ (accessed on August 15, 2011).

"Anasazi: The Ancient Ones." *Manitou Cliff Dwellings Museum.* http://www.cliffdwellingsmuseum.com/anasazi.htm (accessed on July 20, 2011).

"Anasazi Heritage Center: Ancestral Pueblos." *Bureau of Land Management Colorado.* http://www.co.blm.gov/ahc/anasazi.htm (accessed on July 13, 2011).

"The Anasazi or 'Ancient Pueblo.'" *Northern Arizona University.* http://www.cpluhna.nau.edu/People/anasazi.htm (accessed on July 20, 2011).

"Ancient Architects of the Mississippi." *National Park Service, Department of the Interior.* http://www.cr.nps.gov/archeology/feature/feature.htm (accessed on July 10, 2007).

"Ancient DNA from the Ohio Hopewell." *Ohio Archaeology Blog,* June 22, 2006. http://ohio-archaeology.blogspot.com/2006/06/ancient-dna-from-ohio-hopewell.html (accessed on July 10, 2007).

"Ancient Moundbuilders of Arkansas." *University of Arkansas.* http://cast.uark.edu/home/research/archaeology-and-historic-preservation/archaeological-interpretation/ancient-moundbuilders-of-arkansas.html (accessed on June 10, 2011).

"Ancient One: Kennewick Man." *Confederated Tribes of the Umatilla Reservation.* http://www.umatilla.nsn.us/ancient.html (accessed on August 11, 2011).

Anderson, Jeff. "Arapaho Online Research Resources." *Colby College.* http://www.colby.edu/personal/j/jdanders/arapahoresearch.htm (accessed on July 2, 2011).

"Anishinaabe Chi-Naaknigewin/Anishinabek Nation Constitution." *Anishinabek Nation.* http://www.anishinabek.ca/uploads/ANConstitution.pdf (accessed on May 16, 2011).

"Antelope Valley Indian Peoples: The Late Prehistoric Period: Kawaiisu." *Antelope Valley Indian Museum.* http://www.avim.parks.ca.gov/people/ph_kawaiisu.shtml (accessed on August 15, 2011).

"Apache Indian History." *Access Genealogy.* http://www.accessgenealogy.com/native/tribes/apache/apachehist.htm (accessed on July 15, 2011).

"Apache Indians." *AAA Native Arts.* http://www.aaanativearts.com/apache (accessed on July 15, 2011).

"Apache Nation: Nde Nation." *San Carlos Apache Nation.* http://www.sancarlosapache.com/home.htm (accessed on July 15, 2011).

"Apache Tribal Nation." *Dreams of the Great Earth Changes.* http://www.greatdreams.com/apache/apache-tribe.htm (accessed on July 15, 2011).

"The Apsáalooke (Crow Indians) of Montana Tribal Histories." *Little Big Horn College.* http://lib.lbhc.edu/history/ (accessed on July 5, 2011).

Aquino, Pauline. "Ohkay Owingeh: Village of the Strong People" (video). *New Mexico State Record Center and Archives.* http://www.newmexicohistory.org/filedetails.php?fileID=22530 (accessed on July 20, 2011).

"The Arapaho Tribe." *Omaha Public Library.* http://www.omahapubliclibrary.org/transmiss/congress/arapaho.html (accessed on July 2, 2011).

Arctic Circle. http://arcticcircle.uconn.edu/Museum/ (accessed on June 10, 2011).

"Arctic Circle." *University of Connecticut.* http://arcticcircle.uconn.edu/VirtualClassroom/ (accessed on August 15, 2011).

"The Arctic Is…." *Stefansson Arctic Institute.* http://www.thearctic.is/ (accessed on August 15, 2011).

Arctic Library. "Inuit" *Athropolis.* http://www.athropolis.com/library-cat.htm#inuit (accessed on August 15, 2011).

"Arikira Indians." *PBS.* http://www.pbs.org/lewisandclark/native/ari.html (accessed on June 19, 2011).

"Arkansas Indians: Arkansas Archeological Survey." *University of Arkansas.* http://www.uark.edu/campus-resources/archinfo/ArkansasIndianTribes.pdf (accessed on June 12, 2011).

Arlee, Johnny. *Over a Century of Moving to the Drum: Salish Indian Celebrations on the Flathead Reservation.* Helena: Montana Historical Society Press, 1998. Available online from http://www.archive.org/stream/historicalsketch00ronarich/historicalsketch00ronarich_djvu.txt (accessed on August 11, 2011).

Armstrong, Kerry M. "Chickasaw Historical Research Page." *Chickasaw History.* http://www.chickasawhistory.com/ (accessed on June 16, 2011.

"Art on the Prairies: Otoe-Missouria." *The Bata Shoe Museum.* http://www.allaboutshoes.ca/en/paths_across/art_on_prairies/index_7.php (accessed on June 20, 2011).

"Assiniboin Indian History." *Access Genealogy.* http://www.accessgenealogy.com/native/tribes/assiniboin/assiniboinhist.htm (accessed on June 7, 2011).

"Assinboin Indians." *PBS.* http://www.pbs.org/lewisandclark/native/idx_ass.html (accessed on June 7, 2011).

"Assiniboine History." *Fort Belknap Indian Community.* http://www.ftbelknap-nsn.gov/assiniboineHistory.php (accessed on June 6, 2011).

"Athabascan." Alaska Native Heritage Center Museum. http://www.alaskanative.net/en/main_nav/education/culture_alaska/athabascan/ (accessed on June 6, 2011).

Banyacya, Thomas. "Message to the World." *Hopi Traditional Elder.* http://banyacya.indigenousnative.org/ (accessed on July 20, 2011).

Barnett, Jim. "The Natchez Indians." *History Now.* http://mshistory.k12.ms.us/index.php?id=4 (accessed on June 27, 2011).

Barry, Paul C. "Native America Nations and Languages: Haudenosaunee." *The Canku Ota—A Newsletter Celebrating Native America.* http://www.turtletrack.org/Links/NANations/CO_NANationLinks_HJ.htm (accessed on June 5, 2011).

"Before the White Man Came to Nisqually Country." *Washington History Online.* January 12, 2006. http://washingtonhistoryonline.org/treatytrail/teaching/before-white-man.pdf (accessed on August 15, 2011).

Big Valley Band of Pomo Indians. http://www.big-valley.net/index.htm (accessed on August 11, 2011).

Bishop Paiute Tribe. http://www.bishoppaiutetribe.com/ (accessed on August 15, 2011).

"Black Kettle." *PBS.* http://www.pbs.org/weta/thewest/people/a_c/blackkettle.htm (accessed on July 4, 2011).

"Blackfeet." *Wisdom of the Elders.* http://www.wisdomoftheelders.org/program208.html (accessed on July 2, 2011).

"Blackfoot History." *Head-Smashed-In Buffalo Jump Interpretive Centre.* http://www.head-smashed-in.com/black.html (accessed on July 2, 2011).

Blackfeet Nation. http://www.blackfeetnation.com/ (accessed on July 2, 2011).

Boyer, Ruth McDonald, and Narcissus Duffy Gayton. "Apache Mothers and Daughters: Four Generations of a Family. Remembrances of an Apache Elder Woman." *Southwest Crossroads.* http://southwestcrossroads.org/record.php?num=825&hl=Apache (accessed on July 20, 2011).

British Columbia Archives. "First Nations Research Guide." *Royal BC Museum Corporation.* http://www.royalbcmuseum.bc.ca/BC_Research_Guide/BC_First_Nations.aspx (accessed on August 15, 2011).

Bruchac, Joe. "Storytelling." *Abenaki Nation.* http://www.abenakination.org/stories.html (accessed on June 5, 2011).

Brush, Rebecca. "The Wichita Indians." *Texas Indians.* http://www.texasindians.com/wichita.htm (accessed on June 9, 2011).

"Caddo Indian History." *Access Genealogy.* http://www.accessgenealogy.com/native/tribes/caddo/caddohist.htm (accessed on June 12, 2011).

"Cahto (Kato)." *Four Directions Institute.* http://www.fourdir.com/cahto.htm (accessed on August 11, 2011).

"Cahto Tribe Information Network." *Cahto Tribe.* http://www.cahto.org/ (accessed on August 11, 2011).

"Cahuilla." *Four Directions Institute.* http://www.fourdir.com/cahuilla.htm (accessed on August 11, 2011).

Cahuilla Band of Mission Indians. http://cahuillabandofindians.com/ (accessed on August 11, 2011).

"California Indians." *Visalia Unified School District.* http://visalia.k12.ca.us/teachers/tlieberman/indians/ (accessed on August 15, 2011).

California Valley Miwok Tribe, California. http://www.californiavalleymiwoktribe-nsn.gov/ (accessed on August 11, 2011).

Cambra, Rosemary, et al. "The Muwekma Ohlone Tribe of the San Francisco Bay Area." http://www.islaiscreek.org/ohlonehistcultfedrecog.html (accessed on August 11, 2011).

"Camp Grant Massacre—April 30, 1871." *Council of Indian Nations.* http://www.nrcprograms.org/site/PageServer?pagename=cin_hist_campgrantmassacre (accessed on July 20, 2011).

Campbell, Grant. "The Rock Paintings of the Chumash." *Association for Humanistic Psychology.* http://www.ahpweb.org/articles/chumash.html (accessed on August 11, 2011).

Canadian Heritage Information Network. "Communities& Institutions: Talented Youth." *Tipatshimuna.* http://www.tipatshimuna.ca/1420_e.php (accessed on May 19, 2011).

Carleton, Kenneth H. "A Brief History of the Mississippi Band of Choctaw Indians." *Mississippi Band of Choctaw.* http://mdah.state.ms.us/hpres/A%20Brief%20History%20of%20the%20Choctaw.pdf (accessed on June 12, 2011).

Central Council: Tlingit and Haida Indian Tribes of Alaska. http://www.ccthita.org/ (accessed on November 2, 2011).

Cherokee Nation. http://www.cherokee.org/ (accessed on June 12, 2011).

"Cheyenne Indian." *American Indian Tribes.* http://www.cheyenneindian.com/cheyenne_links.htm (accessed on July 4, 2011).

"Cheyenne Indian History." *Access Genealogy.* http://www.accessgenealogy.com/native/tribes/cheyenne/cheyennehist.htm (accessed on July 4, 2011).

"Chickasaw Indian History." *Access Genealogy.* http://www.accessgenealogy.com/native/tribes/chickasaw/chickasawhist.htm (accessed on June 16, 2011).

The Chickasaw Nation. http://www.chickasaw.net (accessed on June 12, 2011).

"Chief Joseph." *PBS.* http://www.pbs.org/weta/thewest/people/a_c/chiefjoseph.htm (accessed on August 11, 2011).

"Chief Joseph Surrenders." *The History Place.* http://www.historyplace.com/speeches/joseph.htm (accessed on August 11,2011).

Chief Leschi School. http://www.leschischools.org/ (accessed on November 2, 2011).

"Chief Seattle Speech." *Washington State Library.* http://www.synaptic.bc.ca/ejournal/wslibrry.htm (accessed on November 2, 2011).

"The Children of Changing Woman." *Peabody Museum of Archaeology and Ethnology.* http://www.peabody.harvard.edu/maria/Cwoman.html (accessed on July 15, 2011).

"The Chilula." *The Indians of the Redwoods.* http://www.cr.nps.gov/history/online_books/redw/history1c.htm (accessed on August 11, 2011).

Chinook Indian Tribe/Chinook Nation. http://www.chinooknation.org/ (accessed on November 2, 2011).

"Chinookan Family History." *Access Genealogy.* http://www.accessgenealogy.com/native/tribes/chinook/chinookanfamilyhist.htm (accessed on November 2, 2011).

"Chippewa Cree Tribe (Neiyahwahk)." *Montana Office of Indian Affairs.* http://www.tribalnations.mt.gov/chippewacree.asp (accessed on June 3, 2011).

"Chiricahua Indian History." *Access Genealogy.* http://www.accessgenealogy. com/native/tribes/apache/chiricahua.htm (accessed on July 20, 2011).

Chisolm, D. "Mi'kmaq Resource Centre," *Cape Breton University.*http://mrc. uccb.ns.ca/mikmaq.html (accessed on May 15, 2011).

"Choctaw Indian History." *Access Genealogy.* http://www.accessgenealogy.com/ native/tribes/choctaw/chostawhist.htm (accessed on June 21, 2011).

"Choctaw Indian Tribe." *Native American Nations.* http://www.nanations.com/ choctaw/index.htm (accessed on June 21, 2011).

Choctaw Nation of Oklahoma. http://www.choctawnation.com (accessed on June 12, 2011).

"Chumash." *Four Directions Institute.* http://www.fourdir.com/chumash.htm (accessed on December 1, 2011).

The Chumash Indians. http://www.chumashindian.com/ (accessed on August 11, 2011).

Clark, William. "Lewis and Clark: Expedition Journals." *National Geographic.* http://www.nationalgeographic.com/lewisandclark/record_tribes_020_5_1. html (accessed on June 19, 2011).

———. "Lewis and Clark: Missouri Indians." *National Geographic.* http:// www.nationalgeographic.com/lewisandclark/record_tribes_012_1_9.html (accessed on June 20, 2011).

"Coast Miwok at Point Reyes." *U.S. National Park Service.* http://www.nps. gov/pore/historyculture/people_coastmiwok.htm (accessed on August 11, 2011).

"Coastal Miwok Indians." *Reed Union School District.* http://rusd.marin. k12.ca.us/belaire/ba_3rd_miwoks/coastalmiwoks/webpages/home. html(accessed on August 11, 2011).

"Comanche." *Edward S. Curtis's The North American Indian.* http://curtis. library.northwestern.edu/curtis/toc.cgi (accessed on July 4, 2011).

"Comanche Indian History." *Access Genealogy.* http://www.accessgenealogy. com/native/tribes/comanche/comanchehist.htm (accessed on July 4, 2011).

"Comanche Language." *Omniglot.* http://www.omniglot.com/writing/coman-che.htm (accessed on July 4, 2011).

Comanche Nation of Oklahoma http://www.comanchenation.com/ (accessed on July 4, 2011).

"Community News." *Mississippi Band of Choctaw Indians.* http://www.choctaw. org/ (accessed on June 12, 2011).

Compton, W. J. "The Story of Ishi, the Yana Indian." *Ye Slyvan Archer.* July 1936. http://tmuss.tripod.com/shotfrompast/chief.htm (accessed on August 11, 2011).

The Confederated Salish and Kootenai Tribes. http://www.cskt.org/ (accessed on August 11, 2011).

U•X•L Encyclopedia of Native American Tribes, 3rd Edition

Confederated Tribes and Bands of the Yakama Nation. http://www.yakamanation-nsn.gov/ (accessed on August 11, 2011).

Confederated Tribes of the Colville Reservation. http://www.colvilletribes.com/ (accessed on August 11, 2011).

Confederated Tribes of Siletz. http://ctsi.nsn.us/ (accessed on November 2, 2011).

Confederated Tribes of the Umatilla Indian Reservation. http://www.umatilla.nsn.us/ (accessed on August 11, 2011).

"Confederated Tribes of the Umatilla Indians." *Wisdom of the Elders.* http://www.wisdomoftheelders.org/program305.html (accessed on August 11, 2011).

"Confederated Tribes of the Yakama Nation." *Wisdom of the Elders.* http://www.wisdomoftheelders.org/program304.html (accessed on August 11, 2011).

"Connecting the World with Seattle's First People."*Duwamish Tribe.* http://www.duwamishtribe.org/ (accessed on November 2, 2011).

Conrad, Jim. "The Natchez Indians." *The Loess Hills of the Lower Mississipi Valley.* http://www.backyardnature.net/loess/ind_natz.htm (accessed on June 27, 2011).

Cordell, Linda. "Anasazi." *Scholastic.* http://www2.scholastic.com/browse/article.jsp?id=5042 (accessed on July 20, 2011).

"Costanoan Indian Tribe." *Access Genealogy.* http://www.accessgenealogy.com/native/tribes/costanoan/costanoanindiantribe.htm (accessed on August 11, 2011).

Costanoan Rumsen Carmel Tribe. http://costanoanrumsen.org/ (accessed on August 11, 2011).

"Costanoan Rumsen Carmel Tribe: History." *Native Web.* http://crc.nativeweb.org/history.html (accessed on August 11, 2011).

Cotton, Lee. "Powhatan Indian Lifeways." *National Park Service.* http://www.nps.gov/jame/historyculture/powhatan-indian-lifeways.htm (accessed on June 1, 2011).

Council of the Haida Nation (CHN). http://www.haidanation.ca/ (accessed on November 2, 2011).

"A Coyote's Tales—Tohono O'odham." *First People: American Indian Legends.* http://www.firstpeople.us/FP-Html-Legends/A_Coyotes_Tales-TohonoOodham.html (accessed on July 20, 2011).

"Creek Indian." *American Indian Tribe.* http://www.creekindian.com/ (accessed on June 12, 2011).

"Creek Indians." *GeorgiaInfo.* http://georgiainfo.galileo.usg.edu/creek.htm (accessed on June 12, 2011).

"Crow/Cheyenne." *Wisdom of the Elders.* http://www.wisdomoftheelders.org/program206.html (accessed on July 5, 2011).

"Crow Indian Tribe." *Access Genealogy.* http://www.accessgenealogy.com/native/tribes/crow/crowhist.htm (accessed on July 5, 2011).

Crow Tribe, Apsáalooke Nation Official Website. http://www.crowtribe.com/ (accessed on July 5, 2011).

"Culture and History."*Innu Nation.*http://www.innu.ca/index.php?option=com_content&view=article&id=8&Itemid=3&lang=en (accessed on May 19, 2011).

"Culture& History." *Aleut Corporation.* http://www.aleutcorp.com/index.php?option=com_content&view=section&layout=blog&id=6&Itemid=24 (accessed on August 15, 2011).

"Culture and History of the Skokomish Tribe." *Skokomish Tribal Nation.* http://www.skokomish.org/historyculture.htm (accessed on November 2, 2011).

Curtis, Edward S. *The North American Indian.*Vol.13. 1924. Reprint. New York: Johnson Reprint Corporation, 1970. Available online from *Northwestern University Digital Library Collections.* http://curtis.library.northwestern.edu/curtis/viewPage.cgi?showp=1&size=2&id=nai.13.book.00000192&volume=13#nav-Edward (accessed on August 11, 2011).

"Dakota Indian Tribe History." *Access Genealogy.* http://www.accessgenealogy.com/native/tribes/siouan/dakotahist.htm (accessed on July 5, 2011).

"Dakota Spirituality." *Blue Cloud Abbey.* http://www.bluecloud.org/dakotaspirituality.html (accessed on July 5, 2011).

"Dams of the Columbia Basin and Their Effects on the Native Fishery." *Center for Columbia River History.* http://www.ccrh.org/comm/river/dams6.htm (accessed on August 11, 2011).

Deans, James. "Tales from the Totems of the Hidery." *Early Canadiana Online.* http://www.canadiana.org/ECO/PageView/06053/0003?id=986858ca5fbdc633 (accessed on November 2, 2011).

Deer Lake First Nation. http://www.deerlake.firstnation.ca/ (accessed on June 5, 2011).

"Delaware Indian Chiefs." *Access Genealogy.* http://www.accessgenealogy.com/native/tribes/delaware/delawarechiefs.htm (accessed on June 8, 2011).

"Delaware Indian/Lenni Lenape." *Delaware Indians of Pennsylvania.* http://www.delawareindians.com/ (accessed on June 8, 2011).

"Delaware Indians." *Ohio Historical Society.* http://www.ohiohistorycentral.org/entry.php?rec=584 (accessed on June 2, 2011).

The Delaware Nation. http://www.delawarenation.com/ (accessed on June 2, 2011).

Delaware Tribe of Indians. http://www.delawaretribeofindians.nsn.us/ (accessed on June 2, 2011).

DelawareIndian.com. http://www.delawareindian.com/ (accessed on June 2, 2011).

Dene Cultural Institute. http://www.deneculture.org/ (accessed on June 10, 2011).

Deschenes, Bruno. "Inuit Throat-Singing." *Musical Traditions.* http://www.mustrad.org.uk/articles/inuit.htm (accessed on August 15, 2011).

"Desert Native Americans: Mohave Indians." *Mojave Desert.* http://mojavedesert.net/mojave-indians/ (accessed on July 20, 2011).

Dodds, Lissa Guimarães. "'The Washoe People': Past and Present." *Washoe Tribe of Nevada and California.* http://www.Washoetribe.us/images/Washoe_tribe_history_v2.pdf (accessed on August 15, 2011).

"Duwamish Indian Tribe History." *Access Genealogy.* http://www.accessgenealogy.com/native/tribes/salish/duwamishhist.htm (accessed on November 2, 2011).

"The Early History and Names of the Arapaho." *Native American Nations.* http://www.nanations.com/early_arapaho.htm (accessed on July 2, 2011).

Eastern Shawnee Tribe of Oklahoma. http://estoo-nsn.gov/ (accessed on June 12, 2011).

Eck, Pam. "Hopi Indians." *Indiana University.* http://inkido.indiana.edu/w310work/romac/hopi.htm (accessed on July 20, 2011).

Edward S. Curtis's The North American Indian. http://curtis.library.northwestern.edu/curtis/toc.cgi (accessed on August 11, 2011).

Elam, Earl H. "Wichita Indians." *Texas State Historical Association.* http://www.tshaonline.org/handbook/online/articles/bmw03 (accessed on June 9, 2011).

Ely Shoshone Tribe. http://elyshoshonetribe-nsn.gov/departments.html (accessed on August 15, 2011).

Etienne-Gray, Tracé. "Black Seminole Indians." *Texas State Historical Association.* http://www.tshaonline.org/handbook/online/articles/bmb18 (accessed on June 12, 2011).

Everett, Diana. "Apache Tribe of Oklahoma." *Oklahoma Historical Society.* http://digital.library.okstate.edu/encyclopedia/entries/A/AP002.html(accessed on July 15, 2011).

"Eyak, Tlingit, Haida, and Tsimshian." *Alaska Native Heritage Center Museum.* http://www.alaskanative.net/en/main_nav/education/culture_alaska/eyak/ (accessed on August 15, 2011).

Fausz, J. Frederick. "The Louisiana Expansion: The Arikara." *University of Missouri–St. Louis.* http://www.umsl.edu/continuinged/louisiana/Am_Indians/8-Arikara/8-arikara.html (accessed on June 19, 2011).

———. "The Louisiana Expansion: The Kansa/Kaw." *University of Missouri-St. Louis.* http://www.umsl.edu/continuinged/louisiana/Am_Indians/3-Kansa_Kaw/3-kansa_kaw.html (accessed on June 17, 2011).

———. "The Louisiana Expansion: The Missouri/Missouria." *University of Missouri–St. Louis.* http://www.umsl.edu/continuinged/louisiana/Am_Indians/2-Missouria/2-missouria.html (accessed on June 20, 2011).

— — —. "The Louisiana Expansion: The Oto(e)." *University of Missouri-St. Louis.* http://www.umsl.edu/continuinged/louisiana/Am_Indians/4-Oto/4-oto.html (accessed on June 20, 2011).

Feller, Walter. "California Indian History." *Digital Desert.* http://mojavedesert.net/california-indian-history/ (accessed on August 11, 2011).

— — —. "Mojave Desert Indians: Cahuilla Indians." *Digital-Desert.* http://mojavedesert.net/cahuilla-indians/ (accessed on August 11, 2011).

"First Nations: People of the Interior." *British Columbia Archives.* http://www.bcarchives.gov.bc.ca/exhibits/timemach/galler07/frames/int_peop.htm (accessed on August 11, 2011).

"First Peoples of Canada: Communal Hunters." *Canadian Museum of Civilization.* http://www.civilization.ca/cmc/home (accessed on June 10, 2011).

"Flathead Indians (Salish)." *National Geographic.* http://www.nationalgeographic.com/lewisandclark/record_tribes_022_12_16.html (accessed on August 11, 2011).

"Flathead Reservation." http://www.montanatribes.org/links_&_resources/tribes/Flathead_Reservation.pdf (accessed on August 11, 2011).

Flora, Stephenie. "Northwest Indians: 'The First People.'" *Oregon Pioneers.* http://www.oregonpioneers.com/indian.htm (accessed on August 15, 2011).

Forest County Potawatomi. http://www.fcpotawatomi.com/ (accessed on June 5, 2011).

Fort McDowell Yavapai Nation. http://www.ftmcdowell.org/ (accessed on July 20, 2011).

"Fort Mojave Indian Tribe." *Inter Tribal Council of Arizona, Inc.* http://www.itcaonline.com/tribes_mojave.html (accessed on July 20, 2011).

Fort Peck Tribes. http://www.fortpecktribes.org/ (accessed on June 4, 2011).

Fort Sill Apache Tribe. http://www.fortsillapache.com (accessed on July 20, 2011).

"Fort Yuma-Quechan Tribe." *Inter-Tribal Council of Arizona, Inc.* http://www.itcaonline.com/tribes_quechan.html (accessed on July 20, 2011).

Gangnier, Gary. "The History of the Innu Nation." *Central Quebec School Board.* http://www.cqsb.qc.ca/svs/434/fninnu.htm (accessed on May 24, 2011).

Gerke, Sarah Bohl. "White Mountain Apache." *Arizona State University.* http://grandcanyonhistory.clas.asu.edu/history_nativecultures_whitemountainapache.html (accessed on July 20, 2011).

"Geronimo, His Own Story: A Prisoner of War." *From Revolution to Reconstruction.* http://www.let.rug.nl/usa/B/geronimo/geroni17.htm (accessed on July 20, 2011).

"Gifting and Feasting in the Northwest Coast Potlatch." *Peabody Museum of Archaeology and Ethnology.* http://www.peabody.harvard.edu/potlatch/ (accessed on November 2, 2011).

Glenn Black Laboratory of Archaeology. "Burial Mounds." *Indiana University.* http://www.gbl.indiana.edu/abstracts/adena/mounds.html (accessed June 7, 2011).

— — —. "The Ohio Valley-Great Lakes Ethnohistory Archives: The Miami Collection." *Indiana University.* http://gbl.indiana.edu/ethnohistory/archives/menu.html (accessed on June 7, 2011).

Glover, William B. "A History of the Caddo Indians." Formatted for the World Wide Web by Jay Salsburg. Reprinted from *The Louisiana Historical Quarterly,* 18, no. 4 (October 1935). http://ops.tamu.edu/x075bb/caddo/Indians.html (accessed on June 12, 2011).

GoodTracks, Jimm. "These Native Ways." *Turtle Island Storytellers Network.* http://www.turtleislandstorytellers.net/tis_kansas/transcript01_jg_tracks.htm (accessed on June 20, 2011).

"Grand Village of the Natchez Indians." *Mississippi Department of Archives and History.* http://mdah.state.ms.us/hprop/gvni.html (accessed on June 27, 2011).

Great Basin Indian Archives. http://www.gbcnv.edu/gbia/index.htm (accessed on August 15, 2011).

Great Basin National Park. "Historic Tribes of the Great Basin." *National Park Service: U.S. Department of the Interior.* http://www.nps.gov/grba/historyculture/historic-tribes-of-the-great-basin.htm (accessed on August 15, 2011).

Greene, Candace S. "Kiowa Drawings." *National Anthropological Archives, National Museum of Natural History.* http://www.nmnh.si.edu/naa/kiowa/kiowa.htm (accessed on July 4, 2011).

"Haida." *The Kids' Site of Canadian Settlement, Library and Archives Canada.* http://www.collectionscanada.ca/settlement/kids/021013-2061-e.html (accessed on November 2, 2011).

"Haida Heritage Center at Qay'llnagaay." *Haida Heritage Centre.* http://www.haidaheritagecentre.com/ (accessed on November 2, 2011).

"Haida Language Program." *Sealaska Heritage Institute.* http://www.sealaskaheritage.org/programs/haida_language_program.htm (accessed on November 2, 2011).

"Haida Spirits of the Sea." *Virtual Museum of Canada.* http://www.virtualmuseum.ca/Exhibitions/Haida/nojava/english/home/index.html (accessed on November 2, 2011).

Handbook of American Indians. "Arikara Indian Tribe History." *Access Genealogy.* http://www.accessgenealogy.com/native/tribes/nations/arikara.htm (accessed on June 19, 2011).

Handbook of American Indians.. "Quapaw Indian Tribe History." *Access Genealogy.* http://www.accessgenealogy.com/native/tribes/quapaw/quapawhist.htm (accessed on June 20, 2011).

"History—Incident at Wounded Knee." *U.S. Marshals Service.* http://www.usmarshals.gov/history/wounded-knee/index.html (accessed on July 4, 2011).

"History: We Are the Anishnaabek." *The Grand Traverse Band of Ottawa and Chippewa.* http://www.gtbindians.org/history.html (accessed May 13, 2011).

"History and Culture." *Cherokee North Carolina.* http://www.cherokee-nc.com/history_intro.php (accessed on June 12, 2011).

"A History of American Indians in California." *National Park Service.* http://www.nps.gov/history/history/online_books/5views/5views1.htm (accessed on August 15, 2011).

"History of Northern Ute Indian, Utah." *Online Utah.* http://www.onlineutah.com/utehistorynorthern.shtml (accessed on August 15, 2011).

"History of the Confederated Tribes of the Siletz Indians." *HeeHeeIllahee RV Resort.* http://www.heeheeillahee.com/html/about_tribe_history.htm (accessed on November 2, 2011).

Hollabaugh, Mark. "Brief History of the Lakota People." *Normandale Community College.* http://faculty.normandale.edu/-physics/Hollabaugh/Lakota/BriefHistory.htm (accessed on July 4, 2011).

Holt, Ronald L. "Paiute Indians." *State of Utah.* http://historytogo.utah.gov/utah_chapters/american_indians/paiuteindians.html (accessed on August 15, 2011).

Holzman, Allan. "Beyond the Mesas [video]." *University of Illinois.* http://www.vimeo.com/16872541 (accessed on July 20, 2011).

———. "The Indian Boarding School Experience [video]." *University of Illinois.* http://www.vimeo.com/17410552 (accessed on July 20, 2011).

Hoopa Tribal Museum and San Francisco State University. http://bss.sfsu.edu/calstudies/hupa/Hoopa.HTM (accessed on August 11, 2011).

Hoopa Valley Tribe. http://www.hoopa-nsn.gov/ (accessed on August 11, 2011).

"Hopi." *Four Directions Institute.* http://www.fourdir.com/hopi.htm (accessed on July 20, 2011).

"Hopi." *Southwest Crossroads.* http://southwestcrossroads.org/search.php?query=hopi&tab=document&doc_view=10 (accessed on July 20, 2011).

"Hopi Indian Tribal History." *Access Genealogy.* www.accessgenealogy.com/native/tribes/hopi/hopeindianhist.htm (accessed on July 20, 2011).

"Hopi Tribe." *Inter Tribal Council of Arizona, Inc.* http://www.itcaonline.com/tribes_hopi.html (accessed on July 20, 2011).

"Hupa." *Four Directions Institute.* http://www.fourdir.com/hupa.htm (accessed on August 11, 2011).

"Hupa Indian Tribe." *Access Genealogy.* http://www.accessgenealogy.com/native/tribes/athapascan/hupaindiantribe.htm (accessed on August 11, 2011).

Huron-Wendat Nation. http://www.wendake.com/ (accessed May 12, 2011).

Hurst, Winston. "Anasazi." *Utah History to Go: State of Utah.* http://historytogo.utah.gov/utah_chapters/american_indians/anasazi.html (accessed on July 20, 2011).

Indian Country Diaries. "Trail of Tears." *PBS.* http://www.pbs.org/indiancountry/history/trail.html (accessed on June 12, 2011).

"Indian Peoples of the Northern Great Plains." *MSU Libraries.* http://www.lib.montana.edu/epubs/nadb/ (accessed on July 1, 2011).

Indian Pueblo Cultural Center. http://www.indianpueblo.org/ (accessed on July 20, 2011).

"Indian Tribes of California." *Access Genealogy.* http://www.accessgenealogy.com/native/california/ (accessed on August 11, 2011).

"Indians of the Northwest—Plateau and Coastal." *St. Joseph School Library.* http://library.stjosephsea.org/plateau.htm (accessed on August 11, 2011).

"Innu Youth Film Project." *Kamestastin.* http://www.kamestastin.com/ (accessed on May 24, 2011).

"The Inuit." *Newfoundland and Labrador Heritage.* http://www.heritage.nf.ca/aboriginal/inuit.html (accessed on August 15, 2011).

"Jemez Pueblos." *Four Directions Institute.* http://www.fourdir.com/jemez.htm (accessed on July 20, 2011).

"Jemez Pueblo." *New Mexico Magazine.* http://www.nmmagazine.com/native_american/jemez.php (accessed on July 20, 2011).

Jicarilla Apache Nation. http://www.jicarillaonline.com/ (accessed on July 15, 2011).

Johnson, Russ. "The Mississippian Period (900 AD to 1550 AD)" *Memphis History.* http://www.memphishistory.org/Beginnings/PreMemphis/MississippianCulture/tabid/64/Default.aspx (accessed June 7, 2011).

"The Journals of the Lewis and Clark Expedition: Nez Percé." *University of Nebraska.* http://www.nationalgeographic.com/lewisandclark/record_tribes_013_12_17.html (accessed on August 11, 2011).

Jozhe, Benedict. "A Brief History of the Fort Sill Apache Tribe." *Oklahoma Historical Society.* http://digital.library.okstate.edu/Chronicles/v039/v039p427.pdf (accessed on July 20, 2011).

"Kansa (Kaw)." *Four Directions Institute.* http://www.fourdir.com/kaw.htm (accessed on June 17, 2011).

"Kanza Cultural History." *The Kaw Nation.* http://kawnation.com/?page_id=216 (accessed on June 17, 2011).

"Kansa Indian Tribe History." *Access Geneology.* http://www.accessgenealogy. com/native/tribes/siouan/kansahist.htm (accessed on June 17, 2011).

Kavanagh, Thomas W. "Comanche." *Oklahoma Historical Society.* http://digital. library.okstate.edu/encyclopedia/entries/C/CO033.html (accessed on July 4, 2011).

— — —. "Reading Historic Photographs: Photographers of the Pawnee." *Indiana University.* http://php.indiana.edu/~tkavanag/phothana.html (accessed on July 6, 2011).

"Kawaiisu." *Four Directions Institute.* http://www.fourdir.com/Kawaiisu.htm (accessed on August 15, 2011).

"The Kawaiisu Culture." *Digital Desert: Mojave Desert.* http://mojavedesert.net/ kawaiisu-indians/related-pages.html (accessed on August 15, 2011).

Kawaiisu Language and Cultural Center. http://www.kawaiisu.org/KLCC_ home.html (accessed on August 15, 2011).

Kawno, Kenji. "Warriors: Navajo Code Talkers." *Southwest Crossroads.* http:// southwestcrossroads.org/record.php?num=387 (accessed on July 20, 2011).

Kidwell, Clara Sue. "Choctaw." *Oklahoma Historical Society.* http://digital. library.okstate.edu/encyclopedia/entries/C/CH047.html (accessed on June 21, 2011).

"Kiowa Indian Tribe History." *Access Genealogy.* http://www.accessgenealogy. com/native/tribes/kiowa/kiowahist.htm (accessed on July 4, 2011).

"Kiowa Indian Tribe." *Kansas Genealogy.* http://www.kansasgenealogy.com/ indians/kiowa_indian_tribe.htm(accessed on July 4, 2011).

*Kiowa Tribe.*http://www.kiowatribe.org/(accessed on July 4, 2011).

Kitt Peak National Observatory. "Tohono O'odham." *Association of Universities for Research in Astronomy.* http://www.noao.edu/outreach/kptour/kpno_ tohono.html (accessed on July 20, 2011).

"Kwakiutl." *Four Directions Institute.* http://www.fourdir.com/kwakiutl.htm (accessed on November 2, 2011).

Kwakiutl Indian Band. http://www.kwakiutl.bc.ca/ (accessed on November 2, 2011).

"Lakota, Dakota, Nakota—The Great Sioux Nation." *Legends of America.* http://www.legendsofamerica.com/na-sioux.html (accessed on July 4, 2011).

"Lakota Page: The Great Sioux Nation." *Ancestry.com.* http://freepages.genealogy. rootsweb.ancestry.com/~nativeamericangen/page6.html (accessed on July 4, 2011).

"Lakota-Teton Sioux." *Wisdom of the Elders.* http://www.wisdomoftheelders. org/program203.html (accessed on July 4, 2011).

Larry, Mitchell. *The Native Blog.* http://nativeblog.typepad.com/the_potawatomitracks_blog/potawatomi_news/index.html (accessed on June 5, 2011).

"Leschi: Last Chief of the Nisquallies." *WashingtonHistoryOnline.* http:// washingtonhistoryonline.org/leschi/leschi.htm (accessed on August 15, 2011).

"Lewis & Clark: Chinook Indians." *National Geographic.* http://www. nationalgeographic.com/lewisandclark/record_tribes_083_14_3.html (accessed on November 2, 2011).

"Lewis and Clark: Crow Indians (Absaroka)." *National Geographic Society.* http://www.nationalgeographic.com/lewisandclark/record_tribes_002_19_21.html (accessed on July 5, 2011).

"Lewis and Clark: Native Americans: Chinook Indians." *PBS.* http://www.pbs. org/lewisandclark/native/chi.html (accessed on November 2, 2011).

"Lewis & Clark: Tribes: Siletz Indians." *National Geographic.* http://www. nationalgeographic.com/lewisandclark/record_tribes_090_14_8.html (accessed on November 2, 2011).

"Lewis & Clark: Yankton Sioux Indians (Nakota)." *National Geographic.* http:// www.nationalgeographic.com/lewisandclark/record_tribes_019_2_8.html (accessed on June 12, 2011).

Lewis, J.D. "The Natchez Indians." *Carolina—The Native Americans.* http:// www.carolana.com/Carolina/Native_Americans/native_americans_natchez. html (accessed on June 27, 2011).

Lipscomb, Carol A. "Handbook of Texas Online: Comanche Indians." *Texas State Historical Association.* http://www.tshaonline.org/handbook/online/articles/bmc72 (accessed on July 4, 2011).

"The Long Walk." *Council of Indian Nations.* http://www.nrcprograms.org/site/PageServer?pagename=cin_hist_thelongwalk (accessed on July 20, 2011).

"Luiseño." *Four Directions Institute.* http://www.fourdir.com/luiseno.htm (accessed on August 11, 2011).

"Luiseno/Cahuilla Group." *San Francisco State University.* http://bss.sfsu.edu/calstudies/nativewebpages/luiseno.html (accessed on August 11, 2011).

"Lumbee History & Culture." *Lumbee Tribe of North Carolina.* http:// www.lumbeetribe.com/History_Culture/History_Culture%20Index. html(accessed on June 4, 2011).

"Métis: History & Culture." *Turtle Island Productions.* http://www.turtle-island. com/native/the-ojibway-story/metis.html (accessed on June 4, 2011).

Métis Nation of Ontario. http://www.metisnation.org/ (accessed on June 4, 2011).

MacDonald, George F. "The Haida: Children of Eagle and Raven." *Canadian Museum of Civilization.* http://www.civilization.ca/cmc/exhibitions/aborig/haida/haindexe.shtml (accessed on November 2, 2011).

"Maidu." *Four Directions Institute.* http://www.fourdir.com/maidu.htm (accessed on August 11, 2011).

"The Maidu." *The First Americans.* http://thefirstamericans.homestead.com/Maidu.html (accessed on August 11, 2011).

"Maidu People." *City of Roseville.* http://www.roseville.ca.us/parks/parks_n_facilities/facilities/maidu_indian_museum/maidu_people.asp (accessed on August 11, 2011).

Makah Cultural and Research Center. http://www.makah.com/mcrchome.html (accessed on November 2, 2011).

The Makah Nation on Washington's Olympic Peninsula. http://www.northolympic.com/makah/ (accessed on November 2, 2011).

Manning, June. "Wampanoag Living." *Martha's Vineyard Magazine.* May–June 2010. http://www.mvmagazine.com/article.php?25216 (accessed on June 9, 2011).

Mashantucket Museum and Research Center. http://www.pequotmuseum.org/ (accessed on June 1, 2011).

Mashpee Wampanoag Tribe. http://mashpeewampanoagtribe.com/ (accessed on June 1, 2011).

"Massacre at Wounded Knee, 1890." *EyeWitness to History.* http://www.eyewitnesstohistory.com/knee.htm (accessed on July 4, 2011).

"Massai, Chiricahua Apache." *Discover Southeast Arizona.* http://www.discoverseaz.com/History/Massai.html (accessed on July 20, 2011).

May, John D. "Otoe-Missouria." *Oklahoma Historical Society.* http://digital.library.okstate.edu/encyclopedia/entries/O/OT001.html (accessed on June 20, 2011).

McCollum, Timothy James. "Quapaw." *Oklahoma Historical Society.* http://digital.library.okstate.edu/encyclopedia/entries/Q/QU003.html (accessed on June 20, 2011).

———. "Sac and Fox." *Oklahoma Historical Society.* http://digital.library.okstate.edu/encyclopedia/entries/S/SA001.html (accessed on June 5, 2011).

McCoy, Ron. "Neosho Valley: Osage Nation." *KTWU/Channel 11.* http://ktwu.washburn.edu/journeys/scripts/1111a.html (accessed on June 12, 2011).

McManamon, F. P. "Kennewick Man." *Archaeology Program, National Park Service, U.S. Department of the Interior.* http://www.nps.gov/archeology/kennewick/index.htm (accessed on August 11, 2011).

Media Action. "Excerpt from Youth-led Interview with Phillip Esai." *Vimeo.* http://vimeo.com/15465119 (accessed on June 6, 2011).

———. "A Portrait of Nikolai." *Vimeo.* 2010. http://vimeo.com/14854233 (accessed on June 6, 2011).

"Menominee Culture." *Menominee Indian Tribe of Wisconsin.* http://www.mpm.edu/wirp/ICW-54.html (accessed on June 7, 2011).

"Menominee Indian Tribe of Wisconsin." *Great Lakes Inter-Tribal Council.* http://www.glitc.org/programs/pages/mtw.html (accessed on June 7, 2011).

Menominee Indian Tribe of Wisconsin. http://www.menominee-nsn.gov/ (accessed June 8, 2011).

"Menominee Oral Tradition." *Indian Country.* http://www.mpm.edu/wirp/ICW-138.html (accessed on June 7, 2011).

Mescalero Apache Reservation. www.mescaleroapache.com/ (accessed on July 15, 2011).

"Metis Communities." *Labrador Métis Nation.* http://www.labradormetis.ca/home/10 (accessed on June 4, 2011).

"Miami Indian Tribe." *Native American Nations.* http://www.nanations.com/miami/index.htm (accessed on June 7, 2011).

"Miami Indians." *Ohio History Central.* http://www.ohiohistorycentral.org/entry.php?rec=606 (accessed on June 7, 2011).

Miami Nation of Oklahoma. http://www.miamination.com/ (accessed on June 7, 2011).

Miccosukee Seminole Nation. http://www.miccosukeeseminolenation.com/ (accessed on June 12, 2011).

"Mi'kmaq Resources" *Halifax Public Libraries.* http://www.halifaxpublicli-braries.ca/research/topics/mikmaqresources.html (accessed on June 1, 2011).

Mississippi Valley Archaeology Center at the University of Wisconsin–La Crosse, "Early Cultures: Pre-European Peoples of Wisconsin: Mississippian and Oneota Traditions." *Educational Web Adventures.* http://www.uwlax.edu/mvac/preeuropeanpeople/earlycultures/mississippi_tradition.html (accessed on June 20, 2011).

"Missouri Indian Tribe History." *Access Genealogy.* http://www.accessgenealogy.com/native/tribes/siouan/missourihist.htm (accessed on June 20, 2011).

"Missouri Indians." *PBS.* http://www.pbs.org/lewisandclark/native/mis.html (accessed on June 20, 2011).

"Miwok." *Four Directions Institute.* http://www.fourdir.com/miwok.htm (accessed on August 11, 2011).

Miwok Archeological Preserve of Marin. "The Miwok People." *California State Parks.* http://www.parks.ca.gov/default.asp?page_id=22538 (accessed on August 11, 2011).

"Miwok Indian Tribe History." *Access Genealogy.* http://www.accessgeneal-ogy.com/native/california/miwokindianhist.htm (accessed on August 11, 2011).

"Modoc." *College of the Siskiyous.* http://www.siskiyous.edu/shasta/nat/mod.htm (accessed on August 11, 2011).

"Modoc." *Four Directions Institute.* http://www.fourdir.com/modoc.htm (accessed on August 11, 2011).

"Modoc Indian Chiefs and Leaders." *Access Genealogy.* (accessed on August 11, 2011). http://www.accessgenealogy.com/native/tribes/modoc/modocindianchiefs.htm

Modoc Tribe of Oklahoma. http://www.modoctribe.net/ (accessed on August 11, 2011).

"Mohave Indian Tribe History." *Access Genealogy.* http://www.accessgenealogy.com/native/tribes/mohave/mohaveindianhist.htm (accessed on July 20, 2011).

"Mohave National Preserve: Mohave Tribe: Culture." *National Park Service.* http://www.nps.gov/moja/historyculture/mojave-culture.htm (accessed on July 20, 2011).

"The Mohawk Tribe." *Mohawk Nation.* http://www.mohawktribe.com/ (accessed on June 7, 2011).

Montana Arts Council. "From the Heart and Hand: Salish Songs and Dances: Johnny Arlee, Arlee/John T., Big Crane, Pablo." *Montana Official State Website.* http://art.mt.gov/folklife/hearthand/songs.asp (accessed on August 11, 2011).

Morris, Allen. "Seminole History." *Florida Division of Historical Resources.* http://www.flheritage.com/facts/history/seminole/ (accessed on June 12, 2011).

Muscogee (Creek) Nation of Oklahoma. http://www.muscogeenation-nsn.gov/ (accessed on June 12, 2011).

Museum of the Aleutians.. http://www.aleutians.org/index.html (accessed on August 15, 2011).

Mussulman, Joseph. "Osage Indians." *The Lewis and Clark Fort Mandan Foundation.* http://lewis-clark.org/content/content-article.asp?ArticleID=2535 (accessed on June 12, 2011).

Muwekma Ohlone Tribe. http://www.muwekma.org/ (accessed on August 11, 2011).

The Myaamia Project at Miami University. http://www.myaamiaproject.com/ (accessed on June 7, 2011).

Myers, Tom. "Navajo Reservation" (video). *University of Illinois.* http://www.vimeo.com/8828354 (accessed on July 20, 2011).

Nametau Innu. "Your First Steps in the Innu Culture." *Musée Régional de la Côte-Nord.* http://www.nametauinnu.ca/en/tour (accessed on May 26, 2011).

Narragansett Indian Tribe. http://www.narragansett-tribe.org/ (accessed on June 1, 2011).

"Natchez Indian Tribe History." *Access Geneology.* http://www.accessgenealogy.com/native/tribes/natchez/natchezhist.htm (accessed on June 27, 2011).

Natchez Nation. http://www.natchez-nation.com/ (accessed on June 27, 2011).

"Natchez Stories." *Sacred Texts*. http://www.sacred-texts.com/nam/se/mtsi/#section_004 (accessed on June 27, 2011).

National Library for the Environment. "Native Americans and the Environment: Great Basin." *National Council for Science and the Environment.* http://www.cnie.org/nae/basin.html (accessed on August 15, 2011).

National Museum of American History—Smithsonian Institution. "Pueblo Resistance: We Are Here." *Mexico State Record Center and Archives.* http://www.newmexicohistory.org/filedetails.php?fileID=23042 (accessed on July 20, 2011).

National Museum of the American Indian. "Central Plains." *Smithsonian.* http://americanindian.si.edu/searchcollections/results.aspx?regid=58 (accessed on July 4, 2011).

— — —. "Prairie." *Smithsonian.* http://americanindian.si.edu/searchcollections/results.aspx?regid=60 (accessed on June 12, 2011).

— — —. "Southern Plains." *Smithsonian.* http://americanindian.si.edu/searchcollections/results.aspx?regid=61 (accessed on June 20, 2011).

"Native Americans: Osage Tribe." *University of Missouri.* http://ethemes.missouri.edu/themes/1608?locale=en (accessed on June 12, 2011).

"Navajo (Diné)." *Northern Arizona University.* http://www.cpluhna.nau.edu/People/navajo.htm (accessed on July 20, 2011).

Navajo Indian Tribes History. *Access Genealogy.* http://www.accessgenealogy.com/native/tribes/navajo/navahoindianhist.htm (accessed on July 20, 2011).

The Navajo Nation. http://www.navajo-nsn.gov/history.htm (accessed on July 31, 2007).

"Nde Nation." *Chiricahua: Apache Nation.* http://www.chiricahuaapache.org/ (accessed on July 20, 2011).

"New Hampshire's Native American Heritage." *New Hampshire State Council on the Arts.* http://www.nh.gov/folklife/learning/traditions_native_americans.htm (accessed on June 5, 2011).

"Nez Percé." *Countries and Their Culture.* http://www.everyculture.com/multi/Le-Pa/Nez-Perc.html (accessed on August 11, 2011).

"Nez Percé (Nimiipuu) Tribe." *Wisdom of the Elders.* http://www.wisdomoftheelders.org/program303.html (accessed on August 11, 2011).

"Nez Percé National Historical Park." *National Park Service.* http://www.nps.gov/nepe/ (accessed on August 11, 2011).

Nez Percé Tribe. http://www.nezperce.org/ (accessed on August 11, 2011).

"Nisqually Indian Tribe, Washington." *United States History.* http://www.u-s-history.com/pages/h1561.html (accessed on August 15, 2011).

Nisqually Land Trust. http://www.nisquallylandtrust.org (accessed on August 15, 2011).

"NOAA Arctic Theme Page." *National Oceanic and Atmospheric Administration.* http://www.arctic.noaa.gov/ (accessed on August 15, 2011).

"Nohwike Bagowa: House of Our Footprints" *White Mountain Apache Tribe Culture Center and Museum.* http://www.wmat.us/wmaculture.shtml (accessed on July 20, 2011).

"Nootka Indian Music of the Pacific North West Coast." *Smithsonian Folkways.* http://www.folkways.si.edu/albumdetails.aspx?itemid=912 (accessed on August 15, 2011).

Northern Arapaho Tribe. http://www.northernarapaho.com/ (accessed on July 2, 2011).

Northern Cheyenne Nation. www.cheyennenation.com/ (accessed on July 4, 2011).

"Northwest Coastal People." *Canada's First Peoples.* http://firstpeoplesofcanada.com/fp_groups/fp_nwc5.html (accessed on August 15, 2011).

"Nuu-chah-nulth." *Royal British Columbia Museum.* http://www.royalbcmuseum.bc.ca/Content_Files/Files/SchoolsAndKids/nuu2.pdf (accessed on August 15, 2011).

"Nuu-chah-nulth (Barkley) Community Portal." *FirstVoices.* http://www.firstvoices.ca/en/Nuu-chah-nulth (accessed on August 15, 2011).

Nuu-chah-nulth Tribal Council. http://www.nuuchahnulth.org/tribal-council/welcome.html(accessed on August 15, 2011).

"Official Site of the Miami Nation of Indians of the State of Indiana." *Miami Nation of Indians.* http://www.miamiindians.org/ (accessed on June 7, 2011).

Official Site of the Wichita and Affiliated Tribes. http://www.wichitatribe.com/ (accessed on June 9, 2011).

Official Website of the Caddo Nation. http://www.caddonation-nsn.gov/ (accessed on June 12, 2011).

Ohio History Central. "Adena Mound." *Ohio Historical Society.* http://www.ohiohistorycentral.org/entry.php?rec=2411 (accessed June 7, 2011).

"Ohkay Owingeh." *Indian Pueblo Cultural Center.* http://www.indianpueblo.org/19pueblos/ohkayowingeh.html (accessed on July 20, 2011).

*Ohlone/Costanoan Esselen Nation.*http://www.ohlonecostanoanesselennation.org/(accessed on August 11, 2011).

Oklahoma Humanities Council. "Otoe-Missouria Tribe." *Cherokee Strip Museum.* http://www.cherokee-strip-museum.org/Otoe/OM_Who.htm (accessed on June 20, 2011).

Oklahoma Indian Affairs Commission. "2011 Oklahoma Indian Nations." *Pocket Pictorial Directory.* Oklahoma City: Oklahoma Indian Affairs Commission, 2011. Available from http://www.ok.gov/oiac/documents/2011.FINAL.WEB.pdf (accessed on June 12, 2011).

The Oregon History Project. "Modoc." *Oregon Historical Society.* http://www.ohs.org/education/oregonhistory/search/dspResults.cfm?keyword=Modoc&type=&theme=&timePeriod=&region= (accessed on August 11, 2011).

U•X•L Encyclopedia of Native American Tribes, 3rd Edition

"The Osage." *Fort Scott National Historic Site, National Park Service.*http://www.nps.gov/fosc/historyculture/osage.htm (accessed on June 12, 2011).

Osage Nation. http://www.osagetribe.com/ (accessed on June 12, 2011).

"Osage Indian Tribe History." *Access Genealogy.* http://www.accessgenealogy.com/native/tribes/osage/osagehist.htm (accessed on June 12, 2011).

The Otoe-Missouria Tribe. http://www.omtribe.org/ (accessed on June 20, 2011).

Ottawa Inuit Children's Centre. http://www.ottawainuitchildrens.com/eng/ (accessed on August 15, 2011).

Ottawa Tribe of Oklahoma. http://www.ottawatribe.org/history.htm (accessed May 13, 2011).

"Our History." *Makah Cultural and Research Center.* http://www.makah.com/history.html (accessed on November 2, 2011).

"Pacific Northwest Native Americans." *Social Studies School Service.* http://nativeamericans.mrdonn.org/northwest.html (accessed on August 15, 2011).

Paiute Indian Tribe of Utah. http://www.utahpaiutes.org/ (accessed on August 15, 2011).

The Pascua Yaqui Tribe. http://www.pascuayaqui-nsn.gov/ (accessed on July 20, 2011).

"The Pasqu Yaqui Connection." *Through Our Parents' Eyes: History and Culture of Southern Arizona.* http://parentseyes.arizona.edu/pascuayaquiaz/ (accessed on July 20, 2011).

"Past and Future Meet in San Juan Pueblo Solar Project." *Solar Cookers International.* http://solarcooking.org/sanjuan1.htm (accessed on July 20, 2011).

Pastore, Ralph T. "Aboriginal Peoples: Newfoundland and Labrador Heritage." *Memorial University of Newfoundland.* http://www.heritage.nf.ca/aboriginal/ (accessed on August 15, 2011).

Paul, Daniel N. "We Were Not the Savages."*First Nation History.* http://www.danielnpaul.com/index.html (accessed on June 1, 2011).

"Pawnee." *Four Directions Institute.* http://www.fourdir.com/pawnee.htm (accessed on July 6, 2011).

"Pawnee Indian Museum." *Kansas State Historical Society.* http://www.kshs.org/places/pawneeindian/history.htm (accessed on July 6, 2011).

"Pawnee Indian Tribe History." *Access Genealogy.* http://www.accessgenealogy.com/native/tribes/pawnee/pawneehist.htm (accessed on July 6, 2011).

Pawnee Nation of Oklahoma. http://www.pawneenation.org/ (accessed on July 6, 2011).

"Pecos Indian Tribe History." *Access Genealogy.* http://www.accessgenealogy.com/native/tribes/pecos/pecoshist.htm(accessed on July 20, 2011).

"Pecos National Historical Park." *Desert USA.* http://www.desertusa.com/pecos/pnpark.html (accessed on July 20, 2011).

"Pecos Pueblos." *Four Directions Institute.* http://www.fourdir.com/pecos.htm (accessed on July 20, 2011).

"People of Pecos." *National Park Service.* http://www.nps.gov/peco/historyculture/peple-of-pecos.htm (accessed on July 20, 2011).

"People of the Colorado Plateau: The Hopi." *Northern Arizona University.* http://www.cpluhna.nau.edu/People/hopi.htm (accessed on July 20, 2011).

"People of the Colorado Plateau: The Ute Indian." *Northern Arizona University.* http://cpluhna.nau.edu/People/ute_indians.htm(accessed on August 15, 2011).

"The People of the Flathead Nation."*Lake County Directory.* http://www.lakecodirect.com/archives/The_Flathead_Nation.html (accessed on August 11, 2011).

"Peoples of Alaska and Northeast Siberia." *Alaska Native Collections.* http://alaska.si.edu/cultures.asp (accessed on August 15, 2011).

"Pequot Lives: Almost Vanished." *Pequot Museum and Research Center.* http://www.pequotmuseum.org/Home/MashantucketGallery/AlmostVanished.htm (accessed June 8, 2011).

Peterson, Keith C. "Dams of the Columbia Basin and Their Effects of the Native Fishery." *Center for Columbia River History.* http://www.ccrh.org/comm/river/dams7.htm (accessed on August 11, 2011).

Peterson, Leighton C. "Tuning in to Navajo: The Role of Radio in Native Language Maintenance." *Northern Arizona University.* http://jan.ucc.nau.edu/-jar/TIL_17.html (accessed on July 20, 2011).

"Pima (AkimelO'odham)." *Four Directions Institute.* http://www.fourdir.com/pima.htm (accessed on July 20, 2011).

"Pima Indian Tribe History." *Access Genealogy.* www.accessgenealogy.com/native/tribes/pima/pimaindianhist.htm (accessed on July 20, 2011).

Pit River Indian Tribe. http://www.pitrivertribe.org/home.php (accessed on August 11, 2011).

"Pomo People: Brief History." *Native American Art.* http://www.kstrom.net/isk/art/basket/pomohist.html (accessed on August 11, 2011).

Porter, Tom. "Mohawk (Haudenosaunee) Teaching." *FourDirectionsTeachings.com.* http://www.fourdirectionsteachings.com/transcripts/mohawk.html (accessed June 7, 2011).

"Powhatan Indian Village." *Acton Public Schools: Acton-Boxborough Regional School District.* http://ab.mec.edu/jamestown/powhatan (accessed on June 1, 2011).

"Powhatan Language and the Powhatan Indian Tribe (Powatan, Powhatten, Powhattan)." *Native Languages of the Americas: Preserving and Promoting Indigenous American Indian Languages.* http://www.native-languages.org/powhatan.htm (accessed on on June 1, 2011).

"Preserving Sacred Wisdom." *Native Spirit and the Sun Dance Way.* http://www.nativespiritinfo.com/ (accessed on July 5, 2011).

"Pueblo Indian History and Resources." *Pueblo Indian.* http://www.puebloindian.com/ (accessed on July 20, 2011).

Pueblo of Acoma. http://www.puebloofacoma.org/ (accessed on July 20, 2011).

Pueblo of Jemez. http://www.jemezpueblo.org/ (accessed on July 20, 2011).

Pueblo of Zuñi. http://www.ashiwi.org/(accessed on July 20, 2011).

Puyallup Tribe of Indians. http://www.puyallup-tribe.com/ (accessed on November 2, 2011).

Quapaw Tribe of Oklahoma. http://www.quapawtribe.com/ (accessed on June 20, 2011).

"The Quapaw Tribe of Oklahoma and the Tar Creek Project." *Environmental Protection Agency.* http://www.epa.gov/oar/tribal/tribetotribe/tarcreek.html (accessed on June 20, 2011).

"Questions and Answers about the Plateau Indians." *Wellpinit School District 49 (WA).* http://www.wellpinit.wednet.edu/sal-qa/qa.php (accessed on August 11, 2011).

"Questions and Answers about the Spokane Indians." *Wellpinit School District.* http://wellpinit.org/q%2526a (accessed on August 11, 2011).

Redish, Laura, and Orrin Lewis. *Native Languages of the Americas.*http://www.native-languages.org (accessed on August 11, 2011).

"Research Starters: Anasazi and Pueblo Indians." *Scholastic.com.* http://teacher.scholastic.com/researchtools/researchstarters/native_am/ (accessed on July 20, 2011).

"The Rez We Live On"(videos). *The Confederated Salish and Kootenai Tribes.* http://therezweliveon.com/13/video.html (accessed on August 11, 2011).

The Rooms, Provincial Museum Division. "Innu Objects."*Virtual Museum Canada.* 2008. http://www.museevirtuel-virtualmuseum.ca/edu/ViewLoit Collection.do;jsessionid=3083D5EEB47F3ECDE9DA040AD0D4C956? method=preview⟨=EN&id=3210 (accessed on May 24, 2011).

Sac and Fox Nation. http://www.sacandfoxnation-nsn.gov/ (accessed on June 5, 2011).

"Sac and Fox Tribe." *Meskwaki Nation.* http://www.meskwaki.org/ (accessed on June 5, 2011).

San Carlos Apache Cultural Center. http://www.sancarlosapache.com/home.htm (accessed on July 20, 2011).

"San Carlos Apache Sunrise Dance." *World News Network.* http://wn.com/ San_Carlos_Apache_Sunrise_Dance (accessed on July 20, 2011).

"San Juan Pueblo." *New Mexico Magazine.* http://www.nmmagazine.com/ native_american/san_juan.php (accessed on July 20, 2011).

"San Juan Pueblo O'Kang." *Indian Pueblo Cultural Center.* http://www.indianpueblo. org/19pueblos/ohkayowingeh.html (accessed on July 20, 2011).

"The Sand Creek Massacre." *Last of the Independents.* http://www.lastoftheinde- pendents.com/sandcreek.htm (accessed on July 2, 2011).

"Seminole Indian Tribe History." *Access Genealogy.* http://www.accessgenealogy. com/native/tribes/seminole/seminolehist.htm (accessed on June 12, 2011).

Seminole Nation of Oklahoma. http://www.seminolenation.com/ (accessed on June 12, 2011).

Seminole Tribe of Florida. http://www.seminoletribe.com/ (accessed on June 12, 2011).

"Sharp Nose." *Native American Nations.* http://www.nanations.com/arrap/ page4.htm (accessed on July 2, 2011).

"The Shawnee in History." *The Shawnee Tribe.* http://www.shawnee-tribe.com/ history.htm (accessed on June 12, 2011).

"Shawnee Indian Tribe History." *Access Genealogy.* http://www.accessgenealogy. com/native/tennessee/shawneeindianhist.htm (accessed on June 12, 2011).

"Shawnee Indians." *Ohio Historical Society.* http://www.ohiohistorycentral.org/ entry.php?rec=631&nm=Shawnee-Indians (accessed on June 12, 2011).

Shawnee Nation, United Remnant Band. http://www.zaneshawneecaverns.net/ shawnee.shtml (accessed on June 12, 2011).

"A Short History of the Spokane Indians." *Wellpinit School District.* http://www.wellpinit.wednet.edu/shorthistory (accessed on August 11, 2011).

"Short Overview of California Indian History." *California Native American Heritage Commission.* http://www.nahc.ca.gov/califindian.html (accessed on August 15, 2011).

Sicade, Henry. "Education." *Puyallup Tribe of Indians.* http://www.puyallup-tribe. com/history/education/ (accessed on November 2, 2011).

"Simon Ortiz: Native American Poet." *The University of Texas at Arlington.* http://www.uta.edu/english/tim/poetry/so/ortizmain.htm (accessed on July 20, 2011).

Simpson, Linda. "The Kansas/Kanza/Kaw Nation." *Oklahoma Territory.* http:// www.okgenweb.org/-itkaw/Kanza2.html (accessed on June 17, 2011).

The Skokomish Tribal Nation. http://www.skokomish.org/ (accessed on Novem- ber 2, 2011).

Skopec, Eric. "What Mystery?" *Anasazi Adventure.* http://www.anasaziadventure. com/what_mystery.pdf (accessed on July 20, 2011).

Smithsonian Folkways. "Rain Dance (Zuñi)." *Smithsonian Institution.* http:// www.folkways.si.edu/TrackDetails.aspx?itemid=16680 (music track) and http://media.smithsonianfolkways.org/liner_notes/folkways/FW06510.pdf (instructions for dance). (accessed on July 20, 2011).

Snook, Debbie. "Ohio's Trail of Tears." *Wyandotte Nation of Oklahoma*, 2003. http://www.wyandotte-nation.org/culture/history/published/trail-of-tears/ (accessed May 11, 2011).

The Southern Arapaho. http://southernarapaho.org/ (accessed on July 2, 2011).

Southern Ute Indian Tribe. http://www.southern-ute.nsn.us/ (accessed on August 15, 2011).

Splawn, A. J. *Ka-mi-akin, the Last Hero of the Yakimas.* Portland, OR: Kilham Stationary and Printing, 1917. Reproduced by Washington Secretary of State. http://www.secstate.wa.gov/history/publications_detail.aspx?p=24 (accessed on August 11, 2011).

"Spokane Indian Tribe." *Access Genealogy.* http://www.accessgenealogy.com/native/tribes/salish/spokanhist.htm (accessed on August 11, 2011).

"Spokane Indian Tribe." *United States History.* http://www.u-s-history.com/pages/h1570.html (accessed on August 11, 2011).

Spokane Tribe of Indians. http://www.spokanetribe.com/ (accessed on August 11, 2011).

Sreenivasan, Hari. "'Apache 8' Follows All-Women Firefighters On and Off the Reservation." *PBS NewsHour.* http://video.pbs.org/video/2006599346/ (accessed on July 20, 2011).

Stands In Timber, John. "Cheyenne Memories." *Northern Cheyenne Nation.* http://www.cheyennenation.com/memories.html (accessed on July 4, 2011).

Stewart, Kenneth. "Kivas." *Scholastic.* http://www2.scholastic.com/browse/article.jsp?id=5052 (accessed on July 20, 2011).

"The Story of the Ute Tribe: Past, Present, and Future." *Ute Mountain Ute Tribe.* http://www.utemountainute.com/story.htm (accessed on August 15, 2011).

Sultzman, Lee. *First Nations.* http://www.tolatsga.org/sf.html (accessed on June 5, 2011).

Swan, Daniel C. "Native American Church." *Oklahoma Historical Society.* http://digital.library.okstate.edu/encyclopedia/entries/N/NA015.html (accessed on August 11, 2011).

"Taos Pueblo." *Bluffton University.* http://www.bluffton.edu/~sullivanm/taos/taos.html (accessed on July 20, 2011).

"Taos Pueblo." *New Mexico Magazine.* http://www.nmmagazine.com/native_american/taos.php (accessed on July 20, 2011).

Taos Pueblo. http://www.taospueblo.com/ (accessed on July 20, 2011).

"Taos Pueblo: A Thousand Years of Tradition." *Taos Pueblo.* http://taospueblo.com/ (accessed on July 20, 2011).

"Territorial Kansas: Kansa Indians." *University of Kansas.* http://www.territorialkansasonline.org/~imlskto/cgi-bin/index.php?SCREEN=

keyword&selected_keyword=Kansa%20Indians (accessed on June 17, 2011).

"Throat Singing." *Inuit Cultural Online Resource.* http://icor.ottawainuitchildrens. com/node/30 (accessed on August 15, 2011).

"Tlingit Tribes, Clans, and Clan Houses: Traditional Tlingit Country." *Alaska Native Knowledge Network.* http://www.ankn.uaf.edu/ANCR/Southeast/ TlingitMap/ (accessed on November 2, 2011).

"Tohono O'odham (Papago)." *Four Directions Institute.* http://www.fourdir. com/tohono_o'odham.htm (accessed on July 20, 2011).

"Totem Pole Websites." *Cathedral Grove.* http://www.cathedralgrove.eu/ text/07-Totem-Websites-3.htm (accessed on November 2, 2011).

"Trading Posts in the American Southwest." *Southwest Crossroads.* http:// southwestcrossroads.org/record.php?num=742&hl=chiricahua:: apache (accessed on July 20, 2011).

"Traditional Mi'kmaq Beliefs."*Indian Brook First Nation.* http://home.rushcomm. ca/-hsack/spirit.html (accessed on June1,2011).

"Tsmshian Songs We Love to Sing!" *Dum Baaldum.* http://www.dumbaaldum. org/html/songs.htm (accessed on August 15, 2011).

"Umatilla Indian Agency and Reservation, Oregon." *Access Genealogy.* http:// www.accessgenealogy.com/native/census/condition/umatilla_indian_ agency_reservation_oregon.htm (accessed on August 11, 2011).

"Umatilla, Walla Walla, and Cayuse." *TrailTribes.org: Traditional and Contemporary Native Culture.* http://www.trailtribes.org/umatilla/home.htm (accessed on August 11, 2011).

"Unangax & Alutiiq (Sugpiaq)." *Alaska Native Heritage Center.* http://www. alaskanative.net/en/main_nav/education/culture_alaska/unangax/ (accessed on August 15, 2011).

Unrau, William E. "Kaw (Kansa)." *Oklahoma Historical Society.* http://digital. library.okstate.edu/encyclopedia/entries/K/KA001.html (accessed on June 17, 2011).

Urban Indian Experience. "The Duwamish: Seattle's Landless Tribe." *KUOW: PRX.* http://www.prx.org/pieces/1145-urban-indian-experience-episode-1-the-duwamish(accessed on November 2, 2011).

The Ute Indian Tribe. http://www.utetribe.com/ (accessed on August 15, 2011).

"Ute Nation." *Utah Travel Industry.* http://www.utah.com/tribes/ute_main.htm (accessed on August 15, 2011).

Virtual Archaeologist. "The Like-a-Fishhook Story." *NDSU Archaeology Technologies Laboratory.* http://fishhook.ndsu.edu/home/lfstory.php (accessed on June 19, 2011).

"A Virtual Tour of California Missions." *MissionTour.* http://missiontour.org/ index.htm (accessed on August 11, 2011).

"Visiting a Maidu Bark House." *You Tube.* http://www.youtube.com/watch?v=fw5i83519mQ (accessed on August 11, 2011).

"The Wampanoag." *Boston Children's Museum.* http://www.bostonkids.org/educators/wampanoag/html/what.htm (accessed on June 1, 2011).

"Washoe." *Four Directions Institute.* http://www.fourdir.com/washoe.htm (accessed on August 15, 2011).

"Washoe Hot Springs." *National Cultural Preservation Council.* http://www.ncpc.info/projects_washoe.html (accessed on August 15, 2011).

"Washoe Indian Tribe History." *Access Genealogy.* http://www.accessgenealogy.com/native/tribes/washo/washohist.htm (accessed on August 15, 2011).

"We Shall Remain." *PBS.* http://www.pbs.org/wgbh/amex/weshallremain/ (accessed on July 20, 2011).

Weiser, Kathy. *Legends of America.* http://www.legendsofamerica.com (accessed on July 20, 2011).

"White Mountain Apache Indian Reservation." *Arizona Handbook.* http://www.arizonahandbook.com/white_mtn_apache.htm (accessed on July 20, 2011).

"White Mountain Apache Tribe." *InterTribal Council of Arizona.* http://www.itcaonline.com/tribes_whitemtn.html (accessed on July 20, 2011).

"White Mountain Apache Tribe: Restoring Wolves, Owls, Trout and Ecosystems" *Cooperative Conservation America.* http://www.cooperativeconservation.org/viewproject.asp?pid=136 (accessed on July 20, 2011).

"Who Were the Lipan and the Kiowa-Apaches?" *Southwest Crossroads.* http://southwestcrossroads.org/record.php?num=522&hl=chiricahua:: apache (accessed on July 20, 2011).

"Wichita." *Four Directions Institute.* http://www.fourdir.com/wichita.htm (accessed on June 9, 2011).

Wind River Indian Reservation. http://www.wind-river.org/info/communities/reservation.php (accessed on July 2, 2011).

Wind River Indian Reservation: Eastern Shoshone Tribe. http://www.easternshoshone.net/ (accessed on August 15, 2011).

WMAT: White Mountain Apache Tribe. http://wmat.us/ (accessed on July 20, 2011).

"Wounded Knee." *Last of the Independent.* http://www.lastoftheindependents.com/wounded.htm (accessed on July 4, 2011).

The Wounded Knee Museum. http://www.woundedkneemuseum.org/ (accessed on July 4, 2011).

Wyandot Nation of Anderdon. http://www.wyandotofanderdon.com/ (accessed May 13, 2011).

Wyandot Nation of Kansas. http://www.wyandot.org/ (accessed May 13, 2011).

Wyandotte Nation of Oklahoma. http://www.wyandotte-nation.org/ (accessed May 13, 2011).

"Yakima Indian Tribe History." *Access Genealogy.* http://www.accessgenealogy.com/native/tribes/yakimaindianhist.htm (accessed on August 11, 2011).

Yakama Nation Cultural Heritage Center. http://www.yakamamuseum.com/ (accessed on August 11, 2011).

"Yaqui." *Four Directions Institute.* http://www.fourdir.com/yaqui.htm (accessed on July 20, 2011).

"Yaqui and Mayo Indian Easter Ceremonies." *RimJournal.* http://www.rimjournal.com/arizyson/easter.htm (accessed on July 20, 2011).

"Yaqui Sacred Traditions." *Wisdom Traditions Institute.* http://www.wisdomtraditions.com/yaqui2.html (accessed on July 20, 2011).

"Yuma (Quechan)." *Four Directions Institute.* http://www.fourdir.com/yuma.htm (accessed on July 20, 2011).

Yuman Indian Tribe History." *Access Genealogy.* http://www.accessgenealogy.com/native/tribes/yuman/yumanfamilyhist.htm (accessed on July 20, 2011).

"The Yup'ik and Cup'ik People—Who We Are." *The Alaska Native Heritage Center Museum.* http://www.alaskanative.net/en/main_nav/education/culture_alaska/yupik/ (accessed on August 15, 2011).

"Yup'ik Tundra Navigation." *Center for Cultural Design.* http://www.ccd.rpi.edu/Eglash/csdt/na/tunturyu/index.html (accessed on August 15, 2011).

"The Yurok." *California History Online.* http://www.californiahistoricalsociety.org/timeline/chapter2/002d.html# (accessed on August 11, 2011).

"Yurok." *Four Directions Institute.* http://www.fourdir.com/yurok.htm (accessed on August 11, 2011).

The Yurok Tribe. http://www.yuroktribe.org/ (accessed on August 11, 2011).

Zeig, Sande. *Apache 8* (film). http://www.apache8.com/ (accessed on July 20, 2011).

"Zuñi." *Northern Arizona University.* http://www.cpluhna.nau.edu/People/zuni.htm (accessed on July 20, 2011).

"Zuñi." *Southwest Crossroads.* http://southwestcrossroads.org/record.php?num=2&hl=zuni (accessed on July 20, 2011).

"Zuñi Pueblo." *New Mexico Magazine.* http://www.nmmagazine.com/native_american/zuni.php (accessed on July 20, 2011).

"Zuñi Pueblos (Ashiwi)." *Four Directions Institute.* http://www.fourdir.com/zuni.htm (accessed on July 20, 2011).

Index

Italics indicates volume numbers; **boldface** indicates entries and their page numbers. Chart indicates a chart; ill. indicates an illustration, and map indicates a map.

history of, *2:* 654–657

language/language family of, *2:* 653, 658

location of, *2:* 653, 654 (map)

name of, *2:* 653

Northern, *2:* 653, 655, 656–657, 658, 660

notable people of, *2:* 666–667

origins and group affiliations of, *2:* 653–654

population of, *2:* 653

relations with other groups, *2:* 714, 734, 793, 913; *5:* 1765, 1768, 1784

religion of, *2:* 657, 658 (ill.)

Southern, *2:* 653, 655, 656, 657, 658, 660, 666

Archaeological sites

of the Alutiiq, *5:* 2087

desecration of, *3:* 1065–1066

Kinishba, *3:* 1060

looting of, as problem, *3:* 1052

preservation of, *3:* 994

Archaeologists, *1:* 354–355; *5:* 1714

Architecture. *See also* Adobe; Buildings

cliff dwellings as, *3:* 983 (ill.), 983–985, 987–988, 988 (ill.)

sacred, of the Pawnee, *2:* 862

sandstone in, *3:* 988

Arctic, *5:* 2055–2158, 2056 (map), 2140–2141

culture of, *5:* 2061–2062

current tribal issues of, *5:* 2062–2066

history of, *5:* 2056–2061, 2059 (ill.)

subsistence in, *5:* 2062

Arctic Circle, *1:* 352, 365

Arctic National Wildlife Refuge, development of oil field in, *1:* 362; *5:* 2064

Arctic tundra, *1:* 352

Arguello, Luis, *4:* 1533

Arikara, *2:* 644, 669–689

arts of, *2:* 683

current tribal issues of, *2:* 686–687

customs of, *2:* 683–686

daily life of, *2:* 677 (ill.), 677–682, 678 (ill.), 679 (ill.), 682 (ill.)

economy of, *2:* 676–677

European contact with, *1:* 384

government of, *2:* 675–676

history of, *2:* 671–674

language/language of, *2:* 670, 675

location of, *2:* 669, 670 (map)

as member of the Three Affiliated Tribes, *2:* 671, 673, 676

name of, *2:* 669

notable people of, *2:* 687–688

origins and group affiliations of, *2:* 670–671

population of, *2:* 669–670

relations with other groups, *1:* 382; *2:* 792, 854, 859

religion of, *2:* 674

trade and, *2:* 475

Arikara War, *2:* 672

Arlee, Johnny, *4:* 1602, 1616

Aroostook Band of Micmacs, *1:* 149, 154, 156, 160

Cultural Community Education Center of, *1:* 159–160

Aroostook Band of Micmacs Settlement Act (1991), *1:* 157

Arroyo Leon, *3:* 1317

Arson by Witches (Jemez Pueblo), *3:* 1193

Arthur, Chester A., *3:* 1072, 1073

Arts. *See under* Arts for specific tribes

Arts in Education, *2:* 537

Asah, Spencer, *2:* 804

Ashevak, Kenojuak, *5:* 2113

Ashini, Daniel, *1:* 447

Assegun, Ottawa and, *1:* 219

Assembly of God

Missouri and, *2:* 820

Nisqually and, *5:* 1930

Skokomish and, *5:* 2002

Spokane and, *4:* 1662

Assimilation, *2:* 795, 797

General Allotment Act and, *5:* 1788

Luiseño and, *4:* 1444

Nisqually and, *5:* 1928–1929

in the Northeast, *1:* 8–9

promotion of ideas of, *3:* 975

Pueblo and, *3:* 1168

self-determination and, *5:* 1719

Waampanoag and, *1:* 320

Assiniboin, *1:* 381–401,; *2:* 644, 647, 936

arts of, *1:* 396–398, 397 (ill.)

current tribal issues of, *1:* 400

customs of, *1:* 398–399, 399 (ill.)

U•X•L Encyclopedia of Native American Tribes, 3rd Edition

F

history of, *5:* 1926–1930
language/language family of, *5:* 1925, 1930–1931
location of, *5:* 1925, 1926 (map)
name of, *5:* 1925
notable people of, *5:* 1940
origins and group affiliations of, *5:* 1925–1926
population of, *5:* 1925
religion of, *5:* 1930
Nisqually National Wildlife Refuge, *5:* 1939
Nisqually Reservation, *5:* 1925, 1928, 1931, 1934
Nixon, Richard, *1:* 116
Niza, Marcos de, expedition, *3:* 1206
No Longer Vanishing (movie), *5:* 1905
Nootka, *5:* 1943. *See also* Nuu-chah-nulth
Central, *5:* 1949
Northern, *5:* 1949
relations with other groups, *5:* 1912
Nootka Sound, *5:* 1822
controversy involving, *5:* 1945, 1947, 1960
native inhabitants of, *5:* 1947 (ill.)
Norse explorers, *1:* 197
Norte, Julio, *4:* 1373
The North American Indian (Curtis), *4:* 1499
North American Indian Anthropology (Ortiz), *3:* 1236
Native American Resource Center at, *1:* 105
North West Company, *1:* 453–454, 454; *4:* 1583, 1675
merger with Hudson's Bay Company, *1:* 454
North West Mounted Police (NWMP) (Mounties), *1:* 386, 408; *2:* 696
Northeast, *1:* **1–349,** 3(map)
assimilation in, *1:* 8–9
Native American treaties in, *1:* 7–8
post-European contact period in, *1:* 4–5
religion in, *1:* 3–4
struggle to preserve heritage in, *1:* 9–10
trade with Europeans in, *1:* 5–7
tribal automony in, *1:* 2–3
Northern Cheyenne Indian Reservation, *2:* 714, 716, 724, 727, 751
Healing Vision Project, *4:* 1399
Northern Lights, *1:* 398
Northern Pacific Railroad, *4:* 1693, 1696, 1696 (ill.)
Northwest Passage, *5:* 2094
Northwest Rebellion (1885), *1:* 405, 454, 456, 467
Not for Innocent Ears (Modesto), *4:* 1379, 1383
Nuclear Free Zone, *1:* 306

Nuclear testing
on Aleutian Islands, *5:* 2123
on Amchitka, *5:* 2117, 2136
Nunavut, *5:* 2065, 2093, 2097, 2112
Nunavut Land Claim Agreement, *5:* 2065
Nuu-chah-nulth, *5:* 1820, 1827, **1943–1962**
arts of, *5:* 1954–1955
current tribal issues of, *5:* 1959–1960
customs of, *5:* 1955–1959
daily life of, *5:* 1951–1954
economy of, *5:* 1950–1951
government of, *5:* 1950
history of, *5:* 1945–1949, 1946 (ill.), 1947 (ill.)
language/language family of, *5:* 1944, 1949–1950
location of, *5:* 1943, 1944 (map)
name of, *5:* 1943
notable people of, *5:* 1960–1961
origins and group affiliations of, *5:* 1944–1945
population of, *5:* 1943
religion of, *5:* 1949

O

O-Ho-Mah Society, *2:* 806
Oakes, Richard, *4:* 1538
Obama, Barack, *1:* 238; *2:* 766, 906, 929; *3:* 1014
Obesity
in the San Carlos Apache, *3:* 1049
in the Tohono O'odham, *3:* 1287
in the Ute, *5:* 1798
Oblone/Costanoan, *4:* 1403
The Oblone Past and Present: Native Americans of the San Francisco Bay Region (Brown), *4:* 1405
Obregón, Alvaro, *3:* 1298
Ocean Power: Poems from the Desert (Zepeda), *3:* 1289
Odjig, Daphne, *1:* 238
Ohitika Woman (Brave Bird), *2:* 931
Ohkay Owingeh. *See* San Juan Pueblo
Ohkay Owingeh Community School (OOCS), *3:* 1228, 1232
Ohlone, *4:* **1403–1418**
arts of, *4:* 1414
current tribal issues of, *4:* 1416–1417
customs of, *4:* 1415–1416

P

Pomo and, *4:* 1515–1516

Pueblo and, *3:* 1111, 1155, 1157–1158, 1159, 1163, 1165

Quapaw and, *2:* 873, 874–875

San Juan Pueblo and, *3:* 1225, 1226–1227

in Southwest, *3:* 972–973

Taos Pueblo and, *3:* 1241–1242

Tlingit and, *5:* 2015

Tohono O'odham and, *3:* 1275–1276

Ute and, *5:* 1785

Washoe and, *5:* 1805–1806

Wichita and, *2:* 951, 953–954, 954–955

Yaqui and, *3:* 1295–1296, 1302, 1303

Yuman and, *3:* 1315–1317

Zuñi Pueblo and, *3:* 1256–1257, 1258, 1259

Spanish Missions. *See also* Mission Indians; Religion

Chumash and, *4:* 1388–1389

Flathead and, *4:* 1605

history of, in California, *4:* 1336–1338, 1338 (ill.)

Hupa and Chilula and, *4:* 1424

Luiseño and, *4:* 1440, 1441–1444, 1442 (ill.), 1443 (ill.), 1450–1451

Mexican takeover and collapse of, *4:* 1340–1341

Miwok and, *4:* 1479, 1483, 1485

Ohlone and, *4:* 1405–1407, 1410–1411, 1412

Spokane and, *4:* 1658

Spanish Trail, *5:* 1716

Special Olympics, *1:* 252

Spence, Ahab (1911–2001), *1:* 423

Spider symbol, *2:* 848

Spirit-Canoe Ceremony, *5:* 1862, 1938

Spirit dancers of the Haida, *5:* 1883

Spirit Doctors of the Tsimshian, *5:* 2045, 2049

Spirit Lake, *2:* 929

Spirit Mountain (Mt. Newberry, Nevada), *3:* 1103

Spirit Rock, *1:* 124

Spivey, Towana, *2:* 541

Spokane, *4:* 1572, **1655–1672**

arts of, *4:* 1666–1667

current tribal issues of, *4:* 1169–1670

customs of, *4:* 1667–1669

daily life of, *4:* 1663–1666, 1664 (ill.), 1665 (ill.)

economy of, *4:* 1662–1663

government of, *4:* 1162

history of, *4:* 1575–1576, 1657–1661, 1660 (ill.)

language/language family of, *4:* 1656, 1662

location of, *4:* 1655, 1656 (map)

as member of COLT, *2:* 687

name of, *4:* 1655

notable people of, *4:* 1670–1671

origins and group affiliations of, *4:* 1656–1657

population of, *4:* 1655–1656

relations with other groups, *4:* 1584, 1599, 1605, 1692

religion of, *4:* 1661–1662

Spokane Falls, *4:* 1670

origin of, *4:* 1610

Spokane Garry, *4:* 1658, 1661, 1670

Spokane House, *4:* 1658

Spokane Indian Days Celebration, *4:* 1669

Spokane Reservation, *4:* 1657, 1663

Sports

in the Great Basin, *5:* 1724

of the Inuit, *5:* 2110–2111

of the Jemez Pueblo, *3:* 1199

of the Mohave, *3:* 1106, 1107

of the Yuman, *3:* 1329

Spott, Robert, *4:* 1569

Spring Festival, *1:* 287

Spruce Tree House, *3:* 985, 987

Squanto, *1:* 324

Square Tower House, *3:* 985

Squatters, *2:* 837

Squaxin, *5:* 1963

Squaxon, relations with other groups, *5:* 1997

Standing Arrow, *1:* 81–82

Standing Rock Reservation, *2:* 906, 921, 929, 931, 935, 938

Standing Tall program, *1:* 462

Star Quilt (Whiteman), *1:* 75

Star society, *2:* 663

Status Indians, *1:* 432

Staying sickness, Tohono O'odham and, *3:* 1284

Steckley, John, *1:* 336

Steptoe, Edward, *4:* 1659

Sterling, Shirley, *4:* 1616

U•X•L Encyclopedia of Native American Tribes, 3rd Edition

T

X

Y